ECONOMIC RESPONSE

ECONOMIC RESPONSE

**Comparative Studies in Trade,
Finance, and Growth**

CHARLES P. KINDLEBERGER

HARVARD UNIVERSITY PRESS

Cambridge, Massachusetts, and London, England   1978

Library of Congress Cataloging in Publication Data

Kindleberger, Charles Poor, 1910-
    Economic response.

    Bibliography: p.
    Includes index.
    1. Europe—Economic conditions—Addresses, essays,
lectures. 2. Europe—Commerce—History—Addresses,
essays, lectures. 3. Finance—Europe—History—
Addresses, essays, lectures. I. Title.
HC240.K453   330.9'4   77-12089
ISBN 0-674-23025-6

For AJ and UW

Preface

The subject of this book is certain economic processes in Western Europe, largely in the nineteenth century. Interest in them, I would hope, lies in the method of comparative economic history, embodied in the subtitle of the book. The chapters are presented in the order in which they were written, although the sequence has been modified slightly for continuity of subject matter. Five chapters—2, 3, 4, 5, and 7—have been published before, and an earlier version of Chapter 6 was given as a lecture in honor of Marc Bloch at the International Center for European Studies at the University of Quebec at Montreal. My thanks for permission to reprint the articles are given to the following periodicals:

"Group Behavior and International Trade," *Journal of Political Economy* 59 (1951): 30-47;

"The Rise of Free Trade in Western Europe, 1820 to 1875," *Journal of Economic History* 35 (1975): 20-55;

"The Formation of Financial Centers," *Princeton Studies in International Finance* 36 (1974): 1-78;

"Commercial Expansion and the Industrial Revolution," *Journal of European Economic History* 4 (1975): 613-634;

"Germany's Overtaking of England, 1806 to 1914," *Weltwirtschaftliches Archiv* 111 (1975): 253-281; pt. 2 (1975): 477-504.

My debts, intellectual and in the book-making process, leave me a hopeless bankrupt. For encouragement in pursuing the method I am especially indebted to Hugh Aitken, Rondo Cameron, Paul Hohenburg, Val Lorwin, and Peter Temin, and to the Council on European Studies. Other intellectual creditors are noted in the separate chapters.

The essays reprinted here and the first version of Chapter 6 were typed at MIT, especially by Marie-Claire Humblet, an able and extraordinarily pleasant secretary, over three years. The final steps of turning the manuscript into book form were carried out in Princeton by Ellen Seiler, by the efficient staff of the Institute for Advanced Studies — and by my wife, who spent three evenings awash in Elmer's glue. I am grateful to them all.

Contents

ECONOMIC RESPONSE

Comparative Economic History

1. It is claimed, with what accuracy I do not know, that fish learn a great deal about water from their first exposure to air. Many of us know from experience that the study of French teaches much about the structure of the English language. "What do they know of England who only England know?" is Kipling's aphorism which makes the same point, most apposite for this work.

In all science there is need for a basis of comparison, for control. In economics we have two broad types of analysis: partial equilibrium, in which one variable is altered with all other elements in the system left unchanged, within the control of *ceteris paribus* (other things equal); and general equilibrium, in which the initial change is allowed to reverberate throughout the system, *mutatis mutandis* (changing those things that ought to be changed). In engineering terms partial equilibrium is without, general equilibrium with, feedbacks. The new economic history and much discussion of economic policy make their points by an attempt to establish the "relevant counterfactual"—What would have happened in the system if Cleopatra's nose had been one-quarter inch shorter, to take an example from history in general? How rapidly would the United States have grown if the railroad had not been invented?[1] What would have happened to the balance of payments of a home country if direct investment had not taken place? (Would industry have continued to export to foreign markets, or were these exports doomed to dry up because of loss of technical monopoly?)[2]

In policy questions, and to a considerable extent in economic history, it is difficult to establish the relevant counterfactual. But one objective test is what actually did happen elsewhere. The technique of comparative economic history, it is suggested, allows us to test a given economic model and to see how general and how special it is by examining the same process or stimulus under other conditions. A historical in-joke, told by Knut Borchardt, economic historian at the University of Munich, is that at every meeting when a paper is read there is always someone who gets up and says, "It was not like that in Breslau." The object of the exercise in comparative economic history is to look at Breslau simultaneously with the Rhineland, the Palatinate, East Prussia, or wherever, comparing regions, provinces, cities, countries—in other words, any reasonable economic unit—and to base generalizations on somewhat disparate examples. American and British economic historians, when contrasted with those of Continental Europe or the British dominions, are perhaps particularly parochial in drawing conclusions from a single historical case.

The questions should not be too grandiose or Toynbee-esque. I have not succeeded in following my own preaching, as will be apparent in Chapter 7, but the comparative economic history I have in mind here deals with segments, sectors, or sections of the economy rather than the broad sweep of general-equilibrium problems such as takeoff, decline, backwardness, business cycles, capitalism, and the like. This is not to fault more daring spirits like Gerschenkron, North and Thomas, Rostow, and Schumpeter,[3] not to mention Marx, Toynbee, Weber, and many more, but to recognize the dangers of wide generalization. The problems in trade, growth, and finance discussed below are quite wide, despite my characterization of them on other occasions as "comparative economic history in the small." Rather than having concern for historical general equilibrium, however, I am interested in the role of technical change, or capital formation, or scientific education in economic growth, or the response of a political economy to far-ranging price change. Problems at this level of disaggregation prove to be quite large enough.

The field may be circumscribed in still another way: by limiting the range of the countries studied. The course in comparative economic systems, as taught in the usual college or university, addresses responses to economic issues of capitalism, socialism, communism, fascism, or perhaps of the United States, Soviet Union, Britain, Japan, China, and India. In a sense every economy is a mixed economy, but proportions in the mixture can vary widely. In these circumstances, in countries with entirely different factors, factor proportions, histories, cultures, and the like, control of the economic variables is weakened and perhaps entirely lost. It is difficult to separate what of the differences in behavior between, say, the United States and the Soviet Union is the result of their different economic systems from what is the result of their disparate social experience. The frequent contrast of China and India raises similar questions of sorting out politico-economic system from cultural difference.

An interesting attempt to delimit the field has been proceeding under the direction of Lloyd Reynolds of Yale University, in a series of twelve volumes entitled *Studies in Comparative Economics*. Eleven scholars studied labor, foreign trade, agriculture, planning, industrial structure, and economic growth in a variety of different countries, with conclusions brought together in a final overarching study.[4] As author of the volume on foreign trade, I may be permitted the view that this narrowing of the field represents an advance on comparative economic systems in the traditional format, but is still some distance from the controlled experiment needed to enable the economist to test his models for generality.

My interest, I suppose, is more in historical economics than in economic history, a distinction illustrated by the complaint of Rosario Romeo in his well-known debate with Alexander Gerschenkron over the primitive accumulation of capital in Italy; he stated that Gerschenkron wanted to understand economic processes in all of Europe, whereas he, Romeo, was interested only in the forces that shaped the economic development of Italy.[5] We can improve economic analysis, I believe, by testing its models against the facts in a variety of contexts, where the conditions in other economies furnish the counterfactual to the single case from which it is dangerous to generalize.

Comparative economic history is of course far from new. Like Molière's *Bourgeois Gentilhomme,* who spoke prose all his life without knowing it, economists and economic historians have been comparing in the large and in the small for some time. Moreover, comparative studies are becoming faddish. There are periodicals such as *Comparative Politics,* started in 1958-59, *Studies in Comparative International Development,* begun in 1965, and *Comparative Polit-*

ical Studies, dating from 1968. The acceptance of the comparative method in social studies and history goes back still further, as attested by the existence since 1955 of a periodical called *Comparative Studies in Society and History.* An informal survey of thirteen volumes of the last journal, however, reveals only four articles that squarely fit the comparable format in economic history, and few in social or other branches of history. After a time a journal accepts papers in which only one country, region, or area is treated, and the comparative element is implicit rather than explicit, the reader being invited in effect to make comparisons with any other situation he happens to know.

One of the best-known comparisons by an economic historians is that of Sir John Clapham, whose study of France and Germany[6] is a classic. But that book has successive chapters on the economic history of France and Germany, and comparison is mainly in the title. One of the finest examples is the article by François Crouzet comparing the economic growth of England and France in eighteenth century.[7] My own effort along the same lines for the same two countries from 1850 to 1950 produced rather negative results.[8] Still another study attempted to ascertain why Belgium industrialized and the Netherlands did not.[9] These tend to be the general equilibrium, big-picture analyses.

Less cosmic in scope is a variety of studies along functional lines:
Agriculture — Boserup, Dovring, Moore, Slicher van Bath;[10]
Banking — Cameron, Goldsmith;[11]
Demography — Richard Easterlin and his students at the University of Pennsylvania;
Education — Anderson and Bowman, Musgrave;[12]
Government — Aitken;[13]
Particular industries — Burn on steel, Hohenberg on chemicals, Kisch on linen;[14]
Labor and labor unrest — Hobsbawm, Kerr and Siegel, Lorwin, Rimlinger on strikes, the three Tillys,[15] and especially the voluminous output of the project directed by Dunlop, Harbison, Kerr, and Myers;
Ports — Böhme, Van Houtte;[16]
Technology — Landes, Musson;[17]
Transport — Girard.[18]
Finally, of course, there is the careful comparative statistical work essential for history, but perhaps not itself the stuff of history, un-

dertaken by Chenery, Denison, Hoffmann, Kuznets, Maddison, the Woytinskys, and a host of others.[19]

Comparative work thus has a long and distinguished record in economic history, but I claim there is still work to do.

Several qualitative points may be made. Comparisons should, I believe, extend over more than two countries, regions, cities, or ports. If one country can mislead the scholar into overly facile generalization, two does not extend the model a great deal. In the studies to follow, the historical record is often very similar in two of the three or four countries examined, and if these happened to be the two countries chosen, a false idea would be obtained. If one were to study the English and Dutch reactions to the fall in the price of wheat after 1879, as I do in Chapter 2, one would conclude that countries clung to free trade; if France, Italy, and Germany happened to be picked, one would believe that the response ran to tariffs. More is better. But there are costs: the need to learn languages, which are going out of style in the United States in favor of mathematics and computer programming; the evident fact that "wider" means "shallower" for a given investment of energy and time, which constitutes the budget constraint for student and mature scholar alike. In some instances two countries will be enough to suggest a broad range of outcomes, as I hope is illustrated in Chapter 7 on Germany's overtaking England. Such examples must be chosen with care to be representative of the broader distribution of cases. It is of some interest that in his 1967 book on banking in the early stages of industrialization covering seven countries, Rondo Cameron and his team arrived at certain conclusions that were subsequently modified when the research was extended to six more examples (and the study of one country was revised).[20] The three, four, or five examples with which the individual can cope with some minimum degree of confidence may not be enough.

As a second point, it is useful to make a distinction between comparative economic history undertaken by teams and that which goes through one head. Team research is fully established in natural science and is making progress in social science. One form of attack is to have separate researchers following a common outline as well as a common point of view. The Center for Economic Growth at Yale tried to collect data for a series of developing countries according to a common design. The Social Science Research Council under Moses Abramovitz is embarked on a parallel series of studies of economic growth in industrial countries. Richard Easterlin's students in demography at the University of Pennsylvania apply the same coherent body of analysis to a series of separate cases of population growth in France, Germany, and so on. Success in these endeavors has a habit of falling short of the hopes of their organizers, for one of two reasons. Forcing the material into a common procrustean bed may mutiliate it and make it less informative than it otherwise would be. More usually, the separate circumstances of a particular case lead the individual investigator to modify the format in many and significant details. In the end each study follows a different model in essential particulars. Small subtle differences and similarities go undetected because with two heads, one does not know everything contained in the other. The benefit of putting the material through one head is that the comparison is closer, tighter. More generalizations — which is what science is about — can be produced.

There are of course costs that offset some, and in many cases doubtless all, of this benefit. The individual researcher has a tighter budget in time, energy, language skills, and historical background than a team. And too deep a familiarity with a particular case can itself be a handicap if it leads the researcher to stress the special features rather than the commonality.

Third, it seems to me important not to hesitate to go beyond economic analysis into other social sciences: political science, sociology, social psychology, and the like. Such extensions must of course be amateurish, as are those in Chapter 2. Nonetheless it is essential not to fall into the jurisdictional fallacy that the economic historian does a better job when he explains everything in economic terms, that limiting the analysis to a single social science is more elegant, more efficient, more scientific. The sociology of science suggests that scientific efficiency and elegance call for the minimum possible sufficient explanation, but do not require confinement to a single discipline. Social sciences are separated by man, not by nature. It is ironic that the German tradition that expounds economic *and social* history differs from the British tradition that separates the two in that it frequently has a smaller social content in its economic history that does British purely economic history.

The present exercises are limited to Europe. The application of the technique can of course be much broader. Professor Charles Issawi, first at Columbia and now at Princeton, is studying successively the economic growth of Egypt, Iran, Iraq, and Turkey. Latin

America lends itself to the technique. Application in eastern Europe and in Southeast Asia is more difficult because of variation in the languages in which material is presented. Some of the literature on the smaller countries of Europe is in English or French, but that tends to be thin, as the treatment of Denmark in Chapter 2 and of Holland in Chapter 5 will reveal. Unhappily, few economic historians have the capacity of a Gerschenkron with sixteen languages at his command, a number of them learned after the age of fifty.

The gravest weakness in the approach exemplified in this book is doubtless its reliance on secondary instead of primary sources. In his vigorous defense of comparative economic history, Fritz Redlich suggests that the technique start with secondary sources and turn to primary material to fill in gaps and plug up holes.[21] This is the ideal. In the instances below, however, I have relied on secondary material, a little contemporary analysis, and occasionally on sources such as speeches, memoirs, and biography—but no primary material. This is historical economics, not economic history. One hopes to be wary in using secondary material, to test one source against another, especially for tightness of economic analysis, and to be particularly aware of the dangers of anecdotism, casual empiricism, and argument by example that fails to consider representativeness. At the same time, I do not feel especially guilty when a friendly critic, Stefano Fenolatea, tells me that I would have had a different view of Premier Cavour's motives in moving to free trade if I had read the fifty-two volumes of the debates on the tariff in the Sardinian Parliament. No doubt. I record the contrary view, but there is no possibility that my faltering pace at reading Italian would warrant even skimming this debate *in extenso*. The argument is not that comparative economic history should replace monographic historiography, but that there is room for a step that goes beyond the latter. It is highly important for Bouvier to investigate the crash of the Union générale bank in 1882 and for Bonelli to dig into the events of the collapse of the Società Bancaria Italiana in 1907;[22] the argument is merely that there is merit in some economist's taking a close look at the two in relation to each other, in an attempt to distill the general from the particular.

Use of secondary sources may stretch the resources of all but the great libraries of Harvard, Yale, Princeton, Columbia, Chicago, Illinois, Berkeley, and Stanford (the Hoover Institution) in the United States, and a handful in England, France, Italy, Germany, and the Soviet Union. The ordinary university library in the United States is fine for American books, less fine for English books, and progressively impoverished in foreign-language works as one moves from French to German to Italian and beyond. Interlibrary loans, moreover, are uncertain and slow. It may be necessary for the mountain to go to Mohammed, that is, for the scholar in advanced research to travel to the library, which restricts the range of topics that can be undertaken by students in course work. The extensive bibliography given here is—sadly—probably beyond the capacity of all but a few major libraries and has been consulted during several sabbaticals.

It may be helpful to explain that the technique as I use it was discovered by accident. In 1949-50, fresh from having worked in government on European questions, I undertook to teach a course at Columbia University on the economy of Europe (commuting once a week from MIT). The course covered a year, and while there was abundant material at hand for the second term on contemporary questions, I found it necessary to study European economic history. This was accomplished in the ample time allowed by a four-hour train ride when traveling by day, and with the generous resources of the Nicholas Murray Butler library at Columbia. In the course of this study I stumbled upon the widely varied reactions of Britain, France, Germany, Italy, and Denmark to the fall in the price of wheat after 1879, and wrote the paper that appears here as Chapter 2. Twenty-five years later I would want to amend it in a number of particulars, as noted in Chapter 8. The paper may nonetheless retain some interest today. And there is no need to rewrite it, since a political scientist has recently done so, with emphasis on domestic politics.[23]

Since the 1951 paper I have been looking, somewhat half-heartedly, for more problems on which the same technique could be used. For some reason that escapes my understanding, it suddenly and belatedly appeared to me that there were a number of issues that could be made to yield fruit through the comparative method. A grant from the Council of Europe made it possible for me to call together a small group comprising Hugh G. J. Aitken, Rondo Cameron, Paul M. Hohenburg, Val R. Lorwin, and Peter Temin. Cameron arranged for a discussion of comparative economic history at an informal meeting of the Sixth International Congress on Economic History, held in Copenhagen in August 1974, and devoted the annual program of the Thirty-Fourth Annual Meeting of the (U.S.) Economic History Association in Philadelphia in September 1974 to "Comparative Economic History: Promises and Problems." The group wrote a proposal to a foundation in an unsuccessful attempt to raise money to support fellowships in comparative economic history, especially stipends for graduate students to learn languages. In the proposal were a number of suggestions for research, which I have in fact undertaken myself. These are set forth below as Chapters 3 to 6.

These four samples of what comparative economic history can be may have some interest for students of current economic policy. They raise questions of whether free trade can be achieved by a convergence of dominant interests alone, or whether it requires some doctrinal or ideological basis advanced by a leading country in the world economic system; and of whether a world financial center is inevitable. In the case of Chapter 5 the merchant of the seventeenth and eighteenth centuries is compared with the multinational corporation of today, the merchant being the key to an information network necessary to achieve gains from trade and to improve quality of output on standard bases to reduce transactions costs and achieve economies of scale. The study on financial centers has only recently been published, but a reader, S. J. Butlin, the distinguished Australian economic historian, has raised by letter the issue whether Switzerland and Canada (and Australia) were slow in selecting a single dominant financial center because they were federal, rather than unitary, states. The evidence of the United States, in which New York was dominant, and of the Federal Republic of Germany, where Frankfurt won out over Düsseldorf and Hamburg, make sweeping generalization dangerous. If I were primarily interested in substance, I should probably pursue this fascinating and important issue and revise the monograph before reprinting it. Since, however, my primary concern is with propagating the method, I leave previously published papers more or less in their pristine form, at the same time calling attention to Professor Butlin's suggestive comment.

It may not be sufficient to practice. Hence I preach. It seems useful to suggest other possible topics for research along comparative lines, or to pose problems, and not to wait until I can perform the research myself. In what follows I draw on the proposal submitted to the foundation, incorporating my own ideas from the initial draft, but the contributions of others as well. An occasional thought is elaborated in some detail to suggest a mode of attack. Other topics are merely indicated. The entire list is given alphabetically in no particular order of importance. It omits a discussion of financial crises on which I am currently engaged, as I have no interest in encouraging competition.

Agriculture

The end of the horizontal extension of agriculture into unused land in the 1860s and 1880s in Sweden, Italy, Silesia;[24]

Land tenure in relation to one or more of a variety of aspects of agriculture: productivity, characteristics of the soil, population retention, human fertility, technical change;

The productivity of land in relation to the social system; why poor land in mountains or along the sea tends to produce republican forms of government, and rich land, an aristocracy,[25] (touched upon in Chapter 6 below).

Bureaucracy

The Gerschenkron thesis on backwardness suggests that the later, economically, that a country develops, the more it must rely on government.[26] This thesis still requires rigorous testing. It is worth contemplating the significance of the widely differing nature of bureaucracy in England, France, Germany, and Italy—bureaucracy as opposed to aristocracy, democracy, or monarchy. I am informed that sociologists have provided no such comparative study despite the interest in the subject of Bendix, Crozier, Weber, and others.[27]

Note that British bureaucracy has been amateur, French technocratic, German dictatorial, and Italian exploitive. And that Germans and Italians are lawyers—the latter mostly with a low grade of educational attainment—whereas top French bureaucrats are magnificently trained in engineering or administration at the *grandes écoles*, and British civil servants typically have taken a first or double-first in greats (classics), modern greats (history and philosophy), or PPE (philosophy, politics, and economics) at Oxford or Cambridge.

The German Junker dominated the civil service because he belonged to a dominant class for whom farming and a military career did not provide full employment.[28] It is especially interesting, ac-

cording to one source, that Italian bureaucracy started out dominated by the Piedmontese of the north, who accompanied Cavour
from the Sardinian into the Italian government and followed his
successors to Florence in 1865 and to Rome in 1870. With the upsurge of industry in the fifteen years after 1895, this group returned
from Rome to Turin, Novara, and Alessandra and entered industry, leaving a vacuum in the national bureaucracy that was filled
by southerners.[29]

As a loose generalization, it may be suggested that farming
regions of a country will dominate the civil service by numbers. In
France this is limited to the lower ranks, where postmen and police
come from the Massif Central, the Pyrenees, and Corsica. Numbers
may be small overall, as in Britain.[30] The leadership may be provided by a nonagricultural class, as in France and Britain.[31] Where
the top ranks are recruited from a feudal agricultural society, as in
Germany and Italy, however, there is likely to be governmental
animosity to industrialization in some respects, along with paternal-
ism in others. The latter is all that Gerschenkron allows for.

To leap from Europe to the United States, note as a crude
generalization that the bureaucracy was dominated by southern
lawyers (that is, educated sons of a land-owning class) until the New
Deal under President Franklin Roosevelt produced a drastic change
and the domination of lawyers from northern cities.

Capital Formation

The role of banking in economic growth;[32]

The financing of the railroad age in England, France, Germany,
Italy (or coal or iron and steel);

The spread of incorporation in Europe (why was it simultaneous
when economic development lagged so far behind in some countries?);

Spectacular bank failures (for example, compare the crash of the
Union générale in France with that of Società Bancaria Italiana
and perhaps others like Baring Brothers, the Royal Linen Bank of
Scotland, and the City of Glasgow Bank).[33]

Confiscation and Sale of Church and Government Property

A fairly recent thesis on Spain has suggested that the sale of confiscated church property was a disaster for the economic develop-

ment of the country because it absorbed savings.[34] Romeo's view, on the other hand, was that the sale of church lands in Italy was part of the primitive accumulation of capital — in Marx's terminology — by which the country built its infrastructure, a necessary condition before private enterprise could form directly productive capital in the period after 1896.[35] I have not searched to see whether the confiscation of church, royal, and noble lands in the French Revolution, the last two reconstituted during the Restoration, have produced one or the other or a still different interpretation. It would be interesting to explore all three cases (and the Tudor expropriation of church lands in the sixteenth century?) to see if the effects were identical or dissimilar in relation to capital formation, attitudes toward land ownership, and other economic activity.

One French writer claims that Napoleon III's slashing of boulevards through Paris under Baron Haussmann in the 1850s served to finance industry by providing owners of city property with liquid claims, which they were then allowed to invest in industrial enterprise.[36] Banks in the Rhineland, moreover, got a start through speculating in church lands when Napoleon's occupation ordered them confiscated and sold.[37] Somewhat analagous is the compensation paid by the British government to owners of slaves in the West Indies in the 1830s. William Gladstone's father, John, put his sizable check largely into railroad securities, thus enabling government to finance the railroads through a form of recycling of credit.[38]

One minor aspect of the seizure of church property was the early use of monasteries and convents as factories. Large and empty, often located in areas where they supported local population, they could house industrial activity[39] where they were not acquired to melt down the copper or lead in the roof, which caused it to fall in. The availability of such buildings helped to reduce the fixed capital requirements of the industrial revolution.[40]

The issue is the circumstances under which a change in ownership of assets stimulates or depresses economic activity. Chapter 5 touches on the question when it considers whether the accumulation of wealth by merchants, used to buy estates, contributed to or subtracted from industrial capital formation.

Demography and Labor

The demographic chasm dug in France[41] and in Italy and Germany by the series of poor harvests in the middle of the nineteenth century;

The peculiar demographic characteristics of coal miners in France prior to World War I, in Silesia and the Ruhr[42] (Professor Michael Haines of Cornell University is now engaged in this research);

Labor participation rates, including those of women, which differ widely from country to country;

Seasonal unemployment in agriculture and the market response;

The growth of similar cities in two or more countries.

Education in Relation to Economic Growth

The economics of education is being explored widely today, and the role of education (both current and historical) in growth, industrialization, scientific research, innovation, and similar aspects of the economy is increasingly under study. I have written a paper myself on technical education in France;[43] although commissioned for a symposium on the French entrepreneur, it could (with more digging) have been comparative. The work of Artz, Ben-David, Cotgrove, Parker, Redlich, Ringer, and Wilkinson is partly organized along national lines, partly comparative; but the field lends itself naturally to the comparative technique.[44] It may also lend itself to overgeneralization of a sociological sort: "In France entrepreneurship typically had origins in banking, commerce and artisanry, and acquired scientific and technical capacities (at the *grandes écoles*) in later generations, whereas in Britain firms were often started by men of scientific attainments whose sons moved away from science to letters, politics, and country living."[45] The role of scientific and technical education in Germany furnishes an obvious contrast to that in both France and Britain.

Imperialism

A host of questions remains to be answered about imperialism: whether it arises inevitably from capitalism, what its effects are in colonies, the extent to which the imperialist power gains or the colonized power loses, and within the aggregates the gains and losses of different groups. The world doubtless needs more monographic literature before the surfeit of existing generalizations can be adequately tested. It seems clear that such generalizations must be based on a variety of cases, however, not just the Boer War or the Belgian Congo at one extreme or Italian Eritrea at the other.

Industries

Particular industries can be studied in expansion and decline, by regions, countries, or specific localities such as cities. It is remarkable that some areas adapt to adversity while others fail, Westphalia adjusting to the pressure of machine yarn imports in linen while Silesia collapsed.[46] It would be interesting to explore why in France the Rouen cotton industry was so sensitive to British imports and Alsatian cotton spinning and weaving were not. Exposure to imports was part of the explanation, but not all. Or why some communities like Barmen and Elberfeld and Lille could effect a move out of linen while others could not.

One particularly interesting aspect of industrial development in Europe in historical terms is embodied in the modern concept of the product cycle. As developed by Vernon, this calls for a good to be developed in one country, imitated abroad, and often to change its long-run efficient location away from the innovating country. The classic example is that of cotton textiles, introduced by Britain, spread everywhere especially for a time to Japan, and then to developing countries in general. In modern times there have been suggestive studies of synthetic textiles, petrochemicals, and semiconductors.[47]

Walther Hoffmann's view of industrial growth relied on something like the product cycle, with a start in textiles, a shift to iron and steel, and finally to engineering industries generally.[48] There is an enormous amount of secondary material that would enable one to study the product cycle in Europe in a single industry. The Italian cotton textile industry is a perfect example, with tariffs applied in 1879 and 1887, stimulating Swiss investment in Italian mills, and the growth of these mills to independence, as finally established by the development of export capacity. Exports were undertaken not to Switzerland in the first instance, but to former Swiss markets in North Africa and in southeastern Europe.

One study approach might be through the formation and later breakup of the European market in, say, cotton textiles. Originally Rouen, Mulhouse, the Zurich Oberland, Saxony, and other areas were protected from one another and from Britain by distance and expensive transport. With the coming of the railroad, natural protection declined; as in customs-union theory, it was followed by creation of trade for effective producers, destruction of trade for the less effective. National and local responses to these effects differed. In some instances, tariffs were sought. Many Swiss firms established subsidiaries abroad.[49] Some localities, as noted for Barmen and Elberfeld, shifted to specialities — ribbons, woven elastic, braid, and the like.

Internal Migration

With growth, movement from the farms into industry and services is inevitable because of Engel's law. Patterns may differ nationally.

The pattern of migration is broadly similar inside France and Britain. Men and women move from the farm to the city in stages. In France, it runs from village, to town, and ultimately to Paris;[50] in Britain, from the village, to the town, to the industrial city in the north; in the south, either to London or abroad.[51] The sharp contrast in readiness to emigrate — the British doing so easily, the French not at all except to Algiers and Tunis — is thoroughly known.

Migration in Italy was either local, to Rome, or abroad. In Germany, external migration stopped fairly abruptly with the boom of the 1850s, but internal migration continued on a long-distance basis, unique among the countries of Europe. Hundreds of thousands of peasants were moved from East Prussia not only to Berlin and Silesia, but clear across Germany to the Ruhr.

A social historian claims that in Norway the migrants who traveled the longest distances from their homes to industry were the most revolutionary.[52] This generalization may not hold for Germany, where the coal and steel towns, built with East Prussian farm labor, stood aside from the regular social life of the area in a submissive way.[53] The phenomenon is thus of social as well as economic interest.

It is claimed today that in Italy the workers who have gone abroad to France, Germany, Switzerland, or Luxembourg are less "angry" than those who have moved from the Mezzogiorno north to Turin and Milan. This could possibly be because they were better off economically. The more likely explanation is that the southern Italians in Turin compare their lot with that of the native workers and feel aggrieved, whereas those outside the country adopt as the relevant counterfactual the position of those still in Abruzzi, Calabria, or Sicily, and regard themselves as fortunate.

Monetary Unification

Unification of Italy in 1860 and of Germany in 1870 furnish striking examples of the integration process, as noted in Chapter 4 on the formation of financial centers. At a time when Europe as a whole is undertaking to integrate its money, the study of monetary unification in Italy and Germany is particularly topical and relevant. To these two cases can be added the formation in 1870 of the Latin Monetary Union among France, Belgium, Switzerland, and Italy. These questions have already been addressed by Professor Koichi Hamada of the University of Tokyo,[54] but more work remains to be done.

Recovery from War

Horst Mendershausen has written a book on German recovery from the two world wars.[55] The substance could be extended to other countries separately and cross-nationally. If appropriate allowance could be made for the extent of war damage and depreciation on the one hand, and for the economic and political setting on the other — very strong requirements indeed — it might be possible to investigate the resilience of economies under particularly exacting circumstances.

Recycling Reparation Transfers

Economic history illuminates current policy issues, and of course vice versa. Among the most promising examples of current problems that require economic historians to rethink their analysis is the recycling of petrodollars after the October 1973 fourfold increase in the oil price achieved by the Organization of Petroleum Exporting Countries (OPEC). The price rise has been compared with a tax on consuming countries, and with the levying of reparation payments. It was seen, however, that it would be impossible to pay the tax, or transfer the reparations to the OPEC countries in real goods immediately, since the less developed OPEC countries were unable quickly to absorb a large increase in imports. It was therefore necessary to pile up petrocurrencies for later drawing down. The process is called recycling.

Such recycling, however, is not a new phenomenon. The Baring loan to France in 1819, the Thiers rente of 1871 subscribed to from abroad and by French investors after selling their foreign securities, the Dawes loan of 1924 and the subsequent flow of capital from New York to Germany were all recycling operations that permitted the money payment of reparations to be made in the short run. Students of transfer of the 1920s — at Harvard under Frank W. Taussig, and in Europe where Keynes, Ohlin, Rueff, and many others worked on the issue — failed to see this key monetary and capital market process, quite different from the role postulated for gold under the price-specie-flow mechanism, and from the exchange rate with transfer under floating. A new comparative economic history is called for that rewrites the old in terms of the monetary approach to the balance of payments.

Regional Approach

William Parker has long maintained that resources are more important than governmental boundaries in determining growth patterns.

Recently both Crouzet discussing England[56] and Pollard discussing Germany[57] have noted that the industrial revolution has been highly localized, less perhaps in relation to natural resources such as coal deposits, than to factors such as the existence of guild regulations. The question can be pursued comparatively.

ONE COULD GO ON, for instance, to topics in trade, transportation, urbanism — but the recitation becomes wearisome. Looking back, it is hard now for me to imagine that there was not a host of topics close at hand in 1950 when I hit on the price of wheat. Chapters 3 on the rise of free trade, 4 on finance, 5 on the role of merchants in industrialization, and 6 on European port cities were in the first draft of the foregoing list when it was drawn up for consideration by the ad hoc committee that was preparing the proposal on comparative economic history. They should doubtless still be on the list, as far from exhausted.

In the 1930s Ring Lardner wrote a book entitled *How to Write Short Stories*. There was a zany two-page introduction, and then just short stories. The introduction to this book is finished: now try the short stories.

Group Behavior
and International Trade

2. The primary tool of analysis in economics is the market. But Walker has expressed the opinion that an economics adequate for prediction and policy must include a theory of extramarket behavior.[1] Polanyi, further, has attempted to demonstrate that the emphasis on the market is likely to be misleading and that a rounded theory of social behavior would include economic drives as only one strand in a broad web of social motivation.[2] The present chapter is designed to suggest that, in certain situations in international trade, a useful tool of analysis may be found in a theory of group behavior at the national level. Unhappily, no theory adequate for the task appears to have been developed. I shall offer a few suggestions about the types of variables with which such a theory should deal.

My method is to take the world decline in the price of wheat after 1870 and to indicate the responses to it in Great Britain, Germany, France, Italy, and Denmark. If a theory of market behavior were sufficient for prediction, it might be expected that the reduction in the price of wheat would lead to increased imports in Europe. Foreign sources of supply would be substituted for domestic. Resources engaged in the production of wheat would shift to other occupations. Some increase in wheat consumption would take place at the expense of other grains, to the extent that wheat would fall in price more than rye, oats, and barley would. Some of these changes did, in fact, occur, but the results were not uniformly of this character.

After I have established the differences in response I shall turn to a series of explanations dependent on nonmarket factors. None of these is completely satisfactory. What appears to be needed is a comprehensive theory of group behavior to deal with groups as large as nations—in particular, a theory that systematically makes allowances for variation in the relation among the subgroups that make up the larger entity.

I am conscious of the amateurish character of the economic history and sociology in what follows, and I am not inclined to apologize for this inevitable shortcoming. Interdisciplinary cooperation must begin with the utilization, however crude, of the products of other social sciences by practitioners in separate fields. I have greatly benefited from the assistance of experts in other fields,[3] but I have been obliged to restrict my use of their techniques, lest my special focus of interest be lost among a host of fine points.

THE MAIN FACTS concerning the world decline in the price of wheat after the American Civil War and its causes are generally understood and accepted. The rapid spread of the American rail network in the 1870s and 1880s made it possible to transport wheat to tidewater more cheaply and in far greater quantities than the canal system had been able to handle. A parallel development occurred in railroad construction from the Ukrainian wheat fields to the Crimean ports. The technological shift from wooden to iron ships—another indirect effect of the Civil War—reduced transatlantic freight rates and those to western Europe from the Crimea. The availability of demobilized manpower, untilled land, and wartime accumulations of money capital, coupled with the development of farm machinery for extensive cultivation, resulted in an expansion of the American supply, which passed the economies of production and distribution on to the consumer in Europe as cheaper wheat. In addition, the weather in the United States was favorable during the 1880s, and yields were high. The European peasant and landowner met increased competition in grain production from overseas.[4]

The difficulties of European wheatgrowers were not caused solely by overseas competition. A series of bad seasons reduced yields and brought about a deterioration in quality. A Royal Commission of Inquiry, sitting from 1879 to 1882, reached the conclusion that the loss of British farm income was primarily caused by untoward weather and only secondarily by foreign competition. The effects of the two causes were not unrelated. In a closed economy, a short crop is at least partially compensated for — so far as farm income is concerned — by an increase in price. In an international, bihemispheric economy, an increase in the local price produced by a series of short crops is likely to be forestalled by imports from overseas.[5]

The view exists, however, that what hurt European agriculture was not overseas competition or any other factor peculiar to agriculture but overall depression, lasting from 1873 to 1896. It is recognized that the price of wheat fell somewhat more than prices in general and this is ascribed to the growth of production in the United States. This relative decline, given by one writer as only 10 percent, is regarded as much less significant for the agricultural depression than was the general fall in prices.[6] The reasoning, however, is not persuasive in the light of price developments on, say, the Copenhagen market, which was unaffected by tariffs. Between 1873 and 1896 wheat fell in price by 53 percent and rye by 48 percent, as compared with a decline of 36 percent in the *Statist*'s index of wholesale prices. And after 1873 American wheat appeared in European markets that had never before seen it, including some cities, such as Trieste, known as export centers for European supplies.[7]

The combination of weather and overseas competition, then, produced potential economic distress for the farming community in the form of short crops and low prices. The remainder of this analysis, for convenience, treats the matter as a question solely of prices. In this connection, some importance attaches to the question of timing. The price of wheat fell from $1.70 to $0.66 a bushel in England from 1873 to 1894, and the sharpest decline was probably that from $1.31 in 1882 to $0.90 in 1886.[8] Action to meet the collapse in the price of wheat was taken, if at all, primarily in response to this pressure. But the nature of the response and the timing differed from country to country.

No ACTION was taken in Britain. The issue had already been settled some years before, in 1846, with the repeal of the Corn Laws. The decline in the world price of wheat produced an improvement in the terms of trade for the rising industrial classes and a basis for lowering, or withholding increases in, the wages of the industrial labor force. The latter, in turn, received a new batch of recruits in the form of agricultural workers displaced from the farm by the unprofitability of wheat growing.

The 1846 repeal of the Corn Laws, fourteen years after the political settlement between the landed gentry and industry and commerce in the Reform Bill, had no immediate economic effect. The period of high farming in Britain continued uninterrupted. British agriculture in general was efficient and profitable from 1837, when the long period of distress after the Napoleonic wars came to end, until 1873. The American Civil War and the Crimean War had helped to postpone the effects of cheap wheat imports, but even in the 1850s there had been no significant effects of the repeal. Land under the plow in Britain reached a peak in 1872 never again attained, even in World War II.[9]

The bad summers from 1875 to 1879, the rinderpest attack of 1877, and the widespread loss of sheep to liver rot in 1879 may have convinced the farmers that their difficulties resulted from the vindictiveness of nature rather than a change in their position in the community. Landowners remained the richest class in the country for several years after the disaster of 1879. By 1886 their relative position had begun to slip.[10] No action was taken to halt the decline in farm prices or to assist the farming community.[11] The dominant group in the society—the rising industrial class—was content to have cheaper food and cheaper labor. Rents fell, young men left the farm for the town, land planted to crops shrank rapidly. The response to the decline in the world price of wheat was to complete the liquidation of agriculture as the most powerful economic force in Britain.

IN GERMANY, France, and Italy the farmer was protected by the imposition of tariffs. In Germany the tariff on grain was enacted first in 1879, after fourteen years of free trade. Duties under this law were almost purely nominal, but rates were raised sharply in 1885 and again in 1887. The timing of tariff enactments in France and Italy was broadly similar, with the exception of the first step and with a significant difference insofar as Italy was concerned. Major increases in grain tariffs took place in Germany and France in 1885 and 1887. In Italy the first step was delayed until 1887, although the second followed quickly in 1888.

The German situation is more properly analyzed in terms of the tariff on rye, which in the period to 1890 was identical to that on wheat. Gerschenkron makes clear that Bismarck's alliance ran not between industry and agriculture as such, but between two powerful components of each, iron and rye.[12] Within industry the interests of the expanding steel industry were opposed to those of the fabricators of metal, who wanted cheap supplies. In this capital-intensive industry, moreover, the level of wages was relatively unimportant. In agriculture the large farms of the Junkers in eastern Germany produced rye as a cash crop for shipment to western Germany and for export. Their interest in high prices should have been opposed by the peasants of northern and western Germany, who bought grain for animal feed and had an interest in low prices. Despite this interest, however, the peasants of Germany politically followed the leadership of the landed nobility and supported tariffs on grain. Gerschenkron claims that they were deluged with propaganda and deluded by the concurrent imposition of tariffs on pigs and other animals—which, however, afforded a much lower level of protection.[13] Even within the ranks of labor there were groups who appeared not to oppose the tariffs.

The enactment of the tariff on wheat in France required the repeal of the Le Chapelier Law of 1791, which forbade associations based upon economic interest. A modification of this law in 1865 had made it possible to establish associations for the improvement of agricultural techniques. Its final repeal in 1884 paved the way for agricultural syndicates, which began by acting as producer cooperatives in the buying of fertilizer and agricultural machinery and in establishing credit unions. Very shortly these groups began to agitate for higher tariffs. The owners of large farms, marketing a higher proportion of their crop for cash than did the owners of small farms, had a greater interest in the price of wheat; but all farmers were affected by it. In only ten of eighty-seven departments of France did grain occupy less than half the tillable land in 1882, and only in one, Corsica, did the percentage fall below 40.[14] There is some evidence that the leadership in the political drive for protection was taken by the cattle interests of Normandy and Brittany. But all parts of the country, from the northern wheat districts to the southern wine areas (suffering from the depredations of *phylloxera*), were united in their zeal to raise the relative level of French farm prices.

The success of efforts to obtain protection for agriculture was aided by a compromise with industrial interests. Agriculture and industry had not always readily adjusted their conflicts of interest. In the time of Napoleon, French commercial policy had favored industrial exports at the same time that it forbade the export of wheat or of agricultural products used by industry. Agricultural interests thereafter tried on several occasions to secure protection on such industrial supplies as hides, wool, oil seeds, and silk, In 1881 the farm interests hoped that commerce and industry would agree to a tariff of 10 percent on foodstuffs in exchange for the concession of freedom to import agricultural raw materials. The compromise of 5 percent, which did not apply to wheat, produced little satisfaction. After the final repeal of the Le Chapelier Law in 1884 and more effective organization, the markedly higher rates of 1885 and 1887 on grain and animals were won with the assistance of threats of retaliation against industry.

Italian tariff policy in the 1870s and 1880s favored industry over agriculture. In 1864 wheat had been subjected to a duty of 0.5 lira per quintal to raise revenue. This was increased to 0.75 lira in 1866 to meet the costs of the war. The tariff revision of 1878, undertaken primarily to regularize the duties of the newly formed kingdom, increased the rate on wheat to 1.40 lire per quintal. These rates were low. In other directions there was no protection for agriculture. Imports of rice and barley, for example, were free of duty. Yet industry enjoyed a considerable measure of protection.

The question of taxes on food was widely discussed. An excise tax of 2 lire per quintal of wheat had been imposed internally in 1869 to improve governmental finances; although vigorously opposed by urban and industrial interests, it continued in effect for fourteen years. The experience with this tax appears to have given the Italian government pause when rising imports of grain from overseas, encouraged by the appreciation of the lire, began in 1884. Three years later, in 1887, the tariff was raised to 3 lire, a full two years after similar action was taken in France and Germany. The rate was increased again to 5 lire in 1888, after the tariff war with France led to the loss of the French market for the wines of southern Italy, to compound the distress of the region.[15] But by this time it was too late. The Italian peasant had already begun to emigrate. Gross emigration across the Atlantic, primarily from agricultural regions of Italy, increased from an average of 25,000 annually in the period 1876 to 1880 to 73,000 in 1885; 83,000 in 1886; 130,000 in 1887; and 205,000 in 1888.[16] The 1888 figure, which is presumed to reflect the period of nominal tariff rates before April 1887, with a time lag, was to remain the peak for thirteen years. Recovery of wheat prices under the impact of the tariffs and other factors slowed the pace of emigration somewhat. Once started, however, the flow became cumulative and self-perpetuating. Early emigrants encouraged first their families and then their relatives and neighbors to follow.

The response of Germany, France, and Italy to the decline in the world price of wheat was to impose tariffs in an attempt to maintain the relative price of wheat and to protect grain producers. In Germany, the movement was led by Bismarck as a step toward a new political alignment of Junkers and steelmakers, but it had the consent of many of those whose interests were adversely affected. In France, agriculture—more or less as a whole—negotiated through the tariff in reaching a settlement with industry. The reluctance of Italian industry to agree to increased tariffs and the delay in imposing them meant that the Italian response to the decline in prices was to quit Europe.[17]

DENMARK—like Britain, the Netherlands, and Belgium—did not impose a tariff on wheat. Instead, it gave up the attempt to compete in the world export market for wheat and became a wheat importer. This shift was incidental, however, to a revolution in Danish agriculture, which was converted from the growing of grain to animal husbandry. Denmark was assisted in responding thus by its proximity to the rapidly industrializing markets of England and Germany, with their expanding national incomes, and by the high income elasticity of demand for butter and bacon. Given the demand, however, there are certain remarkable features of the response of supply that merit investigation. Of particular importance are the middle-sized farm, which predominated in Danish agriculture, the agricultural school system, and the cooperative movement. The second of these at least, and perhaps the whole response to the decline in wheat prices, was deeply affected by the German defeat of Denmark in 1864 and the loss of the province of Schleswig.

Of all the countries of Europe, only in Denmark has the size of the productive unit been stabilized at the medium-sized farm—around fifty acres.[18] In other countries, over considerable periods of time, farm size has increased or decreased. Periodic reversals occur under the influence of such discontinuous events as land reform—primarily the redistribution of church or noble lands and parcellation of peasant strips (or enclosures) when these became too numerous and too narrow to work (that is, extensive farming became more profit-able than intensive). Aside from these turning points, however, farm size appears to have a tendency to increase, as in Hungary, East Prussia, and England up to World War I, or to decrease, as in France, Switzerland, and western Germany. In some countries, like Italy and Poland, the two processes take place side by side. Land purchases by the wealthy, primogeniture, high income taxes, poaching laws, veneration of blood sports in the culture, and the like, tend to increase farm size. Equal inheritance and rapid popu-lation growth tend to reduce the size of the farm unit.[19]

In Denmark a variety of factors appears to have established and maintained the middle-sized farm. The principle of equal inheri-tance has been offset by small family size, by a frontier of the sea to which extra sons could escape, and by easy credit, which enabled farmer-brothers to buy out their share of the patrimony. High land taxes made the maintenance of unproductive estates expensive. But the state intervened from an early date, and continuously (1682, 1725, 1769, 1819), to prevent the aristocracy from adding peasant land to their holdings and to prevent undue subdivision as well. A policy of dividing large holdings into small, but not minuscule, units prevailed for several centuries and was reaffirmed in legislation pro-viding for small holdings in 1899 and 1909. The institution of the middle-sized farm, which happens to be inefficient for grain pro-duction but is well suited to certain types of animal output, goes deep into Danish agricultural life.

The Folk School, or agricultural high school, was originated in 1844 by a remarkable man, Bishop N. F. S. Grundtvig, for the purpose of educating the rural population not in scientific agricul-ture but in "the Danish language and history and . . . its constitution and economic life." Classes are held in the five winter months for men and for three months in the summer for women, normally in some part of the country other than that in which the student lives. The schools attempt to provide the agricultural segment of the pop-ulation with a unity of background and an awareness of the life of the urban population of the country.

The first Folk School was founded in Schleswig. After the loss of the province to Germany, this school was moved to Danish territory. Thereafter the movement spread rapidly.[20] By 1870, before the col-lapse of wheat prices, there were sixty or seventy such schools in the country.

The cooperative movements in Sweden and Denmark have been widely studied. For present purposes, therefore, it is sufficient to make a limited series of points. To sell butter in international trade required bringing the "peasant" butter of uneven taste and texture up to "manor" quality. This meant a standardized product. After the invention of the cream separator, the manufacture of butter could take place on a large scale, even though the labor-intensive production of milk still required the medium-sized farm. Economies of scale in marketing were available not only in butter but in eggs and bacon as well. In this situation the spread of the producers' cooperative movement in Danish agriculture was rapid after the establishment of the first cooperative dairy in Jutland in 1882.[21]

Denmark's response to the decline in world wheat prices, then, was to revolutionize her agriculture and to change herself from an exporter of grains to an importer. It may be observed that the acreage devoted to cereal production in Denmark increased rather than declined after animal industry had developed.

THESE DIFFERENCES in European responses to the decline in the world price of wheat in the 1870s and 1880s may be summarized as follows. In Britain, agriculture was permitted to be liquidated. In Germany, large-scale agriculture sought and obtained protection for itself. In France, where the demography, pattern of resources, and small scale of industrial enterprise favored farming, agriculture as a whole successfully defended its position with tariffs. In Italy, the response was emigration. In Denmark, grain production was converted to animal husbandry. What factors outside the market account for these national differences? A number of attempts have been made to explain at least some of the various responses. The present section undertakes to review and comment upon these efforts.

The most familiar contrast, perhaps, is between the free-trade ideas developed in Britain by Smith, Ricardo, and Mill and the theory of national economy propounded in Germany, especially by Friederich List. A variant of the List doctrine can be found in the "nationalist economics" of Paul-Louis Cauwès in France,[22] although it is difficult to make the case that Cauwès' ideas were more than an aberration in an intellectual atmosphere that was much more sympathetic to the doctrines of the Manchester School. The place of Smith and List in Denmark appears to have been taken by Bishop

Grundtvig, whose métier was poetry and national mysticism rather than economics; and no particular figure rationalized the action taken in Italy. It might be fair to say that the economists of Britain and the national economists of Germany provided the rationale for the action taken rather than its impetus.[23] And the relative unimportance of this function may be indicated by the actions of France and Italy, taken in the absence of any distinctive rationale.

In its vulgar version the foregoing explanation is reduced to the single word "nationalism." Britain adhered to the international system; Germany and France were nationalistic in their responses. But this reasoning has evident weaknesses. Italy's solution was essentially international, or one possible only in an international world, although the attempt was made to apply the "nationalist" solution of tariffs. It could be said that the Italian solution was more international than the British, where the displaced agricultural workers shifted into industry within their own country. The international solution, that is, may involve a shift in international trade or an international movement in factors. The explanation breaks down, further, on the side of nationalism. If we set aside for the moment the subtle differences between the French and the German behavior, the Danish solution, like the French and the German, was a highly nationalistic one—taken without tariffs, to be sure, but in an atmosphere of nationalist emotion. Nationalism and internationalism in this context are compound variables of great complexity. They require, rather than furnish, explanation.

A more elaborate analysis, which fits the present case to a degree, though it makes no mention of it, is that developed by the Danish economist, Carl Major Wright.[24] Wright observes that a country can respond to an adverse change in world market conditions by intervention to correct the world situation, by isolation from it, or by adaptation to it. His book contains a message for small countries like his own. These, he believes, are too weak to intervene in the world market and will not be allowed by the great powers to isolate themselves from it. In consequence, they have to adapt themselves to it. Toward this end he advocates increasing mobility of factors and competition among producers.

The contrast of intervention, isolation, and adaptation is suggestive as far as it goes, but it fails to canvass the alternatives fully or to explain the factors affecting choice among them. France and Germany isolated themselves from the world market, to the extent of the tariff. No country intervened to raise the world price of wheat, though this has been undertaken through international co-operation in the present century. England, Italy, and Denmark all adapted to the change, but in a variety of ways. Since a series of alternative adaptations was available and since adaptation was undertaken by large countries as well as by small, Wright's analysis fails to explain the differences in behavior that did occur. His emphasis on the necessity of small countries to adapt, however, suggests that larger countries are unable to adapt in the same way that is open to small countries. In Britain, for example, some substitution of cattle for sheep occurred, and over a longer period animal husbandry expanded to fill part of the gap left by a decline in crop-lands.[25] But, on the whole, Britain was content to import its wheat and its high-value protein foods as well. British agriculture lacked the energy, the resources, and the ability to devise the institutions that would have been necessary for large-scale conversion from arable cropping to animal husbandry.

Several Continental writers have provided an illuminating framework of analysis against which to contrast the behavior of Italy (and southeastern Europe from Hungary to the Volga) with that of the other countries. For example, F. Delaisi[26] distinguishes between Europe A, lying within a circle drawn through Stockholm, Vienna, Barcelona, Bilbao, and Glasgow, and Europe B, outside the circle. Europe A includes northern Italy, upper Austria, and Bohemia and Moravia, but leaves out Ireland, northern Scotland, and most of Spain. In Europe A, industrialization was possible because of the rise of the bourgeois and their insistence on the spread of education; even in agriculture there was established a basis for rural democracy as peasants acquired land. In Europe B, however, constitutions and parliaments had no roots, illiteracy prevailed, and the bourgeois class was small and timid, working with the aristocracy against the peasant and urban laborer rather than challenging the power of the feudal nobility.

When technological advance made industrialization possible, Europe A adopted it; Europe B gradually collapsed. After 1880 emigration rose sharply from Europe B, comprising particularly Italy, Austria-Hungary, Spain, Portugal, and Finland, as far as Delaisi's statistics went, but including also Russia, Yugoslavia, and Greece. For the countries covered by Delaisi, emigration overseas in the decade 1881 to 1890 amounted to 180,000 annually. In successive decades the annual average climbed to 265,000, 629,000, and 907,000 by 1901 to 1913.[27] In Europe *A*, on the other hand, emigration to overseas areas declined, after hitting new peaks in 1881 to 1885. This was because of the opportunities afforded by the expansion in industry.

This explanation by no means covers the situation in its entirety. Britain was much further along in the urbanization process than was Germany or France. This may help to a degree to explain why industry was ready to permit the liquidation of agriculture and why emigrants from agriculture found their way into cities rather than abroad. After industrialization has started, however, and has reached a point where the process is self-generating and cumulative, the rate of growth should be more important than the existing level of industry. And this pace after 1870 was faster in Germany than in Britain. Nor was industrialization meaningless in France: "While France accepted the new techniques and institutions of industry, and even played a significant role in developing them, she did not permit agriculture to be eclipsed, or to suffer revolutionary change."[28]

As between Italy and Denmark, the quality of agriculture was evidently more important than the proportions of population engaged in rural pursuits (which were of the same order of magnitude after adjustment for definitions of urban life). Delaisi's division of Europe into two, and his discussion of the extent to which the collapsing feudal structure was replaced by modern industrial and national institutions, are interesting. The fact of industrialization and the explanation of its concentration in northwestern Europe, however, fail to account for the differences among the responses of the several countries to the decline in the price of wheat.[29]

NONE OF THE foregoing explanations completely accounts for the differences in response to the market; and perhaps the differences should be approached from the standpoint of a theory of group behavior. To be adequate, such a theory must include not only criteria for differentiating the responses of national groups as a unit but also a system of analysis for interrelations among the subgroups within the larger unit. The existing theory of group behavior appears not to have coped adequately with this sort of question. In the main, social psychologists, sociologists, anthropologists, and so on, have concentrated their attention on the relation of the individual to the group, to the relative neglect of the structure of the very large group (the nation) and of functional groups within it.[30] Where intergroup relations have attracted attention, it has been focused on the problems posed by cultural minorities and the relations between groups differentiated by age, sex, and similar factors, rather than on large functional groups. Without a foundation in scientific literature, the following notions on group behavior are general and tentative.

A group must exist in space and time. To be effective, a group must have a system of communication and a set of common values. The existence of the national group in *space* hardly merits discussion. It is an elementary principle of geography that mountain ridges make the best national boundaries—though they are disliked by the military interests charged with protecting the group—since they are the national barriers of language, culture, and commerce. Rivers provide a system of intercommunication rather than a barrier to it, and a country lying in a great plain, like Poland, has uncertain limits. Water in larger amounts is helpful in demarcating the national space. The existence of Britons as a homogeneous group has been assisted by their insular position, while subgroups are demarcated by highlands. Changes in the national space have an important reaction on national cohesion. The Danish "groupiness," or group consciousness, was enhanced by the loss of Schleswig; the French, by that of Alsace-Lorraine. Italy and Germany, at the same time, gained group solidarity from unification in space.

The existence of a group in *time* is connected with its *set of values*. This must be sufficiently attractive or forceful in the spiritual or emotional life of the group for its members to express their loyalty to the group by remaining a part of it through time and bringing their children up as members. The existence of the group in time suggests a difference between material things and social institutions. Matter can wear out evenly over time; when a functional group recognizes that it is doomed to extinction, however, it is difficult to let it decline slowly at the normal rate of depreciation by refusal to maintain it. When faith in the continuity of the organization or group is lost, the group is likely to disintegrate.

The importance of *communication* to the group is increasingly emphasized by social psychologists working with small functional groups, such as the personnel of factories or unions. It is equally important in larger groups. Switzerland, where four languages are spoken, is cited as an illustration of its unimportance in certain situations. In this case space and a powerful set of values are sufficient to hold the group together. The subgroup of agriculture is typically weaker in cohesion than urban groups because of its dispersal in space and the resultant difficulty of communication among its members. The Folk Schools in Denmark and the formation of agricultural syndicates in France were requirements for the maintenance of the agricultural group in the face of the threat from reduced wheat prices.

An existence in space and a system of communication are not enough to constitute a functional group. The parts of the group must share a sense of identification and emotional involvement and a feeling of participation and purpose before the separate subgroups can be considered to make up a group. This sense of unity and purpose may be enhanced by the existence of an antithetical "outgroup." If the sense is not very strong to begin with, however, the development of an out-group may lead to the disintegration of the "in-group."

The major contrast is between Denmark and Italy. In the former, national feeling was intense, as a result of territorial loss, and social cohesion was high. The rural population felt itself a unit and identified itself with the larger national unit. In Italy, despite the recent unification of 1860, the peasant's sense of belonging to the national group was feeble. A blow to his means of livelihood led to the disintegration of the national group, as far as he was concerned. He withdrew—the type of reaction which the classical economists thought was difficult because of cultural barriers and which, indeed, is today barred by the xenophobia of other national groups. Similar responses took place in the Balkans, the Iberian Peninsula, and throughout the rest of feudalistic Europe.

The weakness of the national group in Europe *B,* to use Delaisi's designation, was a result of the failure of national unity to replace the disintegrated feudal group structure. National groups lacked intercommunication and common values. Illiteracy, for example, ran from 10 percent in the Po Valley in Italy to 30 percent in Florence and Rome, 50 percent in Naples, and 70 percent in Calabria.[31] No new emotional attachment replaced the feudal ties that had bound the peasant to the latifundium. Group cohesion was too weak to meet the challenge and the group, under pressure, collapsed.

The importance of the out-group to the cohesion and efficiency of the national group is illustrated effectively by the role played by German aggression and the loss of Schleswig in the Danish response to the decline in wheat prices. Other examples are not lacking in economic history. The French payment of the five-billion-mark indemnity in 1871 was an act of national dedication—and even immolation. To generalize from this experience to the behavior of exports, imports, prices, and the banking system in similar situations where the group stimulus is absent is a familiar practice of economists,[32] but it is highly questionable.

THE CONTRASTING behavior of Britain, Germany, and France requires an understanding of more than the degree of group cohesion at the national level. Attention must be given to the relations among the separate subgroups. These, to be sure, have a bearing on the overall cohesiveness of the nation: a country in which the subgroups are not sharply differentiated and where a degree of social mobility between them exists is likely to have greater cohesion. For the moment, however, our attention is restricted to the relations among the economic subgroups.[33]

Walker asks, "When do men accept the verdict of the market, and when do they attempt to alter it?"[34] A parallel question can be put for group behavior: When does an ascendant subgroup liquidate another subgroup within the large group, and when does it make adjustment to it? Under what circumstances do relationships among subgroups tend to stay in continuous equilibrium, and when do divergences of interest lead in cumulative fashion (as Marx predicted) to schism and clash? Why did industry allow the liquidation of agriculture in Britain, but not in Germany or France? The question appears not to be a simple one of relative strengths or even of more complex strategies of coalition, such as those suggested in *The Theory of Games*. There was no reason for German steel manufacturing to accept coalition with an essentially backward[35] group of agriculturists or for French industry to make concessions to the prescientific peasant. The answer may be found in areas outside the normal province of the economic theorist or the economic historian. The decisive factors do not appear to lie in the field of economics at all, but in that of sociology.

One clue to intergroup behavior may be found in the notion that not all group relations are competitive. Bateson, the anthropologist, has listed a series of stable interdependent subgroup relationships, which, to be sure, primarily apply to subgroups based on age and sex. These include bipolar relations, such as spectator-exhibitionist, dominance-submission, succoring-dependence, aggression-passivity, and the like, but may extend to more complex arrangements. Among the latter Bateson distinguishes what he calls the "ternary relationship," which contains serial elements but includes face-to-face contact between the first and third elements. The function of the middle member in his illustrations — parent-nurse-child and officer-n.c.o.-enlisted man — is to discipline the third member in the forms of behavior that he should adopt toward the first.[36] The relations of the middle class to the wealthy and to the working classes may partake of this character in some political and social respects.[37]

This clue, by no means unambiguous, may assist in explaining what took place in Germany. Gerschenkron expresses the view that the Junkers deceived the peasants of western Germany, whose interest lay in cheaper grain prices, by provision for a tariff on animals and by other means. The reaction, however, may contain elements of submission of the peasant groups before the will of the Junker with higher status. Residual traces of the feudal relationship existed; probably more important were the battles won for the glory of the national group in 1864, 1866, and 1870. A portion of labor and even the steel barons were content to maintain the economic position of the Junkers, in the face of opportunity to liquidate them, because of the element of status, which for labor outweighed class interest. The leadership and dominance exhibited by the Junker class probably explain the major part of its success in maintaining its position through the Caprivi tariff, World War I, the inflation, and the Nazi regime.

Another clue may lie in that most complex conception, the basic personality type of a culture or subculture. This notion, developed by the social psychologist with the help of anthropological data, denies that human nature is a constant in time or space, but holds that the basic personality type of a culture will condition responses to external stimuli and in turn be altered by them. Of particular importance, it is held, is the way in which a society rears its children.[38]

This matter is far too complex and elusive to pursue here beyond the rough generalization that the basic personality type differs among England, France, and Germany in putting primary emphasis in the culture (below the level of the national group) on, respectively, the individual, the family, and the class. If we accept this, it may assist in explaining why Britain was willing to liquidate agriculture, while France and Germany were not.

Economic and political liberalism, born in Britain, required social mobility to give importance to the individual at the level next below the national group. Mobility in space was provided for Britain, as for Scandinavia and the Netherlands, by the sea, which served as a frontier.[39] At home, despite the class structure, social mobility upward derived from the willingness of the aristocracy to admit successful commercial and industrial interests to the ownership of land and their sons to the public schools. Downward mobility was provided by primogeniture, which drew off the increase in the aristocracy into the middle class. Whatever the facts, the concept of class as a functional subgroup was not recognized in the culture. A blow to a broad economic interest was regarded as affecting not a class but a loose aggregation of individuals.[40] This may account for the passivity of the nation in watching unmoved the liquidation of agriculture in the thirty years after 1879.[41]

The opposition of industry and agriculture in France was more apparent than real; both were concerned not with economic interest as such but with economic interest in a context of the dominant social institution of the family. This has been studied in industry, where the conclusion has been reached that the size of firm which could be kept in the family from generation to generation limited the growth of industry.[42] The unwillingness of the French to emigrate is further evidence. And the continuity of the French farm in the family group from generation to generation is a commonplace.

In Germany the major subgroup, at least at the extremes, was the class. To the extent that the nobility was a farming group in occupation, group solidarity and economic interest were unified in the Junker portion of agriculture, while they were opposed among the peasants. Such conflict of group and economic interest is not, however, unusual: Walker has expressed surprise that the farmers of Australia supported a program of land settlement contrary to their economic interest.[43] But these farmers gained more through the growth in numbers of their group than they lost through the increase of supply. The question was one of class and, within the total class structure, of dominance.

THE DANISH response to the decline in the world price of wheat was by far the most satisfactory, whether in social and economic terms or in economic terms alone. It raised the level of real income for the producer group at the same time as it preserved the gain of cheaper bread for the consumer. Social upheaval was avoided. Was the whole episode an accident? Was this sort of solution possible for the other countries? To what extent is it possible to capitalize disaster in this fashion on a general scale?

The mind of the economist is likely to try to find a parallel in certain situations that occur when wage increases lead to expansion rather than to contraction of output because they provide the incentive to a recombination of factors in more efficient fashion. The classic example is the elimination of the sweatshop through the efforts of union leaders, which increased incomes for both laborers and enterprisers and also reduced the cost of clothing. This was brought about by requiring firms in the garment industry to employ their newly expensive labor efficiently. The market opportunity for combining capital and labor in more efficient fashion had existed before the success of the union drive. Until the system was pushed off dead center, however, the path of least resistance was opposition to the demands of the union.

The parallel is not exact. Dairying to replace grain cultivation had been initiated in the 1860s before the decline in the price of wheat—primarily, however, on large estates.[44] The motive was only partly economic. In part it was observed that the soil was being impoverished by grain crops. There was still another difference. Although a market opportunity offered by the relative prices of grain and butter already existed, it was considerably increased by the decline in the price of wheat in the 1870s and 1880s and the rise in the demand for butter in the growing urban centers of England. A real impetus to the conversion came from the price decline. Particularly remarkable was the capacity of the Danish economy, or polity, to develop the institutions necessary to complete the conversion on a large scale to take maximum advantage of the economic opportunity.

It may be contended that there was a marked degree of accident in the existence of the middle-sized farm, which was inefficient for wheat, and in the development of the agricultural high school, in response to the loss of Schleswig. The explanation for the prevalence of the middle-sized farm would appear to lie deep in the Danish basic personality type, which emphasizes stability rather than growth.[45] The development of the Folk School was perhaps partly an accident, but the Danish peasant had always shown a communicating tendency,[46] and this fact may be more important than the particular form of institution devised at the particular time.

The development of the cooperative in response to a technological need raises more fundamental problems. What factors govern the capacity of a society to develop institutions required to enable it to take advantage of economic, political, and social opportunities? Are these adaptations always accidental? Under certain conditions are they made automatically, or can they be contrived through direction after conscious decision?

Most commentators on the cooperative believe that this development was the product of the prevalence of the freehold in Danish land tenure, together with the high degree of education in Danish farmers. "Tenant farmers will not co-operate because, co-operative accounts being open to inspection, they fear their landlords might raise the rents if it were found that they were prospering."[47] But the emphasis given to the form of land tenure goes deeper than this. The point is that cooperation in Denmark flourished because of the social cohesion that enabled the farmers to create the necessary institutions, when the occasion demanded economies of scale in marketing along with labor-intensive production. The prevalence of freeholds bespeaks equality of status, which makes communication freer in all directions. Education increases the quantity and quality of communication. Together with a high degree of communication, a closely held set of values, and internal social mobility—all of which are interrelated—Denmark had social cohesion. It was this factor that enabled her to create the institutions needed to take advantage of an economic opportunity. In the absence of the economic opportunity, however, the institutions would not have been devised.

In general, then, the flexibility of a society in devising institutions to accomplish its purposes under changing conditions is a function of its social cohesion, which in turn depends upon its internal social mobility, system of communications, and set of values. If social cohesion is high, it may be possible to find a response to external change that will being about a new identification of the interests of the subgroups with those of the total group at an improved level of satisfaction for all. If the system of communication is sufficiently effective, moreover, it may be impossible to isolate the decision-making process, so that the response of the society appears to be automatic.

WHAT I have said can be reduced to some fairly elementary propositions. The response that will be made to an economic stimulus in international trade cannot always be predicted from the nature and extent of the stimulus. It may require a knowledge of the group situation within the separate countries affected. The response may be the disintegration of the group, leading to emigration if that is possible, or, if no such outlet is available, to pathological political behavior. The effect, on the other hand, may range from the liquidation of a particular subgroup in the society for the benefit of others, as in Britain; to the protection of the affected group at the general expense, as in France and Germany; to an inspired act of readjustment undertaken by the group as a whole. Which of these actions will be taken lies deep in the structure of the society. For accurate prediction and policy formation, an adequate theory of the behavior of large groups and their components is needed as an adjunct to the analytical tools of the market.

The Rise of Free Trade
in Western Europe, 1820 to 1875

3. The textbook theory of tariffs and their converse, the movement to freer trade, has more elements than we need for the nineteenth century, but also lacks some. In the usual comparative statics a tariff may be said to have ten effects: on price, trade, production (the protective effect), consumption, revenue, terms of trade, internal income distribution, monopoly, employment, and the balance of payments.

For present purposes we can dispense with the employment effect. The terms-of-trade effect arises only in connection with export taxes; and the monopoly effect must be converted to dynamic form, that increased imports stimulate growth by forcing competition and responsive innovation.

We may illustrate the bulk of the needed effects with the simplest of partial-equilibrium diagrams of a familiar sort. In Figure 1, an import tariff, t, raises the domestic price, P_t, above the world price, P_w (assumed to be unaffected by the tariff), reduces trade from MM to $M'M'$, expands production by MM', and reduces consumption by $M'M$. An increase in rent to producers consists in the quadrilateral a; revenue accruing to the government is represented by b. Removal of the tariff reverses all movements. An export tax as in Figure 2 reduces price and trade, cuts down on producers' rent, increases consumption, reduces production, and earns governmental revenue. Conversely, removal of an export tax raises price, production, and producers' rent, enlarges trade, reduces domestic consumption, loses revenue. In the nineteeth century, when direct taxation was limited, the

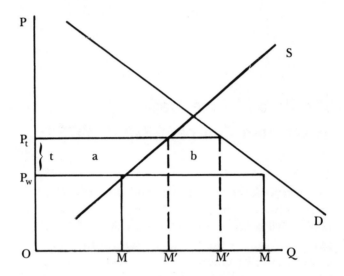

Figure 1.   Import tax in partial equilibrium.

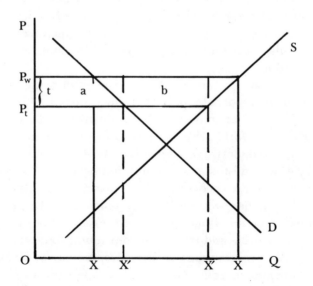

Figure 2.   Export tax in partial equilibrium.

revenue effect could not be disregarded as it is today. Prohibition of exports or imports had in varying degree all other effects on price, trade, production, consumption, redistribution, monopoly, but wiped out revenue (and the terms of trade). This assumed that the prohibition or prohibitive tax was not undermined by smuggling.

Static theory needs two further elements. The first is a theory of incidence. With more than two factors, are rents retained by the initial recipient or are they competed away in bidding for still more scarce resources? The second is another factor, or institutional interest, beyond the normal agriculture and manufacturing, that is, the merchant, with whom may be included shipping. The merchant is interested in maximizing trade not for its impact on production or consumption, but to increase turnover, on which—provided national merchants and ships are used—he earns a return. For trade any goods will do, including those of foreigners which have no impact on domestic production or consumption of the goods in question. (Shipping interests of course insist on the use of national-flag vessels.)

Such is the economic model. Political and sociological elements will be added as required and will include: the view (for example, of Cobden) that free trade leads to peace; trade treaties as foreign treaties in general, desired for reasons of foreign policy, balance of power, and the like; ideology; bandwagon effects; and the need of most men to be consistent. It is especially necessary to indicate the relationships between economic interest and political power.

In his interesting study of the formation of the United States tariff of 1824, Jonathan Pincus asserts that tariff making can be explained by the success or failure of various interests in obtaining rents, the quadrilateral a in Figure 1. In his view the tariff is a collective good, passage of which requires limited numbers of concentrated producers: if the interested parties are diffuse, the fallacy of composition takes over as each element seeks to become a "free rider," leaving the transaction costs of engineering the tariff change to others. This is a theory applicable to representative democracies and leaves little room for executive leadership.[1] Nor does it make allowance for intermediate goods.

That diffuse interests are less well served than concentrated ones in the legislative process is widely accepted in the theory of tariff formation by comparing producers and final consumers. Households count for little in tariff making, since the interest of any one is too small to stir it to the political effort and financial cost necessary to achieve results. With intermediate goods, however, the consumption effect cannot be disregarded; industries that rely on a given import, or on a product exported by another industry, may be as effectively concentrated as producers of final goods.

In the Pincus theory, the movement toward free trade in western Europe would have to be based on the dominance of the interests of consumers of intermediate imports over those of their producers, and of producers of exports over consumers of exported intermediates. A variety of other general explanations has been offered.

In Bastiat's view, the rise of free trade was the result of the spread of democracy.[2] Free trade has also been regarded as the interest of the bourgeois class in England and of the landed aristocracy on the Continent, while protection has been sought by the aristocracy in England and by the bourgeois manufacturing classes on the Continent.[3]

Somewhat more dynamically, Johnson asserts that countries whose competitiveness in world markets is improving tend to move in the free-trade direction, while countries whose competitiveness is deteriorating tend to move to increasing protection. A footnote states, "Outstanding examples are the adoption of free trade by Britain in the 19th century . . . the espousal of freer trade by the United States and Canada in the period after the Second World War."[4]

In what follows we shall find these views insufficiently detailed.

THE BEGINNINGS of free trade internationally go back to the eighteenth century. French Physiocratic theory enunciated the slogan *laissez faire, laissez passer* to reduce export prohibitions on agricultural products. Pride of place in practice, however, goes to Tuscany, which permitted free export of the corn of the Sienese Maremma in 1737, after the Grand Duke Francis had read Sallustio Bandini's *Economical Discourse*.[5] Beset by famine in 1764, Tuscany gradually opened its market to imported grain well before the Vergennes Treaty of 1786 between France and Britain put French Physiocratic doctrine into practice. Grain exports in Tuscany had been restricted under the "policy of supply," or "provisioning," or "abundance," under which the city-states of Italy limited exports from the surrounding countryside in order to assure food to the urban populace. Bandini and Pompeo Neri pointed out the ill effects this had on investment and productivity in agriculture.

The policy of supply was not limited to food. In the eighteenth and early nineteenth centuries there were restrictions on exports in, for instance, wool and coal (Britain), ashes, rags, sand for glass, and firewood (Germany), ship timbers (Austria), rose madder (the Netherlands), and silk cocoons (Italy). The restrictions on exports of ashes and timber from Germany had conservation overtones. The industrial revolution in Britain led further to prohibitions on export of machinery and on emigration of artisans, partly to increase the supply for local use, but also to prevent the diffusion of technology on the Continent. We return to this below.

What was left in the policy of supply after the Napoleonic wars quickly ran down. Prohibition of export of raw silk was withdrawn in Piedmont, Lombardy, and Venetia in the 1830s, and freedom to export coal from Britain was enacted in the 1840s. Details of the relaxation of restrictions are recorded for Baden[6] as part of the movement to occupational freedom. The guild system gradually collapsed under the weight of increasing complexity of regulation by firms seeking exceptions for themselves and objecting to exceptions for others. A number of prohibitions and export taxes lasted to the 1850s — as industrial consumers held out against producers, or in some cases, like rags, against collectors of waste products. Reduction of the export tax on rags in Piedmont in 1851 produced a long, drawn-out struggle between Cavour and the industry, which had to close up thirteen plants when the tax was reduced.[7] To Cavour salvation of the industry lay in machinery and in substitution of other materials, not in restricting export through Leghorn and Messina to Britain and North America.

Elimination of export taxes and prohibitions in nineteenth-century Europe raises doubt about the universal validity of the theory of the tariff as a collective good, imposed by a concentrated interest at the expense of the diffuse. The interests of groups producing inputs for other industries are normally more deeply affected than those of the consuming industries, but it is hardly possible that the consuming is always less concentrated than the producing industry.

THE QUESTION of export duties sought by domestic manufacturers on their raw materials, and of import duties on outputs demanded by producers for the domestic market was settled in the Netherlands in the eighteenth century in favor of mercantile interests.[8] These were divided into the First Hand—merchants, shipowners, and bankers; the Second Hand—which carried on the work of sorting and packing in staple markets and of wholesaling on the Continent; and the Third Hand—concerned with distribution in the hinterland. Dutch staple trade was based partly on mercantile skills and partly on the pivotal location of Amsterdam, Rotterdam, and other towns dedicated to trade in particular commodities, largely perishable, nonstandardized, and best suited to short voyages. The First Hand dominated Dutch social and political life and opposed all tariffs on export or import goods, above a minimum for revenue, in order to maximize trade and minimize formalities. From 1815 to 1830, when Holland and Belgium were united as the Low Countries, the clash between the Dutch First Hand and Belgian producers in search of import protection from British manufacturers was continuous and heated.

The First Hand objected to taxes for revenue on coffee, tea, tobacco, rice, sugar, and so on, and urged their replacement by excises on flour, meat, horses, and servants.[9] They urged that tariffs for revenue be held down to prevent smuggling and to sustain turnover. The safe maximum was given variously as 3 percent,[10] 5 percent,[11] and on transit even as 0.5 percent. Transit in bond and transit with duty-cum-drawback were thought too cumbersome. The Dutch made a mistake in failing to emulate London, which in 1803 adopted a convenient entrepot dock with bonding.[12] Loss of colonies and of overseas connections in the Napoleonic wars made it impossible from early in the period for Holland to compete with Britain in trade. Equally threatening was Hamburg, which supplied British and colonial goods to Central Europe in transit for 0.5 percent revenue duty maximum,[13] many products free, and all so after 1839.[14] More serious, however, was the rise of direct selling as transport efficiency increased. Early signs of direct selling can be detected at the end of the seventeenth century when Venice and Genoa lost their role as intermediaries in traffic between Italy and the West.[15] By the first half of the nineteenth century such signs were abundant. "By the improved intercourse of our time [1840], the seller is brought more immediately into contact with the producer."[16] Twenty years earlier the Belgian members of a Dutch-Belgian fiscal commission argued that "there was no hope of restoring Holland's general trade. Owing to the spread of civilization, all European countries could now provide for themselves in direct trading."[17]

It is a mistake to think of merchants as all alike. As indicated, the First, Second, and Third Hands of the Netherlands had different functions, status, and power. In Germany republican merchants of Hamburg differed sharply from those of the imperial city, Frankfurt, and held out fifty years longer against the Zollverein.[18] Within Frankfurt there were two groups, the English-goods party associated with the bankers, and the majority, which triumphed in 1836, interested in transit, forwarding, and retail and domestic trade within the Zollverein. In Britain a brilliant picture had been drawn of a pragmatic free trader, John Gladstone, father of William, opposed to timber preferences for Canada, enemy of the East India Company monopoly on trade with China and India, but supportive of imperial preference in cotton and sugar and approving of the Corn Laws on the ground of support for the aristocracy he hoped his children could enter via politics.[19] The doctrinaire free traders of Britain were the cotton manufacturers like Gladstone's friend, Kirman Finlay, who regarded shipowners and corn growers as the two great sets of monopolists.

The doctrinaire free trade of the Dutch merchants led to economic sclerosis[20] or economic sickness.[21] Hamburg stayed in trade and finance and did not move into industry. In Britain merchants were ignorant of industry, but were saved by the coming of the railroad and by limited liability, which provided an outlet for their surplus as direct trading squeezed profits from stapling. The economic point is simple: free trade may stimulate, but it may also fossilize.

THE MOVEMENT toward freer trade in Britain began gross in the eighteenth century, net only after the Napoleonic wars. In the initial stages there was little problem for a man like Wedgwood to advocate free trade for exports of manufactures under the Treaty of Vergennes with France, and at the same time to advocate prohibitions on the export of machinery and emigration of artisans.[22] Even in the 1820s and 1830s a number of the political economists—Torrens, Baring, Peel, Nassau Senior—favored repeal of the Corn Laws but opposed export of machinery.[23] The nineteenth century is seen by Brebner not as a steady march to laissez-faire but as a counter-point between Smithian laissez-faire in trade matters and, after the Reform Bill, Benthamic intervention of 1832, which produced the Factory, Mines, Ten Hours, and similar acts from 1833 to 1847.[24]

First came the revenue aspect, which was critical of the movement to freer trade under Huskisson in the 1820s, Peel in the 1840s, and Gladstone in the 1850s. Huskisson and Gladstone used the argument that the bulk of revenue was produced by taxes on a few items — largely colonial products such as tea, coffee, sugar, tobacco, and wine and spirits — and that others produced too little revenue to be worth the trouble. Many were redundant (for example, import duties on products that Britain exported). Others were so high as to be prohibitory or encouraged smuggling and reduced revenue. When Peel was converted to free trade, it was necessary to reintroduce the income tax before he could proceed between 1841 and 1846 with repeal of 605 duties and reductions in 1,035 others. The title of Sir Henry Parnell's treatise on freer trade (1830) was *Financial Reform*.

But Huskisson was a free trader, if a cautious one. He spoke of benefits to be derived from the removal of "vexatious restraints and meddling interference in the concerns of internal industry and foreign commerce."[25] Especially he thought that imports stimulated efficiency in import-competing industry. In 1824 the prohibition on silk imports had been converted to a duty of 30 percent, regarded as the upper limit of discouragement to smuggling. In a speech on March 24, 1826, said by Canning to be the finest he had heard in the House of Commons, Huskisson observed that Macclesfield and Spitalfield had reorganized the industry under the spur of enlarged imports and expanded the scale of output.[26] Both Michel Chevalier[27] and Count Cavour[28] referred to this positive and dynamic response to increased imports in England.

Restrictions on export of machinery and emigration of artisans went back, as indicated, to the industrial revolution. Prohibition of export of stocking frames was enacted as early as 1696. Beginning in 1774 there was a succession of restrictions on tools and utensils for the cotton and linen trades and on the emigration of skilled artisans. The basis was partly the policy of supply, partly naked maintenance of monopoly. Freedom had been granted for the emigration of workmen in 1824. After the depression of the late 1830s, pressure for removal of the prohibition came from all machinery manufacturers. Following further investigation by a Select Committee of Parliament, the export prohibition was withdrawn.

The main arguments against prohibition of the export of machinery and emigration of artisans were three: they were ineffective, they were unnecessary, they were harmful. Ineffectuality was attested to by much detail in the Select Committee reports on the efficiency of smuggling. Machinery for which licenses could not be obtained could be dispatched illegally in a number of ways—by another port, hidden in cotton bales, in baggage, or mixed with permitted machinery—and in a matter of hours. Guaranteed and insured shipments could be arranged in London or Paris for premiums up to 30 percent.

That prohibition was unnecessary was justified first by the inability of foreigners, even with English machinery and English workmen, to rival English manufacturers. Britain had minerals, railways, canals, rivers, better division of labor, "trained workmen habituated to all industrious employments."[29] "Even when the Belgians employed English machines and skilled workers, they failed to import the English spirit of enterprise and secured only disappointing results."[30] In 1825 the Select Committee concluded it was safe to export machinery, since seven-year-old machinery in Manchester was already obsolete.[31]

In the third place prohibition was dangerous. Restriction on emigration of artisans failed to prevent their departure, but did inhibit their return.[32] Restriction of machinery, moreover, raised the price abroad through the cost of smuggling and stimulated production on the Continent. Improvement in the terms of trade through restriction of exports (but failure to cut them off altogether) was deleterious because of its protective effect abroad.

Greater cohesion of the Manchester cotton spinners than of the machinery makers spread over Manchester, Birmingham, and London may account for the delay from 1825 to 1841 in freeing up machinery and support Pincus' theory on the need of concentrated interests. But the argument of consistency was telling. In 1800 the Manchester manufacturers of cloth had demanded a law forbidding export of yarn, but did not obtain it.[33] The 1841 Second Report concluded that machinery making should be put on the same footing as other departments of British industry.[34] It is noted that Nottingham manufacturers approved free trade, but claimed an exception in regard to machinery used in their own manufacture.[35] Babbage observed that machinery makers are more intelligent than their users, to whose imagined benefits their interests are sacrificed, and referred to the "impolicy of interfering between two classes."[36] In the end, the Manchester Chamber of Commerce became troubled and divided by the inconsistency; the issue of prohibition of machinery was subsumed into the general attack on the Corn Laws.[37] In the 1840s, moreover, the sentiment spread that Britain should become the workshop of the world, which implied the production of heavy goods as well as cotton cloth and yarn.[38]

Rivers of ink have been spilled on the repeal of the Corn Laws, and the present chapter can do little but summarize the issues and indicate a position. The questions relate to the Stolper-Samuelson distribution argument, combined with the Reform Bill of 1832 and the shift of political power from the landed aristocracy to the bourgeois; incidence of the Corn Laws and of their repeal, within both farming and manufacturing sectors; the potential for a dynamic response of farming to lower prices from competition; and the relation of repeal to economic development on the Continent, especially whether industrialization could be halted by expanded and assured outlets for agricultural produce, a point of view characterized by Gallagher and Robinson as "free-trade imperialism."[39] A number of lesser issues may be touched upon incidentally: interaction between the Corn Laws and the Zollverein, and the tariff changes in the 1840s; the question of whether repeal of the Corn Laws and of the Navigation Acts would have been very long delayed had it not been for potato famine in Ireland and on the Continent; and the question of whether the term "free-trade imperialism" is better reserved for Joseph Chamberlain's empire preference of fifty years later.

In the usual view the Reform Bill of 1832 shifted power from land and country to factory and city, from the aristocratic class to the bourgeois, and inexorably led to changes in trade policies that had favored farming and hurt manufacturing. One can argue that repeal of the Corn Laws represented something less than that, and that the Reform Bill was not critical. The movement to free trade had begun earlier in the Huskisson reforms; speeches in Parliament were broadly the same in 1825, when it was dominated by landed aristocrats, as in the 1830s and 1840s. Numbers had changed with continued manufacturing expansion, but not much more. Or one can reject the class explanation, as Polanyi does, and see something much more ideological. "Not until the 1830s did economic liberalism burst forth as a crusading passion." The liberal creed involved faith in man's secular salvation through a self-regulating market, a faith that was held with fanaticism and evangelical fervor.[40] French Physiocrats were trying to correct only one inequity, to break out of the policy of supply and permit export of grain. British political economists of the 1830s and 1840s, who won over Tories like Sir Robert Peel and Lord Russell and ended up in 1846 with many landlords agreeable to repeal of the Corn Laws, represented an ideology.[41] "Mere class interests cannot offer a satisfactory explanation for any long-run social process."[42]

Under a two-sector model free trade comes when the abundant factor acquires political power and moves to eliminate restrictions imposed in the interest of the scarce factor, which has lost power. In reality factors of production are not monolithic. Some confusion in the debate attached to the incidence of the tax on imported corn within both farming and manufacturing. The Anti-Corn Law League of Cobden and Bright regarded it as a tax on food, which took as much as 20 percent of the earnings of a hand-loom weaver. Cobden denied the "fallacy" that wages rose and fell with the price of bread.[43] Benefits, moreover, went to the landlord and not the farmer or farm laborer, as rents on the short leases in practice rose with the price of corn.[44] There are passages in Cobden which suggest that the brunt of the Corn Laws fell on the manufacturing and commercial classes rather than labor,[45] but the speeches run mainly in terms of a higher standard of living for the laborer who would spend his "surplus of earnings on meat, vegetables, butter, milk and cheese," rather than on wheaten loaves.[46] The Chartists were interested not in repeal, but in other amenities for the workers. Peel's conversion came with his conclusion that wages did not vary with the price of provision, and that repeal would benefit the wage earner rather than line the pockets of the manufacturer.[47]

In any event, with Gladstone's reductions in duties on meat, eggs, and dairy products, with High Farming (that is, improved farming techniques), and with end to the movement off the farm and out of handwork into the factory, real wages did rise in the 1850s, but so did profits on manufacturing. As so often happens in economic de-

bates over outcomes, history blurred the experiment. Theory suggested that repeal of the Corn Laws would benefit either wages in
manufacturing or manufacturers' profits. It benefited both. Nor
did repeal bring a reduction in incomes to landlords — at least not
for thirty years; the farm response to repeal, and to high prices of
food produced by the potato famine, was more High Farming.

Cobden may have been only scoring debating points rather than
speaking from conviction when on a number of occasions he argued
that the repeal would stimulate landlords "to employ their capital
and their intelligence as other classes are forced to do in other pursuits" rather than "in sluggish indolence," and to double the quantity of grain, or butter, or cheese, that the land is capable of providing,[48] with "longer leases, draining, extending the length of fields,
knocking down hedgerows, clearing away trees which now shield
the corn,"[49] and to provide more agricultural employment by activity to "grub up hedges, grub up thorns, drain, ditch."[50] Sir James
Caird insisted that High Farming was the answer to the repeal of the
Corn Laws,[51] and many shared his view.[52] The fact is, moreover,
that the 1850s were the golden age of British farming, with rapid
technical progress through the decade, though it slowed thereafter.
Repeal of the Corn Laws may not have stimulated increased efficiency in agriculture, but it did not set it back immediately, and
only after the 1870s did increases in productivity run down.

The political economists in the Board of Trade — Bowring, Jacob,
MacGregor — sought free trade as a means of slowing down the development of manufacturing on the Continent. They regarded the
Zollverein as a reply to the imposition of the Corn Laws and thought
that with its repeal Europe, especially the Zollverein under the leadership of Prussia, could be diverted to invest more heavily in agriculture and to retard the march to manufacturing. There were in-
consistencies between this position and other facts they adduced:
Bowring recognized that Germany had advantages over Great Britain for the development of manufacturing, and that Swiss spinning
had made progress without protection.[53] The 1818 Prussian tariff
which formed the basis for that of the Zollverein was the lowest in
Europe when it was enacted — although the levying of tariffs on
cloth and yarn by weight gave high effective rates of protection despite low nominal duties to the cheaper constructions and counts.
Jacob noted that the export supply elasticity of Prussian grain must
be low, given poor transport.[54] "To export machinery, we must im-

port corn";[55] but imports of corn were intended to prevent the development of manufacturers abroad, whereas the export of machinery assisted it. The rise and progress of German manufacturing were attributed to restrictions imposed by France and England on the admission of German agricultural products and wood, but also to "the natural advantages of the several states for manufacturing industry, the genius and laborious character and the necessities of the German people, and . . . especially the unexampled duration of peace, and internal tranquility which all Germany enjoyed."[56]

The clearest statements are those of John Bowring. In a letter of August 28, 1839, to Lord Palmerston he asserted that the manufacturing interest in the Zollverein "is greatly strengthened and will become stronger from year to year unless counteracted by a system of concessions, conditional upon the gradual lowering of tariffs. The present state of things will not be tenable. The tariffs will be elevated under the growing demands and increasing power of the manufacturing states, or they will be lowered by calling into action, and bringing over to an alliance, the agricultural and commercial interests."[57] In his testimony before the Select Committee on Import Duties in 1840 he went further: "I believe we have created an unnecessary rivalry by our vicious legislation; that many of these countries never would have been dreamed of being manufacturers."[58]

From this viewpoint, repeal of the Corn Laws was motivated by "free-trade imperialism," the desire to gain a monopoly of trade with the world in manufactured goods. The Zollverein in the 1830s merely indicated the need for haste.[59] Torrens and James Deacon Hume, among others, had been pushing for importing corn to expand exports in the 1820s, before the Zollverein was a threat.

Reciprocity had been a part of British commercial policy in the Treaty of Vergennes in 1786 and in treaties reducing the impact of the Navigation Laws in the 1820s and 1830s. The French were suspicious, fearing that they had been outtraded in 1786. They evaded Huskisson's negotiations in 1828. But reciprocity was unnecessary, given David Hume's Law. Unilateral reduction of import duties increased exports.[60] Restored to the British diplomatic armory in 1860, reciprocity later became heresy in the eyes of political economists, and of the manufacturing interests as well.

The view that ascribes repeal of the Corn Laws to free-trade imperialism, however, fails adequately to take account of the ideology of the political economists, who believed in buying in the cheapest market and selling in the highest, or of the short-run nature of the interests of the Manchester merchants themselves. It was evident after the 1840s that industrialization on the Continent could not be stopped, and likely that it could not be slowed down. The Navigation Acts were too complex; they needed to be eliminated.[61] The Corn Laws were doomed, even before the Irish potato famine (though that hastened the end of both Corn Laws and Navigation Acts), along with its demonstration of the limitation of market solutions under some circumstances.[62]

As Mill said, "A good cause seldom triumphs unless someone's interest is bound up with it."[63] Free trade is the hypocrisy of the export interest, the clever device of the climber who kicks the ladder away when he has attained the summit of greatness.[64] But in the English case it was more a view of the world at peace, with cosmopolitan interests served as well as national.

It is difficult in this to find clearcut support for any of the theories of tariff formation set forth earlier. Free trade as an export-interest collective good, sought in a representative democracy by concentrated interests to escape the free rider, would seem to require a simple and direct connection between the removal of the tariff and the increase in rents. In the repeal of the Corn Laws, and the earlier tariff reductions of Huskisson and Peel, the connection was roundabout — through Hume's law, which meant that increased imports would lead to increased prices or quantities exported (or both) on the one hand, and/or through reduced wages, or higher real incomes from lower food prices, on the other. Each chain of reasoning had several links.

Johnson's view that free trade is adopted by countries with improving competitiveness is contradictory to the free-trade-imperialism explanation, that free trade is adopted in an effort to undermine foreign gains in manufacturing when competitiveness has begun to decline. The former might better account in timing for Adam Smith's advocacy of free trade seventy years earlier — though that had large elements of French Physiocratic thought — or apply to the 1820s when British productivity was still improving, before the Continent had started to catch up. Actually, free-trade imperialism is a better explanation for the 1830s than for the end of the 1840s, since by 1846 it was already too late to slow, much less to halt, the advance of manufacturing on the Continent.

Vested interests competing for rents in a representative democracy, thrusting manufacturers seeking to expand markets, or faltering innovators trying as a last resort to force exports on shrinking markets—rather like the stage of foreign direct investment in Vernon's product cycle when diffusion of technology has been accomplished—none of these explanations seems free of difficulties when compared with an ideological explanation based on the intellectual triumph of the political economists, their doctrines modified to incorporate consistency. The argument took many forms: static, dynamic, with implicit reliance on one incidence or another, direct or indirect in its use of Hume's law. But the Manchester school, based on the political economists, represented a rapidly rising ideology of freedom for industry to buy in the cheapest and sell in the dearest market. It overwhelmed the Tories when it did not convert them. Britain in the nineteenth century, and only to a slightly lesser extent the Continent, were characterized by a "strong, widely-shared conviction that the teachings of contemporary orthodox economists, including Free Traders, were scientifically exact, universally applicable, and demanded assent."[65] In the implicit debate between Thurman Arnold, who regarded economic theorists (and lawyers) as high priests who rationalize and sprinkle holy water on contemporary practice, and Keynes, who thought of practical men as responding unconsciously to the preaching of dead theorists, the British movement to free-trade was a vote, aided by the potato famine, for the view of Keynes.

FRANCE after 1815 was a high-tariff country that conformed to the Pincus model of a representative democracy with tariffs for various interests, except that (a) there were tariffs for all, and (b) it was not a democracy. The Physiocratic doctrine of laissez-faire for agricultural exports had been discredited in its reciprocal form by the disaster wreaked by imports up to 1789 under the Treaty of Vergennes. The Continental system, moreover, provided strong protection to hothouse industries, which was continued in the tariff of 1816 and elaborated in 1820 and 1822. To the principles of Turgot, that there should be freedom of grain trade inside France but no imports except in period of drought, were added two more: protection of the consumer by regulating the right of export of wheat—a step back from Physiocratic doctrine—and protecting the rights of producers by import tariffs.[66] In introducing the tariff of 1822 for manufactures, Saint-Cricq defended prohibitions and attacked the view that an industry that could not survive with a duty of 20 percent should perish, saying that the government intended to protect all branches together: "agriculture, industry, internal commerce, colonial production, navigation, foreign commerce finally, both of land and of sea."[67]

It was not long, however, before pressures for lower duties manifested themselves. Industries complained of the burden of the tariff on their purchases of inputs, and especially of the excess protection accorded to iron. It was calculated that protection against English iron cost industrial consumers fifty million francs a year and had increased the price of wood—used for charcoal, and owned by the many noble *maîtres de forges*—by 30 percent on the average and in some places 50 percent.[68] Commissions of inquiry in 1828 and 1834 recommended modifications in duties, especially to enlarge supplies that local industry was not in a position to provide and to convert prohibitions into tariffs. A tumult of conflict broke out in the Chamber of Deputies among the export interests of the ports, the textile interests of Alsace and Normandy, the maîtres de forges, and the consumers of iron, with no regard, says the protectionist Gouraud, for the national interest. The chambers were then dissolved by the cabinet and tariffs adjusted downward—in coal, iron, copper, nitrates, machinery, horses. Reductions of the 1830s were followed in the peaks of business by similar pressure for reductions in prosperous phases of the cycle of the 1840s and 1850s.[69]

A troubling question that involved conflicting interests in this period was presented by sugar, for which it was impossible to find a solution agreeable at the same time to colonial planters, shipowners, port refiners, consumers, and the treasury. Colonial supply was high in cost, and a duty of 55 francs per 100 kilograms on foreign supplies was needed to appease the sugar ports. This, however, made it economical to expand beet-sugar production, begun during the Continental blockade, and the sugar ports turned to taxing this domestic production, less heavily at first, but with full equality in 1843. By this time it was too late, and with the freeing of the slaves in 1848, French colonial sugar production no longer counted.

The free-trade movement in France had its support in Bordeaux, the wine-exporting region; Lyons, interested in silk; and Paris, producer of so-called Paris articles for sale abroad (cabinetwork, perfumes, imitation jewelry, toys, and so on). Later Norman agricultural interests in the export to London of butter and eggs teamed up with Bordeaux wine interests to resist the attempts by textile interests to enlist agriculture in favor of higher tariffs.[70]

Intellectual support of free trade led by Bastiat from Bordeaux, and with Michel Chevalier as its most prestigious member, is dismissed by Lévy-Leboyer as unimportant.[71] Nonetheless, Chevalier had an important part in negotiation of the Anglo-French Treaty of Commerce of 1860, and in persuading Napoleon III to impose it on France in the face of the united opposition of the Chamber of Deputies. Some attention to his thought is required.

The prime interest of the Société d'économie politique and of Chevalier was growth.[72] His two-year visit to the United States in 1833 to 1835 impressed him with the contribution of transport to economic growth and contributed to his 1838 major work on *The Material Interests of France in Roads, Canals and Railroads.* American protectionist doctrine of Henry Carey seems not to have affected him. Polytechnician and graduate of the Ecole des mines, Chevalier's first interest in freer trade came from a project to establish woolen production in the Midi, and to obtain cheaper wool.[73] Much of his later reasoning was in terms of the penalty to industry from expensive materials: charging thirty-five francs for a quintal of iron worth twenty imposes on industry "the labor of Sisyphus and the work of Penelope."[74] His major argument, at the Collège de France and in his Examen du système commercial, cited the success of Spitalfield and Macclesfield when Huskisson permitted competition of imports, as well as the experience of the manufacturers of cotton and woolen textiles in Saxony who were worried by the enactment of Zollverein but sufficiently stimulated by import competition so that in two or three years their industry was flourishing.[75] The letter of Napoleon III to Fould[76] talks in specifics of the need to abolish all duties on raw materials essential to industry to encourage production, and to reduce by stages the duties on goods that are consumed on a large scale. In the more general introduction the letter states that "lack of competition causes industry to stagnate," an echo of the Chevalier view. Chevalier himself was one of the judges of the Universal Exposition of 1855 in Paris and noted that France received so many prizes that no one dared confess to being a protectionist.[77]

There were economic purposes behind the Anglo-French treaty

that exchanged reductions in French duties on manufactures for British removal of discrimination against French and in favor of Portuguese wines and brandy, as evidenced by the proposal in France in 1851 for tariffs of 20 percent, 10 percent, and duty free on wholly manufactured goods, semi-finished manufactures, and raw materials;[78] by actual reductions in duties on coal, iron, and steel in 1852 as the railroad boom picked up; and by the legislative proposal designed by Napoleon III in 1855, but not put forward until after the Crimean War, to admit 241 items duty free, reduce tariffs on 19 others, remove all prohibitions, and set a top limit of 30 percent. This last was turned down by the chamber, and Napoleon promised not to submit a new tariff proposal before 1861.

Economic interests were involved, and the theories of great men like Cobden and Chevalier. However, there was more: Napoleon III was starting to engage on foreign adventure. He wanted to rid Italy of Austrian rule by use of arms. The British opposed his military measures, despite their recent use of force in Crimea. The treaty was used to hold British neutrality, as much as or more than to stimulate growth in France. Moreover, it did not need to be submitted to the chamber. Under the constitution of 1851, the emperor had the sole power to make treaties, and such treaties encompassed those dealing with trade.

The move was successful both politically and economically. With the help of the French armies, Italy was unified under the leadership of Piedmont, and French growth never faltered under the impetus of increased imports. French industries met competition successfully and checked the growth of imports after two years.[79] While the effects of the treaty are intermingled with those of the spread of the French railroad network, it "helped to bring about the full development of the industrial revolution in France."[80]

Further, it added impetus to the free-trade movement in Europe. This was under way in the early 1850s, following repeal of the Corn Laws. The Swiss constitution of 1848 had called for a tariff for revenue only, and protective duties were reduced progressively from 1851 to 1885. The Netherlands removed a tariff on ship imports and a prohibition against nationalization of foreign ships. Belgium plugged gap after gap in its protective system in the early 1850s, only to turn around at the end of the decade and adopt free trade down the line. Piedmont, as we shall see, and Spain, Portugal, Norway, and Sweden (after 1857) undertook to dismantle their protective and prohibitive restrictions.[81] With the Anglo-French treaty the trickle became a flood. France, Germany, Italy, and Britian engaged in negotiating reciprocal trade treaties with the most-favored nation clause.[82]

Following the French defeat at Sedan in 1870 and the abdication of Louis Napoleon, the Third Republic brought in the protectionist Thiers. The Cobden treaty was denounced in 1872. Reversal of policy waited upon repeal of the Le Chapelier law of 1791, taken in the heat of the French revolution against associations, which forbade economic interests to organize. Dunham claims that a country with leadership would have accepted a moderate tariff in 1875, but that the free traders had neither organization nor conviction, that is, they had too many free riders.[83]

The French movement to free trade was taken against the opposition of the separate interests,[84] in the absence of strong export interests, with an admixture of economic theory of a dynamic kind, and imposed from above. The motivation of that imposition was partly economic, partly—perhaps even mainly—political. Moreover, it had a bandwagon effect in spreading freer trade.

In the French case, the leadership overwhelmed the concentrated economic interests. That leadership earned its surplus, to use Frohlich, Oppenheimer, and Young's expression, in a coin different than economic, that is, in freedom to maneuver in foreign policy. It may be possible to subsume increases in leadership surplus in this form into an "economic theory of national decision-making" with costs to vested interests accepted in exchange for political benefits to a national leader, ruling by an imposed constitution, the legitimacy of which is not questioned. The effort seems tortured.

As MENTIONED EARLIER, the Prussian tariff of 1818 was regarded when it was enacted as the lowest in Europe.[85] But the duties on coarse yarns and textiles were effectively high, since the tariff was levied by weight. Jacob in 1819 noted that the "system of the Prussian government has always been of manufacturing at home everything consumed within the Kingdom; of buying from others, nothing that can be dispensed with," adding, "As scarcely any competition exists, but with their own countrymen, there is little inducement to adopt the inventions of other countries, or to exercise their facilities in perfecting their fabrics; none of these have kept pace."[86] Baden, on joining the Zollverein, which adopted the Prussian tariff for the totality, believed itself to be raising its tariff level when it joined.[87] What Baden did, however, was to acquire enforcement: its long border previously had been effectively open.

The Prussian tariff dominated that of the Zollverein, organized in the years from 1828 to 1833, primarily because Prussia took a very liberal view of tariff revenues. Most goods by sea entered the German states via Prussia, directly or by way of the Netherlands, but the text of the Zollverein treaty of 1833 provided that the revenues from the duties after deduction of expenses would be divided among the contracting states according to population.[88] Prussia thus received 55 percent, Bavaria 17 percent, Saxony 6.36 percent, Württemberg 5.5 percent, and so on; Prussia was said in 1848 to have sacrificed about two million thalers a year, exclusive of the fiscal loss sustained by smuggling along the Rhine and Lake Constance.[89] This can be regarded as a side payment made by the beneficiary of income distribution under Pareto-optimal conditions to gain its policy, or as the disproportionate share of overhead costs of the collective good saddled on the party that most wanted it.[90]

Despite adjustments made in Prussian customs duties between 1819 and 1833, the tariff remained low by British standards. Junker grain growers were hopeful of importing British manufactures in order to sell Britian more grain. Junker bureaucrats, brought up on Adam Smith and free trade by instinct, were fearful that highly protective rates would reduce the revenue yield.[91]

Outside of Prussia plus Hamburg, Frankfurt, and the other grain-growing states of Mecklenburg, Pomerania, and so on, there was interest in higher tariffs; but apart from the Rhineland, there was little in the way of organized interests. Von Delbrück comments that Prussia and Pomerania had free-trade interests and shipping interests, but that outside the Rhineland, which had organized chambers of commerce under the French occupation, there were few bureaucrats or organs with views on questions of trade and industry. Nor did the Prussian government see a need to develop them.[92]

Saxony was sufficiently protected by its interior location so as not to feel threatened by low tariffs—which, as mentioned, were not really low on coarse cloths. On joining the Zollverein, Baden was concerned over raising its tariff and worried lest it be cut off from its traditional trading areas of Switzerland and Alsace. It fought with the Zollverein authorities over exemptions for imported capital equipment, but gradually with Bavaria and Württemberg, evolved into a source of pressure for higher tariffs on cotton yarns and iron. Fischer points out that the request for lifting the duty on cotton yarns from two talers per centner to five was resisted by the weavers of Prussia (the Rhineland) and Silesia.[93]

Cotton yarns and iron were the critical items. Shortly after the formation of the Zollverein a trend toward protection was seen to be under way.[94] The Leipzig consul reported a new duty on iron to the Board of Trade in February 1837 and observed that the switch from imports of cotton cloth to imports of yarn pointed in the direction of ultimate exclusion of both.[95] Bowring's letter of August 1839 noted that the manufacturing interest was growing stronger, that the existing position was untenable, and that tariffs would be raised under the growing demands and increasing power of the manufacturing states, or would be lowered by an alliance between the agricultural and commercial interests.[96]

Open agitation for protection began two and one-half years after the formation of the Zollverein, when the south pushed for duties on cotton yarns. Linen yarns and cloth went on the agenda in 1839 and iron, protection for which was sought by Silesian and west German ironwork owners, began in 1842.[97] But these groups lacked decisive power. The Prussian landed nobility covered its position by citing the interests of consumers,[98] and Prince Smith, the expatriate leader of the doctrinaire free traders, in turn tried to identify free trade and low tariffs with the international free-trade movement rather than with the export interests of the Junkers.[99] The tariff on iron was raised in 1844, those on cotton yarns and linen yarns in 1846. Von Delbrück presents in detail the background of the latter increases: he starts with the bureaucratic investigations into linen, cotton, wool, and soda, with their negative recommendation; continues through the negotiations, in which Prussia was ranged against any increase and all the others in favor; and concludes that the Prussian plenipotentiary to the Zollverein conference was right in not vetoing the increase, as he could have done, since a compromise was more important than the rationally correct measure of this or that tariff.[100] The head of the Prussian Handelsamt (commerce office) was not satisfied with the outcome of the conference, but had to accept it.

From 1846 on, the direction of Zollverein tariffs was downward, aided first by the repeal of the Corn Laws and second by the Cobden-Chevalier treaty. With the increases of the 1840s and English reductions the Zollverein tariff, which had started as one of the lowest in Europe, had become relatively high. Von Delbrück was one of the doctrinaire free traders in the Prussian civil service and remarked in 1863 that he had been trying for a reduction in the tariff on pig iron for seven years, since the tariff reform of 1856, which reordered but did not lower duty schedules. He also wanted a reduction in the tariff on cotton cloth; duties on woolens were no longer needed. The opportunity came with the announcement of the Anglo-French treaty. He noted that Austria had gone from prohibitions to tariffs, that the Netherlands had reformed its tariffs with a 5-percent maximum on industrial production, and that the levels of Italian duties were lower than those in Germany. "Could we stay away from this movement? We could not."[101]

Bismarck was no barrier to the Junker bureaucracy. His view about tariff negotiations was expressed in 1879 in the question, "Who got the better of the bargain?" Trade treaties, he believed, were nothing in themselves but an expression of friendship. His economic conscience at this time, he said later, was in the hands of others.[102] Moreover, he had two political ends that a trade treaty with France might serve: to gain her friendship in the Danish question (which led up to the Prussian war of 1864); and to isolate Austria, which was bidding for a role in the German confederation.[103] Austrian tariffs were high. The lower the levels of the Zollverein, the more difficulty she would have in joining and bidding against Prussia for influence. The Zollverein followed the 1863 treaty with France with a series of others.

Exports of grain from Prussia, Pomerania, and Mecklenberg to London as a percentage of total English imports hit a peak in 1862 at the time of the Civil War[104] and proceeded down thereafter as American supplies took over. The free-trade movement nonetheless continued. Only hesitation prevented a move to complete free trade at the peak of the boom in 1873.[105] There is debate about whether or not the crash later in the year triggered off the return to protection in 1879. Victory in 1871 had enlarged competition in iron and cotton textiles by including Alsace and Lorraine in the new German empire. Radical free traders and large farmers achieved the reduction in duties on raw iron in 1873 and passed legislative provision for complete removal in 1877.[106] But Lambi notes that *Gewerbefreiheit* (freedom of occupation) had caused dissatisfaction and in some versions subsumed free trade.[107] By 1875 the iron interests were organizing to resist the scheduled elimination of iron duties in 1877.

The difference between the 1873 depression, which led to tariffs, and the 1857 crisis, which did not, lay in (a) the fact that the interests were not cohesive in the earlier period, and (b) that Britain did not keep on lowering duties in the later period as it had in the first.[108] On the first score the Verein Deutscher Eisen- und Stahl Industrielle was formed in 1873, after vertical integration of steel back to iron mining had removed the opposition between the producers and the consumers of iron. This supports the view of the effectiveness of concentrated interests in achieving their tariff goals when scattered interests will not—though again it has nothing to do with representative democracy. On the other hand, the free traders also organized; in 1868 the Kongress Nord-Deutscher Landwirte was organized, and in 1871 it was broadened to cover all Germany. In 1872 a Deutsche Landwirtschaftsrat was formed.[109] Many of these organizations and the once free-trade Congress of German Economists were subverted and converted to protection after 1875, but a new Union for the Promotion of Free Trade was formed in September 1876.[110] German economic interests as a whole became organized, and the struggle was among interests concentrated on both sides.

Abandonment of the opposition of the landed interests is perhaps critical. Consumers of iron in machinery, they opposed tariffs on iron up to 1875, but with the decline in the price of grain and the threat of imports, their opposition collapsed. It might have been possible to support tariffs for grain and free trade for iron, but inconsistency is open to attack. After von Delbrück's resignation or discharge in April 1876, Bismarck forged the alliance of bread and iron. As widely recounted, he had strong domestic political motives for higher tariffs on this occasion, as contrasted with his international political gains from lower tariffs up to 1875.

In general, however, the German case conforms to the Stolper-Samuelson explanation: the abundant factor wants free trade; when it becomes relatively scarce, through a gain in manufacturing at home and an expansion of agriculture abroad, it shifts to wanting tariffs. Doctrine was largely on the side of free trade. List's advocacy of national economy had little or no political force. His ultimate goal was always free trade, and his early proposal of 10-percent duties on colonial goods, 15-percent on Continental, and 50-percent on

British was more anti-British than national.[111] In the 1840s he was regarded in Germany, or at least by the Prussians, as a polemicist whose views were offered for sale.[112] Bismarck is often regarded as the arch-villian of the 1879 reversal of Zollverein low tariffs, but it is hard to see that his role was a major one.

ITALIAN MOVES in the direction of free trade prior to 1850 were tentative and scattered. The abandonment of the policy of supply in Tuscany in the eighteenth century has been mentioned earlier, as well as the removal of prohibitions on the export of raw silk in Piedmont, Lombardy, and Veneto. Lombard and Venetian tariff policies were largely imposed by Austria, which was perhaps not wholly indifferent to local interests and to the promotion of industry.[113] Piedmont concluded a series of trade treaties with the larger states, especially France and Britain, and in 1847-1848 explored a tariff union with Tuscany and the papal states.[114] But the major initiatives were taken after Cavour became minister of agriculture, industry, and commerce, then minister of finance (1851), and then prime minister (1852). The low tariffs that Cavour achieved for the Kingdom of Sardinia were subsequently extended to Italy as a whole after its unification in 1860 under Cavour's leadership and were followed by a series of trade agreements lowering import duties still further.

As a young man, Cavour had visited France and Britain—once in 1833-1835 and again in 1842-1843. Like Chevalier, whose lectures he attended during the second visit, he was interested in growth through banks, public works, and especially market forces encouraged by freedom of trade. He knew Babbage, Nassau Senior, Cobden, de Tocqueville, Sismondi, Cherbuliez, Michelet, Pellegrino Rossi (an Italian free-trader, resident in Paris), Chevalier, and Faucher, and wrote long papers on English Poor Laws, the Irish question, and the Corn Laws.

Cavour was attacked as a doctrinaire who deserted a tried and effective system to follow an abstract theory,[115] but has been defended by biographers as having "a genius for the opportune."[116] His fifty-two speeches on the tariff question as finance minister had high educational quality, says Thayer, and achieved an economic revolution. There are views that Cavour's successful pressure for free trade represented economic interests. He was a large landowner, and the low tariff has been said to "reflect clearly the interests of the large landowners."[117] Piedmont agriculture was related to western European markets for rice, silks, wine, and hides.[118] The application of Piedmont's low tariff to all of Italy has been said to have assured the interests of the ruling classes of Britain and France.[119]

For the most part, however, it seems evident that in following low-tariff policies in the Kingdom of Sardinia in the early 1850s and in Italy after unification in 1860, Cavour was operating on the basis of a theory. His views were widely shared. Prodi notes that the liberal faith in freedom through the market in 1860 not only triumphed but remained sure and irrefutable. There were some like Cappellari who wanted to reduce tariffs slowly as industry was getting ready to export, as in England, and like Martello who was conscious of the differences between Italy and England and elastic in his application of Adam Smith to Italy.[120] For the most part, however, the tariff problem was ignored in Italy until the inquiry of 1870. Industrialists, led by the wool manufacturer Rossi, disliked the Piedmont low tariff and especially the twenty or more trade treaties that followed. Limited transport over land meant, however, that there was no unified domestic market for local manufacturers to exploit.

Clough[121] observes that the advantages that were supposed to devolve automatically from the free movement of goods in international commerce did not seem to accrue to Italy. For one thing, loss of custom revenues upset the finances of first Sardinia and then Italy, despite a vigorous expansion of trade.[122] Customs duties had provided 14.7 million lire out of a total revenue of 69.4 million.[123] Secondly, the balance of payments turned adverse, partly—perhaps mainly—as a result of Cavour's and his successors' programs of public works. Piedmont ran up a large debt, which later devolved on the Kingdom of Italy. In 1866 it became necessary to halt redemption of the lira in gold, and the depreciation of the currency during the *corso forzoso* (forced circulation) alleviated some of the effects of competitive imports. But the spread of the railroad in the 1860s and the low tariff policies proved ruinous to industry, especially in the south. The Sardinian tariff schedule by and large was at the same level as those of Modena, Parma, and Tuscany, well below that of Lombardy in most goods, though higher in others, but far below the levels of the papal states and especially of the Kingdom of the Two Sicilies (Naples).[124] After a long period when the country was "strangely deaf" to the troubles caused by the low tariff,[125] the Commission of Inquiry was launched in 1870, the tariff was raised in 1878, and a new system of high tariffs on industry, modified by trade agreements favoring agriculture, was instituted in its place.[126]

MY FIRST CONCLUSION from this survey was that free trade in Europe in the period 1820 to 1875 had many different causes. Whereas after 1879 countries reacted quite differently to the single stimulus of the fall in the price of wheat—England liquidating its agriculture, France and Germany imposing tariffs (though for different political and sociological reasons), Italy emigrating (in violation of the assumptions of classical economics), and Denmark transforming from producing grain for export to importing it as an input in the production of dairy products, bacon, and eggs (see Chapter 2)—before that, the countries of Europe all responded to different stimuli in the same way. Free trade was part of a general response to the breakdown of the manor and guild system. This was especially true of the removal of restrictions on exports and export taxes, which limited freedom of producers. As more and conflicting interests came into contention, the task of sorting them out became too complex for government (as shown in *Gewerbeförderung* in Baden and the refinement of the Navigation Laws in England) and it became desirable to sweep them all away.

Part of the stimulus came from the direct self-interest of particular dominant groups, illustrated particularly by the First Hand in the Netherlands. In Britain, free trade emerged as a doctrine from the political economists, with a variety of rationalizations to sustain it in particular applications: antimonopoly effects, increased real wages, higher profits, increased allocative efficiency, increased productivity through innovation required by import competition. In France, the lead in the direction of free trade came less from export interests than from industrial interests using imported materials and equipment as inputs, though the drive to free trade after 1846 required overcoming the weight of the vested interests by strong governmental leadership, motivated by political gain in international politics. The German case was more straightforward: free trade was in the interest of the grain-exporting and timber-producing classes, who were politically dominant in Prussia and who partly bought off and partly overwhelmed the rest of the country. The Italian case seems to be one in which doctrines developed abroad, which were dominant in England and in a minority position in France, were imported by strong political leadership and imposed on a relatively disorganized political body.

Second thoughts raise questions. The movement to free trade in the 1850s in the Netherlands, Belgium, Spain, Portugal, Denmark, Norway, and Sweden, along with the countries discussed in detail, suggests the possibility that Europe as a whole was motivated by ideological considerations rather than economic interests. That Louis Napoleon and Bismarck would use trade treaties to gain ends in foreign policy suggests that free trade was valued for itself, and that moves toward it would earn approval. Viewed in this perspective, the countries of Europe in this period should not be considered as independent economies whose reactions to various phenomena can properly be compared, but rather as a single entity that moved to free trade for ideological or perhaps better doctrinal reasons. Manchester and the English political economists persuaded Britain, which persuaded Europe—by precept and example. Economic theories of representative democracy, or constitutional monarchy, or even absolute monarchy may explain some cases of tariff changes. They are of little help in western Europe between the Napoleonic wars and the Great Depression.

The Formation
of Financial Centers

4. It is a curious fact that the formation of financial centers is no longer studied in economics, perhaps because it falls between two stools. Urban and regional economics, which concern themselves with cities, discuss the location of commerce, industry, and housing but rarely that of finance. (Exceptions should perhaps be made for Canada[1] and for France.[2]) Pred's study of urban growth in the United States deals exclusively with commerce and industry, with no mention of banking or financial markets.[3] A 1973 survey of U.S. urban economics mentioned finance only once in the text and referred to no work on the subject in a bibliography of 438 items.[4] Only the study of the New York metropolitan area led by Vernon devotes attention to it.[5] At the same time, a vigorous new literature on money and capital markets and their role in economic development takes no interest in geographical location or the relationships among financial centers.[6] Apart from a sentence or two, one would think that the money and capital market was spread evenly throughout a given country.

The "geography of finance," to borrow Kerr's phrase, is relevant to contemporary issues as well as being of considerable historical interest. Contemporary relevance is provided partly by the tasks of building money and capital markets in developing countries, which McKinnon[7] and Shaw[8] regard as vital to economic development—more important, indeed, than foreign aid or export expansion. Among developed countries there is the issue of which center, if any, will emerge as the leading money and capital market of the

European Economic Community if it achieves monetary integration. Economic analysis may not be equal to the task of predicting the answer to this question, or of recommending the policy measures a government or intergovenmental body should follow if it wishes to affect the outcome of the market process.[9]

Historically, an explanation is needed about why money and capital markets were centered at the capital in Great Britain, France, and Germany, but not in Italy, Switzerland, Canada, the United States, or Australia. One can formulate an aspect of the issue as a riddle: What do the Midlands Bank, the Crédit lyonnais, and Dresdner Bank, the Banca Tiberina, the Bank of Nova Scotia, and the First Boston Corporation have in common? The answer: Their executive offices are located in a different place from that implied by their names—the Midlands Bank in London, the Crédit lyonnais in Paris, the Dresdner Bank in Berlin (from 1892 to 1945), the Banca Tiberina (after 1879) in Turin (not along the Tiber), the Bank of Nova Scotia in Toronto, and the First Boston Corporation in New York. The two historical curiosities can be combined. A year after the Midlands Bank transferred its headquarters from Birmingham to London in 1891, there was a simultaneous movement of the Schaffhausen'schen Bankverein from Cologne to Berlin (that is, from a provincial city to the capital) and of the Eidgenössische Bank from Bern, the capital, to Zurich. The affinity of finance and location is underlined by the fact that so many banks have places rather than functions (such as Merchants, Farmers) in their names. (Private banks, where confidence is all-important, are named for people.)

A historical approach is also called for, because if analysts have little interest in spatial finance, the same cannot be said of their grandfathers. Two generations ago, before and after World War I, economics displayed an interest in the functions of and relations among financial centers that is rare in current research. Fanno had a chapter on the centralization process in banking and money markets that included geographic centralization.[10] Powell presented a detailed account of the processes by which congeries of isolated banks were formed into a financial structure centered on London, with many physiological analogies, including natural selection and survival of the fittest.[11] The most highly developed analysis, however, was provided by Gras, the economic historian, who described the stages of development from village and town to metropolitan economy, specifying the development of specialized financial institutions as a metropolitan function.[12]

In the pages that follow, a comparative analysis is presented in literary rather than statistical or econometric form. It is perhaps unnecessary to defend the comparative method after having shown that the administrative capital sometimes serves as the financial center and sometimes does not. I go further, however, and suggest that the study of single cases, valuable as it is, frequently tempts the economic historian to rely too heavily on single analytical models and that the comparative method, for limited problems at least, is of value in showing what is general and what special in historic process. The qualification that the comparative method is most effective with limited problems — as a rule, of a partial-equilibrium sort — reflects concern that, as the analyst moves from one country, society, polity, or economy to another, general-equilibrium issues like business cycles, stages of growth, and backwardness embody too many degrees of freedom to enable him to generalize with confidence.

That the comparative historical account is qualitative rather than quantitative derives from the limitations of the writer, the magnitude of the task of deriving comparable data from a wide number of countries, and an interest more in process than in detailed outcome. Even such an impressive study as that of Goldsmith, which shows conclusively that financial machinery becomes more elaborate as a country grows in productive process, does not examine the detailed processes, particularly the spatial ones.[13] Extending this study to measure the process described would make it unduly long.

The next section of this chapter briefly reviews the literature on the location of cities and their functions, the roles of money and capital markets in the development process, and the evolution of banks and banking. Its main purpose is to identify the economies inherent in a central organization of financial markets and banking machinery, and to show why financial centers tend to be organized spatially in a hierarchy, with a single center as the keystone of the arch. The description is limited largely to banks and banking, with little explicit attention to other elements of money and capital markets. Some reference is made to clearinghouses, stock exchanges, government and private security markets, mortgages, foreign bonds, and insurance, though none to factoring, consumer finance, or pension funds. As economic growth proceeds, the importance of banks as financial intermediaries diminishes relative to other institutions, but it is always strategic.

This concentration on the why of a single financial center is followed by seven case studies designed to show the processes by which a given locality is chosen. I deal with England, France, and Germany, where the political capital became the financial center as well. The contrast between the English and French centers, on the one hand, and the German, on the other, is provided by their respective political histories, especially the late unification of Germany in 1870, which furnishes a sort of "instant replay" of the process. Later sections deal with the Italian and Swiss examples, each with late unification, in 1860 and 1848 respectively, but different from the German case because the financial center turns out to be a city different from the political capital. Canada and the United States furnish examples of financial centers that are emerging in countries developed from the wilderness; here again, the political and financial leadership chose different sites. The Canadian experience is of particular interest. The country felt obliged to free itself successively from money- and capital-market reliance on London and New York, experienced two shifts of the financial center, from Halifax to Montreal, then—long-drawn-out and still incomplete— from Montreal to Toronto. Lately, moreover, a relatively independent market has begun to develop in Vancouver.

The final section deals in summary fashion with the question of a world financial center, arching over and connecting indirectly national money and capital markets. London held the position during most of the nineteenth century, though with challenges from France and Germany. In the twentieth century a shift to New York occurred, and a second shift is now in progress from New York to the Eurodollar market. That market is spread all over the world; but its heart, to use a well-worn image, beats in the American and British banks in London. I conclude by seeking to use the lessons derived from the historical studies to throw light on the question of whether a financial center for the European Economic Community will emerge, and if so where.

Banking Development and the Metropolis

A recent spate of books has focused anew on the role of banking in economic development. Two of the earliest writers in the field were Hoselitz and Gerschenkron, who emphasized especially the role of the Crédit mobilier, founded in 1852, in stimulating rapid industrial expansion in France.[14] German banking was said to be as powerful as the steam engine.[15] These leads were followed up and developed by Cameron, in his own book on France and in the case studies he edited.[16] Some of these cases, particularly Austria, Italy, and Spain, suggested that banking may or may not make a positive contribution to economic development, depending not on the personal qualities of the bankers but on the "structural characteristics of the system, and the laws, regulations and customs."[17] The contribution of the Crédit mobilier to the industrial development of France has also been downgraded;[18] its interests, and those of many of its imitators, lay in speculation, not in industrial growth.

Much of this historical literature, however, focused on banking as an agent of growth through stimulation of demand. By contrast, the analytical contributions of Goldsmith, McKinnon, and Shaw emphasize the role of banking in mobilizing and allocating liquid resources. Goldsmith points out that the development of financial intermediaries "accelerates economic growth and improves economic performance to the extent that it facilitates the migration of funds to the best user, i.e. to the place in the economic system where the funds will find the highest social return."[19] Shaw equates "deep" with "liberalized" finance, which opens the way to superior allocations of savings by widening and diversifying the financial markets in which investment opportunities compete for the savings flow. In his only reference to space, he goes on: "The market for savings is extended . . . Local capital markets can be integrated into a common market, and new opportunities for pooling savings and specializing in investment are created."[20] McKinnon's emphasis is on raising the rate of interest on financial capital to equality with the rate of interest on real capital.[21] This makes it worthwhile for entrepreneurs to save in money form for later investment and increases the availability of external finance; entrepreneurs who would otherwise be limited to their own savings are thereby enabled to start businesses sooner and on a larger scale. Financing trade and production at a rate of interest equal to the return on real assets is a shot in the arm to development. Integration of capital markets eliminates local and sectoral monopoly and monopsony, but especially stimulates the formation of savings and its pooling.[22] Here is an echo of Powell's reference to banking as a "magnet which pulls out hoards."[23]

As noted, these discussions of banking innovation and financial intermediation or deepening lack a spatial dimension. Financial centers are needed not only to balance through time the savings and investments of individual entrepreneurs and to transfer financial capital from savers to investors, but also to effect payments and to transfer savings between places. Banking and financial centers perform a medium-of-exchange function and an interspatial store-of-value function. Single payments between separate points in a country are made most efficiently through a center, and both seasonal and long-run surpluses and deficits of financial savings are best matched in a center. Furthermore, the specialized functions of international payments and foreign lending or borrowing are typically best performed at one central place that is also the specialized center for domestic interregional payments. (This is not always the case. For twenty years after Berlin became the undisputed center for German domestic finance, Hamburg continued its role as the leading city for foreign-trade finance.)

To limit ourselves again to domestic interregional payments, the efficiency of a single center is akin to the contribution to utility of a single numeraire. Each locality deals not with each other locality in making and receiving payments, but with a single center; $n-1$ conduits are needed instead of $n(n-1)/2$. Small localities are typically clustered about a provincial financial center but are linked to others through the central financial market. When country clearing was established in London in 1858, the National Provincial Bank thought it "preposterous" for a bank at Manchester to collect a check on Newcastle upon Tyne through London.[24] At that time, the National Provincial Bank had offices in Manchester and Newcastle, whereas its banking office in London was opened only in 1866. Later, however, the National Provincial Bank must have cleared among its branches through a central point such as London. French centralization of distribution through Paris has been much criticized; the efficiency of central clearing for such purposes as moving artichokes from Dijon to Bordeaux obviously declines as costs of transport rise. But for money payments, there can be no doubt of the efficiency of a central financial market as the apex of a national system, and of a single international market as the apex of national financial centers. An African student once complained to me that Latin American payments to a country such as Kenya were made in dollar checks on New York; he was persuaded that the system was devised to enable imperialist extortionists to exploit the periphery. He found incredible the truth that the centralization of payments and use of a vehicle currency are efficient.

As an efficient system of payment develops, utilizing the medium-of-exchange function of banking, firms find themselves able to economize on working balances by centralizing them at the metropolitan pivot. Companies above a certain size tend to establish financial offices in the metropolis to deal in financial markets as well as to finance a larger flow of payments with smaller working balances. Increasingly competitive security markets provide larger and cheaper security issues for those who need capital, as well as more liquid investments for lenders. Economies of scale are found not only in the medium-of-exchange and store-of-value functions of money, but also in the standard-of-deferred-payment function insofar as it relates to loans, discounts, and bond issues.[25]

The origins of banking are diverse. Elementary textbooks imply that they can be traced mainly to the storage function of goldsmiths, but this is oversimplification. The goldsmiths in England, congregated in London, were an important source of private banking, but by no means as important as merchant houses. Other bankers originated as scriveners or notaries, tax receivers or tax farmers who lent out funds being held for remittance to the treasury, court bankers who provided advances and personal services to profligate princes, and industrial companies that paid wages in tokens, moving a stage beyond the truck system (payments in commodities), and found that the tokens remained in circulation. Some manufacturers lent out business profits rather than plowing them back in industrial expansion. But the majority of bankers started as merchants, gradually becoming specialized in the financial side of commerce. Ten of fourteen private bankers in Liverpool—a commercial city, to be sure—sprang from wholesale houses.[26] Often a merchant devised a system for making or collecting payments at a distance and was asked to perform such services for others. The Bank of England was started during the Nine Years' War by wine merchants who, as they sold their stocks and had no opportunity to replace them, found themselves with liquid capital. Beer also resulted in capital accumulation that in a number of instances led the brewer into banking.

Both banking and commerce involve the overcoming of distance, and the geographical pattern of banking was linked to commerce. Cities are typically located at a break in transport; such a break must lie across a trade route.[27] London, Paris, Cologne, Rome, and Montreal lie on major rivers at the first ford or shallow part up from the sea. Berlin lies at the point of transshipment for bulk cargoes moving from the Oder to the Elbe.[28] Lyons and Frankfurt were historic fair towns on international caravan trails, and the *furt* in Frankfurt stands for ford — the ford of the Franks on the river Main. As we shall see, the coming of the railroad, a major innovation in transport in the nineteenth century, changed the character of banking and the location of some financial centers, and only timely action by communities to influence the shape of the railroad network prevented other changes adverse to them.

Not all commodities are identical in their impact on transport or the location of financial activity. It is possible to construct a "staple theory" of finance, at least for the early stages of banking development, to explain the particular impact of different commodities on the size and pattern of financial flows. Seasonality of financial requirements is one aspect; unique production processes, a need for bought inputs, and time needed to consume outputs are others. Ports are dominated by particular commodities financed in certain ways: Liverpool by cotton and wheat, Glasgow by sugar and tobacco, Cherbourg by cotton, Bremen by cotton and coffee (financed in London), and so on. This in turn affects their financial development.

The mechanism by which the location of a city, the transport network, and the economic characteristics of the goods and services in which an area specialized, determined the financial pattern was partly Darwinian and partly the result of deliberate action by government or private individuals. The Darwinian evolution of the banking pattern is illustrated by depressions that wiped out both badly located banks and bankers and those who were well located but incautious. State policy is reflected by the centralizing policies of the Bank of France and French government, which in 1848 eliminated the provincial banks established during the 1830s, and by the decentralizing pressures in Canada and the United States. The strength of regional banking in France in the period before World War I was in spite of, not owing to, state action — which typically operated at that time to discourage regional autonomy. At the private level, local action fostered means of transport and opposed rival financial centers. Of great interest, banks, bankers, corporation head offices, and the like deliberately changed locations, often saving face by professing loyalty to their birthplace. Goldstein and Moses describe Webber's game-theoretic model of location decisions under uncertainty with the assumption that "once the firm is located, it is impossible to relocate."[29] For banks, as will be evident later, such an assumption lacks historical validity.

Some allowance must also be made for pure accident. I am informed by Juan Linz that Bilbao flourishes in Spain as the second financial center outside of Madrid because Prieto, the Socialist finance minister in the 1930s, came from that region and saved its banks while allowing those of Barcelona to fail. The history of European and North American banking is filled with accounts of bankers' quarrels based on personal, social, political, and religious differences, which may or may not be superficial rationalizations of deep-seated economic forces.

In terms of Harold Innis' "staple theory," which ascribes economic outcomes to the characteristics of different commodities or products that dominate economic life at any one time, banking starts out to serve the needs of sovereigns and nobles; develops in connection with commerce; then, less personally, with governmental finance; next with transport, including shipping, canals, turnpikes, and railroads; then with industry; and finally with intermediation in insurance, mortgages, consumer finance, factoring, pension funds, and the like. In a highly developed setting like New York or London, the money market in a broad sense includes (a) a money market with many specialized segments for commercial paper, acceptances, collateral loans, treasury bills, federal funds (in New York), certificates of indebtedness, and the like, and (b) a capital market, both private and governmental, dealing in new issues and secondary distribution, together with (c) trading in commodities, foreign exchange, bullion (in London, Paris, and Zurich), and, to a lesser degree, ships and ship charters, and insurance.[30] The borrowing and lending pattern starts locally and extends to a national center, with perhaps intermediate regional stops, finally becoming international. Specialization grows in instruments and functions and by hierarchical market. Inflations, depressions, wars, and the like distort or intensify the pattern.

The hierarchical character of financial specialization was originally discussed in 1922 by an economic historian, N. S. B. Gras, who developed a theory of stages of metropolitan development in which finance was the apex.[31] There is a national credit market in a country, but it is spatially concentrated in a hierarchical pattern. As summarized by Duncan,[32] Gras traces through four phases the growth of the metropolis to serve a hinterland: (a) commerce, (b) industry, (c) transport, (d) finance. Finance is more concentrated than commerce, industry, or residence. In 1929, four counties had one-quarter of the savings deposits in the United States—a poor measure of financial concentration—whereas eleven counties shared one-quarter of retail sales, and twenty-seven counties shared one-fourth of the population.[33] In 1955, New York had $4.4 billion of nonlocal loans, compared with $1.2 billion for Chicago and $490 million for San Francisco—another measure of metropolitan character.[34] Similar data for Canada in the 1960s are given later in this chapter.

Cities, according to Vernon, attract industries or services in which there is great uncertainty and need for face-to-face contact, those in which speed of interaction is a requisite.[35] Unstandardized outputs lead to agglomeration as a convenience for the shopper. The port of New York attracted the wholesalers, who pulled in the financial institutions, which attracted the central offices of national corporations.[36] A detailed study of New York's financial functions supports this view and discusses the external economies arising from specialization, joint facilities, and the services of other industries such as printing.[37] Shopping convenience is mentioned, but perhaps too little is made of the fact that the broader the financial market, the greater the liquidity of security issues, with the result that lenders and borrowers from other regions will transfer to that market their gross demands and supplies, not just net excess demand or supply. The borrower pays a lower rate of interest and/or is able to issue a larger loan. The lender acquires a qualitatively different investment because it is traded on a broader secondary market, which is why he is willing and often eager to accept a lower interest rate.[38] Insurance companies are less centralized than most other segments of the money and capital market because of a pronounced perference by consumers in the United States for locally issued insurance policies.[39]

In addition to economies, there are diseconomies that work against centralization and favor regional markets. The foremost is cost of information, which gives local credit markets an advantage in dealing with small firms in an area. Unfamiliarity with local personalities and character may discourage central money and capital markets from lending locally. The difference in time is another diseconomy of centralization that has supported the growth of North American markets as against European, the Eurocurrency market as against New York, and the West Coast of North America as against Toronto-Montreal and New York. Direct communication by telephone or telex must be simultaneous; when it spans many time zones, it involves a dislocation of the working day for at least one party. This is another specific illustration of the cost of dealing in finance at a distance; the foremost is the loss of information obtainable only with face-to-face contact. Still a third diseconomy of centralization is crowding, which made for the building of hundreds of offices in midtown Manhattan after World War II and induced one bank, the First National City Bank, to move its head office from downtown to midtown Manhattan. The same phenomenon had been evident in London, with a banking community in the West End of London, separate from the city, for the convenience of wealthy clients in Mayfair. The London and Westminster Bank, formed in 1836, communicated through its name that it was one of the few banks that operated in both the city and the West End.

Not a diseconomy so much as a discrimination is the tendency of governments and private persons to favor their compatriots over foreigners, even at the expense of higher cost or lower profit — an implicit or explicit mercantilist attitude.

Up to a certain high degree of concentration, positive externalities and economies of scale appear to outweigh diseconomies and favor centralization. The continuous reduction in the costs and difficulties of transport and communication over the last two hundred years has favored the formation of a single world financial market.

London as the Financial Center of England

Prior to about 1750 there was little country banking in England. Large incorporated banks existed in Scotland, and the Bank of England was established in London in 1694; there were also many private bankers there. The Bank of England had a monopoly of joint-stock banking in England. Private banks were allowed to issue notes, but their size was limited by the fact that they could have no more than six partners.

Beginning about 1750 there was an upsurge of banks in the country. The dozen or so existing at that time doubled by 1772 and reached four hundred by 1800.[40] Bankers with large families or trusted relatives tended to establish a separate firm in the city in addition to one in the country. The father of the four Baring brothers had come to Exeter from Germany as a wool and serge merchant and had gone into banking in 1717; fifty years later the brothers divided up — two in London and two in Exeter.[41] And Abel Smith II, son of the tax receiver Thomas Smith who remitted funds to London through his connections as a mercer with goldsmith bankers, started a Nottinghamshire bank in 1757, a London bank in 1758, a Lincoln bank in 1775, and a bank at Hull for the Russian trade in 1784.[42] Much of the activity of these banks was remittance. Landlords living in London received their rent twice a year in May and November, so that the banks were called upon at these times to provide London bills.[43] The West End banks, which served the landed interests, were particularly involved in government securities.[44] In addition, in prosperous times country banks accumulated deposits which they remitted to London for investment. Testifying before the Bullion Committee in 1810, Mr. Richardson, a bill broker, said:

In some parts of the country there is little circulation of bills drawn on London, as in Norfolk, Essex, Sussex, etc . . . I receive bills to a considerable extent from Lancashire in particular, and remit them to Norfolk &c where the bankers have large lodgments and much money to advance on bills of discount.[45]

Bagehot added in 1873 that the distribution of the bill-brokers' customers remained much the same after sixty years,[46] and his text speaks of funds from agricultural counties such as Somersetshire and Hampshire, with good land but no manufactures or trade, being invested in the discount of bills from Yorkshire and Lancashire.[47]

The numerous country banks, hard hit by the deflation following the Napoleonic wars, generated a campaign, led primarily by Thomas Joplin, a timber merchant from Newcastle, for adoption of the Scottish system of joint-stock (incorporated) banking with branches. The panic of 1825, in which many small country banks disappeared, brought the adoption of joint-stock banking in 1826; but within a radius of 65 miles from London the privilege of issuing notes was reserved to the Bank of England. (The bank sought to provide an element of stability for the country banks by opening branches outside the 65-mile area.) With the renewal of the bank's charter in 1833, further legislation was required. This was interpreted, against the wishes of the Bank of England, as permitting joint-stock banks of deposit, if not joint-stock banks of note issue, within 65 miles of London. The result was the establishment outside the radius of many banks with the right of note issue. Inside the area only a few banks were started, as the issuing of notes was deemed the principal source of profit. The outstanding one, which survives today, is the London and Westminster.

The other four of the five great joint-stock banks of 1967 (reduced to four by the merger of the National Provincial with the London and Westminster in 1968) were originally provincial. Lloyds was started as a private bank in 1765 in Birmingham by a successful Quaker metal trader. Members of the family set up a London firm in 1770; the last partner of both the London and Birmingham houses died in 1807. The Birmingham bank remained private until 1865, when it began a series of mergers and amalgamations that converted it from a provincial to a city and national institution. Mergers of 1884 with two private banks (Messrs. Barnett, Hoares, Hambury, and Lloyd; and Bosanquet, Salt and Co.) brought the bank effectively to London. The head office remained in Birmingham, but the center of gravity shifted rapidly to London.[48] The need to acquire branches and to establish the bank of London came from difficulties in balancing the demand and supply for investments. In 1866 a shareholder was opposed to branching, but the chairman pointed to the need to attract funds.[49] Then, as the branch movement grew and banks were acquired in areas of surplus funds, the opposite necessity to find an outlet for funds in London became imperative — a process of unbalanced growth. According to Sayers, "A main attraction for joining Lombard Street was the prospect for fuller and more remunerative employment of surplus cash."[50] Integration of the national capital market can be seen in the tension caused by the original practice of paying 2.5 percent on deposits in Birmingham, while in Lombard Street the rate varied with the bank rate. When the bank rate rose above 4 percent, some depositors were tempted to move cash to London. This tendency existed before amalgamation with the London banks, but became accentuated thereafter. Only much later, in 1920, when a 7-percent bank rate had made the London rate apply far out into the country, was the problem resolved by establishing a single deposit rate for the entire bank.[51]

The history of Midlands Bank is similar to that of Lloyds. It started early, in 1836, as a joint-stock bank, but moved slowly, acquiring only six branches in the next fifty years, all near Birmingham. By 1889 it had absorbed eight provincial banks, including substantial ones in Lancashire and Wales. At this point the Birmingham Banking Company, another smaller rival of Lloyds, followed Lloyds' example in acquiring a London connection.[52] Like modern multinational corporations, which invest defensively, following the leader to prevent it from stealing a march, the Midlands Bank merged with the Central Bank of London in the same year. So as not to offend Birmingham, it was stated that the London bank had imposed among its conditions "a sine qua non that the head office must be in London, and half-yearly meetings of stockholders in January in Birmingham and July in London." The Baring crisis of 1890 sped the process of amalgamation when Lord Goschen, chancellor of the exchequer, shocked the banks by calling their reserves inadequate. By October 1898 the business of the Midlands was judged ill-balanced: "Our country business is out of all proportion to our Metropolitan business," and the head office was too small. This was corrected by merging with the City Bank of London.[53] The bank's biographers regard the process as the outcome of an irresistible trend in English banking; Surrey and Kent and the suburbs of London — not the agricultural counties this time — were lending surplus funds to the industrial areas of the Midlands and the West Riding (Yorkshire). The head office was the channel through which resources flowed far more efficiently than under the old agency and bill system.[54] There was danger for local banks which became too heavily involved in separate industries: Bradford in wool, Oldham in cotton, Sheffield in steel.[55]

On occasion, however, there was safety in being off by oneself. Prior to its merger with the Midlands, the Bank of Wales had little trouble in the crises of 1857 and 1866, largely because its business was predominantly Welsh.[56] On the other hand, the Northumberland and Durham Bank failed in 1857 — whether, as one story has it, because the bank had loaned almost £1 million of its £2.5 million assets to a single company, Derwent & Co., which was working mineral rights owned by the bank's Jonathan Richardson,[57] or because £250,000 of small bills on Newcastle shopkeepers, probably good in themselves, were not discountable outside Newcastle.[58] Integration is good in good times; in bad times, it is good if you have the trouble and the rest of the world helps, bad if the trouble originates outside and is communicated inward.

The National Provincial Bank and Barclays developed differently. The National Provincial was organized as a joint-stock company in 1833, with £1 million of capital, a board in London, but banking operations in a series of branches outside the 65-mile limit. Some existing banks were taken over; many new ones were created. The geographical spread was wide: Gloucester, Stockton, Darlington, Kingsbridge, Manchester, Ramsgate, Newcastle, Emlyn, and so forth. As Withers notes, "In those days of slow communication and transport it must have required no ordinary courage . . . in an era of political and industrial unrest and wild speculative fever, to open for business, and to establish liabilities in places as remote as Darlington in the north and Exeter in the west."[59] The provincial banks were given a certain amount of local autonomy but were under the general management of London. In 1866, when the bank had 122 offices, it opened for business in London. This involved giving up the right to issue notes.

The calculations that led to this decision — to exchange the right of note issue amounting to nearly £450,000 for banking operations in London — have not been made explicit. The rise of railroad communication, development of London clearing, and, after the Bank Act of 1844, spread of payment by check rather than by notes, plus the development of limited liability for banks as well as other shareholders in 1857 and 1862, may all have played a role. In 1858 the National Provincial was opposed to clearing in London and to the substitution of checks for country banker drafts and notes.[60] By 1865 it found the trends irresistible. If the testimony of other banking histories is applicable, the London agency banks were probably earning profits on a surplus of funds generated in the branch network; the branch banks could appropriate the profit by investing the funds themselves. It would be interesting to know whether the decision was influenced by the possibility of improving intrabank settlements in London.

The last of the giant joint-stock banks, Barclays, was created in 1896 from an amalgamation of twenty private banks then doing business in various parts of England, with histories stretching back many generations. The three largest were Barclay, Bevan, Tritton,

Ransom, Bouverie & Co. of London, itself a merger of a city and a West End bank; Gurney and Co. of Norwich; and Jonathan Backhouse of Darlington. Seven of the twenty original banks were firms in which there were Gurney interests. The merger combined a valuable London business with strong connections in the eastern counties, the southwest, and the northwest.[61] Amalgamation reflected the view that the day of the private general banker was ending and that national networks both made for efficiency in payments and protected the banker from undue dependence on other banks for funds or outlets. In particular, country banks with considerable surpluses of funds to invest required assured outlets, partly in the industrial counties but partly abroad. The necessary division of surplus funds could be made only in a central capital market, with the net excess of each branch-banking network made available for lending abroad through the discount market and the stock exchange.

In concluding the discussion of England, it is hardly necessary to explain how London became the metropolitan apex of the financial network. Whether with the correspondent system, the Bank of England branches in the provinces, or the nationally spread joint-stock banks with their head offices also in the provinces, the system had no choice but to center in London. London had an ancient banking tradition and it was a major port, the capital seat, and the hub of the railroad network; all forces were brought to bear on this locality, which was itself somewhat divided between the city and the West End. The different banking systems in Ireland and Scotland reached across their boundaries and linked up with London.

After the railroad was built in 1830, London was accessible from all parts of the country. Howard Lloyd went to London from Birmingham one day a week from 1884 to 1902 and, after his retirement in that year, attended a weekly board meeting from his country place until his death in 1920.[62] In 1899 one partner of Smiths spent three days a week at Nottingham and one each at London, Newark, and Mansfield.[63]

London was not the only port; much foreign banking business had been conducted through Liverpool, the cotton and grain port, and through Glasgow and Dundee, which specialized respectively in tobacco and jute. The centralization process occurred through failure, merger, or a change of headquarters. Three American banks, the so-called W-banks—Wiggins, Wildes, and Wilson—failed in the crisis of 1837,[64] and the Bank of Liverpool did not survive the crisis of 1857; the Royal Bank of Liverpool failed in 1847 and stopped payment a second time in 1867. W. & J. Brown & Co., which remained afloat in 1837, added British capital and opened a London branch during the Civil War, when cotton was scarce; it closed down the Liverpool operation in 1889. Other Liverpool banks were absorbed at the end of the century, like the Liverpool Union Bank, which was taken over by Lloyds in 1900. The takeover required courage, Sayers states, as Liverpool valued its independence.[65] When Lloyds tried to absorb the Manchester and Liverpool District Bank in 1903, there was an outcry. The *Manchester Guardian* protested that the "strongest, best conducted and most prosperous of the so-called country banks should not lose its identity."[66] Financing was separated from the handling of commodities and concentrated away from the port of entry. Henry Bell, who became general manager of Lloyds in 1913, had started his banking career in a private bank in Liverpool. He worked for a time with the Liverpool Union Bank, where he gained experience in the financing of cotton, corn, timber, and provisions. When the Liverpool Union was taken over by Lloyds, he was soon transferred to the head office in Birmingham, and in 1903 was transferred again to manage the City office in Lombard Street. There he turned his Liverpool experience in commodity finance to such good account that he ended up as general manager of the entire Lloyds Bank.[67] Successful men, management, and techniques all converge upon the center.

Two of the smaller national joint-stock banks survived into the 1960s, with head offices in Lancashire but large London branches. The Manchester and Liverpool District Bank kept its identity until 1962, despite amalgamations, but changed its name to District Bank in 1924 when it achieved national status. By the same token, the Bank of Liverpool grew through merger to national scope, permitting its acquisitions to retain their original London agents, until in 1918 it was dealing with five private bankers. It then merged with Martin's Limited, with a head office in Liverpool but a separate board in London. In due course, after a death, the parochial name was altered to Martin's Bank.[68]

As they became national, banks experimented with various degrees of uniformity of practice and decentralization.[69] In the end, "the principal characteristic of the British money market is the decentralization of granting credit, while at the same time the various banking institutions are closely connected by the placing of their actual reserve in the hands of one note-issuing bank."[70]

That coiner of physical images, Ellis T. Powell, quoted the 1858 Select Committee on the tendency of deposits to gravitate to London, the center of commercial activity, adding, "The expression 'gravitates' is singularly felicitous, though it is possible that the Committee did not realize how rapidly the mechanism of the Money Market was being modelled on the lines of the Solar system."[71]

Paris in France

The development of banking in France differed sharply from that in England. Centralization had been a feature of French life since the time of Louis XIV, but the French Revolution scattered banking back to its origins in Geneva or Germany, or overseas. With the peace these merchant banks returned to Paris; they began to slough off speculation in merchandise and to open subsidiaries in ports such as Le Havre to finance imports of cotton.[72] Apart from the ports, however, the development of credit markets was slow and they were poorly integrated. Emile Pereire wrote in 1834 that there were no banks outside of Paris, in contrast with England, which had five or six hundred.[73] The disconnected character of money and capital markets is illustrated by the fact that Dijon paid 9 or 10 percent for discounts, while Paris paid 4 percent and Lyons as little as 3 percent.[74] Lyons, however, found money tight each spring when it paid for silk from Italy. The seasonal tightness applied to all of rural France, which shipped funds to Paris in the first half of the year and got them back with the harvest after August.[75]

Napoleon, who established the Bank of France at the turn of the century, sought to unify the national credit system by establishing subsidiaries of the bank in the provinces to improve the circulation of specie and drafts. With the Restoration, the Bank of France abandoned this policy on two grounds, the difficulty of finding the local buyers for Bank of France stock needed to qualify as regents of the provincial *comptoirs,* and the scarcity of three-name paper, which was all the bank would rediscount. The alternative was to establish regional banks to mobilize local savings more effectively. Such banks got off to a good start in Rouen, Nantes, and Bordeaux — all ports — and others were begun in the 1830s in Le Havre,

Lille, Lyons, Marseille, and Dijon, but under restrictions. The Bank of France decided that it needed a monopoly of the note issue and limited the regional banks on the paper they could discount, the size of the notes they could issue, and the ability to redeem notes in Paris.[76] In the financial crisis of 1848 the Bank of France allowed the regional banks to fail, so as to take over the note issue, and returned to a program of comptoirs.

One of the fundamental reasons for developing local institutions was the fear that the Bank of France would order the provinces to restrict credit in a crisis without regard for local conditions.[77] As we have seen in the case of England, however, integration and separation can each be a help or a hindrance in periods of stress, depending upon where the liquidity squeeze strikes.

With a fractured national market, some localities experienced unique conditions owing to specialized foreign relations. While Paris served as an intermediary between sources of capital such as Vienna, Frankfurt, Strasbourg, and Basel and outlets such as Rouen, Saint-Quentin, and Ghent, Lyons had its special connection with Geneva, and Mulhouse with Basel.[78] Marseille was continuously bled for specie by Spain, Corsica, Algiers, and the Black Sea.[79]

In contrast with these cities, which were linked into two or more banking networks, the countryside went its own way. Bankers were often landed proprietors rather than merchants, with an interest in lending to agriculture and in equipping large estates, but they were dominated by security, prudence, tradition, and routine. The banking leadership was in Paris, and the small country banks chose not to follow it.[80]

With the foundation of the Crédit mobilier and the large credit banks—the Crédit lyonnais, Société générale, Comptoir d'escompte, and others—in the 1850s and 1860s, the money and capital market of France became better interconnected but no less centralized with the passage of time. The Crédit mobilier and the Société générale started in Paris and undertook large-scale lending for railroads, ports, and other public works, but did not finance local industrial activity. Established in the silk capital at the entrepôt for foreign trade to Switzerland and Italy, the Crédit lyonnais spread out a network of branches—first in the Languedoc and then throughout the country—to draw funds not to Lyons but to Paris. The history of the bank is discussed in detail in two books, one an account of the years from 1863 to 1882,[81] the other one of the few studies of credit networks by a geographer.[82]

Bouvier follows with great precision the move of the bank from Lyons to Paris. Started by Henri Germain, son of a silk manufacturer, who received a substantial dowry from his wife, daughter of another silk family, its early investments were industrial and regional. Most were in difficulty by 1870. In some cases, such as the widely discussed firm La Fuchsine, manufacturers of a synthetic dye, the difficulties of the firm were intensified by the greed of the bank in seeking quick profit rather than careful development. Mme Germain died in 1867, and M. Germain was remarried in 1869 to a Parisian. He was elected to the Chamber of Deputies, and this required his presence in Paris. Bit by bit he spent a greater proportion of his time in Paris. He did not visit the head office in Lyons once during 1881, and the head office was actually shifted to Paris in 1882. Even in 1879, the head of the subagency at Béziers asked whether he could not deal directly with Paris rather than going through Lyons.

In 1871 the bank made very large profits in the Thiers rente. From then on its task was to collect savings from all France, but especially from the Lyons hinterland, to funnel to Paris for investment in foreign bonds. "Drainage" (with a French pronunciation) was the function of the branch network, the accumulation of deposits. Towns like Grenoble, Annecy, and Creusot, which had thriving industry and building and needed loans, were to be avoided. Loans were provided to commerce, the fruitgrower, the cattle feeder, and the abbatoir, but not to industry. The minister of finance made the same objection in relation to Lille in 1835: "It is rare that banks adapt to and prosper in cities of factories. There is little hope of keeping the notes of the bank in circulation for very long."[83]

The change in the personal interests of Henri Germain from Lyons to Paris are of course symptomatic rather than causal. The decline in silk manufacturing in the Lyons area reduced the demand for finance and left Lyons "a gold mine for savings." Germain and the *hauts banquiers* of Paris, Geneva, and Italy who started the bank with him were interested only in lending to large and established industry, as was true of Paris banking generally. Where such loans were not available, foreign loans served instead.

Little change in this process was produced by the rise of the so-called "industrial banks," or *banques d'affaires,* founded in the 1870s. Most disappeared in the Great Depression or in the crash of 1882, which also engulfed the Union générale. Those that survived did so by hoarding their profits on the Thiers rente. With recovery, from 1896 on, moreover, their investments were highly similar to those of the deposit banks, in foreign bonds and established companies.

Under these circumstances the demand for local credit had to be filled locally in regional credit markets, which sprang up in competition with the national market. In 1910, and again in 1929, small regional banks that had not merged with or been driven under by the large Paris-led firms organized to resist the domination of the center. In 1910 the four-hundred-member Syndicat central des banques de province met at Bordeaux.[84] In 1929 the Crédit industriel et commercial, in cooperation with several other institutions, organized the Union des banques régionales pour le crédit industriel.[85] The movement flourished, particularly in the north, in Lorraine, and in Haute Savoie.

In the north, the Crédit du nord emerged as one of the strongest of the regional banks in France. With its head office in Lille in 1848, it established a few branches—Armentières in 1878, Tourcoing in 1884, and Paris in 1889, before expanding more rapidly after 1894.[86] It is of particular interest that it remained a regional bank and did not move its head office to Paris. Other vital regional capital markets in Lorraine and Haute Savoie undertook to finance the expansion of Briey iron ore after 1870 and the development of hydroelectric power generation, aluminum, and other electric metallurgical and electric chemical industries.[87] The Charpenay bank failed in 1931, receiving no assistance from the Bank of France. A well-known writer on French banking has accused the Bank of France of fostering greater centralization in the twentieth century by actively competing with the regional banks for local paper.[88] The small regional banks were able to compete with the national institutions because their deposits were mostly at term, as opposed to sight, and they were able to maintain much lower reserve ratios, in some cases as low as 3 to 4 percent, against 12 percent or so for the larger banks.[89]

Beyond the private and deposit banks, centralization of the capital market in France was accentuated by government institutions, not only the Bank of France but also such national institutions as the

Crédit foncier (1852), Crédit agricole (1860), and Caisses d'epargne (1881, later merged with the Caisse de dépôts et de consignations). To this day, savings banks do not invest locally, as is generally the case in the United States, but divert their funds to Paris, where they are administered by a single decision-making unit, most recently as an adjunct to the planning process.

The choice of Paris over other central locations need not be explained. Tradition, administrative centralization, the communication network laid out in a star with Paris as the center, all attest to the pull of the capital. Apart from the regional banks, there was no resistance to the centripetal force. By 1900 the Lyons bourse had been left behind and was characterized as a museum piece, despite some revival during the German occupation of France in 1940 to 1942, when it was in the unoccupied zone.[90] After World War II the movement continued, with the transfer to Paris in the single year 1950 of the head offices of three major Lyons companies, including the Comptoir de textile artificiel, whose president continued to live in Lyons but worked in Paris during the week.[91] The movement of international, largely American companies to France in the 1950s and 1960s accentuated the trend and finally elicited a program to move industry and head offices out of Paris to the provinces.

Berlin in Germany

The emergence of a single financial center in Germany has taken place twice, on both occasions in connection with war: first, in the rise to dominance of Berlin over Cologne, Frankfurt, Darmstadt, Dresden, Leipzig, and Hamburg after the victory of Prussia over France in 1871; and, second, in the gradual emergence of Frankfurt as the financial capital of West Germany, following the isolation of Berlin at the end of World War II. In both instances the process was partly political and partly economic.

Prior to 1870 Germany was made up of at least thirty principalities, republics, and kingdoms. These varied in size from cities like Frankfurt and Hamburg to the large state of Prussia, which encompassed a wide area from Frankfurt north to the sea and then east — including East Prussia and Silesia — with its capital at Berlin. Prior to the reduction of internal barriers in 1818, the establishment of the Zollverein in 1834, and the construction of the railroad in the 1840s, the constituent elements of Prussia often pursued separate

policies because of physical separation. Private banks were local—
the Rothschilds in Frankfurt, the Oppenheims in Cologne, Bleichröder and Mendelssohn in Berlin, Heine and Warburg in Hamburg.
Beginning with the creation of the Schaffhausen'schen Bankverein
in 1848 on the ruins of Schaffhausen & Co., which had failed, two
waves of bank formation took place, from 1850 to 1857 and from
1866 to 1873, from the victory of Prussia over Austria to the onset of
the Great Depression, with hardly any pause for the Franco-Prussian War in 1870.[92]

In a passing moment of absent-mindedness, the Prussian government in 1848 granted the Schaffhausen'schen Bankverein permission to create an incorporated bank. But when the bank sought to
grow by adding to its capital and moving to Berlin in 1853, it was
refused permission.[93] Its by-laws did not specifically provide for
branches. Tilly states that Berlin in the 1850s was the ideal place to
start a bank, although he fails to say why—presumably because of
its security activity in the finance of railroads.[94] To get around the
refusal of the Prussian government to permit further incorporated
banks, Cologne financiers, led by the Oppenheims and Gustav
Mevissen and with French financial support, started the Bank für
Handel und Industrie, known as the Darmstädter Bank, in Darmstadt, Hesse, a few miles from Frankfurt-am-Main and outside Prussian jurisdiction, where money was plentiful. The statutes were for
the most part copied from those of the Schaffhausen'schen Bankverein charter of 1848, but went beyond these to include provisions
patterned after the Crédit mobilier of 1852, permitting loans and
participations for its own account, underwriting, issuance of bonds,
and powers to effect mergers and consolidations of various companies.[95] The bank quickly opened an agency in Frankfurt and followed that with agencies in Mainz, Berlin, Heilbronn, Mannheim,
Breslau, Leipsig, and, considerably later, in Hamburg and Stuttgart.[96] The Frankfurt agency was converted to a branch in 1864.

In 1856 another way was found around the Prussian refusal to
grant bank charters, by using the form of Kommanditgesellschaft
auf Aktien, a limited partnership with transferable shares.[97] Scores
of banks were created, among them the conversion of the private
bank of Hansemann, founded in 1851, into the Diskontogesell-
schaft, the Berliner Handelsgesellschaft (both of them in Berlin and
both with Cologne money), the Norddeutsche Bank, and the
Deutsche Vereinsbank at Hamburg.[98]

The participation of Cologne bankers in operations in Darmstadt and Berlin, and via them throughout the German states, raises the question whether there was a national German or at least a Prussian-Saxon money and capital market as early as the 1850s. Cologne had no security market of its own, finding it easier to use Berlin and Frankfurt, or even Brussels and Paris.[99] At this stage Frankfurt and Berlin specialized in security markets: Frankfurt loaned to princes, towns, and foreign states, but not to industry and not for railroads.[100] The thesis of Tilly's study of the Rhineland banks is that German industrialization of the period was achieved not through the careful planning of an efficient state bureaucracy but in "thousands of profit-oriented decisions made by capitalist entrepreneurs operating throughout Prussia"—and especially in the Rhineland.[101] The implication is that the decisions were decentralized. Karl Marx said of Germany that there was "no Isaac Pereire but hundreds of Mevissens on the top of more Crédit mobiliers than Germany has princes."[102] But Mevissen was himself the president of the Darmstädter Bank, Luxemburg Bank, Schaffhausen'schen Bankverein, Bank für Suddeutschland, Kölner Privatbank, and the Berlin Handelsgesellschaft, in addition to being president of a railroad, and he sat on the boards of six mines and two industrial companies, typically as chairman of the executive committee.[103] Other Cologne bankers like Hansemann, Camphausen, and Oppenheim moved freely between banking in Berlin and Cologne and business operations in the Ruhr. Eichborn was a banker in Berlin and an industrialist in Silesia. Private bankers such as Bleichröder and Mendelssohn in Berlin worked alongside the joint-stock banks and corporations, especially in the issuance of securities.[104] For Prussia, at least, and for Germany as a whole, excluding Bavaria, Württemburg, Baden in the south, and the Hansa cities in the north, the banking network solidified rapidly in the 1850s.

Hamburg was different. It clung longer to merchant banking and was slower to specialize than other parts of Germany. Its interests lay in foreign trade, in shipping, and in overseas finance rather than in domestic railroads and coal and steel. Regarded by the rest of Germany as the "English city," and itself disdainful of Prussian leadership until the successes of 1870, its banking was tied more closely to London than to Berlin. In 1857 this foreign connection almost led to disaster. The speculative excess in grain produced a crisis that spread from New York to Liverpool to London to Scandinavia to Hamburg, where a number of private houses could not meet their obligations and ship captains were unwilling to discharge their freight for fear of not being paid. Appeals for a silver loan were made to Rothschild, Baring, and Hambro in London; to Fould and Napoleon III in Paris; and to Amsterdam, Copenhagen, Brussels, Dresden, Hanover, and Berlin.[105] Fould, who was the father-in-law of Heine, the Hamburg banker, telegraphed back: "Your dispatch is not sufficiently clear." The Berlin ambassador indicated that Brück and the Kaiser would not help. At the last minute, as an anti-Berlin gesture, the Austrian government sent a train with 12 million talers of silver, known as the *Silberzug,* which saved the private banks of Merck, Godeffroy, Donner, John, Berenberg, and Gossler & Co. after the discount rate had reached 10 percent.[106] Shortly thereafter, Hamburg moved to specialized banking and the foundation of joint-stock banks, the Norddeutscher Bank and the Commerz- und Diskontobank.

With Prussian successes in the 1860s, German banking became increasingly concentrated in Berlin. The defeat of Austria deprived Frankfurt of its counterweight against the power of Prussia; from having been an imperial city and a free city, it became, in Böhme's expression, a Prussian provincial city. The functions of the Frankfurter bourse in dealing with state loans passed to Berlin. Among private banks Bleichröder, Mendelssohn, and Warshauer in Berlin flourished in their security dealings, while Bethmann, Erlanger, and Rothschild in Frankfurt found their clientele shrinking.[107] It seems evident that the ascendancy of Berlin over Frankfurt was political, but there are other explanations—the nimbleness and skill of the Berlin bankers[108] and the greater importance of railroad issues over those of state entities.[109] Each contains a portion of the truth. But Berlin had not made its start by specializing exclusively in railroad securities: the Prussian State Bank and the affiliated Seehandlung had undertaken some industrial development finance well before 1840. Nor had Frankfurt monopolized state issues. After the fire of 1842 Hamburg floated a loan of 34.4 million mark banco through one Hamburg and two Berlin houses. Issued in Berlin, much of the original amount was bought in Hamburg, and all had been repatriated by 1846.[110] Berlin was thus a capital market for more than Prussia before 1850.

When the Reich was founded by unifying Prussia and the other German states, the several monies in circulation were consolidated by adoption of the mark; the several banks of issue were absorbed into the Preussische Staatsbank, which emerged in 1875 as the Reichsbank. In the boom that immediately followed victory, however, there was a rash of bank creations, the most important new banks being the Deutsche Bank in Berlin and the Dresdner Bank in Dresden, both in 1872. The Deutsche Bank was started by a group including Adalbert Delbrück and Ludwig Bamberger, the former a private banker, the latter a member of the Zollverein Parliament and an economic expert who had worked in Paris banks during an exile after 1848. The bank's founders wrote to Bismarck in February 1870 indicating their intention to devote the bank to foreign trade. Outside the United States, the finance of world trade at that time was in the hands of the French and British. Georg von Siemens, a cousin of the electrical-equipment manufacturer, was general manager of the Deutsche Bank. He was completely persuaded of the high national purpose of making German trade independent of British credit and of filling "the gap in finance of external trade."[111] The bank was located in Berlin, "the importance of which is indicated by the eagerness with which the Frankfurt capital market comes to meet it."[112] It also enlisted some Hamburg capital.[113]

In actuality the Deutsche Bank had little success in foreign finance and found it impossible to operate in that field from Berlin. Its first step in March 1871 was to open a branch in London, in cooperation with two Frankfurt banks. It then established branches in Bremen and Hamburg in 1871 and 1872, respectively, "because of the difference in foreign exchange in inland and coastal towns, and the rather sharp differences in inner and coastal trading practices."[114] Von Siemens' biographer insists that the requirements of overseas trade were decisive for the foundation of the Deutsche Bank but notes that business was not limited to foreign trade; he justifies expansion on the domestic front by the need to have the bank's acceptance signature widely recognized.[115] In the crisis of 1873 a number of banks failed and the Deutsche Bank took over several of them. In the beginning it restricted itself to state loans, communal loans, and railroad securities and held back from founding industries and issuing securities. Gradually, however, it built a syndicate of banks to move into industrial finance and underwriting. The finance of foreign trade was forgotten or put aside because of the need to build domestic roots;[116] lending to foreign borrowers, but not finance of German foreign trade, was undertaken in the

1890s. Foreign-trade finance remained the province of the Hansa cities, particularly Hamburg with its strong ties to London.

Victory in 1871 brought to the capital the Därmstadter Bank from Hesse and the Mitteldeutsche Creditbank from Frankfurt. The crash of 1873 produced a lull in the movement, and then came the Dresdner Bank in 1882, the Schaffhausen'schen Bankverein in 1892, the Commerz-und Diskonto Bank from Hamburg in 1892. Whale comments that these Berlin offices were at first only branches but soon grew to be coordinate head offices that rather eclipsed the original head offices.[117] The process is set forth in more detail in the centennial volume of the Commerz Bank.[118] The Mitteldeutsche Creditbank, which had started in Sachische Meiningen in 1856 because it had been refused permission to locate in Frankfurt, opened its Berlin office, as noted, in 1871. From 1889 on it began a policy of building local branches both in Frankfurt and in Berlin. By 1905 there were six such offices in Frankfurt, including Hoechst and Offenbach-am-Main, and seventeen in Berlin. These numbers reflect "the gradual shift of weight to the capital and the squeezing out of Frankfurt from its leading position as bank and stock exchange city."[119] When Anton Gustav Wittekind retired in 1912 after forty years of leadership, two successors were appointed, one in Berlin and one in Frankfurt.

The move of the Commerz Bank from Hamburg to Berlin was more complex, as befitted a surrender by the possessor of a proud heritage. Founded in Hamburg in 1870, the Commerz Bank saw its early hopes dashed by the crisis of 1873. Deciding to follow the fashion of the times and found a subsidiary in Berlin, it absorbed the private banking house J. Dreyfus and Co. of Frankfurt-am-Main, which had acquired a Berlin subsidiary in 1891. The merger gave rise to some competition in Frankfurt, but the Commerz Bank's chief interest from the first had been in Berlin. In 1899 it embarked on a policy of branch offices in Berlin, followed by more branches in Hamburg. The Frankfurt office of J. Dreyfus was given up in 1897 in favor of a *commandite* with the reconstituted firm. Even this was ended in 1908. In 1905 the Commerz Bank merged with the Berlin Handelsbank, bringing it a head office for its subsidiary and fourteen deposit branches. By 1914 the bank had eighteen branches in Hamburg and forty-four in Berlin.[120]

Riesser attacks a statement that banks in Germany differed from those in Britain in that the British banks moved from the provinces to London, whereas those in Germany moved from the capital to the provinces.[121] The latter process started only after 1897, when the big banks had finished moving to Berlin. Then came the filling out of the national system in directions and areas hitherto neglected, exactly as individual British banks had done.[122]

German experience differed from that of the rest of the Continent and North America in that the metropolitan financial center for the country did not also serve for intermetropolitan dealings. Berlin had borrowed and lent abroad in the first half of the century, when the German capital market was fragmented, just as had Frankfurt, Cologne, Hamburg, and Augsburg.[123] With the unification of the German capital market after 1871, domestic functions focused on Berlin and finance of foreign trade on Hamburg. The Diskontoge-sellschaft had worked closely with the Norddeutsche Bank of Hamburg since the early 1860s. Although the Deutsche Bank established a Hamburg subsidiary in 1872, it became effectively interested in overseas operations only in 1886.[124] The Darmstädter Bank opened a subsidiary in Hamburg in 1890, the Dresdner in 1892, and the Mitteldeutsche in 1896. Wiskemann observes that Bismarck's interest in capital exports was not exclusively political.[125] The "imperialistic phase" of German capital lending began after his dismissal. However much it might rival Britain in shipping and in direct rather than entrepôt purchasing, Hamburg did not challenge London in finance, whether from inability or disinclination.

The position of Berlin as a transfer point for transport between the Elbe and Oder rivers and its subsequent development as a railroad center have been mentioned. Friedrich List characterized it as an important communications center as early as 1833.[126] Two scholars, one a social historian, the other an economic historian, have suggested that part of Berlin's importance lay in the fact that it was midway between the Ruhr and Upper Silesia.[127] Borchardt's other reasons seem more compelling—the concentration there of the Prussian authorities, the German imperial authorities, and the central bank, and the preference of associations and other organizations for that city, its easy access to Hamburg, and the like. The German geographer W. Christaller developed the theory that a central location tends to be chosen as a metropolis, but this view has since been discredited by the abundance of counterexamples, such as New York and London.[128] Even to the extent that the central-place theory retains validity, there is no reason why it should be central between heavy industries that are competitive rather than complementary. The break-in-transport theory of metropolitan location requires connections between intercommunicating portions of a common hinterland, not a point on the ridge of equal delivered prices between competitive suppliers.

AFTER WORLD WAR II, with the isolation of Berlin and the formation of zones of occupation, the major banks were broken up. In 1945 the Deutsche Bank, for example, was divided into ten branch institutes in the three western zones of occupation. With the relaxation of Allied control in 1952, these were amalgamated into three regional banks, the Süddeutsche Bank in Frankfurt, the Rheinische-Westfälische Bank (later Deutsche Bank West) in Düsseldorf, and the Norddeutsche Bank in Hamburg. When permission was granted in 1957, these three were reunited into the Deutsche Bank AG, with a legal seat at Frankfurt but with three "central offices" remaining in the three cities indicated, each of which had several members on the common management committee. In the mid-1960s the central office in Hamburg was reduced in status. In 1974 Frankfurt dominated Düsseldorf on the board of directors, with eight directors to Düsseldorf's five, and weekly board meetings held mainly in Frankfurt. The general secretary of the Deutsche Bank explained that Frankfurt had become the main focus of the bank because of the city's status as the most important financial center of postwar Germany. The Bundesbank was there, the Frankfurt bourse had the greatest turnover of all the exchanges in the German Republic, and both of the other so-called Grossbanken had their head offices in Frankfurt.[129]

In the same fashion, the Commerz Bank of Hamburg was divided into ten successors, reassembled into three in 1952, and into one in 1958. Various directories in the 1960s gave the location of its head office as Düsseldorf. In 1974 the head office was in Frankfurt.

It is of some interest that Cologne, the city nearest to Bonn, the postwar capital of the German Republic, was never in contention. Düsseldorf, which gave Frankfurt the greatest competition, is the trading and financial city of the Ruhr, with its heavy industry. Hamburg and Frankfurt were chosen by the British and American authorities respectively as the seats of their occupation forces in Germany. After the moratorium on foreign investment in Germany was removed, the head offices of American-owned multinational corporations gravitated to Frankfurt, partly because of its large and efficient international airport and partly because of the American governmental presence there, although the decisive element in that presence was shortly moved to Bonn.

The fragmentation of German financial (and political) areas and their reunification in West Germany reflect the U.S. political preoccupation with decentralization and the reality of the forces pushing in the direction of a single financial center. In the initial stages U.S. policy harbored, or at least fostered, the illusion that each of the ten *Länder* might have a central bank and a separate monetary policy. When the occupation forces were withdrawn, Land banks were quickly unified in a Bank Deutsche Länder, later transformed into the Bundesbank. The American effort at decentralization represented an idealistic (ideologic?), interesting, but futile experiment.

Italy—Turin, Florence, Rome, or Milan?

In her account of the rise of the New York money market, Myers states: "There occurred a separation between the political and financial capitals which is peculiar to America. In Europe the two are generally the same: London, Paris, Berlin are the seats both of government and of the money market."[130] Milan, Zurich, and Amsterdam attest to the fact that this is not always the case. As we shall see, moreover, the formation of the Italian financial center was more complex than this statement implies.

Italy, of course, had an ancient tradition in banking. Venice and Florence were banking centers in the Renaissance; Lombard Street in London was named after immigrant bankers from Milan and its surrounding area. In the late eighteenth century, when port cities were banking centers, Genoa, the capital of Liguria, was a flourishing trading town with a developed financial community. There was a smaller financial community down the coast at Leghorn. With its magnificent port, Naples was the commercial and financial center of the Kingdom of Two Sicilies, with the whole south of Italy as its hinterland. Its importance is indicated by the fact that the Rothschilds established a branch of their house there after the Napoleonic wars.

As the northern city-states lacked a substantial hinterland,[131] the small city-states declined, and Italy reached the middle of the nineteenth century without a substantial banking center in the north outside of Genoa. As late as 1844, Genovese were convinced that Turin could not become a banking center.[132] Attempts to create banks in Milan failed between 1821 and 1847, and Lombardy had to rely on capital imports from France during the period of seasonal financial stringency caused by silk.[133] With the unification of Italy in 1860 under the leadership of Count Cavour of Piedmont, Turin became the capital of Italy, and the banking center as well. Lombardy, which had been liberated by the Kingdom of Sardinia in the course of the unification struggle with Austria, held back from wholehearted support of "Italy" and insisted on local autonomy. Rome and the papal states were not to be acquired until 1870.

The financial difficulties of the regime led to foreign borrowing and to the selling off of royal and church land. Rivalry developed in France between the Pereires and the Rothschilds over which could stake out a dominant position in Italy. Both were interested in banking and the finance of state and public works, largely railroads. Speculative fever in Paris stimulated the Crédit mobilier to found the Società Generale di Credito Mobiliare, and the Société de crédit industriel et commercial to start the Banca di Credito Italiano. The Engish ambassador joined the Ricasoli family of Florence to found the Banca Anglo-Italiana, again in Turin. In all, thirteen banks of ordinary credit (roughly equivalent to joint-stock banks in Britain or commercial banks in the United States) were founded in Turin from 1860 to 1866, including the notorious Banco Sconto e Sete (Bank of Discount and Silk). Elsewhere in the north there were three leading private banks in Genoa, four in Milan, and one in Leghorn. In 1865 Florence became the capital. In 1866 de Boullay of Paris started a new bank in Florence, which sold American mortgages and shares in the tax collections of Lecce. It quickly suspended payments. The Credito Mobiliare, which for thirty years was to be the most important bank in Italy after the Banca Nazionale, the predecessor of the Bank of Italy, transferred its head office to Florence in 1865.[134]

Gerschenkron has ascribed the development of Italy after 1896 to the industrial investments of the Banca Commerciale Italiana and the Credito Italiano, which were founded with largely German funds.[135] The question inevitably arises why the Credito Mobiliare and the Banca di Credito Italiano did not produce the same result thirty years earlier. Cameron indicates that, if a banking system is to be effective, government must assure minimal conditions of both financial and political order and refrain from random ad hoc interference.[136] Cohen, who supports the Gerschenkron thesis for the end of the century,[137] explains the earlier failure by the poor development of financial institutions, their geographic limitation to the north and central parts of the country, and their general inefficiency.[138]

The banks of the 1860s were supported in 1871 and 1872 by a new wave of foreign banks, including the Banca Italo-Germanica, which started in Florence, moved to Rome, and developed branches in Naples, Milan, and later Trieste and Leghorn. This bank speculated unwisely and collapsed in 1874. Another with a similar experience was the Banca Austro-Italiana. Both names indicate that nationality was not a critical factor at this stage and that German banks as well as French banks could fail. Somewhat longer lived was the Banca Generale, founded in Rome in 1871 with Milanese and foreign capital.[139] Luzzatto comments that these bank failures were unimportant in an economy which was four-fifths agricultural and not integrated through cheap transport.[140] Losses were suffered mainly by foreign speculators, plus some Italians in Turin and Genoa, and, in minor measure, in Florence, Milan, and Leghorn.

Despite the abortive attempts to shift the financial center to Florence when it became the capital in 1865 and to Rome when the capital was finally established there in 1870, Piedmont and its capital, Turin, remained the financial center of the country from 1860 to 1890. The Banca Tiberina, which had close associations with the Banco Sconto e Sete, moved north from Rome in 1879 and maintained its legal seat in Turin until 1889.[141] Its purpose was to enlarge its capital for speculation in Roman real estate, and it sought capital not only from the Banco Sconto e Sete but also from the Banca Nazionale. In 1884 the Banca Napoletana was transformed with the help of the Banca Nazionale and new Genovese, Turin, and Swiss capital into the Banca di Credito Meridionale for the purpose of investing in Neapolitan real estate under the regulations of a law of the same year.[142] The Credito Mobiliare seems to have moved back from Florence to Turin to be in the action (although I find no explicit mention of a date) and to have participated alongside the Banca Generale in lending to the steel and shipbuilding complex at Terni, to railroads, and for housing, especially in Rome. One of the six banks of issue, the Banca Romana was also deeply involved in the financing of Roman expansion. The note circulation of the Banca Nazionale reached its limit in 1866 and the limit was raised.[143] The Banca Tiberina began to fail and it was saved. Two matters caused crisis to erupt — the tariff war with France in 1887, which provoked the withdrawal of French capital, and the revelation that the Banca Romana had violated its statutory note-issue limit, leading to a political scandal. The result was the failure of the Credito Mobiliare and the Banca Generale, the forced amalgamation of the seven banks of note issue (including the Banca Nazionale and the Banca Romana) into the Bank of Italy, and the collapse of Turin as the financial capital of Italy. The failure of the Credito Mobiliare is sometimes ascribed to the death in 1885 of its leader, Balduino. While he was alive, the bank's speculations were happy. In his contemporary annual articles on Italian financial affairs, Pareto blamed the failures on the fact that the banks engaged in affairs patronized by the government; he advised the Banca Commerciale Italiana and the Credito Italiano to refrain from such activity.[144] Under Balduino's successor, Bassi, the Credito Mobiliare entered into building speculation in Rome and Naples.[145] The Banca Generale lost heavily in Terni, in railroads (the Ferrovie Meridionale), in Milan, and in foreign investment. Luzzatto notes that its Crédit mobilier-type operations were pursued from the Rome head office, and that the Milan branch went in for strictly commercial banking.[146]

The wave of liquidation from 1887 to 1893 removed Turin from leadership and put Milan and Genoa ahead. The larger Lombard and Ligurian banks built branches in Piedmont, including its capital, Turin, and Piedmont's depositors shifted their funds to them.[147] In the nineties the Banca Commerciale Italiana was established in Milan; the Credito Italiano started with its head office in Genoa and ultimately moved it to Milan.[148] The former was purely German in origin, started by Bleichröder and the Deutsche Bank. The latter took over the Milan remnant of the Banca Generale and had German, Belgian, and Swiss stockholders. In 1898 a Società Bancaria Milanese was started, was transformed into the firm Weill-Schott Brothers and Co., and absorbed another private bank in Milan. It expanded rapidly in boom conditions, acquired the Banco Sconto e Sete in 1904, kept on expanding, and in 1907 was dominated by its Genovese group. The Bank of Italy supported it, being interested in developing a third large bank in Lombardy, in Liguria, and above all in Genoa. Bonelli notes that the bank lacked central direction, with its Milan office entirely unaware of the risks taken in Genoa.[149] When the international money market tightened in the crisis of 1907, the Società Bancaria Italiana, as it was now known, collapsed despite the efforts of Stringher of the Bank of Italy to save it. This left Milan as the undisputed financial center *in* Italy. The more interesting question is whether it was the financial center *of* Italy, that is, whether the Italian financial system was still unintegrated or had coalesced into a unified structure.

The critical questions in this abbreviated account of the geography of Italian banking from 1860 to the First World War are, Why was Rome not the financial center? If not Rome, why did Turin lose out to Milan? What role in the choice between Turin and Milan was played by the nationality of the foreign sources of capital and direction?

The reasons for the rejection of Rome seem evident. It became the capital late, it was badly located in relation to the productive parts of Italy, and its transport connections were poor. In no sense could it be called a metropolis with an economic hinterland for which it provided service. Rome, in fact, was a parasitical city. The church sucked income from the rest of Italy and the world, and the services it rendered in return were spiritual, and economically elusive. Savings were limited, the demand for capital for investment in housing very large. It was a sinkhole for capital, not a functioning pivot for allocating capital throughout the country.

The rise of Milan to pre-eminence over Turin has been attributed to the excesses and scandals of 1887 to 1893, the loss of prestige of France relative to Germany after 1871, the deep cleavage between France and Italy over the tariff agreement of 1887, and the political banking of Germany, with its Lombard connections. In my judgment, more cause should be attributed to the locational aspects. Turin got the jump on Milan with the Fréjus pass and the Mt. Cenis tunnel in 1870, the latter projected under Cavour in 1859 before unification. Cavour's policies concerning railroads, canals, and economic development generally gave the Kingdom of Sardinia (Piedmont and Sardinia) a head start in economic development, but easy access to France was a vital aspect. When the Gotthard tunnel was finished in 1882, the position of Piedmont was weakened and that of Milan strengthened;[150] the completion of the Simplon tunnel in 1906 intensified the central character of Milan and the increasingly peripheral character of Piedmont.

A hypothesis emerging from this review is that Italian financial integration did not take place until 1893 and that it had an important role in the economic upsurge that occurred between then and World War I, much along the lines predicted by Shaw and McKinnon. Prior to that time the capital market was fragmented, despite a certain amount of branch banking, the active roles of the Banca Nazionale and the government, and the close connections of banks in Turin and Rome on a few investments (largely housing and such railroads as were left over by foreign investors). Such a hypothesis would explain why German Crédit mobilier-type banks succeeded in stimulating the Italian economy when French banks of the same character could not. Turin industry grew rapidly after 1893, but it was financed by the Banca Commerciale Italiano and the Credito Italiano, except for the automobile industry, which used the Turin bourse.[151] From 1860 to 1885 Italy, even central and northern Italy, was not an integrated financial market. When it became one, economic development spurted.

A Single Center in Switzerland?

Forty years ago Schwarzenbach made the case that Switzerland differed from France, England, and Holland in not having a single financial center but, rather, three: Zurich, Basel, and Geneva.

In contrast to other financial centers . . . the money market in Switzerland is not concentrated in any one city. This fact is chiefly due to the political organization of Switzerland as a confederation of twenty-five states (cantons) which have wide powers of local government. As an outgrowth of territorial and historical factors, a strong individualism exists which is responsible for the lack of uniformity in the social and economic structure of the various states. Consequently there has developed no single preponderant business or financial center such as Paris in France, London in England, or Amsterdam in Holland.[152]

This statement was hardly true. Of the seven large commercial banks in being forty years ago, five had their largest office, if not the nominal head office, in Zurich and two in Basel;[153] of the seven stock exchanges, only Zurich, Basel, and Geneva were of any importance, and the Zurich turnover was from two to four times greater than that of Basel, with Geneva an also-ran.[154] Switzerland provides a classic case of the formation of a single financial center, since it started with many, of which Zurich was originally not particularly important compared with Geneva, Basel, Bern, or Winterthur. Zurich emerged as the financial center at the end of the nineteenth century, despite the connections and traditions of Geneva and Basel and the fact that the governmental seat was at Bern after confederation in 1848. Zurich's success can be ascribed to its focal location in the railroad age, especially after the building of the Gotthard tunnel, and to the pushiness of its bankers.

Geneva and Basel were old banking communities with long-established connections. Geneva's lines ran to Lyons, which had a great Swiss colony, the so-called *Nation suisse*,[155] and to Paris, where its Protestants mingled freely with the Huguenots and Jews of the *hautes banques* and the Bank of France. Many Parisian bankers had spent the Revolution and especially the Terror in Geneva, although others installed themselves in Zurich, Neuchâtel, Lausanne, or Winterthur.[156] With the return of peace, fifteen out of twenty-two hautes banques in Paris were said to be of Genevese origin.[157] The traditional names of Burchardt, Iselin, and Stahelin were long associated with Basel banking, lending to Switzerland generally but principally to Baden, as far north as Karlsruhe and Stuttgart, and to eastern France in competition with Paris, especially to Besançon, Mulhouse, Strasbourg, and Nancy.[158] Mulhouse was even called the daughter of Basel finance.[159]

Zurich had some tradition in foreign banking going back to 1750, but it was hardly a significant town one hundred years later. It was less important than Geneva or Basel and about on a par as an economic center with Winterthur, when it started its meteoric rise in 1850. Its population increased elevenfold between 1850 and 1910.[160] In World War I its position in the interior of the country, away from the belligerents' borders, resulted in the concentration there of international transactions.

Zurich's development can be illustrated by an account of the Union Bank of Switzerland, which was formed from an amalgamation in 1912 of the Bank of Winterthur, established in 1862, and the Toggenburger Bank, originally of Lichtensteig and later of St. Gall in eastern Switzerland. The Bank of Winterthur started out bravely as a banque d'affaires in the boom of the 1860s, in discounts, industrial-security issuance, and railroad promotion. From the 1850s,

Winterthur was connected by railroad with Zurich, Frauenfeld, Schaffhausen, and St. Gall. The town fathers, proposing to make the city a center for storage and transshipment of goods, built a weighing house, a municipal granary, and a storage warehouse at the time they formed the Bank of Winterthur. By 1872 the bank was on a solid footing with a flourishing business throughout German Switzerland.

In 1873 the city embarked on a foolhardy scheme to build a "Swiss National Railway" in order to make Winterthur a link in the network running from Lake Constance to Lake Geneva, bypassing Zurich, Bern, and Lausanne. Part of the inspiration was pique against Zurich, the capital of the canton in which Winterthur was situated, and against Alfred Escher, "the strongest personality in economic and political life at the time,"[161] president of the Schweizerische Kreditanstalt, which he founded in 1856, president of the Northeastern Railroad, and later promoter of the Gotthard tunnel. The threat of Winterthur to Zurich and Escher was met by prompt and effective action by the Northeastern and Central railroads. The Swiss National Railway went bankrupt in 1878, and the city had to issue debt to make good its share of the loss when assets of the company in which 31 million Swiss francs had been invested were sold at auction to the Northeastern Railroad for less than 4 million.[162]

"If you can't lick them, join them." Already in the 1870s there had been a demand for the Bank of Winterthur to establish a foothold in the business center of Zurich. As Winterthur stagnated and Zurich flourished, the bank moved at the very end of the century to shift its center of gravity. In 1897 it acquired a participation in a Zurich banking and stockbrokerage firm, but this proved to be unsatisfactory and was given up in 1901. The bank then strove to overcome its prejudice against branches and in 1906 acquired the Bank of Baden's Zurich office, which had been established in the 1890s. Part of the stimulus was the rising strength of Escher's creation, the Swiss Credit Bank, growing with the city of Zurich, his success in railroading, and the threat of the Swiss Banking Corporation. The corporation, started in midcentury as a syndicate of private bankers calling itself the Bank Corporation, formed into a bank, the Basler Bankverein, in 1870. In 1895 it merged with the Zürcher Bankverein to form the Swiss Bank Corporation.[163] The Swiss Credit Bank and the Swiss Bank Corporation belonged to the "cartel of

Swiss banks" formed in 1897 to place the loans of municipalities and cantons. The cartel excluded the Bank of Winterthur, which then formed a rival group. The Bank of Winterthur merged with the Toggensburger Bank of eastern Switzerland in 1912, started branching into French Switzerland in 1916, and went into Italian Switzerland in 1920. Its last penetrations into Basel and Bern occurred in 1920 and 1923.

A history of the bank, Union Bank of Switzerland, asserts that it was inevitable after the formation of the Zurich office that Zurich should become the heart and center of the institution. The "administrative offices" were kept in Winterthur and St. Gall, and annual meetings of stockholders alternated between them from 1912 to 1945. There was one managing director for Winterthur and Zurich and one for Lichtensteig and St. Gall; they acted alternately as chairman of the annual meeting. "Gradually the Toggensburger chairman for Lichtensteig and St. Gall gave precedence to Winterthur, and after his death in 1921, the two-consul system fell into desuetude."[164] In World War I the foreign-exchange business of Zurich grew, and this encouraged the concentration of the Union Bank's commercial business in Zurich. Even before the war, that branch had been making rapid progress in the handling of its stock-market and credit operations. A new building was completed in Zurich in 1917, and a year later the accounting department was moved there from Winterthur. From then on the board of directors held all its regular meetings in the Zurich building. In 1912 the management had comprised two ex-Winterthurers and two ex-Toggensburgers. One retired, and three new managers from Zurich were brought in, including the head manager, Paul Jaberg. Another death left the Zurich preponderance at three of five.[165]

Of further interest, the Swiss National Bank (the central bank, created in 1905 after a legislative proposal for its establishment had been rejected by referendum in 1894) has been domiciled in Bern since 1935, but effectively it is divided between Bern and Zurich. The seat of management is Zurich, and two of three departments are located there — discounts, foreign exchange, and secured loans in one, giro and auditing in the other. The third department in Bern deals with note issue, cash reserves, administration, and the fiscal agencies for the federal government and the federal railways.[166] This division of functions brings to Zurich all subjects that involve uncertainty and need for face-to-face communication (ex-

cept those involving the federal government) and leaves routine
questions — except possibly cash reserves — for another location.

There is a question today whether telex and the telephone have
made Basel, Geneva, and Zurich one financial center, with no real
distinction among them. Are the distances between Zurich and
Basel and the language barrier, if one adds Geneva, so slight as to
be negligible? I think not. Some American corporations, such as
Investors Overseas Service, may have chosen Geneva because it has
been a more international community than Zurich ever since the
location there of the League of Nations in 1919. Moreover, the
French-speaking atmosphere may be more attractive to international corporations than *Schwytzerdütsch* or even *schriften Deutsch*.
But Zurich clearly dominates. The gnomes are the gnomes of Zurich, not of Switzerland. The location in Basel of the Bank for International Settlements — a 1930 decision dictated by the route of the
railroad — and in Geneva of the league and its successors, the Economic Commission for Europe and the European offices of the
United Nations, keep those cities alive administratively and as
banking centers. But Zurich is the focus.

Even had it not been for its traditional banking relations to
France, Geneva would have held on to some (perhaps most) of its
role as a distinct financial center because of the cultural differences
between French- and German-speaking Switzerland. It is of interest
to contemplate whether Geneva would have outstripped Zurich if
Suisse romande had been larger and wealthier than the German-
speaking parts. Lugano in a small way remains a separate financial
community, linked to Italy by ease of communication as well as by
language and separated from the rest of Switzerland by the Alps,
however much tunneled. But Ticino is a very small proportion of
total Switzerland. Geneva, the Vaud, Neuchâtel, and the other
francophone portions are substantial both in numbers and economically. It is likely but not certain that cultural differences made for
separation of financial functions.

Switzerland, I conclude, is not very different in financial agglomeration from other European cases. Tradition, the federal form of
government, the seat of government in Bern, the international roles
of Basel and Geneva, and the financial relations of those cities with
particular hinterlands abroad, at least historically, were overwhelmed by the central location of Zurich at a crossroads. The
crossroads was partly arbitrary and man-made, if we accept the

Union Bank's account of the role of Escher, which I have not pursued in depth. Zurich benefited from the accident of World War I, which inhibited development of the two financial markets on the border; Geneva, with its relations with France, and Basel, connected to Germany exclusively after the loss by France of Alsace-Lorraine, may to some extent have neutralized each other. While there can be no doubt that Geneva and Basel are today closely connected with Zurich and with each other, Zurich is the financial capital of Switzerland, and an international money and capital market, though not the political capital, which is in Bern.

A final point: Measured by total assets, Zurich would stand out, but not so much as when measured by the assets of commercial or private banks. This is because of the large role of the cantonal banks, the first of which was established in Bern in 1834. Restricted to particular cantons, they do not move. Their total assets rose ahead of those of "discount banks" and "other banks" in the 1870s and by 1910 constituted four-fifths of the banking total.[167] But the cantonal banks put half their funds into mortgages, where the national market is less perfect than in bills of exchange, commercial loans, or stock-exchange securities. (In the 1960s, it took a difference of almost 2 full percentage points in savings-bank interest rates to move savings-bank funds from the East to the West Coast of the United States, indicating that in this capital market integration proceeds slowly.) The cantonal banks do not constitute so much an exception to these remarks as a different story.

Toronto vs Montreal in Canada

Initially, I intended to limit this exercise in comparative economic history to Europe, and thus to countries at broadly the same stage of development and with similar factor proportions. The more I considered Canada, however, the more I observed certain interesting and perhaps unique features. I therefore deal here with Canada, and later, as a companion piece, briefly with the United States.

Chartered banking in Canada began after the Napoleonic wars. The Bank of Montreal opened its doors in 1817 without a charter. The first chartered bank, according to Neufeld, was the Bank of New Brunswick, opened in 1820.[168] The centenary volume of the Bank of Montreal claims 1821 as the date for its charter, but royal assent was not received until 1822, putting the bank two years behind its New Brunswick neighbor.[169] Then quickly followed the formation of the Quebec Bank, the Bank of Canada (not the central bank started in 1936, but a Montreal bank established by American citizens), and the Bank of Upper Canada.

With a large Scottish population, initial Canadian practice followed the Scottish tradition of branch banking rather than the English, and the Bank of Montreal opened agencies in Quebec, Kingston, and York in the first year, 1817. Kingston and York (now Toronto) were in Upper Canada (now Ontario), so that the tension between Montreal and Toronto, or between the provinces of Quebec and Ontario, may be said to have started early. In the same year the Bank of Canada founded an agency in Kingston. The Bank of Montreal opened an agency in New York in 1853, the first such agency and one of only two as late as 1870.[170] The Bank of British North America was organized in London in 1836 and within a year opened branches in Toronto, Montreal, Quebec, St. John, Halifax, and St. John's, Newfoundland.[171]

While Montreal handled the export of furs and the import of general merchandise, Nova Scotia throve on shipbuilding from as early as 1761 to 1874, when wooden ships lost out to ironclads. The major banks in Nova Scotia were the Halifax Banking Company, formed in 1825 from Collins, an earlier private bank; the Bank of Nova Scotia, organized in 1832 as a counterweight to the monopoly of the Halifax; and the Merchants Bank of Halifax (later the Royal Bank of Canada), proposed during the Civil War, when shipbuilding had its last expansion. The two largest firms, heavily indebted to the Merchants Bank, passed into receivership in 1885. The Merchants Bank "now realized that if enterprises of national importance were to be financed, the bank must become national in scope, with [sufficient] capital and reserves that its position could not be shaken by local losses."[172] The bank resolved in that year to extend its operations to Montreal and, after establishing a branch there, opened agencies in the east and west of the city.[173] In twelve years, the focus of the bank had shifted from Halifax to Montreal. In 1898 Duncan of the Halifax branch ceased to be in sole command of the bank, though he remained for one more year in charge of the head office in Halifax and the branches in the Maritimes and Newfoundland. With the upsurge of business the Montreal manager, Pease, was made general manager; the name was changed from the Merchants Bank of Halifax to the Royal Bank of Canada; branches were opened as far away as Vancouver; and some 5,000 new shares of $250 par were sold to prominent Americans. At the annual meeting of 1906 it was proposed to change the head office from Halifax to Montreal, "the natural center for expansion." This was accomplished the following year.[174]

The decision of the Bank of Nova Scotia took place more slowly. Again, a personnel change was the occasion:

One of the first important decisions made by the new general manager — a title which replaced the old Scotch form of "cashier" in 1898 — was the removal of the Bank's executive office from Halifax to Toronto in March, 1900. The change was a natural outcome of the westward turn of events which followed closely on the linking of far-flung provinces by the Canadian Pacific and other railway systems and was a necessary step if the Bank were to play a leading role in the new prosperity and economy of the twentieth century. Many of its Maritime customers had already become dominion-wide concerns, and important connections which it had established in Ontario, Quebec and Winnipeg, necessitated banking facilities free from the delay attendant upon correspondence between these points and Halifax. It is a matter of pride to the citizens of Nova Scotia that the Bank still retains its head office in Halifax, and that year by year the shareholders meet on the fourth Wednesday in January in the Maritime home of their institution — now a splendid new building completed last year and fittingly used for the first time by the directors and shareholders at the hundredth annual meeting in January, 1932.[175]

At almost exactly the same time, in 1899, Max Aitken (later Lord Beaverbrook) became secretary to a Halifax firm at the age of twenty. He arranged a merger between the Commercial Bank of Windsor and the Union Bank of Halifax, which presumably transferred the focus of that bank's operations from Nova Scotia to Ontario. Later, he formed an investment concern, Royal Securities, in Halifax, which operated in new ventures, mergers, reorganizations, and the like. This was moved from Halifax to Montreal in 1906.[176]

Puzzling in the foregoing is the lack of a single magnet: Montreal, Toronto, Windsor, and again Montreal. It is tempting to say that Montreal was the attraction in 1887 when the Merchants Bank of Halifax (Royal Bank of Canada) made its decision, and delay in the case of the Bank of Nova Scotia produced a different choice because of developments between 1887 and 1900. Moreover, the choice of Windsor in 1899 is odd unless the Commercial Bank was Aitken's second or third choice for merger with the Union Bank. But then why Montreal again in 1906? And why, once the Royal Bank had established itself in Montreal and Toronto outstripped it—a supposition we are about to examine—why did not the Royal Bank or the Bank of Montreal move to Toronto? The Bank of Montreal declined relative to the Canadian Imperial Bank of Commerce, located in Toronto,[177] but presumably not enough to warrant the expense and wrench of transferring to the livelier site.

The decline of Halifax as an early financial center needs no further explanation, but the drawn-out resolution of the competition between Toronto and Montreal is perplexing. Toronto started to compete with Montreal in the 1850s, was beaten back in the 1860s when a financial crisis followed the end of the Civil War in the United States, and then began a long rise to rival status. With the western boom and the wave of British investment in Canada after 1896, Toronto gained further, even though much of the capital from London was handled through Montreal. After World War I, there were still further gains for Toronto but no clear-cut ascendancy. Toronto continued to gain and ultimately surpassed Montreal as a financial center, but the latter did not give way, as had Cologne, nineteenth-century Frankfurt, Lyons, Turin, Philadelphia, Baltimore, and Boston. The money market in Canada is said to be centered in "Toronto and Montreal," or reference is made to the interest differential between New York and "Montreal-Toronto."[178] The Royal Commission on Banking and Finance refers to foreign-exchange brokers of Montreal and Toronto, or to the dealer inventories of the secondary security market as "concentrated in Montreal and Toronto."[179] The Bank of Montreal and the Royal Bank retain their offices in Montreal, whereas the three smaller but faster-growing (till 1960) chartered banks—the Canadian Imperial Bank of Commerce, the Bank of Nova Scotia, and the Toronto-Dominion Bank—are headquartered in Toronto.[180] Since 1960 the Bank of Montreal and the Royal Bank have grown in total assets relative to the Toronto three, but with regard to security deals, the Royal Commission in 1964 observed:

The main volume of business has remained concentrated in Montreal and Toronto with the latter tending to grow in relative importance in response to the westward shift of Canadian economic activity and the replacement of overseas countries by the United States as the primary source of external capital.[181]

Yet Montreal is as close to New York as is Toronto and should not have suffered when New York replaced London as the source of overseas investment in stocks and bonds issued by Canadian entities.

Let us leave aside the question of whether Montreal or Toronto is the more important money and capital market for this or that financial instrument. The more interesting question is whether Toronto is emerging as the single financial center of Canada by a process drawn out at much greater length than in other countries, or whether the two centers have been stabilized in an exceptional cooperative relationship. In 1947 Masters wrote, "Rivals, their capital structures became and remained closely linked."[182] This has been the standard view until very recently. It now appears, however, that Toronto has overtaken and surpassed Montreal. So drawn out is the process, however, that Montreal banks seem to be under no pressure to move their head offices or their major money-market or foreign-exchange activities to the Ontario financial capital. The diseconomies of disarticulation are, in some inexplicable way, not very pressing.[183]

Gras distinguishes four stages — commerce, industry, transport, and finance — through which a town must pass en route to becoming a metropolis.[184] For the early period during which Toronto came out from under the shadow of Montreal, we are fortunate in having a history that explicitly uses Gras's model. Masters' study is focused on the period from 1850 to 1890, when Toronto triumphed over its other rivals and emerged as the dominant financial center of the province.[185] Along the way, there was a continuous struggle with Montreal, a struggle marked by the desire to avoid financial domination by New York.[186] The major episodes in that struggle were construction of the Grand Trunk railroad and the early Welland and St. Lawrence canals; transfer of the government account from the Bank of Upper Canada in Kingston to the Bank of Montreal in 1864; the failure of the former in 1866; the determination of E. H. King, general manager of the Bank of Montreal, to pattern banking legislation after the National Bank Act in the United States, shifting from branch to unit banking to keep ahead of challenging banks and requiring banks of issue to hold government debt, thus relieving the Bank of Montreal; and the struggle over the Canadian Pacific Railway terminus in the 1870s. The details are perhaps too complex for a non-Canadian readership. The central point is that in the

1860s Ontario was alarmed at the growing strength and dominance of the Bank of Montreal, which it believed to be draining loanable capital from Ontario to Montreal.[187] Determined to resist this development, Ontario made political efforts to bring transportation routes to and through Toronto, created and fostered banks such as the Bank of Commerce in 1866 and the Dominion Bank in 1870, and influenced banking legislation.[188] Toronto's population rose from 45,000 in 1861 to 210,000 by 1901, while Montreal's grew from 90,000 to 270,000. Thereafter, as money and migrants poured westward, Toronto continued to gain on Montreal, but not so much as to crush it as a financial center.

Several factors account for the rise of Toronto as a rival of Montreal in addition to the transport system, the development of the west, and policy initiatives by Torontonians. One is the shift of investment from railroads to mining. St. James Street in Montreal specialized in railroad securities, while Toronto specialized in mining stocks. In manufacturing, moreover, Montreal tends to have older industries: clothing, textiles, food and tobacco products, and railway equipment, as well as machinery and aircraft, whereas the Golden Horseshoe from Niagara to Toronto and around the western end of Lake Erie, the Torontonian hinterland, specializes in flour milling (old), steel, automobiles, agricultural implements, and electrochemical and electrometallurgical industries based on Niagara power.[189] Casual empiricism suggests that the income elasticity of Ontario's industry outweighs that of Quebec.

Another factor is the change in the source of external capital from Britain to the United States. Britain's gateway to Canada was naturally Montreal. New York had the choice of going up the Hudson all the way or turning west via the Erie Canal. Direct investment, however, strongly favored Toronto. Table 1, showing employment percentages in Canadian-, U.S.- and U.K.-owned firms in Canada indicates sharp differences by province. There is, of course, no assurance that the location of production facilities governs the location of head offices of investing companies, which in turn have an effect on the location of financial facilities. United States corporations could locate production facilities in Ontario but have Canadian corporate headquarters in Montreal, in communication with the U.S. head office in New York, but this pattern is unlikely. With New York virtually equidistant from Montreal and Toronto, it makes sense for companies such as General Motors, whose produc-

Table 1.   Manufacturing employment in selected provinces of Canada, by nationality of control of firms, 1961 (percent of total).

	Canadian	United States	United Kingdom
Atlantic provinces	78.67	6.05	15.15
Quebec	75.95	16.84	6.35
Ontario	62.39	30.71	6.10
Canada	70.48	22.54	6.16

SOURCE: Ray, "Regional Aspects of Foreign Ownership," p. 49.

tion facilities are in the Middle West and whose finance is in New York, to choose Toronto over Montreal in the interest of efficient communication between U.S. headquarters and Canadian production. Where a U.S. company has only a single factory in Canada, moreover, head office and plant are probably located together. Toronto may also be favored by U.S. businessmen because of the identity of language and the similarity of culture.

But what must be explained is less the rise of Toronto than the lack of greater decline of Montreal until the 1970s. Part of the explanation may lie in governmental policy, which urged the two main banks to keep their head offices in Montreal. Unlike the central bank's position in England, France, Germany, or Switzerland, but similar to that of the Bank of Italy in Rome, the Bank of Canada remains in the capital, Ottawa, where it was established in 1935. Ottawa is located in Ontario, but on the Quebec border. The Porter Commission notes that until recently the bank's senior personnel "have made only infrequent visits to the financial centers of Toronto and Montreal," and that visits of financial people to Ottawa, while always welcome, are made only for some specific purpose or complaint and do not provide the "frequency of contact needed."[190] The remark is addressed to the question of the efficient functioning of Canadian financial machinery, which requires frequent face-to-face contact among governmental and private financial decision makers. There are recent indications that the diffidence between central and commercial bankers noted by the Porter Commission has diminished or disappeared. It is perhaps going too far to read into the discussion a hint that the Bank of Canada remains in Ottawa because it is unable or unwilling (given the bicultural nature of the dominion) to choose between Toronto and Montreal.

Canada is one of the few countries where geographers as well as historians have studied metropolitan development, using the Gras model. Geographers, along with economists, are surprised that relations between Toronto and Montreal have for so long been complementary rather than competitive, and that the country fails to conform to the model of metropolitan primacy. In population the ratio of the largest to the next largest city is 1.2 in Canada, compared with 2.3 in the United States and 7.5 in France.[191] Almost 350 miles apart, Toronto and Montreal overwhelm the rest of Canada but not each other, as Table 2 shows. Financial concentration reaches more than 90 percent in the two cities in stock-market activity, and here Toronto is far ahead. In all else, it has been a draw.

Geographic analysis throws more light on the separate claims of Toronto and Montreal to metropolitan supremacy by comparing the inbound and outbound passenger traffic of the two cities with that of other major Canadian cities. The nul hypothesis is that such traffic will conform to the gravity model, in which predicted traffic

Table 2.   Selected data for indicated metropolitan centers[a] in Canada, about 1961 (percent of Canadian total).

	Montreal	Toronto	Vancouver	Next ranking city
Population (1961)	11.6	10.0	4.3	2.6 (Winnipeg)
Population (1966)	12.2	10.7	4.4	2.5 (Winnipeg)
Service receipts and retail sales	13.4	13.8	5.4	3.1 (Winnipeg)
Value added in manufacturing	17.9	19.8	4.0	5.3 (Hamilton)
Checks cleared at clearinghouses	26.8	37.3	6.0	7.1 (Winnipeg)
Income tax paid	12.7	19.0	6.1	3.6 (Winnipeg)
Assets of leading corporations	38.1	36.7	6.3	5.0 (Calgary)
Value of stock-market transactions	26.3	67.1	6.3	0.2 (Calgary)
Domestic airline passenger traffic[b]	17.6	23.3	10.9	6.6 (Edmonton)

SOURCE: Kerr, "Geography of Finance in Canada," tables 16-1 to 16-6, 16-8.
[a] Metropolitan census areas.
[b] Leading airports outbound plus inbound (1965).

between any two cities is some constant times the product of the two populations divided by the square of the distance between them. The model predicts well for most pairs,[192] but high residuals — positive and negative — have significance (see Table 3). The residuals suggest that Toronto has particularly close relations with distant cities, and that Sudbury, a large mining town, has limited relations with the cities nearby, presumably because it is specialized and because it deals with the world through Toronto. It is equally of interest that St. John's and Halifax have heavy interaction in the provinces, probably because they are so removed from other centers, whereas London and Windsor, both important manufacturing towns, deal little with each other, presumably because their relations go through Toronto. Airplane traffic is not as useful an index of financial interaction as check clearings would be, but it throws an oblique light on the phenomenon.

The centripetal tendencies in Canada, then, are less forceful and much slower than those observed in Europe.[193] Canada first detached its monetary and capital relations from London and turned them toward New York. Montreal balanced between London and New York. Toronto then rose to assert independence from Montreal, with some duality: "One group of finance capitalists were to continue to shuttle back and forth between Toronto and Montreal, while others, including mining men, were to be just as solicitous in cultivating the New York market."[194] The dominion built up "To-

Table 3.   Pairs of cities with high positive and negative residuals.[a]

High positive residuals in descending order of importance	High negative residuals in descending order of importance
Toronto — Vancouver	London — Windsor
St. John's — Halifax	Sudbury — Quebec
Toronto — Winnipeg	Sudbury — St. John's
Toronto — Calgary	Sudbury — Fort William
Toronto — Edmonton	Sudbury — Regina
Toronto — Halifax	Sudbury — Ottawa
Toronto — St. John's	Sudbury — Montreal
Vancouver — Winnipeg	Sudbury — Edmonton
Vancouver — Montreal	Ottawa — Montreal
Vancouver — Ottawa	Moncton — St. John's

SOURCE: Kerr, "Metropolitan Dominance in Canada," table 16-11.
[a]Calculated by relating airline passenger traffic of the cities to the product of their populations divided by the square of the distance between them.

ronto-Montreal" as a counterweight to New York, fostering a market in Treasury bills in the 1950s and a day-loan market, which enabled the Bank of Canada to control the money supply by internal operations rather than resort to New York funds.

In the same fashion, under the leadership of the Bank of British Columbia, Vancouver has set out to build its own money and capital market; in its foreign-exchange operations, it deals in U.S. dollars directly with banks in Seattle, San Francisco, and Los Angeles, rather then through Toronto-Montreal.[195] One reason, of course, is the difference in time zone, and distance (that is, the cost of wire services) may be another. It is paradoxical, except perhaps in terms of differences in rates of growth, that Canadian banks should abandon one coast—Nova Scotia—and cultivate the other.

The arguments for and against regional financial independence are summed up in a sentence from the Porter report apropos of stock markets, but applicable in general to money and capital markets:

While a single national exchange would concentrate all trading, cause the markets to be broader and more resilient and might reduce trading costs per unit, it would fail to take account of the country's significant regional variety and of the need of local exchanges to provide a center for the shares of smaller and less nationally-known companies.[196]

Contrast this with the remark quoted earlier from the Royal Bank's fiftieth anniversary celebration volume that if "enterprises of national importance were to be financed, the bank must become national in scope, with [sufficient] capital and reserves that its position could not be shaken by local losses."[197]

New York as the Financial Center of the United States

The rise of New York as the financial center of the United States, winning out initially over Boston, Philadelphia, and Baltimore in the first quarter of the nineteenth century, and beating back, so to speak, later challenges from Chicago and St. Louis, is sufficiently familiar that it need not occupy us for long. It is, moreover, well chronicled in Albion,[198] Gras,[199] and Myers[200] and has been more recently analyzed in Robbins and Terleckyj.[201] Of the financial dominance of New York since 1825 there is no doubt. The remarkable feature is that it was maintained despite persistent attempts to defeat it—from the early efforts of rival cities, the Second Bank of the United States in Philadelphia, and the National Bank Act of 1863 to the attempt embodied in the Federal Reserve Act of 1913. Economies of scale in money and finance proved stronger than the institutional enactments against them.

Prior to the end of the Napoleonic wars, there was no clear ascendancy of one North Atlantic American port over the others. Each had its hinterland. After 1815, well before the completion of the Erie Canal, New York took steps to pull ahead. British supplies accumulated during the war were dumped there. When commission merchants threatened to hold them back for higher prices, New York enacted an auction law that made all sales final and forbade withdrawing goods once offered for sale. Jobbers, wholesalers, and country merchants flocked to the port. In 1818 a New York merchant started the first liner service, by sailing packet to Liverpool; a ship left promptly on schedule whether it had a full cargo or not. These actions created a demand for sterling. To provide a supply, merchants, shippers, and bankers—at that time indistinguishable from one another—sought the financing of cotton and grain. Planters, always needing to buy more land and slaves, were continuously in debt. New York bankers advanced them funds to ensure that cotton bound for Liverpool from New Orleans, Mobile, Savannah, or Charleston would be shipped coastwise to New York and then across, a diversion of 200 miles which after 1850 proved physically unnecessary. The Erie Canal, projected in 1818, was finished in 1825. That same year New York bankers advanced a large loan to the state of Ohio to divert the grain trade from the Ohio and Mississippi rivers to the canal and New York.[202] Baltimore was slow in building the Chesapeake and Ohio Canal. It was still under construction when the opportunity came to build the Baltimore and Ohio Railroad. Philadelphia tried to meet the competition with the Main Line Railroad, built betwen 1827 and 1837. But this route was clumsy and inefficient. It ran by rail from the city to the Susquehanna River and by boat to the Alleghenies, with produce hauled over the mountains by stationary engine. By 1842 Boston had tunneled the Berkshires with the Boston and Albany Railroad but still had to rely on the Erie Canal for western produce. Supplementing the canal by the New York Central on a water-level route, New York stayed ahead.[203] When Andrew Jackson destroyed Philadelphia's Second Bank of the United States in 1836, New York's position was assured.

A good illustration of the pull to New York is the experience of

Alexander Brown and Sons of Baltimore. The father came to the United States from Ulster in 1800, opened an Irish-linen warehouse in Baltimore in that year, and distributed bulky goods through Maryland and Virginia. He took William, one of his four sons, into partnership in Baltimore in 1805, sought to open a branch in Philadelphia in 1806 and again in 1809, but succeeded through his son John only in 1818. By this time William was in Liverpool, and Liverpool and Philadelphia had outstripped Baltimore. By 1825 it was clear that New York was the most interesting center, and in that year son James opened Brown Brothers & Co., primarily to promote the interests of the Liverpool house, William and James Brown & Co. While Baltimore remained the head of the family enterprises until Alexander's death in 1834, for the last years of his life the backbone of the commission business was the sale in New York or shipment to Liverpool of the cotton sent by southern correspondents. The first New York circular of Brown Brothers & Co. in 1825 indicated correspondents in New Orleans, Mobile, Charleston, Savannah, and Huntsville.[204]

Others to desert Baltimore were George W. Peabody, Elisha Riggs, and William W. Corcoran. Peabody, originally from Boston, teamed up with Riggs to serve as London commission agent. The American end of Peabody and Riggs moved to New York in the late 1830s and subsequently broke up, with Peabody founding in London the firm that later developed into J. P. Morgan & Co.[205] Riggs then went into the securities business with Corcoran and at some stage, probably at the time of the Mexican War, both moved to Washington to deal in U.S. securities. Here is the direct pull of the capital. Note, however, that neither made an optimal choice in terms of maximizing wealth; the Riggs Bank and the Corcoran securities business, while profitable, remained small compared with New York operations.

New York attracted people as well as goods and money. Most came from Connecticut and Massachusetts (south of Cape Cod and west of Worcester, beyond which the pull of Boston dominated), with few, apart from the Stevens family, from New Jersey. New Englanders captured the New York port about 1820 and dominated its business until after the Civil War.[206] The analogue is with the Scots in banking and accounting in London. While I have no definitive explanation for the divergent behavior of New Jersey and Connecticut, the answer is likely to be found in the different character of the soil, flat and relatively rich on the one hand, hilly and rocky on the other.

As New York became the financial center of the country, the practice developed of maintaining bankers' balances in the city. A substantial seasonal movement had to be handled. New York funds were built up during the harvest and movement of crops and drawn down during the rest of the year. New York funds bore a premium exchange rate over those in Philadelphia and other centers, a fact that was resented by other parts of the country. Measures were taken by states to prevent the drain of funds to New York; for example, Connecticut in 1848 required a minimum reserve of 10 percent in vault cash, and in 1854 prohibited lending out of state more than one-quarter of a bank's capital and surplus, and required that loans be made within the state up to the amount of capital and surplus before any could be loaned outside. None of these devices proved effective. Country banks found New York paper and deposits among the safest and most reliable investments. As in England, provision was made in New York State for the redemption of notes issued by country banks either at their seats or in New York, Troy, or Albany, a further incentive to build up New York balances.[207] The city served as an intermediary between Europe and the south and west, and balanced the country movement of cash on a seasonal basis as well.

The National Bank Act of 1863 furnished legal recognition of the New York banks' role as the ultimate banking reserve of the country. The original legislation provided that country banks could keep as little as two-fifths of the mandatory 25 percent reserve in vault cash and deposit the remainder in a national bank in one of eight cities: Boston, Providence, New York, Philadelphia, Cincinnati, New Orleans, Chicago, and St. Louis. Banks in the eight cities had to hold their entire reserve in currency. This was hard on the reserve cities outside New York; they normally kept funds in New York, but now had to hold only currency reserves. Revision of the law in 1864 provided for eighteen "redemption cities," enlarged from the previous list, and allowed banks in those cities to keep half their 25 percent reserve in New York. "Country banks" were permitted to maintain two-fifths in deposits in a national bank in any redemption city. In effect, New York was a central reserve city and the other seventeen were reserve cities.[208]

In 1887 the legislation was amended again to permit any city of more than 200,000 inhabitants to become a central reserve city. Chicago and St. Louis accepted, "determined to wrest from New York its prestige and financial preeminence."[209] St. Louis complained to little avail that merchants making payments to other cities bought drafts on New York rather than sending checks on St. Louis banks.[210] Bank balances rose rapidly in the two cities, but those in New York did not slow down. Chicago and St. Louis attracted deposits from their areas, but cities even farther west and farther south kept correspondent balances in New York.

The Federal Reserve Act of 1913 represented an extension of resistance to the financial domination of New York. Gras in 1922 said it "struck a heavy but not a death blow."[211] The statement seems exaggerated even for its time. New York remained the leading financial center, unchallenged by the eleven places chosen as regional centers for the other districts. Because branch banking was permitted in California, individual institutions like the Bank of America grew to be among the largest in the country, though the New York State requirement of unit banking failed to prevent New York banks from dominating the country in size and number.

The Federal Reserve Act was based on the theory that regional money and capital markets would develop around the locations of the twelve district banks. The act implicitly contemplated separate monetary policies for the twelve districts. A structure of rates developed, the lowest rates being charged customers in New York, for example, with higher rates as size of city decreased and as one moved from north and east to south and west.[212] Fluctuations in the rate were wider in New York than in the outlying portions of the market.[213] But there was only one money market and only one monetary policy, focused on New York. Discount and open-market policies were unified. New York's facilities were more specialized, more competitive, and more available to other regions. Half the loans of New York City's banks were for borrowers outside the city, as contrasted with 8.2 percent for Chicago, 7.8 percent for Dallas, and 6.3 percent for San Francisco—the three nearest competitors.[214] New York was also the center for international finance.

Here is a clear example of economies of scale. The financial center was a port, but the connection of finance to ports had diminished. It was neither an administrative capital nor a central location. Its dominance continued in spite of the strong resistance implicit in populism, in spite of political steps to reduce its role, in spite of New York's own insistence on unit rather than branch banking, and in spite of efforts to create other financial centers by legislation.

The 1959 move of the head office of the First National City Bank from Wall Street to a midtown location on Park Avenue raised a series of new questions. Have the economies of centralization been exaggerated, or is modern communication reducing them? Is propinquity to corporate head offices for bank decision makers more important than ready access to other banks, law offices, and financial markets for Treasury bills, foreign exchange, commercial paper, stocks, bonds, and the like? The bank left the bulk of its check handling in downtown Manhattan, close to the other banks and the clearinghouse but far from headquarters. It was understood that this would create some problems. In London, City banks acquired West End banks (by merger rather than by building new branches in competition with existing institutions) to serve the convenience of nonfinancial clients. In New York, the same forces threatened to reverse the centralization process.

International Financial Centers

The same concentration that produces a single dominant financial center within a country (with the possible exception of Canada) tends to result in the emergence of a single worldwide center with the highly specialized functions of lending abroad and serving as a clearinghouse for payments among countries. Banks, brokers, security dealers, and the like establish branches in such centers. The process is similar to that which takes place within a country, although the barriers of exchange risk and higher transaction costs prevent it from being carried as far.

Court, merchant, and security banking spread internationally, as it did within countries, by the process of branching. Originally these functions were usually performed by large families of male members. The court banking performed by the five Rothschild brothers moved out after the Napoleonic wars to Vienna, Frankfurt, Naples, Paris, and London. Alexander Brown used his four sons to extend his merchant banking business from Baltimore to Philadelphia, New York, Boston, and Liverpool. (It has been suggested that one of the reasons for extending Alexander Brown and Sons in space, apart from efficiency, was that Alexander found it difficult to live near his most dynamic son, William.)[215] Early American bankers in France, such as Welles and Greene, who were associated with Welles cousins in Boston, went to Paris and Le Havre in 1817, and Fitch and Co. of New York established a branch with a brother in Marseille in the 1830s.[216] In the early 1860s, the eight Seligmann brothers went from New York and San Francisco to Frankfurt, Paris, and London (the central financial capitals rather than the ports) and to Amsterdam and New Orleans, largely to sell U.S. securities.[217] The Philadelphia banker Drexel, who had moved there in 1837 after dealing in foreign exchange in Louisville, Kentucky, had three sons. One of them, Joseph William Drexel, set up an allied firm in Paris in 1867. He teamed up with J. P. Morgan in New York in 1871 to provide a network for selling U.S. securities in Europe in close cooperation with his brothers in Philadelphia.[218]

It is not entirely clear that there was a dominant financial center in Europe prior to 1870. It seems doubtful that the economies of scale had extended far enough that one center existed. American banks went to London, Liverpool, Paris, and Marseille. London bankers established themselves in Paris, and Baring Brothers teamed up with Hope and Co. of Amsterdam. Prussia placed loans abroad in Hamburg, Frankfurt, Kassel, Leipzig, Amsterdam, and Genoa in the 1790s.[219] By 1820 it was borrowing in Amsterdam on foreign issues, and in Frankfurt on domestic; Amsterdam was the first trading city on the Continent for public loans—Prussian, Austrian, and Russian. Interest rates differed widely among financial centers.[220]

British foreign lending at short term was stimulated by the usury laws of 1571, which limited interest charged to a stipulated rate that successively declined from an original 10 percent to 8 percent in 1623, 6 percent in 1660, and finally 5 percent in 1713, until their repeal in 1854. Akin to the interest ceilings of Regulation Q in the United States (which did not apply to foreign time deposits, allowed foreign banks to earn high interest rates in New York, and enabled them to bid for dollar deposits, thus stimulating the movement of funds to the Eurodollar market in the late 1950s), acceptances on foreign bills permitted charging commissions as well as interest, thereby avoiding the usury laws, as some domestic borrowers complained.[221] By the time the usury laws were eliminated, this man-made distortion no longer had importance in stimulating the flow of British capital abroad, inasmuch as British savings exceeded domestic demand at going rates of interest and the efficiency of the London market kept transaction costs low.

By the mid-1820s Britain was a substantial exporter of capital on long-term account. In one view, Britain had a monopoly of capital exports until 1850, when France moved in, largely for *la gloire* (that is, capital exports in the service of national policies).[222] This view is not universally shared. Crick and Wadsworth express an opposite opinion:

During the early years of the 19th century, Paris had held pride of place as the principal international banking center, but subsequently London steadily overtook her . . . After suspension of specie payments by the Bank of France in 1848, London banks became busier in international affairs, with more and more bills domiciled in London.[223]

Both statements seem insufficiently qualified. As Cameron has shown, French bankers experimented with international lending in the 1830s and 1840s but came into their own in foreign issues in the 1850s and 1860s, led by the Crédit mobilier and the Rothschild Paris house, which transferred their intense domestic rivalry to the international arena.[224] Whether London or Paris was the leader in the second quarter of the century, the role was contested during the twenty years after 1850, and Paris finally lost out:

All great communities have at times to pay large sums in cash, and of that cash a great store must be kept somewhere. Formerly there were two great stores in Europe, one was the Bank of France and one was the Bank of England. But since the suspension of specie payments by the Bank of France [in the war of 1870] its use as a reservoir of specie is at an end . . . Accordingly London has become the sole great settling house of exchange transactions in Europe, instead of being formerly one of two. And this preeminence London will probably retain for it is a natural preeminence. The number of mercantile bills incalculably surpasses those drawn on any other city . . . The pre-eminence of Paris partly rose from a distribution of political power.[225]

Even this statement, written immediately after the events of 1871 and 1872, is put too strongly. London emerged as the undisputed leader in international finance after 1873, especially outside the Continent, but Paris was by no means completely in the shadow.

The pivotal role of London was enhanced by the part it played in transferring the Franco-Prussian indemnity. The new German government ended up with substantial claims in sterling, which, along with the Vienna stock-market crash, helped to precipitate the Great Depression.[226]

Whether London focused so heavily on foreign lending that it neglected the provision of finance to domestic industry is a familiar issue, incapable of clearcut answer. The presumption is that it did not. Numerous industries required large amounts of capital: for a long time, railroads; then shipping, iron and steel, cotton, banking, and finance; later coal, public utilities, and communications. The London Stock Exchange was responsive to the capital needs of these industries.[227] In addition, private companies went public in manufacturing and such profitable enterprises as brewing. Investors wanting trustee securities lost their taste for industrial shares and preferred foreign railroad and government bonds.[228] On the whole, however, domestic and foreign lending are complements, not substitutes, even though in the British case they were cyclically opposed.

After 1870 France did not contest British financial leadership. On the contrary, on such occasions as the Baring crisis of 1890 (when the London market was threatened with panic because of the failure of the major bank, Baring Brothers, which was deeply involved in speculation in Argentine land bonds), France supported London with a gold loan from the Bank of France to the Bank of England. While the apex of the financial system of the world was London, foreign balances were also maintained by central banks in Paris and Berlin, like provincial cities in a national system.

Germany's attempt at resistance, led by the Deutsche Bank, and its failure have been detailed earlier in this chapter. Hamburg was prepared to challenge London's pre-eminence in shipping and to support the German program of naval construction,[229] but not to contest the financial position of London. It had a special place in financing German trade and in providing a market for northern securities,[230] but it was too provincial vis-à-vis Berlin in domestic matters and vis-à-vis London in international ones. While the Deutsche Bank, with a few others, opened a branch in London, it contested British financial hegemony mainly in the narrow arena of the Ottoman empire, or took on the Italian clients of the weakened French.

New York's challenge to the dominance of London has been traced back to 1900. In his report for 1904 the U.S. Comptroller of the Currency recommended that national banks with more than $1 million of capital be allowed to accept bills of exchange and establish foreign branches. In the panic of 1907 American banks borrowed more than $100 million from Europe to overcome the inelasticity of the money supply. As a result, Abrahams states, it became clear that the American economy had grown too large to be carried by Europe and that an American solution was necessary.[231]

As in 1870, however, it was war that turned positions sharply. J. P. Morgan & Co. provided an early credit to the French government against gold deposited in the vault of the Morgan, Harjes bank in Paris. In 1916 three leading American banks, the Guaranty Trust, the Bankers Trust, and J. P. Morgan, organized a syndicate under which 175 American banks made loans under acceptance credits to 75 French firms. During World War I a number of commercial-bank branches that had been opened in France and Britain in the early years of the century were expanded and new ones were established, to serve both governmental finance and industry, but especially to handle monies for the U.S. Army.

Further branches were organized after the war in a massive expansion, which subsided after the 1920 boom. H. Parker Willis, in his Introduction to Phelps, spoke of the "unfavorable experience gained by some American banks which went hastily into foreign countries during the years 1919 and 1920."[232] Substantial foreign lending by Wall Street began with the success of the Dawes loan in 1924, but declined after June 1928 when the stock-market rise diverted attention to that outlet and tight money hit the domestic and foreign bond markets. Foreign, especially German, borrowing shifted to the short-term market and finance paper, slowed down in 1930, and stopped completely after the Standstill Agreement of July 1931.

From 1914 on London had difficulty maintaining its role as a center for foreign reserves and a source of short- and long-term credit. The rise of New York produced two reactions — anguish at the loss of leadership and relief at the shifting of responsibility. The head of the London City and Midland Bank (as it was known then) "publicly wept" over the passing of sterling supremacy, while the head of the Hong Kong and Shanghai Bank was enthusiastic about the rise of New York credits, telling Benjamin Strong — "and most

English bankers agreed with him"—that New York must carry some of the load for financing the world's commerce.[233]

I have dealt elsewhere[234] with the hiatus created in the interwar period by British inability to serve as a lender of last resort for Europe and by U.S. unwillingness, at least until the Tripartite Monetary Agreement of September 26, 1936, to take over the task. In this view the 1929 depression was the consequence of an ineffective transition of the financial center from London to New York. No new center rose to challenge the old ones and to wrest financial supremacy or responsibility from them. Instead, in this instance an old center lost the capacity to serve as the center of the world financial system, and the most promising candidate for the position was unwilling or unable to fulfill the responsibilities.

From 1936 on, and especially during World War II, the United States increasingly accepted world financial leadership. The first steps were governmental. The Anglo-American Financial Agreement of 1946 represented a "key currency" approach in which, first, sterling would be restored to health as a means of rebuilding the financial system, so that the sterling area could play an important, and possibly even coequal, role with the dollar. In the first Marshall Plan discussions, however, in June 1947, Clayton and Douglas rejected the suggestion of Bevin and Dalton that the United States undertake a new program of assistance to Britain, after which they would approach Europe in "financial partnership."[235] Gradually the New York market recovered its interest in lending abroad, at long term and short. New York was the world financial center from the early 1950s until the end of the decade, when the Eurodollar market began to develop.

As the emphasis in this chapter is historical, little will be said of the transition from New York as the leading financial center back to London as the principal location of the Eurodollar market, or of the breakdown of the Eurodollar market with the events of August 1971, the Smithsonian devaluation, and the floating period begun in February 1973. Several points about the process should be made, however. First, U.S. banks and security dealers increased the number and size of their European branches in the 1960s. Early in the decade the major efforts abroad of New York banks in London were as dealers in dollars seeking to escape first Regulation Q and later capital controls. In the crunch of 1966 and 1969-1970, however, a number of banks throughout the United States went to London not to lend but to be in position to borrow dollars to add to their reserve balances in the United States. Second, much of the foreign branching was defensive investment. Banks went abroad not so much to earn profits as to avoid losing clients; as American corporations moved abroad, their bankers went with them. Third, with the forced devaluation of the dollar in August 1971, the Smithsonian Agreement of December 1971, and the period of floating in response to adverse speculation beginning in February 1973, the Eurodollar bond market substantially dried up.

After the second devaluation, trade payments and long-term contracts came to be denominated in currencies other than dollars. While borrowers were willing to go short of dollars, private parties outside the United States were less willing to go long. In Eurocurrency and Eurobond markets, the dollar was less widely used. No single currency took its place, however; the deutsche mark, Swiss franc, Japanese yen, and, to a lesser extent, Dutch guilder and Belgian franc severally replaced the dollar as international money. As the dollar declined in world financial use, no other currency or center, for the time being at least, rose to take its place. The international payments mechanism thereby lost the efficiency that comes from centralizing payments.

One possibility is that the European Economic Community may develop as a money and capital market to replace the Eurodollar market in the world financial system.

A Financial Center for Europe?

Will European economic integration, specifically the formation of the European Economic Community, result sooner or later in geographic financial centralization? To pose the question is to review the forces that in the past have led to the formation of financial centers.

(1) *A European currency*. Is a European currency necessary to the development of an efficient money and capital market? The answer is almost certainly yes. The Segré report proposed to achieve an integrated money and capital market — presumably concentrated in space, although the issue was not addressed — by removing national restrictions on lending and harmonizing regulations.[236] The resul-

tant market, however, would still have been divided by currency. The Werner report recognized that integration of financial institutions implies development of a single money,[237] although currencies having permanently fixed exchange rates, by the Hicks theorem, are a single money in all but the trouble and expense of exchange transactions. In some views it is necessary to go further and develop common long-term assets that are included in the portfolios of participating nations.

The London capital market operates in sterling, while New York and the Eurodollar markets operate in dollars. The movement toward world financial integration has been set back by currency realignments and floating. The development of a European capital market serving world as well as European needs probably requires a European currency.

History suggests that this is conveniently accomplished by taking an existing money and converting others onto it. In Germany, the Prussian thaler was adopted after conversion from silver to gold, but it was called the "mark" after the currency used in Hamburg. In Italy, the process was more complex and involved reduction of ten separate currencies to four and then to one, the one being the new lira of Piedmont, which had taken the lead during the political unification. The process took a decade.[238] If a national currency—say, the deutsche mark—is chosen as the basis for new currency called the *ecu* (both an acronym for European Currency Unit and an ancient French coin), it might confer an advantage on the established financial center associated with the chosen currency, in this case Frankfurt. It is likely that Berlin benefited from the choice of the Prussian thaler and Turin from that of the Piedmont lira.

An attempt to create an entirely new currency would presumably not affect the ultimate choice of a particular financial center, assuming that the currency was successfully established and the agglomeration process envisaged actually took place. Some unexpected side effects would probably occur. There is, of course, the question of whether the public would in fact go over to the synthetic currency. The 1958 conversion of the old to the new franc by dividing by 100 affected children and tourists more than it did the French population, which continued for a number of years to use the old franc as a unit of account. On the other hand, the conversion of sterling to the decimal system in 1970 was relatively painless. Money is established not by fiat but by public acceptance, and public acceptance in nine countries of a synthetic new money cannot be guaranteed. Such acceptance is necessary, however, to the creation of a single financial center.

(2) *A central bank*. The development of a European money ultimately requires a European central bank, and meanwhile a pooling of foreign-exchange reserves. It is not evident that the latter must have a physical embodiment and staff; the former will. If a single central bank—the Bank of England, the Bank of France, the Bundesbank, or any other—were chosen as the European central bank and other central banks were merged into it, its existing location might well have an effect on the ultimate choice by the market of a physical center. The example of the Bank of Italy in Rome, far from the financial center in Milan, makes this uncertain, however.

In any case history suggests that the choice of one among a number of competing centers is normally evaded in the process of merging banks. The new European central bank would probably begin as a "federal reserve" system in which the various central banks started as separate units but ultimately became fully articulated subordinate parts. The managing board might be located in a nonfinancial center comparable to Washington, Ottawa, or Bern. With the passage of time one regional bank would come to dominate the others, as New York dominates Boston, Philadelphia, and Richmond. Location of the board in a place like Strasbourg, for instance, would probably have little attractive force.

(3) *An administrative capital*. If the administrative machinery of the European Economic Community, including the European central bank, were located in an existing financial center, it would be likely to serve as a magnet to other financial institutions and to attract them into a single primary location. The creation of a new capital would surely not, as Rome, Bern, Washington, Ottawa, Canberra, and a host of other examples testify. Other factors would have to be at least neutral—with enough tradition, savings available for investment throughout the Community, and the like. This suggests an interesting question: If France persuaded the EEC to choose Paris over Brussels as its capital, would France's strong postwar tradition in opposition to foreign lending stand in the way of financial concentration?

(4) *Tradition*. Tradition and skill favor London as the financial

center, but it is doubtful that these are enough. Savings are also necessary, so that dealers can make a market, lend when the rest of the market is borrowing, and sell out of inventory when the rest of the market is buying. London's success in capturing the lion's share of the Euromoney market arose from the presence there of major branches of U.S. banks, which provided savings. British savings are limited in amount; are concentrated in institutionalized form, such as insurance and pension funds that no longer flow into foreign investment; and are in any case held at home by investment controls. It is conceivable but unlikely that skill and tradition are enough to bring the European financial center to London on the basis of brokerage, with the British participants not taking a position. The Interbank Research Organization, studying the future of London as an international financial center, recognizes that Britain is unlikely to be a major exporter of capital but proposes that it operate as an entrepôt, with Europe as its hinterland.[239] The picture is not persuasive.

(5) *Economies of scale.* Clustering develops when the high risks of an activity can be reduced by continuous interchange of information.[240] It is possible but expensive to communicate by telephone and telex, and many financial functions involving uncertainty are better performed face-to-face. Robbins and Terleckyj note that the central financial district of lower Manhattan minimizes communications costs.[241] In 1960 a financial house with 120 lines to New York houses would have paid $420 monthly rental if located in New York, $230,000 if in Chicago, and $640,000 if in Los Angeles. While presumably communications costs have declined in the intervening years (costs are not so high as to prevent the head offices of a limited number of banks from being located in Toronto and Montreal in Canada, or Basel and Zurich in Switzerland), they are not likely to be so low as to eliminate all tendency to clustering. A network of banks located in all the financial capitals of Europe — London, Paris, Frankfurt, Amsterdam, Brussels, Milan, and Zurich — would not be cheap.

Note the unimportance of clustering for new security issues. Syndicates in new issues comprise firms located virtually everywhere. But secondary markets must be concentrated so as to eliminate the need to search over wide distances for price information or to maintain continuous interchange. While long-distance arbitrage does take place in some securities, such as kaffirs (gold-mining stocks) between London and Johannesberg and between major European markets and New York, the number of securities handled in this manner is limited; efficiency in handling a large number of issues is sacrificed to efficiency in handling a diffuse market through arbitrage.

Robinson has said that the secondary market is unimportant for coporate bonds, as most investors keep them until they mature or are otherwise retired.[242] This does not seem to be borne out for the Eurobond market, if one can judge by the number of articles devoted to "the major weakness of the Euro-bond market . . . trading rather than issuing."[243] In addition, costs of the continuous exchange of price information among traders must be covered. The six leading traders—three of them American firms—were located in London, Brussels, Geneva, and Zurich in 1969; today the leaders are in Frankfurt, Paris, Luxembourg, and some centers in Canada and the United States.[244] Furthermore, there are problems of delays in payment and delivery of bonds. To meet these, the Morgan Guaranty Trust Company organized "Euroclear" in Brussels in 1968, Barclays Bank International founded Eurobond Clearing House in London in 1969, and a group of Luxembourg banks organized a Center of Delivery of Euro-Securities in Luxembourg (CEDEL) in 1971. That such arrangements were unsatisfactory is indicated by these events: (a) Barclays Bank International abandoned the Eurobond Clearing House and substituted a different system of Registered Depository Receipts;[245] (b) Euroclear and CEDEL agreed to collaboration after long negotiations sponsored by the Association of International Bond Dealers; and (c) the Morgan Guaranty Trust Company decided to sell Euroclear while making an agreement to render it banking services for five years. This last step represents an improvement by eliminating the control of the clearinghouse by a single bank. At the time it was stated that the number of participants in Euroclear had risen from 74 in 1968 to 376 in 1972.[246]

In 1971 Kohn suggested that there was no need for a single center for the secondary market—"the true marketplace."[247] While "in any particular time one locale is more attractive than another," he said,[248] the market really has no center at all—not London or Luxembourg, Frankfurt or Brussels, Paris or Geneva; it is a mistake to expect all market makers to buy or sell freely in all circumstances. This verdict seems appropriate only for a period of transition or flux before an efficient centralized system has been developed. Another possibility is that the secondary market for securities could be linked up among widely separate centers by a computer-based system of bid and asked prices, supported by a regional system of security depositories. In the United States, the National Association of Security Dealers started the first of these in 1971 and the Depository Trust Company of New York, with eight regional depositories in six states, provided the second in 1973. Although it is far from clear what volume of security dealings would be necessary to cover the capital expense of establishing such a system in Europe, it seems likely that in time there will be no need for a central location for secondary markets in securities.

Other centripetal forces remain, especially the need for face-to-face communication with bankers, lawyers, security dealers, and borrowers and lenders. Telephone and telex have moderated these centralizing tendencies but have not destroyed them. Nor is the picture telephone likely to provide a substitute for face-to-face communication in the flesh.

The achievement of economies of scale in a concentrated center — an evolutionary and time-consuming process, as the historical record shows — has been disrupted by the 1971-1974 currency realignments and floating. When and if a European currency is established or the Eurodollar recovers strength and is reestablished as international money, the need for scale economies is likely to lead ultimately to agglomeration. Present participants in the Eurocurrency and Eurobond markets may be content to remain where they are and deal with one another by telex and telephone (this is more likely for the Eurocurrency market and for new issues than for the secondary market), but new entrants will be drawn to optimal locations, probably a single place. Banks and security dealers located in many centers will cut down on the less efficient locations in periods of recession and expand the efficient ones when recovery comes, in spite of the decline in cost of communication. While the experience of Euroclear, CEDEL, and Barclay's suggests that the choice lies between Brussels and London, the outcome is likely to depend on other factors. Economies of scale predict one center, but not which one.

(6) *A central location.* The Christaller view that the metropolis chosen as the financial center must be centrally located[249] probably holds at the extremes: Edinburgh, Copenhagen, Rome need not apply. It cannot count for much in Europe among London, Paris, Frankfurt, Brussels, or Amsterdam (or Geneva or Zurich if Switzerland were to join the European Economic Community). Probably even Hamburg or Munich would not be ruled out for failing to stand at the epicenter.

But need the European financial center be in Europe? Could it again be New York, with London, Paris, Frankfurt, and the rest linked to one another by means of their connections with Wall Street? Can Europe be integrated financially by an outside center, as it is to some degree integrated in the field of labor by Mediterranean workers who have no roots in any one place, and in industry by American corporations that are more mobile than their European counterparts? Such an outcome is possible and, as indicated, there is some interest in the United States in developing policies to restore New York to world financial leadership. The immediate outlook is not propitious, given the dim view the world takes of the dollar. Over a longer view, moreover, the time differences round the world make a European center, rather than one in North America or Asia, more efficient in integrating European financial markets.

(7) *Transport.* While metropolitan centers have grown at breaks in transport, it is usually possible today to adjust transport to function. A few communities, like Wellington, New Zealand, are so hemmed in between mountains and sea that a major airport can be developed only at exorbitant expense. Small cities may have difficulty supporting the costly transport facilities necessary for effective communication. Existing facilities are likely to be taken into account to avoid constructing new ones. On the whole, however, there are few limits among European cities.

(8) *Headquarters of multinational corporations.* Might banks, perhaps starting with U.S. banks, drift into a single center or build up their offices in such a center, perhaps putting those offices in charge of European branches, if a number of multinational corporations, particularly those of U.S. ownership, were to congregate? The reason for attributing particular behavior to foreign corporations and foreign banks is that, in the context of European integration, they are more mobile than "native" corporations and banks.

American corporations in Canada are likely to be located in a more economic pattern than Canadian corporations, since the latter will resist leaving the places in which they started. In Canada, however, the location of the U.S. parent corporation may cast an economic shadow across the border, as Ray has suggested.[250] The location of U.S. subsidiaries in Europe is likely to reflect no such influence. French corporations, by contrast, may move their headquarters from Lyons to Paris, but they are unlikely to continue further to London, Brussels, or Frankfurt.

What governs the choice of location for the headquarters of an American firm in Europe? Initially, investment was often made in Britain, on the basis of similarity of language and culture; in a particular country from which forebears of the firm's decision makers had migrated to the United States; or in centers thought to be agreeable, especially Paris. Later, but before the Common Market, it was frequently judged necessary to produce in each country in which the firm wanted to sell: "To sell in France, produce in France." The advent of the Common Market, and the conversion of the Six into the Nine, has changed this less than had been anticipated. With time, however, and as the European Economic Community seems more solid and less ephemeral, other firms may follow the pattern of IBM, which is said to have rationalized its production to take advantage of the elimination of tariffs, or of Ford Motor Company, whose major facilities exchange parts between Antwerp and Cologne.

What is relevant, however, is not the location of production facilities but of company headquarters. In Germany after World War II, companies were attracted to the American military headquarters in Frankfurt. Today more and more American companies seem to develop an affinity for the headquarters of the Commission of the European Communities in Brussels.[251] Sales headquarters may be divided culturally between Latin and Germanic countries, in some cases splitting Switzerland between two European headquarters. Financial headquarters of some companies have been located in London. Where a company has one headquarters, and it was not established in the last fifteen years in Brussels, it has typically been where the firm has its largest production facilities, or in London or Paris. If there is a trend, it is probably to Brussels.

With one exception, major American banks in Europe have not

designated any one branch to head up their European network. London, Brussels, Paris, Frankfurt, Zurich, Geneva, and Rome report separately to the head office, and coordination among them is directed from New York. It is not evident that this is efficient. It is likely, rather, that the matter will be allowed to continue unresolved, pending the emergence of a particular location as the dominant center.

(9) *Culture*. For cultural reasons a single financial center may not emerge. Cultural factors perhaps contributed to the stalemate between Toronto and Montreal and, according to some authors, to the survival of Basel and Geneva as financial centers in spite of the competition from Zurich. French corporations stay in Paris, Belgian in Brussels, Dutch in Amsterdam, and German in Düsseldorf, Hamburg, and Frankfurt. International cooperation among such banks as the Crédit lyonnais, the Banca Commerciale Italiana, the Deutsche Bank, and Morgan Guaranty Trust remains voluntary for separate deals; there is no true merger, with unified decision making. Historical evidence predicts that the emergence of a true financial center would be preceded by takeovers, mergers, and amalgamations, but in the last fifteen years these have been few.

This is perhaps the crux. If there is no integration beyond tariff removal and collaboration in international economic negotiation, there will be no single European financial center apart from the world system. Like the banks in the hinterland of St. Louis and Chicago that kept correspondent balances in New York, European financial institutions will operate partly within the Community and partly outside. During the period of the Eurodollar, the separate financial markets of the Six were more effectively joined with the Eurodollar maket than they were with one another. If a European center emerges as the apex of the world hierarchical system and Europe does not achieve effective integration, sections of the capital market in Europe may even be linked to the center through outside connections, as part of the world feeder system.

(10) *Policy*. Governmental policy can accelerate or slow down the emergence of a given city as the primary financial center, but it can probably not change the outcome. Pushing too hard for centralization will create resistance, while strong efforts at decentralization can be overcome by private forces. It is uncertain whether the United States could recreate in New York a financial center for the

world after its maladroit handling of the troubles of the dollar. Whether the Swiss or German authorities can prevent their financial capitals from being developed to serve as a world center is less uncertain. It is difficult to use exchange control to prevent inflows of hot money, but governments can forbid development of the positive insitutions that will effectively employ foreign monies in domestic and foreign lending.

Policy requires more than governmental agreement. The Segré report on the unification of the European capital market was widely praised, but nothing happened. No European country was deeply committed to building a well-functioning European capital market. Accordingly, I predict — very tentatively — that Brussels will emerge as the financial center of the European Economic Community, for the following reasons. It serves as headquarters for the commission; it attracts foreign corporations and will ultimately attract foreign and European banks; and it tolerates the world intellectual medium of exchange, the English language. The process will be long and drawn out, for commitment to European integration does not go deep. France will push the advantages of Paris as the federal administrative center, and incidentally the center for financial institutions, but with little likelihood of consent from the other members. Sterling is too weak, and British savings too unavailable, to advance London's claim for consideration. While the advantages of centralization are less compelling than they were in the middle of the nineteenth century, they still exist. Thus I predict that, despite cultural resistance and only with difficulty, centralization will take place, but not before the late 1980s.

Commercial Expansion
and the Industrial Revolution[1]

5. The problem examined in this chapter is the relation between the commercial expansion of the seventeenth and eighteenth centuries and the industrial revolution. In particular it is asked whether a commercial revolution — that is, a discontinuously rapid increase in commerce — was necessary to, sufficient for, or merely contributed to the industrial revolution. If commercial expansion was not needed in advance of an industrial revolution, was it required as a concomitant? Are different types of merchants needed at different stages of industrial evolution or revolution? In particular, is there a possibility that at a fairly advanced stage of industry the mercantile function may best be taken over by the industrial firm that undertakes direct buying and direct selling; and that continued performance of the middleman function by the merchant community may inhibit technical change by acting as a filter between producer and consumer, blocking communication between them?

In the early stages of the industrial revolution, the merchant has been thought to have contributed to industrialization in various ways: by extending the market for outputs; by increasing the range and reducing the cost of available inputs; through capital accumulation; to some extent as a source of entrepreneurial ability; by directly and indirectly increasing purchasing power; by inducing rationality in business procedures and widening economic horizons.[2] Additional points, somewhat less compelling, made elsewhere are the merchant's importing of foreign techniques and his serving as a cause of growth of large towns and industrial centers.[3]

The method employed here is to study the role of merchants in a number of countries that are not widely dissimilar. The activities of merchants in general are first analyzed, then the ties between commerce and industry in four countries: Holland, Britain, France, and Germany. In particular, I examine the hypothesis that the commercial revolution produced the industrial revolution in Britain; a commercial revolution in Holland failed to lead to an industrialization process; and industrialization occurred in Germany based on direct selling and buying by industrial firms, without the need for or the benefit of a flourishing commercial network. I then explore which of these general views, if they are verified, applied in France. Limitations of time and capacity prevent extending the examination to the Italian city-states with their commercial expansion of the twelfth to fifteenth centuries, or to Spain engaged in colonial trade via Seville and Cadiz in the sixteenth and seventeenth centuries. Mere mention is made of Swiss experience in textiles and watches.

Commerce may be foreign, and within foreign, continental and overseas; or domestic, and within domestic, national, regional, or local. The term *merchant,* moreover, covers a wide spectrum of individuals engaged in various activities that overlap, but the central focus of which may differ in significant ways. The literature mentions the great merchant or Merchant Adventurer, the merchant-banker, merchant-shipper, merchant-manufacturer, stapling merchant, wholesaler, retailer. In French distinctions, not always identical, are made among *négociant, armateur* (ship-outfitter), *marchand, détailleur, boutiquier;* in German among *Grosskaufmann, Kaufmann, Händler;* in Holland among First Hand, Second Hand, and Third Hand. Differences among various writers in the same country and *a fortiori* between countries make precision about numbers difficult, if not possible. In the main, I shall consider overseas trade on the one hand, and the wholesaler at the national level on the other; I am specifically not concerned with retail shopkeepers.

The functioning of the merchant must of course be specified in historical time, since his role has been continuously evolving. Gras traces this evolution from the traveling, unspecialized merchant of the Middle Ages, who played a role especially in moving goods as well as financing, buying, and selling them, and the sedentary specialized merchant who followed him, and who operated from his counting house (and perhaps a warehouse), increasingly specialized by commodities, by function (export, import, shipping, finance, insurance), and by area.[4] Specialization by commodities was linked to specialization by function, since when a sedentary merchant was also a shipowner or outfitter, for example, he found it necessary to provide different commodities for both outbound and return voyages, whereas specialization in commerce without shipping made it possible to deal with limited numbers of products down to one. The specializing merchant, however, was exposed to greater risk as commodity quality changed, or old markets were closed off, leaving his knowledge obsolete and him without a continuing function. After the eighteenth century, direct buying and selling reduced the roles of merchant and merchant nation.

The mercantile function can be divided analytically into two parts, which we may represent by ideal types: the "gains-from-trade" merchant who buys cheap and sells high in arbitrage fashion, and the "value-added" merchant who concerns himself especially with the quality of goods, and among particular aspects of quality with delivery date or timeliness. The distinction of course is overdrawn, since transport and finance in transit add value to goods in the arbitrage case, and gains from trade are reaped where the merchant is deeply concerned with standardization, quality control, and prompt delivery. Moreover, the merchant who brings primary products from the Baltic, Mediterranean, East Indies, and America to Amsterdam for stapling in gains-from-trade operations generally improves the quality of the goods—refining sugar, curing tobacco, roasting coffee, repacking grain to prevent spontaneous combustion, breaking bulk, and the like. The distinction is nonetheless a useful one and runs between joining markets and altering markets by upgrading goods, standardizing them, and economizing on inspection and handling. In both cases the merchant provides information, in the first instance on where goods exist and where they may be needed, in the second of what kinds of goods should be produced to satisfy consumer demand at minimal cost.

Most emphasis in the commercial revolution has been on the gains-from-trade merchant, who uses his information and courage to obtain large rents when he is successful. The value-added function has perhaps been neglected. To avoid the risk that the goods bought and financed will be rejected by the purchasing merchant or the ultimate consumer, the merchant first inspects, say, textiles closely — not only at the fair or in the cloth hall, but in his warehouse under strong light — and then undertakes to full, shear, bleach, size, dye, or otherwise finish the cloth for the market. New qualities are sought to displace old standards and penetrate additional markets.

The distinction between the gains-from-trade and the value-added merchants, while loose, is broadly that between the First Hand in Holland, which dealt, bought, and sold goods from overseas, and the Second Hand, which sorted them, inspected, arranged for bleaching and dyeing when needed, and then repacked. It is not far from Adam Smith's separation between the speculative-merchant, who can sometimes acquire a considerable fortune by two or three successful speculations, and the slow accumulator in a single industry, who seldom makes a great fortune in consequence of a long life of industry, frugality, and attention.[5] Smith claimed that the only difference between the competent retailer and a great merchant was the quantity of capital:

Besides possessing a little capital, he must be able to read, write and account, and must be a tolerable judge too of, perhaps, fifty or sixty different sorts of goods, their prices, qualities, and the markets where they are to be had cheapest. He must have all the knowledge, in short, that is necessary for a great merchant, which nothing hinders him from becoming but the want of sufficient capital.[6]

This underrates the qualities that Smith detects in the speculative merchant: boldness and foresight, including the boldness in the value-added merchant of urging new varieties of products on producers and consumers.

When the knowledge used by the gains-from-trade merchant has been widely diffused, his contribution is ended. Direct buying and selling replace his intermediary role. Similarly the specialized merchant who develops a particular product for a particular market faces a crisis when a new, better quality displaces his. He may sell the old product in new markets, or more likely a new set of merchants may take over selling the old product in new markets. On this score, the fact that merchants in many societies seek to make a fortune and withdraw from economic life into politics, gentle life, or rural pursuits is helpful. Capital accumulated in commerce may be invested in land, government stock, canal, turnpike, and later railroad securities, used to build spacious houses or chateaux, and consumed; hence it is unavailable for industry. Some will be diverted to banking and recycled into other commerce. But the social aspirations of most successful merchants, which induce them to withdraw from trade, serve an economic and political purpose. When the merchants continue on, they block economic change and tend to perpetuate oligarchies that may be republican but are not democratic.

FOR PRESENT PURPOSES the commercial revolution, ignoring the Hanseatic cities, the Italian city-states, and Seville and Cadiz, began in the United Provinces of Holland. Favored by location in the days of sailing ships, at the crossroads of traffic between the Atlantic (and Mediterranean) and the Baltic, and representing a "land of cities intimately united by an all-pervading network of waterways,"[7] the Dutch developed colonies, shipbuilding, shipping, herring fisheries, and the so-called stapling trade. The linkage from trade to local production led to shipbuilding, and success in shipbuilding in the seventeenth century gave Holland an advantage in fishing for herring along the British east coast in the North Sea. Herring were also bought from Scandinavia and packed with salt obtained from Portugal. Baltic grain was repacked in the stapling ports with Second Hand skill, which prevented it from exploding in the heat of the Mediterranean. Linens from Europe exchanged against woolens from Britain were both bought and sold in Amsterdam, after having been finished at Haarlem with local supplies of acid whey for bleaching, along with seaweed from the Mediterranean and ashes for lye obtained from many points. The First Hand bought, financed, and brought the goods to Holland, and later shipped them on to their ultimate destination. The Second Hand sorted, inspected, finished, and repacked them. The Third Hand wholesaled them to the hinterland. All dealt in the highly developed commodity and financial markets of Holland.[8]

Dutch shipping is said to have embodied few innovations, but to have made effective use of all existing techniques. Design was specialized between naval and merchant vessels, so that the latter could be more lightly built — not having to carry cannon — and could be cheaper and more efficiently sailed. When protection was needed, as against pirates, the ships were convoyed. Dutch shipbuilding, it was said, would have provided Adam Smith with a more striking example of the division of labor than pinmaking.[9] The Dutch ship known as the *fluyt* was standardized; as many as one a day could be built in the yards of Saandam, which used labor-saving machinery, especially winddriven sawmills and great cranes to lift and move heavy timbers. Timber was imported from the Baltic duty-free, and large inventories were maintained — for as many as four or five thousand ships.[10] With a crew of ten against one of thirty for an equivalent English vessel, freight rates in Dutch ships were one-third to one-half lower in peacetime than those of any rival. Since it was always easy to find a ship bound for Amsterdam, stapling there was often cheapest even when it was the longest way around.[11]

Dutch stapling stimulated other industries besides shipbuilding and its related ropemaking, canvas, and naval supplies, and fishing, including herring, cod, and whaling. There were cheese and gin, plus the finishing of colonial products and textiles. Haarlem, as mentioned, specialized in bleaching; Leiden in weaving, based on imported wool from Spain; and Amsterdam in silk. The revocation of the Edict of Nantes in 1685 brought to the Netherlands from France Protestant immigrants estimated by Scoville at fifty to seventy-five thousand. Included among them was a number of entrepreneurs who undertook silk manufacture in Haarlem and Utrecht, as well as production of velvet and linen in the French manner. The stimulus was short-lived, however, compared with that in commerce and finance, and France recaptured the market for these products after the Peace of Utrecht in 1713.[12]

Dutch successes in the sixteenth and seventeenth centuries were not limited to commerce, exploration, shipbuilding, and fishing, but extended to public works — especially land reclamation, not only in Holland but in England, France, Sweden, and elsewhere[13] — and to agriculture. The Dutch entrepreneur, workman, farmer, and seaman seem to have been characterized by energy and innovation. This industry and vitality are the only basis on which one can make sense of Adam Smith's remark that the "carrying trade is the natural effect and symptom of great wealth, but it does not seem to be the cause of it."[14] Or perhaps a distinction is being made between the carrying trade (shipping) as such, and commerce with large gains from trade. Smith recognized that Holland was the richest country of Europe — though there is some lag here, as marks of decline of the Dutch and upsurge of the British were apparent by 1700 and clear by 1730. But in his identification of commerce with manufactures and merchants with artificers, Smith does not recognize that unlike England, Holland was a country with commerce but not manufactures.

The decline of the Dutch economy after about 1730 is variously explained. Three wars against the British in the seventeenth century and two against the French in the early eighteenth were surely major factors. On narrow economic grounds these destroyed capital, cut trade routes, raised taxes, which were levied on consumption, and thus raised wages. In broader sociological terms they drained the economy of its energy and innovative capacity. Not only did trade decline, but also shipbuilding, textile production, fishing, and agriculture. Dutch industry, sailors, innovators, and capital went abroad. Many industries expired without a fight.[15] In 1670 the Dutch considered themselves superior to the British in energy and ability as well as in capital and material resources. In 1779 a Leiden clothier complained of the general lack of initiative among Dutch industrialists, and a deep-rooted aversion to experimenting with new methods: "a lack of initiative and enterprise in many industries and to some extent in agriculture in striking contrast to 100 years previously."[16] Cipolla believes this decline in capacity to meet economic challenges is typical of all empires — a three-generation effect that applies to societies as well as to families. "The Dutch of the seventeenth century were great innovators. By the end of the 18th century they were incapable of keeping up with progress taking place outside their boundaries."[17]

Such sociological explanation is rejected by a recent study of the comparative industrial growth of Belgium and the Netherlands in the first half of the nineteenth century, which comes down squarely on the explanation of high wages in Holland as the cause of failure to industrialize.[18] Other explanations relate to lack of mineral resources, especially coal, inadequate demand, and governmental policy, specifically free trade, insisted on by the First Hand as a traditional protector of their gains from stapling.[19] High wages clearly would make it difficult for Dutch industry to compete in existing industries that used existing methods with countries that paid lower wages, especially if Dutch capitalists provided to Dutch and foreign industry at equal rates. But Dutch wage rates were high only in the provinces of Holland and Zeeland; they were low in Utrecht, Friesland, Overijessel, Gelderland, and Groningen. More

fundamentally, the impact of high wages is damaging to industrialization only in a static model. In a dynamic model high wages stimulate innovation, as Habakkuk points out for the United States in the
nineteenth century, and Crouzet for Britain in the eighteenth.[20] In
the sixteenth century, the Dutch went into trade for lack of land.[21]
In the early period, a dynamic model applies; in the later, a static.
The change from dynamic to static model may be more significant
than parametric shifts in either.

Nonetheless, the Dutch experience makes clear that commercial
success is not sufficient for industrial success, and that flourishing
and highly specialized commerce poses risks while it earns large gains
from trade. England set out to challenge Dutch supremacy in trade,
with the Navigation Acts and acts of war. Hamburg represented
another threat. But the Dutch emporium declined under direct
trading even without the aid of mercantile policy. Exeter serges,
which had first gone via London and Holland to Spain and Portugal, cut out first London, and then Holland, after bringing the dyeing and finishing stages to Devon.[22] German linens ultimately
skipped Haarlem on their way to British ports.[23] The proportion of
Bordeaux exports that went to the United Provinces bound for Germany and the Baltic declined from 53 percent in 1717-1721 to 21
percent in 1764-1766, while that of exports direct for the "North"
rose from 10 percent to 51 percent.[24] From having been the "regulating granary" of Europe, Holland by the nineteenth century was
merely a dumping ground.[25]

Long-distance trade by sea need have no connection with domestic industry. It is not clear whether this is accidental ("the absence of
any large export industry which could form the solid backbone of
exports and domestic investment"[26]) or in the nature of colonial
trade. A reviewer of an eight-volume work on Bordeaux notes that
"just like Athens in the classical period, or Carthage in the Roman
epoch, or Venice in the XVIth century or Amsterdam in the
XVIIth, Bordeaux found itself operating, in the XVIIIth century,
as a center for the deposit and distribution of a flood of goods which
passed from one hemisphere to the other . . . left behind by all those
ports like London, Le Havre or Marseilles which were connected to
the great European industrial centers."[27] "A merchant is not neces-
sarily a citizen of any country," said Adam Smith. "It is in a great
measure indifferent to him from what place he carries on his

trade."[28] Smith's understanding of trade is not always complete: he believed that the merchant employed in exchanging corn from Königsberg for wine from Portugal brought both to Amsterdam because he felt uneasy separated from his capital and wanted to see it badly enough to compensate for the double charge involved in loading and unloading.[29] This ignores the stapling functions of quality control through grading, packing, storing, and the like. But "merchants knew perfectly well in what manner [commerce] enriched themselves. It was their business to know it. But to know in what manner it enriched the country was no part of their business."[30]

To the extent that the entrepreneurship thesis is valid, it differs in Holland (and Hamburg and Marseille) from the formulation applicable in Britain and most of France. Dutch merchants did not withdraw their capital to buy land and enter the nobility as the British and French sought to. There was too little land available.[31] The First Hand closed ranks, formed a tight oligarchy, resisted new entry, and moved gradually out of trade into conspicuous consumption and banking. Moreover, it was international, not domestic banking, and like Dutch trade unconnected with domestic industry. Charles Wilson overstates the case when he writes that finance became the handmaiden of the industrial revolution in England, but in Holland the mistress of a plundered and bankrupt household.[32] Holland's commercial role went into sharp decline by 1750; its financial role, despite crises such as those of 1763 and 1772, lasted until the Napoleonic wars. In the long run, finance remains more concentrated and is slower to cultivate direct relations outside the center than is commerce.

IN HOLLAND the commercial revolution was not followed by an industrial revolution. In Britain it was. But the British were not seeking to expand commerce as a basis for industrialization when at the end of the sixteenth century and throughout the seventeenth they deliberately set out on mercantilist lines to rival Dutch commerce. On the contrary, they were bent on taking over the Dutch monopoly as Florence had taken over Venice's.[33] The Duke of Albermarle later said, "What we want is what the Dutchmen have."[34] Sir Josiah Child listed fifteen respects in which the English should imitate the Dutch,[35] because with his compatriots he wanted to take over the rents inherent in Dutch gains from trade. To the extent that the commercial revolution in Britain determined the subsequent changes in industry—"perhaps determined" them[36]—it was accidental rather than by design.

Like its Dutch counterpart, the East India Company was established at the end of the sixteenth century. In 1614 a group of London merchants tried to escape the monopoly of textile finishing by forbidding the export of undyed cloth.[37] The effort broke down by 1622. A proclamation of 1615 urging the use of English ships found little favor with Yarmouth, Hull, or London merchants.[38] Half a century later, however, those policies began to take effect. The Navigation Acts were adopted in 1651, strengthened in 1660, and supplemented in 1663 by the Staple Act, which monopolized the carrying trade of the colonies.[39] New Amsterdam was exchanged for Surinam after the Second Anglo-Dutch War and rechristened New York. Export restrictions were applied in wool in the time of Edward III and again in 1660; the earliest restriction on export of machinery was that on the stockingframe in 1698. At the same time measures of protection of British industry were begun (and continued throughout the eighteenth century) in iron, linen, sailcloth, and to keep out calico in an effort to protect woolens.

A revolution in British trade consisted in the "sudden and rapid growth in re-export trade from negligible to one third of exports in 1699-1701."[40] In the hundred years after 1660 "the English merchant class was able to grow rich, to accumulate capital, on middlemen's profits and on the growing shipping industry which was needed to carry cheap sugar and tobacco, pepper and saltpeter on the ocean routes. Although re-exports and these imports called for no investment in home industry, but only in trade, this could be called the commercial revolution."[41]

As Dutch commercial vitality in colonial products diminished, that of Britain (and France) rose. The initial monopoly of London in the established trading companies and under the Methuen treaty of 1703 with Portugal made the outports restive. The west coast ports were better located for Atlantic trade; Bristol, Liverpool, Exeter, and Glasgow moved into triangular trade with West Africa and the West Indies and American colonies, and direct trade with the American colonies. Glasgow specialized in Virginia and Maryland tobacco, by 1750 outstripping London, Whitehaven, Bristol, and Liverpool,[42] and stapling it for Amsterdam and French ports by virtue not of value added in sorting, packaging, and the like, but on the basis of the monopoly of British ports conferred by the Navigation Acts.

The great West Indies merchants like John Pinney[43] or John Gladstone[44] were "speculative merchants," forced into sugar plantations largely by the necessity to take over the properties of those to whom they sold slaves on credit or advanced funds for other purposes. The record shows little interest in improving such plantations, beyond hiring the most efficient overseer possible. John Gladstone never visited the Indies, and John Pinney's "great pride" was "to be considered as a private country gentleman."[45] Both had more money than they knew what to do with. The Pinney merchant house speculated in cotton and sugar and once put £10,000 into the Great Western Cotton Works.[46] For the most part it invested its profits and slave compensation money in English land, government securities, and railway shares.[47] John Gladstone supported the industrial revolution to the extent of contributing to the education of artisans and workers through the Mechanics and Apprentices Library.[48] He toyed briefly with the idea of buying a country bank that had suspended payments in Gloucester in 1825,[49] but the deal fell through. For a man without pretensions to enter the aristocracy, there were not many investment outlets apart from houses and estates before the railroad boom and limited liability. "He knew little of industry, for the world of a Liverpool merchant prince was distinct from that of factory owner."[50]

The connections of gains-from-trade commerce with industry were limited. To a small degree Bristol went in for staple-based industries. It had twenty sugar refineries in operation in the middle of the eighteenth century, glass making for home demand and exports, tobacco processing, a chocolate industry established in 1731, and a range of metal manufacture.[51] But the city lost ground in the eighteenth century for a variety of reasons — delays in modernizing the harbor and the lack of a hinterland caught up with progress in the industrial revolution.[52] This reverses the causation from industry to commerce. It savors of understatement to say "not all overseas trade had industrial consequences."[53] Glasgow was important in colonial trade and in manufacturing, but there was no connection between the tobacco fortunes and the cotton factories.[54] Merchants became landowners,[55] bankers, or plantation owners overseas, not industrialists. Minchinton was forced to deny Williams' claim that "profits from West African and West Indian trades provided one of the main streams of accumulation of capital in England which financed the industrial revolution."[56]

Recent research, to be sure, has concluded that the industrial revolution did not need large flows of capital from commerce apart from working capital furnished by merchants. Fixed capital needs were small, and expansion was financed by plowed-back earnings.[57] As will be shown, South Wales was an exception in iron and copper, but not in tinplate or coal. For the most part, however, the industrial revolution was not characterized by a discontinuous leap in rates of savings and capital formation, as many economic historians have long thought.

At the other end of the analytical spectrum from the Merchant Adventurer seeking large gains from trade in overseas operations was the value-added merchant who operated internally to create a national market within Britain. Bit by bit a mercantile system evolved, starting with a single emporium or relay center which, like Amsterdam in the seventeenth-century world, served as a hub for the system while information was a scarce input and transactions costs high and gradually was replaced both by direct connections that bypassed the initial pivot and by the development of new and more efficiently located markets in some commodities, such as Manchester for cotton, cotton yarn, cotton grey-goods, and finished cottons.

London was the initial relay, for domestic as for foreign trade. The monopoly in foreign trade was man-made; that in domestic trade was an evolutionary construct. In 1677 the city had 1,686 merchants — although it is not altogether clear what this means in the absence of unambiguous definitions. London was the entrepôt of England, with the postal system at its inception in the seventeenth century radiating out along five or more great roads, one rate being charged for a letter to or from London and double that for letters between other parts of the country, on the theory that all letters went to, from, or through the capital.[58]

Trade was local, national, and international. In the early stages both national and international trade went through London. International trade separated itself first to the outports.[59] The merchants of Leeds and Wakefield finally gained full control of the Yorkshire export trade and by 1740 were routing it through Hull, rather than London.[60] Inland traders were less important than exporters in the first half of the eighteenth century, but seem to have used London still to a considerable extent.[61] In import-competing goods with no export market, national marketing took place through London merchants, whether in silk, as illustrated by Sir Thomas Lombe in London, or ribbons, manufactured in Conventry but sold through twelve merchant-manufacturers with warehouses in London and Coventry.[62]

The evolution of the process is seen in detail in cotton. In the first half of the eighteenth century, London was the center for the greater part of the sale of Manchester goods, home and foreign, and a merchant like Joseph Hague made a fortune in London as both importer of cotton for Lancashire and dealer in cotton goods.[63] The change to Manchester took place more rapidly in cloth than in raw cotton, where London remained the main port until 1795 — a decade after the industry had begun exporting cloth. London lost out in cloth slowly after 1780, and rapidly from 1790, when Liverpool, Manchester, and Glasgow merchants took over. Ultimately Glasgow cloth was marketed through Manchester.[64] At the end only surplus stock was sent to London.[65] In the nineteenth century began the movement of some manufacturers into the merchant function — buying cotton in Egypt and the United States and dispatching cloth to commission agents at home and abroad.[66] The industry was one, however, in which the merchant system remained powerful and prevented wide development of direct selling. Woolens moved to direct trading.[67] In cotton textiles, failure to eliminate the merchant led to an unnecessarily large number of separate qualities of product, since the merchant lacked motive to induce the customer to change specifications, however arbitrary, and could transfer orders from one manufacturer to another until he found one who would fill them.[68] Like Amsterdam or London as a trading relay, the merchant is efficient at a certain stage of economic development and dysfunctional beyond it. In the functional stage it is important to have trade develop with the scale of industry. Thereafter it helps to have the merchant ready to withdraw. The speculative merchant finds no difficulty in withdrawing provided that he is attracted into the high-prestige vocations of banking or public service, or the high-prestige avocation of country life.

Between the pure types of gains-from-trade and value-added merchants broadly represented by the tobacco importer of Glasgow and the cotton-yarn specialist of Manchester lay a wide number who combined both functions. Perhaps the woolen trades provide the best illustration. In the seventeenth century Exeter was the scene of a flourishing export trade in woolens woven in Devon. The dependence of weaver on merchant is illustrated in Tiverton's action when a merchant died in 1765 in sending to Exeter for another.[69] Exeter first shipped its serges to London, which relayed them to Amsterdam for finishing and distribution on the Continent. London took the finishing away from Amsterdam. Then Exeter shipped direct to Amsterdam. Later Exeter took over the finishing from London and Amsterdam and shipped direct to Hamburg, Oporto, and Cadiz.[70] While these changes were occurring, however, Norwich came to the fore in worsteds and Devon serges began to decline. As early as 1714 Sir John Elwill, a leading Exeter merchant, in writing to a Dutch client noted that "mixt serges [were] not worn by Many Sort of people as formerly." Wilson suggests that "it is not altogether fanciful to seek part of the explanation for failure in the relative weakness of the link between manufacturer and merchant. In Devonshire the two functions were often separate; in Norwich and Yorkshire they were often combined."[71] After a brief glory, Wilson notes, Norwich — which had benefited from London merchants — gave way to Yorkshire, where the link was most strong. (Bowring put the point more generally in 1872: Exeter's decay he attributed to want of men of sufficient means and wide views to create new branches of trade when the old had gone.[72])

To a considerable extent, however, the Yorkshire experience has been misinterpreted. A great deal of the difficulty has been caused by Heaton's attention to Benjamin Gott, a merchant who went into manufacturing and built Bean Ing, a vast mill in which all the processes from sorting the wool to packing the finished pieces were carried on under one roof. By 1800 the mill housed a thousand operatives. Heaton called Gott only an Industrial Half-Revolutionary, because all his weavers worked handlooms and he supplemented their output by purchasing heavily from small domestic clothiers.[73] (Compare Gras, who called Sir Thomas Lombe, a London merchant who financed a silk throwing mill of the Italian pattern on the Derwent River in 1718, the morning star of the industrial revolution, not the rising sun,[74] because his mill used waterpower instead of steam.) Others besides Gott moved from merchanting into manufacture: the Luptons,[75] John Edwards, and Law Atkinson.[76] The outcry to which this change of profession gave rise has created a misleading impression. With very few exceptions merchants did not enter manufacturing. When successful they put their fortunes into land, annuities, government stock, canals, and turnpikes, entered public life, or retired to the country. Some like William Denison invested in land but did not retire to the country; he was interested in land for its safe return.[77] But the gentlemen merchants of Leeds provided neither capital nor entrepreneurship for the industrial revolution.

They did, however, extend the market, and this by upgrading quality and pushing on delivery dates. Yorkshire's share of British exports of woolens rose from one-fifth in 1700 to one-third in 1772 to three-fifths in 1800. It was accomplished, states Wilson, by concentrating on the cheap end of the market in both woolens and worsteds and leaving to East Anglia (Norwich) the better worsteds, to the West Country (Cotswold) the fine broadcloths, and to Devon (Exeter) the serges.[78] Cloth was bought in cloth halls or purchased direct from the clothiers, but in any event was brought to the merchant's workshop after purchase and inspected.[79] No one paid attention to the lead seal testifying to measurements. The cloth was sheared, fulled, dyed, and sized by the merchant in his workshop, or on order under his direction. Price was not an issue in exports as compared with quality. "William Denison bullied his clothiers about delays and inferior workmanship and occasionally threatened withdrawal of his custom, but never attempted to dictate prices."[80] Initially Yorkshire woolens were relayed by way of London, then Amsterdam, then sold direct to Europe. In due course the European market died down; expansion shifted to transatlantic trade with the American colonies, and after interruption from 1770 to 1783 with the United States. With each major shift in the trade, new merchant houses came to the fore and old houses either failed or withdrew. The shift from the German and Portuguese trade to America, for example, meant new risks, especially much longer extensions of credit and new names.

The extension of the market underlined by Adam Smith was far from unimportant, but it tended to move parallel to rather than in anticipation of increase in production. Davis claims that the process of industrialization in England from the second quarter of the eighteenth century relied importantly on colonial demands for "nails, axes, firearms, buckles, coaches, clocks, saddles, handkerchiefs, buttons, cordage and a thousand other things."[81] In nails, the nailmonger stood between the nailmaker and the export merchant, serving especially the colonial trade; he grew rich and turned banker.[82] This did not involve financing industry directly, but rather more trade.

The major systematic provision of entrepreneurship and finance from commerce to industry is found in the iron and copper industry of South Wales. Here the industry was organized from the beginning in large units, and in those branches of industry that started small — coal and tinplate — there was little London and Bristol mercantile capital. In iron, however, the demands of war brought both merchants and their capital: Anthony Bacon came to Cyfarthfa Furnace at Methrhy Tydfil in 1765, joined subsequently by the London merchants Richard Crawshay, Alexander Raby, Sir Benjamin Hammett, Henry Smithers, the Thompsons, Harfords, and Grenfells. John regards the process as an exception to British development. South Wales had raw materials or access to them — coal, iron, copper, tin — but lacked an industrial tradition comparable to that of the Midlands, Lancashire, or Yorkshire. When war cut Britain off from Russian and Swedish iron ore, an opportunity presented itself with few local resources to take advantage of it. London and to a much lesser extent Bristol merchants brought capital and entrepreneurship. Similar opportunities did not present themselves elsewhere.[83]

In frequent other cases trade and industry were linked in the early eighteenth century, but nothing came of it. At an early nonspecialized stage merchants were involved in all kinds of manufacture. The firm of Sutton and Cotesworth started as tallow chandlers and corn merchants in Newcastle; traded internationally in grindstones, glass bottles, lead, and salt among exports, flax, hemp, madder, whalebone, and wines among imports; manufactured candles and sword steel; mined coal and grindstones; and produced salt.[84] Joseph Pease of Hull invested in trade, shipping, underwriting, and whaling and founded a bank, but preferred to think of himself as an industrialist, engaged in oil-seed crushing, white lead, whiting, soap and paint making, cotton spinning, and through his son-in-law distilling and copper mining. Jackson calls him "one of the great entrepreneurs of the 18th century."[85] He can hardly have contributed to the industrial revolution.

There were of course revolutionary figures in trade: Strutt, who financed Arkwright's patent for the roller spinner and subsequent patents,[86] Robert Owen, David Dale, Samuel Oldknow—but they came from the country drapers' shops, not from the merchant princes.[87] In an anonymous 1883 account of early fortunes,[88] only three of twenty-eight industrial fortunes resulted from production of one who had started in trade. Sir John Brown was apprenticed to a cutlery merchant, having wanted to be a merchant as a boy despite family resistance, started to make his own cutlery, gradually moved into other steel products such as files, and ended up making railway spring buffers. Titus Salt set himself up as a manufacturer to spin alpaca wool after trading in it, because he could not induce Bradford spinners to spin that fiber. William Bass was a carrier of beer, then a trader, and finally a brewer. But these connections run between the humblest of the value-added merchants, rather than the merchant bankers, and not at all between the gains-from-trade merchant princes and industry. David Dale, who built the New Lanark cotton mills outside Glasgow, was not one of the hundred forty pre-1776 Glasgow merchants making fortunes in tobacco, but started as an apprentice in a silk mercer's house, imported linen yarn, went into banking, and only then into cotton spinning.[89]

Trade thus grew with the industrial revolution, rather than starting it, as Bairoch also demonstrates.[90] In fact, it is just as well that merchants who do make great fortunes withdraw from trade. Gains-from-trade merchants have to make a fortune in a few years because their rents are likely to be competed away rapidly. Value-added merchants are usually capable of making only a few major improvements in the organization of trade or a change in product before they settle into a routine. To make a fortune and clear out leaves the coast clear for new families to enter and adjust to evolving conditions. Such new families may not exist, as noted earlier for Exeter.

If, then, the commercial revolution was the expansion of overseas trade in colonial goods—sugar, tobacco, tea, and coffee—the merchant's role was not central to the industrial revolution. The value-added merchant aided industrialization in two ways: by urging improvements and by expanding the market, and perhaps in a third way, in the usual case, by removing himself from the economic process after a limited period and unblocking what would otherwise be a barrier to change. The process of building the market proceeds by stages — first through a relay point like London and a relay institution like the merchant. As information becomes widespread and change slows down, to maintain the old circuits is inefficient.

FRENCH FOREIGN TRADE expanded somewhat faster than that of the United Kingdom during the eighteenth century, and trade of some ports — notably Bordeaux, the real exports of which grew at a compound rate of 4.1 percent per year — much faster. Fortunes were made not only in Bordeaux, but in Marseille, Nantes, Saint-Malo, Rouen, Le Havre among ports, and by the great merchants (négociants) of inland cities like Paris, Lyons, Amiens, Beauvais, and Le Mans. Much of the trade of the ports, however, as with Amsterdam, Bristol, Liverpool, and Glasgow, was only loosely coupled with domestic production in France and thus had little to do with the industrialization process. Within France there was a commercial and equally an industrial evolution — without the discontinuity one finds in the Britain of the last quarter of the century. The négociants reaped large gains from trade and amassed big fortunes. Some went into banking. Many bought seigneuries (land estates) and offices (annuities) available from the king, including ennoblement. To a greater extent than in Britain, ports were populated by foreign merchants, or Protestants of French origin, usually nominally converted to Catholicism, whose loyalties ran partly or wholly to fellow religionists and family members abroad. The internal market developed first through the relay of Paris, and to a lesser extent of Orleans and Lyons, but these were finally overcome through direct shipments. Annual and semiannual fairs gave way in the eighteenth century to continuous distribution.

French economic historiography has given us a rich detailed picture of the position of the separate ports, and of the textile trades of Beauvais and Le Mans, based on archives and notarial records, admiralty accounts, rolls for special taxation, and individual marriage contracts, testaments, and bankruptcy proceedings. The prosperity of the ports resulted primarily from overseas trade. Trade of the Middle Ages in wheat, salt, and wine gave way after the middle of the seventeenth century, especially in the last quarter, to preoccupation with sugar and slaves and to a lesser degree with coffee, cotton, and indigo. Saint-Malo and Nantes were deeply engaged in fishing off Newfoundland for cod, which was dried or salted for distribution to the Catholic peasantry of France, as well as (along with salt beef from Ireland) to slaves in the Antilles. In the course of the eighteenth century Bordeaux prospered especially because of her window on the Atlantic and her good relations, based on the ancient trade in wine, with Holland and the Baltic, to which excess supplies of sugar, coffee, and indigo were relayed.

Nantes (and its neighbor Lorient) had the privilege of the French East India Company (until 1769) and was a center of trade in spices. Its success, most marked in the first half of the century, was owing to its accumulation of capital from the East Indian trade and its three-way trade in slaves and sugar. Well placed for the movement to the interior of high-value products like spices, its long-run disability lay in poor road and river connections with Paris.[91] The salt, cod, sugar, drugs, and spices brought to Le Mans from Nantes had to be transshipped from boat to horse and cart at Malicorne.[92] Bordeaux was not much better situated. It could supply planters in Martinique and Santo Domingo with flour, wines, brandy, and salted food, cod transshipped from Brittany, or beef from Ireland; but it was far from the manufacturing centers of France. Crouzet claims this was not important, since the biggest export item was textiles and they were not heavy.[93] Inward shipments were handicapped by high transport costs, administrative and customs obstacles, not to mention low incomes. The cargoes comprised Spanish wool, salt, and dried fish, and above all, sugar and coffee. Soap, dried fruits, rice, drugs, perfumes, and oils came by water from Marseille.[94] Elsewhere Crouzet suggests that if trade was regarded as a superficial phenomenon in France, so was it in the United Kingdom, and that Bordeaux, Nantes, and Rouen furnished the colonies with textiles to clothe the slaves, materials for sugar mills, sails, cordage, and cannon for ships.[95] The list seems skimpy. Meyer produces a longer one for Nantes, nearer to the manufacturing centers than Bordeaux: luxury articles wanted by the planters (furniture, silver, books, clothes); food for slaves: dried cod from Newfoundland, salt beef and butter from Ireland and Brittany; food for the planters: flour, grain, wine, brandy; construction materials: bricks, lime, wood; cheap cloth for the salves. He calls them of "mediocre" or "feeble" value.[96] Commercial expansion was not a strategic factor in the growth of industry, nor did the international conjuncture spread to the peasantry—whose economic life was rather dominated by the state of the harvest well into the nineteenth century.

If overseas commerce did not help greatly with demand, there remains the question of capital formation. Fortunes were made at Nantes and Bordeaux in ten to fifteen years, Arthur Young said.[97] Many of these were consumed in the purchase of seigneuries and the building of chateaux. Others found their way into banking. Some went abroad. Foreign merchants never completely dominated the merchant communities of France, but they frequently led them. Bordeaux was a melting pot; at the top of its society were foreign merchants, living assembled at Chartrons and connected through the "Protestant international" to Huguenots and other Protestants not only at other French ports but at Amsterdam, London, and Geneva.[98] Not all foreigners were Protestants; among them were Irish and English Catholics, themselves religious and political refugees as were the Huguenots from France. As the total number of négociants recorded by Carrière in Marseille rose from 275 at the beginning of the eighteenth century to 750 near the end, on the eve of the French Revolution, the percentage of foreigners went from 10 to 18, and the percentage of French from the Languedoc and Dauphiné, largely Protestants if nominal converts, from 9 to 28.[99] Some Huguenot capital was exported from France following the revocation of the Edict of Nantes, particularly in the wave of penalties against failure to abjure Protestantism begun ten years before 1685 and lasting as late as 1730.[100] It was easy for merchants and shippers to export gold, silver, jewelry, furniture. Van Harzel, a Dutch Protestant, who possessed the second largest fortune in Nantes in 1715—400,000 livres—escaped in 1730 with his entire wealth.[101] French contemporaries and later scholars made a great deal of this loss, and of the dependence of Marseille and even Nantes merchants on Swiss funds of the "Protestant diaspora,"[102] but this dependence was later denied.[103] The Protestant infusion of the *négoce,* however important, owes a great deal to the movement of Protestants excluded from charges and *offices,* and with inhospitable farmland, off the southern slopes of the Massif Central to

Bordeaux and Marseille.[104] Foreigners participated when a port failed to maintain representatives abroad — as Marseille, not deeply engaged in northern trade, let Swiss, German, British, and Dutch agents buy, rather than itself seeking to sell.[105] In some views foreigners filled a vacuum left by French disdain for commerce.[106] Or the high proportion of foreigners could possibly be regarded as a supply response, with excess German potential merchants, limited by the closed ranks of the Hanseatic cities and anxious to join the race for fortunes, finding a place in French ports and even in the West Indian islands. Jean-Jacques Bethmann, the richest shipowner and one of the greatest merchants in Bordeaux, was of Frankfurt-am-Main origin, and there were many others.[107] Spanish and Portuguese Jews expelled from their countries were not numerous, but some of them were among the most prominent merchants. Abraham Gradis had many friends in high places, was owed money by the Marshal of Richelieu and the Duke of Lorges, and died, some years after a loss of 2,700,000 livres tournois, with a fortune of 10,000,000 — second only to that at 15,000,000 in 1791 of the Languedocian François Bonaffé, a Protestant who married a Creole in Guadeloupe.[108]

As in Britain, there are a few examples of close connection between commerce and industry. The Dolle brothers, originally from the Dauphiné, made money in commerce with the Antilles, via the fair of Beaucaire, and moved to buy plantations in the French West Indies rather than land in France. In 1787 they explored the desirability of going into linen weaving in Grenoble to assure a supply of cloth for their slaves.[109] This conveys a hint of market failure, that adequate supplies would not be available at appropriate times and prices when needed, although perhaps the prospective investment was nothing more than an outlet for surplus funds. More apposite, but also more debated, is the Huguenot shipowner Antoine-Jean Solier, who took funds fron his coreligionists in the calico printing (*indiennes*) trade, whether in Switzerland to which they had been expelled by the revocation of the Edict of Nantes, or after their return to France in the Oberkampf plant at Jouy.[110] Solier et Cie was a négociant in general as well as a specialist in import of undyed calico from India, and it is not certain that Swiss participation in this trade was more significant than any other.

One odd connection between trade and commerce led through

land. The merchant retired to the country on an estate, but then entered industry as a *maître de forges* on the basis of iron discovered on the property and woods available for charcoal. Le Nicolais of Laval was a *négociant blanchisseur* who acquired the forge of Aron in this way.[111] Another was Narcisse L., associated with his father in the wine trade in Paris, who in 1833 took on interests in mines and blast furnaces.[112] The equivalent in Glasgow was the tobacco merchant whose land turned out, or was known in advance, to bear coal and led its owners into the coal, salt, or iron business.[113]

Rouen and Le Havre were more closely connected with industry, Rouen more than Le Havre, which participated in the colonial trade. Woolens and linens of northern France were sold at fairs at Caen and Guilbray and shipped over Rouen when exported. More important were the growth of the cotton textile industry, based on cotton imported from the West Indies, and the putting-out system operated by Rouen merchants. "Siamoises," a mixture of linen and cotton patterned after the dress worn by the ambassador of Siam and the members of his suite in 1684, were one specialty. Total production rose rapidly in Rouen and its parishes from 50,000 pieces in 1717 to 489,000 in 1767; these were exported as well as sold within France.[114] As Britain mechanized, Rouen tried to follow suit, with the aid of British workers, merchants, and manufacturers. Fortunes were perhaps made more quickly in the colonial trade, either directly or via Cadiz, than by industry, and in banking, which was closely associated with Paris. Rouen was more like Liverpool, Bordeaux like Glasgow — except that Liverpool was associated with an innovative textile center, Rouen with an imitative. It was badly hurt by the Eden treaty of 1786, which lowered duties on English textiles and earthenware.

Apart from Rouen, the *grand négoce* of the ports had a limited connection with the industrial evolution of France. The same was not true of the great merchants of the inland cities, insofar as they have been studied. France is a hexagon, closed against the outside world, but connected internally by a communication network. Until the eighteenth century this network operated commercially with Paris as the entrepôt, pivot, or relay. In the sixteenth century the brightly colored cloths of Paris and Rouen were being sold in the Languedoc by merchants traveling to fairs.[115] At the end of the seventeenth and beginning of the eighteenth centuries, Paris began to be eliminated by direct selling. In 1650 Beauvais sold two-thirds of its linens to Paris and Lyons, with the rest sold locally or exported over Rouen. In 1690 exports had gained at the expense of Paris, and direct relations had been established by Beauvais merchants with Montpellier, Toulouse, and other inland cities. By 1730 the role of Paris had shrunk to very small proportions. Lyons, however, sustained its trade. In the early period it had been a relay point for the south. Later it served as a stapling place for exports to Switzerland and Italy.[116] Over the eighty years from 1690 and throughout the rest of the eighteenth century, exports grew to a preponderant position because of the competition at home from cotton cloths. The high-quality *demi-holland* of the seventeenth century became an export staple because of the loss of home demand. By diverting the existing supply to new outlets, the Danse, Motte, and other mercantile dynasties relieved the pressure on Beauvais manufacturers to keep up with technological change and thus contributed indirectly to their fossilization and ultimate decline.

Paris remained the relay longer for the newer goods in greater demand. While Oberkampf at Jouy (after 1759) sold no indiennes in export markets, it used Paris as a center of consumption and for redistribution to distant points. Alongside this network, however, developed direct marketing through the established textile centers such as Abbeville, Amiens, Beauvais, and Troyes, and the establishment of depositories that handled shipments to fairs.[117] There was of course specialization. One Parisian *indienneur*, Dubois, sold four-fifths of his output in the provinces; another, Jarry, sold mostly in Paris.[118] In silk, another high-grade product, as well as in printed cottons, Lyons sold through Paris throughout the century, apart from export sales. Two-thirds of domestic sales went through the relay of Paris, rather than directly, and the "overpowering superiority of Paris limited the direct intervention of Lyon négociants in the rest of the country."[119] Even in silk, however, Paris was a rival but did not dominate.[120]

There were some interesting features in the trade of *étamine*, a loosely woven light woolen cloth in which Le Mans and the surrounding cities specialized. The number of négociants in Le Mans engaged in this product was seven in 1712, a dozen toward the middle of the century.[121] It is stated that these négociants followed the extension of the master manufacturers "or at least did not precede it," but became the masters of the trade by buying, finishing, and shipping the cloth.[122] Le Mans and its surrounding towns specialized in étamine dyed black, which was sold in large quantities to monks and nuns within France and in Italy as well. Domestic sales through fairs were handled largely by merchants from Paris or other towns, rather than by the *marchands/drapiers merciers* of Le Mans, who existed in large numbers, or the Le Mans négociants.[123] Like demi-holland, étamine lost out to cotton textiles and also suffered from deterioration in the quality of wool. Paris merchants dropped out of the trade, leaving the great merchants of Le Mans with only overseas trade.

The account of textiles in the province of Maine provides a footnote on Paris as a relay in the "curious commercial circuit" in linens. The Le Beauvais Abbey in Le Mans bought linen for shirts, underpants, and stockings from Alençon, 20 miles to the north and slightly west, each year from 1713 to 1730. These were delivered at the end of January or beginning of February, like other linens brought from Rouen for surplices, table linen, and handkerchiefs, by a certain Marigner, wholesale cloth merchant of Paris, 65 miles to the east of Le Mans.[124] Dornic suggests that the explanation lies in the state of the local roads in winter. Another possibility is that until direct selling took over, especially in the declining products that lost out in the French luxury market, the relay of Paris remained critical. In foodstuffs, of course, it continued at Les Halles in Paris until the market was moved to Orly in the 1960s.

By the middle of the eighteenth century Paris, like London and Amsterdam, was shifting from trade to finance. It continued to invest in trade, through the trade of the ports. One scholar states bluntly that Paris in the eighteenth century was a financial, not a commercial, city,[125] but this presumably would apply more fully to the second than to the first half of the century. Funds were invested but little in industry. Le Couteulx, Paris banker and Rouen merchant, invested in textile manufactures in Rouen, but mainly trafficked in Spanish piasters through his Cadiz branch.[126] Paris was a relay for money that went back to the ports and to foreign trade, when it was not used to buy privileges from the court, rather than into industry. At the same time the commercial network within France, if not the superficial but profitable trade of the ports, evolved side by side with the progress in production.

GERMANY HAS BEEN CHARACTERIZED as an economy without highly developed commerce, and one that sprang directly from traditional society to industrialization without passing through an extended commercial development.[127] In the early nineteenth century a British observer characterized Münster as having "little commerce," claimed that the "commerce of Hanover [is] inconsiderable despite the connection of Bremen" and further that "a body of merchants and manufacturers, who by their capital give employment to numerous workmen, and who like country gentlemen are too rich to be dependent on the smiles or frowns of the court, is not to be found in Prussia."[128] Bavaria was marked by the lack of a considerable group of great merchant families and long-distance trading houses.[129] In Baden merchants were mistrusted as swindlers and speculators, and the task of industrial development (*Gewerbeförderung*) was to protect and strengthen the middle class against them.[130]

This picture is perhaps one-sided, leaving out as it does the Hanseatic cities (Cologne, Bremen, Hamburg, Lübeck), the Rhineland, and Frankfurt-am-Main, in which merchant communities were highly developed. Cologne had sunk back from a leading position in international commerce as Antwerp and Rotterdam proved better located for stapling. In its turn Lübeck, the site of Thomas Mann's novel of a merchant dynasty, *Buddenbrooks* (1910), lost out to the better-located Hamburg and Bremen. These cities, however, developed their own merchant dynasties, with Hamburg especially strengthened by displaced Huguenots at the beginning of the eighteenth century and by refugees from the French Revolution at the end. Hamburg specialized in short-haul trade to the Baltic and above all to London. It became known as the "English city." Bremen developed long-distance traffic, especially transatlantic, in tobacco, cotton, and rice. Hamburg dominated in sugar, coffee, hides, tropical wood, and wines. Bremen complained that it lacked an export product, as Hamburg had grain and the Baltic ports grain and wood.[131] Frankfurt was the gateway for British goods to southern German states.

Frankfurt and Hamburg differed profoundly in social and political ways. Frankfurt was a creation of the Prussian king, who established the Frankfurt fair there, at the major crossing of the east-west trade route of central Europe. When the Zollverein was formed under Prussian leadership, Frankfurt found membership irresistible. Hamburg was republican, oligarchic, devoted to trade, shipping, and finance to the exclusion of all else. The leading merchants associated but little with bureaucrats from the government, refused to accept titles, and frowned on intermarriage with Prussian officers.[132] In contrast to Augsburg, whose merchants were anxious to be ennobled, the city not only forbade ennoblement as a strict rule as early as 1276, a regulation renewed in 1658 and practiced throughout the seventeenth century, but stated on the earliest of these occasions that no knight could live in the city.[133] Hamburg was a miniature Holland, populated by gains-from-trade merchants with stapling commodities produced for the most part at a distance. It resisted incorporation in the Zollverein and the Reich until the patriotic surge of 1870, and even then it remained a free port, rather than an integral economic member of the empire, for another decade and half. Within Frankfurt, moreover, there was a difference of view between the patrician merchants who wanted to stay out of the Zollverein and the new group who succeeded in winning adherence.[134] The difference corresponds roughly to that between the gains-from-trade leading merchants, interested in overseas trade and especially in British goods, and the value-added men, concerned with developing the local market.

Limited economic development in most of the German states (especially poor transport connections among them), and political separation, led to stunted commercial growth outside the Hanseatic states, Frankfurt, and the Rhineland. The Rhineland and Westphalia were different from the other German states even before guild restrictions were eliminated by Napoleon at the end of the century. Merchant networks large and small were much more fully developed. Barmen and Elberfeld concentrated in textiles, particularly bleaching and dyeing, with the former emphasizing production, the latter marketing. What is impressive about these two cities is their capacity to shift as comparative advantage was lost — from linens to cotton and then to ribbons and embroidery. When high wages and English competition with machine-made cottons made it necessary, a plant was moved across the river to Gladbach-Rheydt. By the end of the eighteenth century the Rhineland mercantile elite with customers throughout Europe, especially France, the Netherlands, and London, was a close-knit oligarchy, cut off from the aristocracy as the English and French were not, and turned inward into a life of luxury—horses, servants, finishing schools for daughters, wine, jewelry, and speaking French. Of three hundred mercantile houses in Frankfurt, two hundred forty were of German origin and in 1776 some fifty to sixty of them were from Barmen and Elberfeld.[135] Similar mercantile houses existed in Krefeld and Münster, not to mention Cologne.

Silesia was otherwise. The linen trade flourished from the sixteenth century only when Dutch and English merchants by-passed the guilds because they could not adjust to the requirements of foreign markets.[136] By the late seventeenth and eighteenth centuries Silesian linen dominated the world and produced a class of wealthy merchants who loaned out their profits in mortgages to the aristocracy and, when they could, acquired estates.[137] When linen lost its overseas market to cotton, the only response was lower wages and fraud and adulteration.[138]

The merchant class in the Rhineland seems to have furnished entrepreneurs for industry, but from the petty merchant class rather than the *Grosskaufmänner*. A study of Rhenish and Westphalian entrepreneurs notes that many of them in the nineteenth century came from merchant families of the previous century.[139] Zunkel comments that whereas in Britain entrepreneurs came largely from artisans, in Germany merchants played at least an equal role.[140] These small merchants, *Kaufmänner* rather than *Grosskaufmänner* of the sort found in Hamburg, went from putting-out (the cottage industry served by merchants who brought raw materials and took away furnished goods) into manufacturing—like J. G. Brugelmann, who built the first mechanized cotton-spinning works at Ratingen near Düsseldorf in 1783, five stories high, with 1,600 spindles, and partly but not entirely powered by water.[141] Until 1830-1850 foreign trade and financing of foreign trade were largely in Dutch hands. Krupp, Stinnes, Haniel, Liebrecht, and Ehrenbold also moved from trade to production in iron and coal in the first half of the nineteenth century.[142] Mannesmann at Remscheid was a printer and merchant who started a file factory in competition with British imports.[143] "It was not the successful handworker who made it big, but his son, who, converted from being a powerfully capitalized merchant, used the corporate form, and hired a technical man who remained in the second rank."[144] On the other hand, in Switzerland in the textile industry, factory pioneers were technical people, not financial, trade, or managerial.[145] Elsewhere, however, Braun noted that north of the Alps there formed a local stationary class of merchants, united in guilds parallel to the handwork guilds of the city, who were interested in innovation, achievement oriented, and busy not only in trade, traffic, and finance but also in production. He cites the Geneva watch industry, along with the Zurich textile industry, as linked to city merchants who, once the restrictions of the ancient regime were lifted, put forth a tremendous burst of energy.[146]

A few strands of information on merchants investing in industry exist for Germany and are set forth below. The information is available only for the period after that of our primary interest and is highly fragmentary. It suggests, however, that merchant wealth provided one important source of capital in new companies. It is assumed that these merchants were the value-added type rather than gains-from-trade overseas traders.

The explanation given for underrepresentation of merchants in Germany as contrasted with Britain and France has various elements: first, the late unification of the country and the failure at an early stage to build an entrepôt or relay pivot apart from the fairs of Frankfurt and Leipzig; second, the disdain with which German social values regarded commercial pursuits, holding the merchant in lower status than the industrialist, in contrast with Britain where the opposite ranking obtained; and third, the early bureaucratization of the firm, with direct buying and selling combined with production in a single business entity.

The low standing of commerce in Germany (other than the Hanseatic cities and Frankfurt-am-Main) contrasted with the higher status of the nobility and the military, of course, and of industry as well. Merchants were scorned as tradespeople, *Händler* opposed to heroes, in Sombart's book *Helden und Händler,* contrasting the Germans and the British. The term contained anti-Semitic prejudice as well as a sense of economic and social inferiority vis-à-vis the British.[147] The three-generations-from-shirtsleeves-to-shirtsleeves did not apply in Germany, nor was there opportunity to gain acceptance in an open aristocracy.[148] Purchase of land in Prussia was forbidden to all but the nobility until 1807,[149] although there was brisk trade in land along the coastal lands such as Mecklenburg and Holstein. After 1807 there is evidence of rich merchants buying estates,[150] and of farms that had been in the same family for two or three hundred years changing hands three, four, or even six times in ten to fifteen years.[151] Sartorius von Waltershausen is quoted to the effect that in the 1820-1830 agricultural crisis 80 percent of aristocratic landlords lost their estates;[152] presumably not all were broken up and sold off piecemeal to land-hungry peasants. Later estates were purchased. But the rule broadly held: while bourgeois were permitted to purchase estates after the Stein-Hardenberg reforms and aristocrats to enter trade, for the most part the old barriers to social integration held.

Industrialization on a significant scale in Germany came in the middle of the nineteenth century and relied on direct buying and merchants. There is some debate about when German industrial take-off occurred,[153] but for our purposes a difference of twenty years is inconsequential. In mining, distribution of coal was regulated by the state, subject to price control, and did not need to rely on a mercantile structure.[154] Railroads were large-scale and so, quickly, were iron and steel. In the earliest stages of getting started, when the firm consisted in thirty-five workers, Albert Poensgen, of the steel tubing plant of Poensgen & Schoeller, took over all mercantile activities of the firm personally, especially supervising the routine purchasing of inputs by two employees after Dutch merchants failed to perform what he had expected from them.[155]

In the new electrical and chemical industries, bureaucratic organization took place from the beginning. Siemens and Halske was started by a military engineer, Werner Siemens, and quickly acquired a manager in another military man, Wilhelm Meyer. Initial sales were of telegraphic installations for the military forces of Prussia and the Russian government. By 1872 Siemens noted the necessity to write to customers in advance of undertaking production. "Only thus can our fabrication constructions be very cheap, good, and quickly delivered."[156] The middleman was eliminated before he had taken hold, in an effort to speed up technical progress Kocka observes that the monopoly in education which the merchant class had had earlier was eroded by general universal education, and that rather than rely on a mercantile network, large companies enforced standardization, undertook communication of goods and prices, delivered goods to inventories of shops, sold by sending samples over distances, and undertook direct contact between buyer and seller.[157] Dye companies initially marketed abroad through export firms in the developing countries, and through wholesale firms in Europe and the United States. These agents were allowed, however, to carry only one firm's lines. After 1885 they went to direct selling.[158] The chemical industry required intimate contact between producer and consumer to ensure proper use of frequently dangerous materials, but also of products that had to be employed in exact ways to achieve efficient results.[159]

Did the absence of a well-knit system of markets hurt? Political reality more than the absence of mercantile connections was responsible for the fact that prior to Zollverein and the railroad, Germany was not one country but a juxtaposition of a number of half-closed economies. With Zollverein and the railroad, a large German market quickly substituted for innumerable local markets.[160] It has frequently been claimed that Germany was poor in capital prior to 1950. Sombart observed that great fortunes were rare, and the man with a mere half-million talers was regarded as rich.[161] Hamburg at midcentury is said to have had a hundred millionaires in mark banco (equivalent to 500,000 talers) as opposed to only seven or eight in Cologne.[162] But as Borchardt has made clear in a classic article, it is hard to give credence to the widely held view that Germany's lag behind Britain in the early nineteenth century was the result of lack of capital. Capital markets, like goods markets, were fragmented and underdeveloped, but banking institutions (and foreign credits) responded quickly to the demand for capital for such large projects as railroads and iron foundries; once started, they proceeded on reinvested profits.[163] The so-called German way to industrialization may have been delayed by the absence of an antecedent capital market built on mercantile credit, but not for long.

No ATTEMPT has been made to compare numbers of merchants at various periods in Holland, Britain, France, and Germany, or to evaluate such statements as that England in 1721 had two-thirds the number of merchants of all Europe put together, though Amsterdam in 1671 handled ten times as much trade as London with one-twentieth of the retailers.[164] The secondary sources are weak on the merchant communities of London and Paris because of their great size and complexity and because of the destruction of the Paris archives in 1871.[165] A few qualitative conclusions can perhaps be drawn, however.

The widely held view of the contribution of the merchant to industrialization seems clearly exaggerated insofar as the profits of gains-from-trade commerce are concerned. These fortunes are neither necessary nor sufficient to stimulate industry. They are typically consumed by being invested in nonindustrial outlets, including banks, which finance primarily trade or foreign governments, and land, government stock, annuities, and *offices*. When industry catches hold, it largely uses trade credit and finances itself with plowed-back profits. In large-scale industry—South Wales iron and German joint-stock companies, for example—one can find investor contributions from merchants and, especially in the latter case, from banks. They are the exception.

Nor do merchants typically become manufacturing entrepreneurs, unless one limits the discussion to the putters-out of the proto-industrialization period. Again there are exceptions, like Benjamin Gott among the value-added merchants. The great majority of merchants who made fortunes moved out of business into banking, politics, or rural pursuits. Where there was no aristocracy to imitate—perhaps the agriculture of the area did not produce a surplus that needed to be guarded, or could be expropriated by the landed aristocracy and military—merchant oligarchies formed, tended to dig in, and ultimately led to mercantile decay. The moving on of successful merchants served the economic function of removing what might otherwise have developed into a hindrance to change.

The value-added merchant is a unit in an information network. In the early stages information is needed to see what can be produced and what is needed or sought and where. Surveillance of quality and delivery timeliness are two aspects of information control. Division of labor between the producer and his intelligence-gathering collaborator permits maximum efficiency. With success comes fossilization, at which stage the merchant network is a barrier to change, with the result that it is helpful to have him ready to retire. Where he clings to the old ways, decay ensues.

One general force that acted to reduce the role of the merchant was universal education. The rents earned by both types of merchants were initially based on their monopoly of calculation and languages. Apprenticeship was expensive and consisted in instruction at home and in the offices of associates abroad. Money and opportunity costs limited entry. But the spread of education brought down the rents of merchants through competition. With information cheap, direct connections rendered the middleman obsolete when he was not dysfunctional.

In sum, the commercial revolution was neither sufficient nor necessary for the industrial revolution, as the cases of the Netherlands and Germany prove. This does not deny that commerce can be helpful, by providing capital for agriculture and for social overhead, if not for industry; by training entrepreneurs for petty commerce like the putters-out, if not the great merchants; and especially by achieving scale in growing industries through value-added merchants. It may also be that a commercial revolution was necessary — if not sufficient — in the first industrial revolution in Britain, if it was not necessary in a country that industrialized enough later to depend less on standardized products and more on tailor-made production embodying software. There can be little doubt that the contributions of the value-added merchant to the industrial revolution (standardization, quality control, prompt delivery dates, and upgrading) were vital — a lesson overlooked all too frequently in socialist and developing countries today. But the maxim "commerce leads to industry" is too simple.

European Port Cities[1]

6. My goal in this chapter is exploration of a small corner of
what one may think of as the Galbraith "big picture," modified by the North-Thomas institutional and the Innis stapling theories of economic history. In Galbraith's terminology the scarce factor of production at a given place and stage
in economic development earns monopoly returns, which it
converts, in part at least, into social prestige and political
power. Under feudalism, with a manor system, land was the
scarce resource; control over land, often in the form of
ownership, gave rise to nobility. In the North-Thomas view,
nobility exchanged protection of serfs and their goods for
service and a share of the crop. The economic transaction
had elements of compulsion in it, as serfs were tied to the
soil to prevent them from making a better bargain. However, it acquired a degree of legitimacy from the charismatic
leadership of the nobility, to cast the matter in the mode of
Max Weber. In a less generous interpretation, the nobility
served as a sort of Mafia that exchanged protection, primarily from other members of the same class, for a prominent
fraction of the result of the peasants' toil.

With the rise of commerce, and later industry, capital became the scarce factor; businessmen — the bourgeoisie — insisted on their right initially to vote, ultimately to dominate
political decisions. In due course the vote became general-
ized from property to persons. With a century or more of
industrial growth, affluent societies developed in which
capital had become no longer scarce, and in fact was abundant. In these societies, runs the self-serving view of the aca-

demic pundit, knowledge is the scarcest resource; intellectuals and what Galbraith calls the technostructure have risen to esteem, high material rewards, and frequently decision-making authority in political and business life.

I do not wish to quarrel with the broad-brush outline of this picture, but rather to refine it to a limited extent, then to fill in some detail regarding port cities, especially in Europe.

RICARDO made clear many years ago that not all land is equally productive. Rich land that earned large rents to be captured by the aristocracy in whole or in part was matched at the other end of the spectrum by no-rent land that was unable to support nobility. Weber observed that in ancient Greece land in the plain accumulated in the hands of the nobles, while the hillsides that could not produce a rent were everywhere held by the peasantry.[2] Braudel made similar observations of the Mediterranean in the Middle Ages, noting that mountains made for democracy, while plains were suited to the aristocratic form of government.[3] Joseph Marshall, a British civil servant traveling through Germany in the eighteenth century, noted:

It is always to be remarked that the gradations of freedom are ever to be found in mountainous countries; in general such are free; but even under absolute monarchs they enjoy more liberty than the subjects of the same prince who inhabit plain countries.[4]

Rappard has examined the topography of Switzerland with its separate cantons prior to confederation in 1848 and found democracies in the poor Alpine districts (Uri, Schwyz, Unterwald, Zug, Glaris, Appenzell), patrician aristocracies in the plains, corporative oligarchies in commercial cities, and an assortment of monarchies and aristocracies, ecclesiastical and secular, absolute and qualified in mixed cases.[5] In southern Germany — the Türinger Wald, South Mecklenberg and the Schwarzwald — there were no nobles because the soil was thin and a surplus could be acquired only from extensive holdings.

Differences among nobles also frequently related to the quality of the soil. The Junkers in the north and east of Germany were originally relatively poor and knew how to milk; in Bavaria, nobility did not undertake farm work. In France, a gentleman himself was not permitted to plow more than four *charrues* — a small portion — of his land without losing status.[6] In Haute-Provence in the sixteenth century the nobleman "lived alongside his peasants, cleared the land as they did, did not scorn a plough and till the ground, or to carry wood or dung on the back of his donkey. He was a constant irritation to the Provencal nobility . . . Here there were no rich, well-fed clergy to be envied and mocked; the priest was as poor as his flock."[7]

Land is more complex as an agricultural input than simply rich bottom and poor hillside land. Feudalism could not get a hold amid the farms and forests of Norway, according to the social historian Bull, because of the scattering of population over wide areas poorly connected by road. The steward of the lord could not manage more than ten peasant holdings in a neighborhood; others were days' journeys away by horse and boat. Peasants were thus free, not only in the sense of owning their land, but they were never submitted to bondage, hereditary taxes, or compulsory labor. The monarch had difficulty raising taxes, and to pay for wars at the beginning of the eighteenth century sold off the land owned by the royal house since the Middle Ages.[8]

A similar absence of nobility, or very weak nobility where it existed, holds for North Friesland, stretching from the United Provinces in the west to Schleswig in the east. This North Sea coast is separated from the rest of Europe by moor and heath, rimmed by dikes. Constantly under threat of flooding, its population must be mobile. They are sea folk with "little time for cities, noble knights, artists or thinkers."[9]

The drainage and irrigation needed to make some land usable are both collective goods, in which benefits and costs cannot be separately allocated but must be assigned communally. In Spain irrigation "communities" known as *huertas* allocated costs of building and maintaining the channels, pipes, and ditches needed to distribute water, divided it fairly upstream and downstream, and among individual users in separate areas. Valencia had also a separate problem of drainage in low-lying swamps (*marjals*), which called for the same kind of collective, institutionalized will to take care of benefits external to the individual. "Municipal councils, herding and fishing collectives, and irrigation communities were characteristic of a society in which feudal customs had taken but shallow root."[10] In the fens of Britain there was less cooperation, but a particular institution, the Commission of Sewers, developed with its courts of sewers to determine responsibility for maintaining the drainage system, and to allocate costs of collective works.[11] The heavy costs of draining the fens in the seventeenth century, carried out by the Dutch engineer Cornelius Vermuyden, resulted in an arrangement under which the Earl of Bedford advanced the capital and received in return 95,000 acres of the reclaimed land.[12]

Fishing offers a still more limited prospect for supporting nobility. Poor because of the absence of the Malthusian preventive check of delaying marriage to wait to inherit land, the fishing population of the North Sea was further devastated from time to time by the mysterious disappearance of the herring shoals for years at a time.[13] Above all, fishermen are mobile. Or so one would have thought. But Braudel upsets this easy generalization:

The whole of Dalmatian society moreover was dominated by hierarchy and discipline . . . Even in recent times an entirely leisure class of *Sjor* or *Signori* existed above a proletariat of humble gardners and fishermen. "A fisherman," says Cvijic, "fishes for himself and for a *Sjor* with whom he is closely associated. The *Sjor* considers him as almost one of his household and the fisherman refuses to sell his fish to anyone else."[14]

The purpose of this chapter, however, is to examine ports and their economic, social, and political peculiarities. There will be national differences, and differences across time: ports that are independent states, called "autocephalic" by Weber, largely Italian, with an exiguous hinterland, but in the case of Venice and Genoa, colonial empires for a time;[15] some with merchants who amass fortunes and retire to the country to join the aristocracy or gentry, if they can gain admission, especially in France and Britain; traditional republican oligarchies like Hamburg, that resist the landed gentry of the hinterland and stand aloof; weak nobilities in the city itself, as in Italy, though with investments on terra firma in Venetian country estates. Virtually all are oligarchic, republican, but not democratic.

Moreover, ports specialize by commodities, by types of shipping, and especially by relations with the economy of the hinterland they may be said to serve. In one view applied to France, there are two countries: the agricultural society and economy of the interior, focused on Paris and Versailles, with thousands of small towns thirty miles (or a day's ride) apart; and the rim of port towns, Marseille, Bordeaux, Nantes, Saint-Malo, Rouen, plus interior market centers on international trade routes like Lille, Lyons, and Strasbourg.

The "other France," particularly represented by the ports, in effect belonged more to the Atlantic world than to the self-contained, isolated, rural France dominated by Paris.[16] But it is necessary to start more generally with cities. In the limits of a brief discussion it is impossible to provide an orderly chronological account of developments in a number of countries, even if it were possible in the limits of competence. This chapter will therefore move about among the centuries to some degree and extend the analysis in Chapter 5 backward to Venice and Genoa.

CITIES IN EUROPE emerged initially from administration and commerce, and only belatedly from industry. Administration and commerce are mixed in some degree, as the administrative city has local markets at a minimum, and the commercial city has its own government. Before the days of the large industrial cities like Manchester, Essen, or Roubaix-Tourcoing, there were of course crafts in all cities. Prior to the industrial revolution, the major distinction ran between administrative cities that were the seats of temporal and spiritual government (that is, with a palace and a cathedral) and commercial cities with fairs, docks, warehouses, and exchanges.

Capital cities — both administrative centers handling the "money, messages and men"[17] required for governing, and commercial centers dealing in goods — were typically found at the point where a major inland trade route crosses a formidable river upstream from the sea: Paris on the Seine, London on the Thames, Rome on the Tiber, Seville on the Guadalquivir, Cologne on the Rhine. Berlin was the major transshipment point between tributaries that almost connected the Elbe and the Oder rivers. Other inland ports were Frankfurt-am-Main on the ford (*furt*) used by the Franks to cross the Main, and places like Lyons, Basel, and Montreal up rivers below falls where boats of a certain draft had to stop.

Weber distinguished among the consumer city, the producer city, and the market city, the first being identical with the administrative classification, the second with the industrial, and the third with the commercial entrepôt center.[18] The consumer-administrative city was patrician in government and hierarchical; the commercial city was run by a confraternity or oligarchy.

This set of distinctions would have to be modified somewhat to embrace financial centers and university towns. The first tend to

conform to commercial centers on inland routes, and to administrative centers which also have or once had substantial market activity.
University towns produce an intellectual and cultural topography
that sometimes fits the administrative-commerical-financial hierarchy, as in Paris and Vienna, and sometimes diverges sharply, as in
Oxford, Cambridge, and if I may say so, Cambridge, Massachusetts. Unified countries like Britain, France, and Spain produce a
different distribution of cultural centers than countries like Germany and Italy, long made up of city-states or principalities, each
typically with its own court and concert hall, and often too a university.

The function of a city is to transact business, whether economic,
political, or intellectual. Certain types of transactions must be
carried on face to face, especially where ideas are subject to rapid
change or where it is necessary to achieve explicit understanding to
avoid the possibility of error. Commerce, finance, law, advertising,
government, high-style industry, entertainment, and so on, in
which tastes change rapidly and the consumer must be consulted
constantly, can be conducted only where population is dense and
where face-to-face contact is readily achieved. In today's world the
telephone is not enough, much less the mails. Cities are required as
the nodes of high-density information networks.[19]

The relationship among various cities in a country is a function of
many aspects of its national life, including the degree of centralization or decentralization, which in turn grows out of historical
relations among king, nobility, and bourgeois; the timing of national unification; the nature of the unification process; and
similar factors. Paris has long dominated France, with the possible
exception of the ports. When Prussia took the leading role in
German unification, Berlin — already an administrative and cultural
capital because of the Prussian court — acquired dominant financial
functions as well. In Australia, Brazil, Canada, and the United
States, to cite only a few examples, a separate capital was created to
avoid the domination of a single large city that antedated unification.

AN AHISTORIC VIEW of ports — in location economics, for instance
— sees them as nodal points in a transport pattern that leads to the
agglomeration of economic activity at a point in space. Market-

oriented export activities gather there, such as automobile assembly, pulled toward the overseas market but halting, if only temporarily, at the water's edge. Supply-oriented import activities reach out to overseas sources, without actually leaving, and industries to process imported raw materials gather at the stage where bulk is broken or, at a minimum, some change in transport method is required. Oil refining, tobacco curing, sugar refining, ore smelting, soap making, grain storage, flour milling, coffee roasting and grinding, tea packaging, or bottling of beverages imported in the cask are typical activities of a port, along with more obviously related activities such as shipping, shipbuilding, ropemaking, and the like. In Cambridge, Massachusetts, the air outside my building used to be redolent of chocolate or soap, depending on which way the wind was blowing, and on occasion rubber, from a tire-reclaiming plant that may or may not have been port related. (I am happy to say that research activities have now displaced these odors.) Boston is famous for baked beans and Indian pudding, both made with molasses. When Boston was a major sugar port in the eighteenth century, hogsheads of molasses were broken down into flagons and jugs, and bulk molasses in Boston was abundant and cheap.

In historical perspective, however, the location-theory approach would be misleading except for high-value goods, notably exotic products from the East such as pepper, dyes, china, silk, and — after the discovery of America — coffee, sugar, tobacco, and precious metals, and bulk products that could be shipped their total route by water. Coal, wheat, salt, wine, fish, timber, and woolens could not be transported any considerable distance overland before railroads, unless by rivers and later canals. Ports dealt to a considerable extent with one another, rather than with the hinterland. The molasses of Boston had to be consumed, by and large, not more than a wagon's ride from the docks. Bordeaux was in closer touch with Amsterdam than with Lyons. First Venice, then Amsterdam, London, and Hamburg became what the literature of the eighteenth century called emporia, relays, or stapling places; these locations imported goods over long distances, undertook a few finishing processes; subtracted some of the product for local consumption, and shipped the rest on to another port within its narrow rim. Price notes the distinctions among shipping points, shipping centers, limited markets, and general markets for tobacco that was collected in

Maryland and Virginia and readied for shipment to Britain, largely Glasgow.[20] An equivalent hierarchy of ports existed at the receiving end: Glasgow, the specialized center grown rich under the Navigation Acts that required all tobacco from the colonies to be shipped to Britain, subtracted about 15 percent of the total; and then French, Dutch, and German ports, which broke bulk into smaller and smaller quantities. Tobacco was a valuable product. Coal from Newcastle was available cheaply only in ports, as its cost doubled ten miles from dockside. Between coal and tobacco and spices lay a wide range of products. Only those at the upper end in value per weight were moved in international trade from or to points far from sea and river ports.

Until about the turn of the nineteenth century, larger ports were in varying degrees financial as well as commercial centers. Not only were London, Paris, and New York financial centers but also Liverpool, Le Havre, Hamburg, and Baltimore. Economies of scale changed that, and bankers in large numbers moved from the lesser port cities to the dominant centers. After the French Revolution and the rise of the empire, Paris took over the financial roles of Rouen, Nantes, Bordeaux, and Marseille, partly as a result of the Continental system that cut these ports off from their North Sea and Baltic, Atlantic, and Mediterranean networks, but also because when trade was restored, the function could be performed with greater efficiency in Paris. In due course the banking functions of Lyons, the great inland port on the route from France to Italy and Switzerland, were also transferred. Cities specialized in handling goods or money — a few like London and Hamburg for a while, in both — but typically Paris would give up on internationally traded goods, Bordeaux on money.

Ports specialize by function. Just as Glasgow dominated the Atlantic tobacco trade in the eighteenth century, so Liverpool commanded cotton and grain in the nineteenth and Bristol sugar, slaves, and the Newfoundland run. Hamburg specialized in North Sea trade, especially to the Baltic and London, whereas Bremen developed larger oceangoing ships for bulk cargoes in tobacco (after the War of Independence ended the application of the Navigation Laws to that trade, and with an interval for the Continental system) and in coffee and cotton. Le Havre and Rouen were above all cotton ports, Nantes specialized in spices and slaves, Bordeaux in wine for export (a local product with a river, the Gironde, for unifying the catchment basin) and sugar for import, Marseille in soap. In the emigrant trade from Germany in the middle of the nineteenth century, Bremen with the larger ships took passengers all the way to the United States; Hamburg staged them there via London and Liverpool. For every migrant who embarked at Hamburg between 1836 and 1848, nine left by way of Bremen.[21]

The United States lies outside our scope in this chapter, but a similar functional analysis exists for Boston, New York, Philadelphia, Baltimore, Norfolk, and intermediate shipping points, cities, and lesser ports. Boston specialized in fish and timber, Philadelphia in wheat and flour, especially when rising British consumption after 1760 converted that country from an exporter to an importer. There was no major port that traded tobacco; it was bought for Glasgow from shipping points rather than sold to Glasgow by an exporter on the eastern seaboard.[22]

Ports differ in efficiency for different cargoes by reason of their linkages to surrounding territory. Rotterdam was an exchange port between river and sea, ideal for bulk cargoes like coal and later petroleum; Antwerp's original growth depended on trade in wool and woolens, later on superb road and rail connections. Hamburg had both.[23] Bremen suffered from lack of space and especially from the absence, despite the Weser River connection, of an outward bulk cargo comparable to Hamburg's grain from Brandenberg and Mecklenberg or Rotterdam's coal from the Ruhr. In Bremen and Nantes a merchant was a shipowner first, a merchant second; in Hamburg and Bordeaux, the order was reversed.[24]

Perhaps the most fundamental distinction among ports, however, turns on their relationship with the hinterland. The Fox view that French ports belong to an Atlantic network economy more than to France has been mentioned. The more usual view is that some have close ties to the hinterland, others do not. In the previous chapter Olivieri was quoted to the effect that Athens, Carthage, Venice, Amsterdam, and Bordeaux did not have close connections to European industrial centers, whereas London, Le Havre, and Marseille did.[25] The distinction is related to that made between the gains-from-trade merchant who buys goods where they are cheap and sells them where they are expensive, with some minimal processing in addition to relaying, and the value-added merchant who is concerned to improve the product for the market, sometimes undertaking the finishing process himself, but in all instances interested in upgrading the product, standardizing it, controlling quality, and meeting delivery dates. As noted in Chapter 5, these are ideal types; in the real world the distinctions blur. The gains-from-trade merchant is associated with the great entrepôt stapling centers, however; the value-added merchant tends to affiliate with the industrial centers like Leeds, Manchester, Beauvais, Le Mans, and Barmen that are not ports, as well as with the ports like Antwerp, Rouen, Lyons (if the last be allowed), and Gothenburg. Not all ports are without a hinterland, as Fox implies. Braudel notes the "*some ports* [my emphasis] are without a hinterland," the functions of the port — the fusion of a fortress and a market — being enough to create a *town*.[26]

PRESENT INTEREST in the relation of ports to hinterland does not extend to Athens or Carthage but begins with Venice, a republic with a doge elected by the patrician oligarchy. Olivieri is a little severe in suggesting that Venice was a mere stapling center with no indigenous production. In addition to the Arsenal, which constructed merchant and naval galleys for Venetian use with elaborate division of labor, interchangeable parts, and great efficiency, Venice produced for export (largely to Byzantium) a wide range of luxury products, especially glassware, soap, silks, jewelry, leatherwork, and fine woolens, which it exchanged for grain, cotton, spices, sugar, and so on in competition with Genoa.[27] In the early period the Venetian traders were nobles, not landed, having moved from the land in the early years of the Renaissance to the island city to seek fame and fortune, but no less noble for that, says McNeill.[28] Later, having made their fortunes and experiencing intense competition from the Dutch and English, who were competing in woolens and soaps by questionable methods,[29] they moved back to the country and lived a city life there.[30] The city economy of Venice declined over the sixteenth century, says Rapp, not so much because of the development of new routes to Asia via the oceans, in contrast with the land routes leading to the eastern Mediterranean, as because of direct competition in the Mediterranean of Dutch and British merchants. "Venice slept the sleep of the rich."[31] Luzzatto suggests that with her foreign trade cut off by mercantilism, Venice lost out by failing to develop a productive interchange with its hinterland.[32] If he means agriculture, this is questionable, as capital was invested in drainage and irrigation as well as in magnificent estates, but agriculture failed to produce great wealth. Nor can he mean an industrial hinterland, since trade in all but luxury goods was efficient only by water.

With the gradual slipping of Venice, Genoa took over in trade and finance. In the sixteenth century it carved out a prominent role in distributing Spanish and Portuguese precious metals to France and Germany, as well as trading wheat, wine, and spices, and running monopolies in salt and wool. There was virtually no hinterland, nor any local industry. In Genoa some textiles were produced—largely silk before the nineteenth century—and paper. To a degree the port served as the outlet to the Mediterranean for Milan and other industrial parts of Lombardy before the rise of Marseille to the west and Leghorn, the specially designed port for Florence, to the east and south.[33] Expert in finance, with goods flowing from all over the world to the free port, as it was declared in 1608, Genoa grew rich with little outlet for its wealth except palaces in the city, productive farms in Milan or Naples, and government bonds in Spain, Rome, and Venice.[34] There was no stimulus to local agriculture in a city perched on the shore at the edge of the mountains, nor any in industry. In 1785 Genoa was called the poorest state in Europe with the richest citizens. The Genovese were said to be the richest creditors in Europe with France, Austria, Russia, Spain, and Denmark in their debt, and interest receipts of 17 million lire a year from France alone. In addition, they owned one-third of the feudal estates of Naples, of Piedmont, and of the papal states. Contemporaries considered that foreign investment depressed economic activity and weakened the spirit of enterprise, as old entrepreneurs were converted into rentiers.[35]

The financial ascendancy of Genoa lasted about fifty years at its peak, from 1570 to 1620, before Amsterdam took over. Genoa never had a hinterland until railroad tunnels penetrated the mountains to Turin in the nineteenth century. The Continental blockade, the efforts of Austria (which dominated Lombardy) to divert trade to Trieste, the tunneling of the Alps (which linked Turin and Milan directly to northern Europe by road and rail), and finally the Suez canal in 1868 left Genoa in the wings. The decline of commerce and the failure to stimulate agriculture or industry led to emigration from Liguria throughout the eighteenth century.

Venice and Liguria were both republics, the usual political pattern for trading cities with their own administration—that is, not subject to the jurisdiction of a wide national government. Nobility existed, but it soon cut a weak figure. At unification in northern Italy, there were no rich landlords outside of Count Cavour and his small circle to carry the tasks of public life. Nobility did not imply wealth or power, nor did it convey feudal or military privileges, as in Germany, or maintain a tradition of government, as in Britain.[36] There were differences of course among provinces and changes through time. In Lombardy a patrician lost status if the family had not held office in three generations, or if a member participated in a base trade.[37] It can be claimed that a managerial elite must maintain an "active, inquisitive, energetic mode" and that "landlords and tax collectors who squeeze goods and services from a sullen and resentful peasantry may have a far less stimulating experience."[38] But old wealth from commerce, if not sustained by an interest in agriculture, government, or industry, equally may lose its capacity to keep a people or class energetic. The ports of Venice and Genoa grew rich on the stapling trade, with some Venetian production of luxury exports, and declined in due course without fructifying sectors other than finance in Genoa.[39]

Amsterdam was the stapling center par excellence. Its location at the English Channel entrance to the North Sea, connections by river with Germany, France, and Belgium, and the daring and skill of its shipbuilders and seaman led it to excel in what Adam Smith calls "distant trade." Colonial products were brought to Europe via Amsterdam either directly or at one remove, such as from Bordeaux, and the exchange of Baltic grain and fish for Mediterranean and Iberian salt and wine took place also in Amsterdam. Connected with its commercial success were Dutch achievements in fishing for herring, and in shipbuilding with standardized designs, extensive division of labor, and power tools—windmill driven before the age of steam.[40] Although Amsterdam was not identical with the United Provinces of Holland, it dominated them; and the Dutch republic reflected the typical political pattern of a self-administering city-state—republican, not democratic, and highly oligarchic. The country was run by the First Hand, the overseas merchants, and especially by the Heeren ("lords") who ran the Dutch East India Company. The Second and Third Hands, who did the processing of the stapled goods and wholesaled them locally, had very little voice in affairs. Membership in the councils of the United Provinces was hereditary in many cases, and children of eight, nine, or ten years of age occasionally had seats.

In the previous chapter I observed that Dutch merchants did not withdraw their capital from trade to participate in conspicuous consumption, in emulation of an aristocracy, because of nonavailability of land, although I cited a dissenting opinion.[41] Further testimony has come to hand to suggest that they did actually withdraw their capital. Carter states that the rich capitalists who were putting money into English funds were also building palatial country houses; she quotes Montesquieu, who compares Amsterdam in 1729 to Venice, where magnificent palaces were built instead of fleets.[42] Buist cites John Hope, who in 1767 "entered upon a process of aristocratization which gradually alienated him from the everyday affairs of the firm," as he acquired five great houses within fifteen years and spent his time traveling between them with guests.[43] The suggestion has even been put forward that the transformation from urban merchant to country gentleman led the ruling oligarchs to lose interest in and support for the navy and turn their attention to land armies to protect their estates. The transition from trade to finance, and especially foreign investment, also lessened interest in convoys and naval escorts and may have marked the beginning of the downturn of trading fortunes.[44] The navy was an inordinate expense for the United Provinces, but if the stapling trade was to survive in an era of repeated Anglo-Dutch and then Anglo-French wars, it was a necessary one. In the end, the Continental system and occupation of the provinces by Napoleonic forces put Amsterdam, which had never had a hinterland, permanently in the shadow of London and even Hamburg.

Goods came and went to and from Amsterdam. So did people. A sizable colony settled in London as agents of Dutch capitalists, and in other ports and colonies all over the world. At the same time, Holland had its doors open to persons of all kinds seeking to find refuge from persecution elsewhere (such as Jews and Huguenots) or merely to improve themselves, like the refugee merchants driven from Antwerp by the blocking of the Scheldt River in 1572, who contributed to the success of Dutch trade.[45] Weber notes that traders and financiers are everywhere skeptical or indifferent to religion.[46] (Newport, Rhode Island, a port city with no hinterland or catchment basin, and dominated in its location by Boston and New York, is said to have done as well as it did by the tolerance derived from the views of Roger Williams, which attracted to the town a conspicuous number of Jews and Quakers.[47])

The Hanseatic city of Hamburg was like Amsterdam in many respects. Starting from a position well behind other ports, but with an ancient tradition going back at least to the twelfth century, it gained rapidly through the eighteenth century, particularly after the loosening of the Navigation Laws in the 1820s. Apart from ship-building and local crafts, there was no industrial production of consequence. An ancient tradition despised nobility.[48] Hamburg's interest in world trade and colonies, and its specialization in trade with Britain, led it to be regarded in the rest of Germany as the "all-English city," that is, as non-German. In return, there exists to this day in Hamburg and Schleswig the view that Egypt starts south of the Elbe. In contrast with those in Britain who made fortunes on foreign trade, bought places in the country, rebuilt them in grand style, and lived the life of the squirearchy, in Hamburg business ambition and love of solid work were (are?) passed down to sons even by rich fathers, and fashionable idleness occurred only as a rare exception.[49]

A detailed contrast has been drawn by Böhme between Hamburg and Frankfurt-am-Main, an inland port, if it belongs in the category at all, but a commercial and financial city with a very different tradition and history than Hamburg.[50] Hamburg had trade without production, a very small and uninfluential group of handworkers, no guilds to speak of, leading merchants and bankers who were Lutheran rather than Catholic and interested in overseas trade. In Frankfurt, on the other hand, there was a division in the ranks of merchants between those interested in having the city serve as a gateway for foreign goods, a group closely allied to the court bankers, and a more numerous group of those who wanted to trade in local products with the German confederation. The two groups split over whether to join the Zollverein. In 1836 the so-called "English-goods party" was beaten, and Frankfurt became a member of the Zollverein — to the disgust of Hamburg and Bremen, which held out (Hamburg for another forty-five years). Prussian victories in 1864, 1866, and 1870 were too much to enable Hamburg to withhold joining the empire, but her proud status as a free port was maintained by agreement with the reluctant Berlin government for seventeen years after German unification.

Frankfurt merchants and bankers specialized. In contrast, the Hamburg merchant was

a trader restless, a spying head, always pregnant with speculation, always cautious, never fully certain. He conducts his own trade, and buys on speculation and for his own account in foreign harbors and cities, taking them to another foreign city, to sell them to foreigners, or to an inlander. He is often at the same time a commission agent, a banker, shipowner, forwarder and participant in insurance . . . in contrast to the Frankfurter, an all around man.[51]

Like all commercial cities, both were open to foreigners in the Netherlands' tradition of asylum: Hamburg had its Goddefroys and de Chapeaurouges; Frankfurt its de Neufvilles, deBarys, and d'Orvilles.[52] But Hamburg was republican, and Frankfurt loyal to its tradition of imperial privilege at the time of the Holy Roman Empire.

Issues concerning French ports relate to internal differences among them on the one hand, and to differences between ports as a whole and interior towns. Arthur Young raised the first set of questions two hundred years ago, and Adam Smith — along with Edward Whiting Fox of the present day — the other. The form of government of the French ports could not be oligarchic, since the cities were not independent like the Italian city-states or Hamburg, nor did they dominate the national public as did Amsterdam merchants in the United Provinces of Holland.

Traveling through France immediately before the French Revolution, Young drew a contrast among Rouen, Bordeaux, and Nantes, the first with a hinterland of cottage industry, the second with the spillover of wealth into improved agriculture, the last with no interaction of any sort with the country about it. The sharpest contrast for this agricultural observer was between Bordeaux and Nantes, the countryside around the former having

many new and good country seats of gentlemen, well built and set off with gardens, plantations, etc. . . . . the effects of the wealth of Bordeaux,[53] while within three miles of Nantes there was the most incredible agricultural blundering and ignorance.

This is a problem and lesson to be worked at, but not at present . . . What a miracle that all this splendour and wealth of the cities should be so unconnected with the country.[54]

The vineyards around Bordeaux, of course, had been commercialized by nobles and wealthy merchants alike. Like the rich Parisians of the eighteenth century with a "farm" in the Beauce, the bourgeois of Bordeaux owned a domain with vines.[55]

En route from Rouen to Le Havre, Young found a scattering of country seats, and was glad to see them, but

farmhouses and cottages everywhere, and the cotton manufacture in all . . . to Havre de Grace the approach marks a flourishing place: the hills are almost covered with new little villas, and many more are building.[56]

The distinction between Bordeaux and Rouen/Le Havre in their effects on agriculture may have almost nothing to do with the nature of the trades (stapling in Bordeaux and drawing on an industrial hinterland in Rouen) and turn more on commercialization of agriculture in which Paris, as just noticed for the Beauce, played a major role. Rouen is in Normandy, and Normandy alone of the provinces of France experienced the enclosures, farmed on an adequate average scale, and sought improved efficiency.[57] Wealth invested by merchants in agriculture around Nantes was immobilized,[58] and that invested in the small wine plots around Bordeaux failed to produce changes in the peasantry.[59] In Britain, the merchant was regarded by Adam Smith as the "best of improvers" in agriculture.[60] It is hard to make the case that this was true of France except for the Paris area.

This leads into the larger issue of the "other France," and whether the port cities, connected with one another, had virtually no contact with the interior and the sociopolitical system. Young's expressed wonderment about Nantes uses "cities" in the plural as if the "splendour and wealth" of all cities were disconnected from the country. Adam Smith, who spent more than two years in France as tutor to the Duke of Buccleugh, claimed that the inferior ranks in mercantile and manufacturing towns there—he often failed to separate commerce from industry—differed from those in towns with a court. The first were in general "industrious, sober and thriving," the second "generally idle, dissolute and poor, as at Rome, Versailles, Compiegne and Fontainebleau." "If you except Rouen and Bordeaux, there is little trade or industry in any of the Parlement towns of France."[61] Marseille moved at a slower pace than Bordeaux in the eighteenth century, but like the latter had an economic rhythm unconnected with that of France as a whole.[62]

There is some uncertainty whether French merchants who made fortunes wanted to join the first France. The view is widely held that they did.[63] The large foreign and Protestant element in the merchant community on the whole did not.[64] Jean Pellet, a baptized Huguenot merchant at Bordeaux, did, and was rather mocked on that account; his prestige, it was said, proved unequal to his fortune.[65] In Marseille, merchants did not move rapidly to ennoblement. The négociants had their country seats and an occasional chateau, but were content to stay in trade generation after generation.[66]

Historians rather than this historical economist must render a verdict on Fox's thesis of two Frances, geographically bound together but economically and socially separate and politically antagonistic. Whether this view illuminates or explains much of French history from the Fronde revolts of the seventeenth century to the French Revolution and its aftermath in the Restoration and the July monarchy is beyond me. One can question perhaps whether Fox makes enough of Colbert's mercantilism and of the interest of Louis XIV in naval power and hence ports, even commerce — not from the viewpoint of taxation alone, but of *grandeur* and *gloire*. In an interesting study Josef Konvitz notes the plans under Louis XIV for rebuilding Rochefort and Marseille, the one a naval base, the other a purely commercial city.[67] Perhaps the fact that Rochefort was rebuilt in monumental style, and because of the opposition and sabotage of the merchants Marseille was not, supports the Fox thesis.

Were there two Britains? Surely not. The oceanborne trade of Glasgow, and to a lesser extent Bristol, was only weakly connected to the hinterland and closely linked to the Atlantic trade. London was both an entrepôt for world goods relayed to other destinations, and a port exporting domestic production and importing for domestic consumption. Elsewhere — Edinburgh, Newcastle, Hull, Exeter, and Liverpool — ports were umbilically connected with exports of British produce, imports for British use. But this is related to geography too, and the facts are that no spot in the British Isles is more than 110 miles from a deep-water port, and that most industrial locations are connected by water—or were after the canal building of the eighteenth century. In France and Germany, there are ports and hinterland. In Britain, it is almost as if the whole country is the outskirts of the port, and there is no deep hinterland. In this setting the successful British merchant and financier could move quickly to join the gentry into which he was welcomed.

OUR EXPLORATION of ports perhaps says little beyond the statements that the character of economic life has repercussions on the sociopolitical institutions that develop in a given area, that cities are different from the country, that port cities differ from other cities, and that port cities differ one from another in the ways they specialize. It would have been illuminating to have been able to penetrate to deeper generalizations, if such are possible, to discover uniformities between the functions of different ports and their social attitudes. Some of the questions that remain belong to sociology rather than to economic history or historical economics, such as why do British merchants allow themselves to be drawn off into the gentry, or actively seek admission to it, whereas the successful Hamburg merchant disdains co-option of this sort? Even this query has an economic aspect, as noted in the previous chapter, since part of the problem with merchants is to get them out of the way when their function is altered by the loss of their monopoly of knowledge through diffusion or technical change.

Inconclusive as a study of this superficiality must be, it does demonstrate, in my judgment, the benefits of the comparative approach to the analysis of ports. The experiences of Amsterdam and London, Amsterdam and Hamburg, Hamburg and Bremen, London and Glasgow, Antwerp and Rotterdam, Genoa and Venice, Bordeaux and Nantes—all differ. Some of the differences relate to ascendancy at different points in historical time, others are the result of geography or the social matrix. One can learn much from the study of a single port over time, in an evolving setting; but more, much more, by making comparisons.

Germany's Overtaking
of England, 1806 to 1914[1]

7. The subject of economic rivalry has renewed relevance in the last third of the twentieth century, when American hegemony in economic matters is slipping. An inevitable corollary is the question of which if any new economic power will take the place of the United States on the world stage: Japan? Germany? China? A dark horse like Brazil? A Toynbee view of the world may be too rigid, but it is not without value to study economic growth and development in comparative terms, emphasizing not only catching up[2] but also falling back and decline. One could focus equally well on the outstripping of the United Provinces of Holland by Britain in the eighteenth century, the rivalry of Germany and the United States vis-à-vis Britain in the period after 1850, or the rapid advance of Japan relative to the United States from 1955. The choice for this chapter is to focus on the catching or possible overtaking of Britain by Germany in the nineteenth century, or from 1806 after the Battle of Jena to 1914, prior to World War I.

Germany as Apprentice, 1806 to 1848

The major emphas of the chapter is on German economic development, and only the last quarter is on decline in Britain. I shall follow to some degree Rostow's breakdown of German economic growth: 1806 to 1850 for the "preconditions," 1850 to 1872 for the "takeoff," and 1873 to 1913 for the "drive to maturity"; this is not to accept a Rostovian theory of "stages" or to worry much about the question of timing, which occupies so much space in Hardach's useful article.[3] Whether one selects the Zollverein or the revolution of 1848 as the turning point preceding what Gerschenkron would call the "great spurt" is of little consequence so long as it is well understood what was happening when.

It is worth spending a moment to explore what is meant, if anything, by such expressions as "overtaking," "catching up," and "falling behind." One could use measures of overall income or income per capita, although the well-known difficulties of comparing different national incomes in real terms give one pause. Leaving those difficulties aside, we can say that Germany overtook Britain in real income per capita only in the 1960s, and not at all in the nineteenth century. A crude measure of growth is the percentage of employment in agriculture. By this yardstick Britain is still far ahead of Germany. Or perhaps one ought to measure not output so much as consumption; this favors Britain in the short run because of her smaller proportion of income used for investment. One can take overall or per capita measures, or rates of change; there are economists who bring Samuel Johnson up to date by asserting that the first derivative is the last refuge of a scoundrel. Or the growth of productivity per weighted index of factor inputs. Or capacity to transform, that is, to adapt to changes in economic variables. Or capacity to develop new industries. A less subtle measure would relate to economic power defined in some sense such as Hawtrey used[4] — the ability to deliver firepower at a distance, a definition that peculiarly favored the insular position of Britain with her big navy. Or steel production. Or the rate of growth in competitive export markets. Or foreign lending. On each of these measures there will be somewhat different results. Germany never caught up with Britain in agriculture, textiles, shipping, or overseas banking. In the development of new industries, Germany was pressing her hard in the 1880s; in steel, in the 1890s. German overall investment overtook British in the 1870s. By Rostovian stages the German takeoff occurred sixty to seventy years after the British,[5] but the end of the drive to maturity becomes simultaneous.

The question is one of substance, and it was asked as early as 1827 by one Johann Conrad Fischer — a Swiss, to be sure, but one who spoke for Central Europe or the Continent as a whole: "Out of what origin and through what means has not industry but the spirit and the idea of industry and its kind and manner arisen in England and when will the Continent come to a knowledge of its power and a culmination will be reached in England?"[6] Fischer first visited England in 1794 at the age of twenty-one, and for the last time in 1851. The biggest changes, in his view — he was a metallurgist who started out as a coppersmith and ended independently discovering crucible steel, so that he probably knew little of cotton textiles — occurred between 1794 and 1814. In the earlier year, Britain had nothing that the Continent lacked except the steam engine. In 1814 progress had been made in numerous industries, and changes taken place that he had not suspected. The British (by the 1820s) were masters of the Continent in fire, reflecting the advantages of physics and chemistry.[7] The Napoleonic wars were a hothouse of developments in metallurgy and machinery for Britain, but not for the Continent, and put Britain far ahead of, say, Germany.

Parenthetically, this brings up another moot issue of economic overtaking — whether Britain overtook France only during the Napoleonic wars or, rather, early in the eighteenth century. New research by Crouzet, Lévy-Leboyer, and others suggests that there was no enormous development gap between France and Britain prior to the Napoleonic wars, and that France if anything grew faster than Britain during the previous fourscore years, after having been even with her in 1685 and fallen behind in the period from the Revocation of the Edict of Nantes to John Law.[8] During the wars themselves Britain clearly outstripped France; but my intuition tells me to be skeptical about the conclusion that the gap, if any, was really very small in 1780 or favored France. France was ahead in a number of lines, such as glass and fine porcelain, but she had experienced no fundamental commercial or agricultural revolution, as Britain had, nor the first ten years of the industrial revolution. Moreover, French topography and balanced regions inhibited the joining of various parts of the country into a national market, as had occurred for a number of products in Britain. The rapid expansion of foreign trade had been superficial. Specialization and exchange were noteworthy to Adam Smith in 1776, who observed that Birmingham and Sheffield were three times as efficient as the Continent — an order of magnitude that admits little doubt — and competition under the Eden Treaty of 1786 proved painful to French producers in textiles (apart from silk), and porcelain, iron, and hardware to an extent that made continuation of the treaty, had not the French Revolution intervened, highly doubtful. A study of levels of output and income per capita in France and in England at various points in the eighteenth century and again in, say, 1820 would be highly valuable as an addition to our knowledge. I have little doubt that it would show Britain decisively ahead. But to return to Germany.

The Germans impressed Mme de Stael in 1810 as sluggish — poets and thinkers, musicians and metaphysicians. By 1910, says Lowie, they were the Yankees of Europe.[9] The early retardation is commented on widely, and frequently given a numerical estimate. In 1800, a German writing an English friend said that business in his country was in the same condition as that in Britain of seventy to a hundred years before.[10] Benaerts put Germany in 1820 fifty years behind on the road to the machine age,[11] but later indicated that with the help of foreign ideas, foreign capital equipment, and a distinctive German role, the country made up in twenty years an industrial lag of half a century.[12] In the Rhineland the lag in cotton spinning is said to have lengthened from ten years in 1800 to twenty in 1850.[13] Part of this phenomenon was the result of inadequate capital, which made it difficult for plants started under the Continental system to survive when British industry regained access to the market. Part was today's familiar problem of a widening gap between the developed countries and the less developed, with faster growth in the former. Britain was growing rapidly, and Germany had not yet gotten going.

German handicaps were many. Agriculture was still caught in the grip of the manorial system, three-field rotation, and compulsory crop selection (*Flurzwang*). There had been improvement in agriculture,[14] but no agricultural revolution. Industrial production was organized by guilds, patents, privileges. Commerce was stunted.[15]

The freeing of the serfs by vom Stein and Hardenberg was a direct consequence of the defeat of Prussia at Jena in 1806. In the occupied territories of the Rhineland, Napoleon had directly commuted peasant services to rents. His effect in the east was indirect, because the aristocracy felt the need to respond to the desires of the masses of suppressed serfs in order to get support for the war. The process was drawn out, and in the course of it land in the east ended up in Junker hands, whereas in the west the peasant controlled the land with a burden of debt or dues.

As in agriculture, so in handicraft. Napoleon broke up the system in the west, destroying guilds, secularizing church lands, and introducing more modern commercial law. In the south and east the process was a prolonged one and reached its culmination only with the revolution of 1848, which established *Gewerbefreiheit,* or occupational choice. Earlier *Gewerbeförderung* had had its positive as well as its negative side. The entrepreneur who had been awarded a privilege or patent, occasionally a site, buildings, or even capital, was regulated as to quality of output, limited in the amount of wood he could consume, needed permission to export, and the like. Foreign enterprise was controlled. The system carried the seeds of its own decay. As Fischer points out for Baden, complications became endless.[16] Improved transport made for overlap and conflict among the regulations of the locality, the Grand Duchy, and later the Zollverein. The ambiguities of patent laws were cited by an inventor in 1835 as one reason why Germany was a hundred years behind England.[17] But the system of discrimination, privileges, and exemptions proved so difficult to administer that it had to be swept away and Gewerbefreiheit substituted. Freedom of occupation was introduced in Berlin as early as 1810, along with an employment tax devised by the French and reutilized by Hardenberg to repair the damaged finances of the state.

As noted earlier, the role of commerce in Germany in this period was limited. There were Hanseatic cities—Hamburg, Bremen, and Lübeck—which did a thriving external business in the Baltic, the North Sea, and across the Atlantic, though not in the Mediterranean where the British navy refused to protect German shipping against pirates and the Germans had no protection of their own. An earlier Hansastadt, Cologne, had slipped in position as oceangoing ships became larger and could no longer readily ascend the Rhine. Cologne's international position declined to that of being a satellite of first Antwerp, then Rotterdam and Amsterdam. The internationally oriented Hansa cities and Frankfurt, another externally oriented city, had limited connections with the interior. Hamburg built a tradition of being an English, rather than a German, city and was the last independent unit to join the Zollverein—doing so by conversion from a free port, and "not without repugnance,"[18] some seventeen years after it had joined the empire.

Frankfurt gave up earlier—in 1836, only two years after the Zollverein was established. Its international mercantile and banking traditions went far back to its role as a site for fairs on a medieval trade route on the ford of the Franks over the Main. These traditions were still powerful in 1810 when French occupation officials burned 185 chests of English goods owned by Frankfurt merchants in front of the town gates, only to have the Frankfurt bankers refuse to renew the discount on French bills, which produced bankruptcies in Strasbourg, Nancy, Rheims, and elsewhere.[19] The Continental system was soon overturned, but Britain continued to count on Frankfurt as a base, along with Hamburg, from which to smuggle goods into Prussia and other German states. With the formation of the Zollverein, new pressures arose to trade more with the German states and less with the outside; and in 1836, four hundred Frankfurt merchants, the "new men," voted to join the Prussian customs union, having been offered a favorable bargain on the division of customs receipts and special provision for admission of foreign goods to the fair despite the opposition of the lords of the Senate, the stock exchange, and the "English goods" party. The Hansa cities and Hanover were disgusted with Frankfurt's action, and more than one British observer considered that the city lost by the action.[20]

In 1790 three hundred rulers in Germany levied tolls as they pleased,[21] and there were eighteen hundred customs frontiers; between Strasbourg and the Dutch frontier on the Rhine were thirty customs houses. The process that led to the Zollverein started with the Prussian tariff of 1818. It was a low tariff, strongly influenced by the views of the Physiocrats and of Adam Smith. Smith's views were highly popular among the Prussian bureaucracy, and constituted a sort of bible, so much so that the provincial leader Vincke wrote in 1796 that he made it a practice to start each day by reading a passage from *The Wealth of Nations*.[22] Mercantilism in the early Prussian setting had meant monopolies, privileges, prohibitions, premiums, and subsidies to achieve export surpluses, rather than the construction of internal markets with emphasis on uniform coinage, codes of commercial law, and standards. Even with the liberal tariff rates of 1818, the merchant class in Germany developed slowly, thus forgoing the benefit from a commercial revolution in rationality and calculation on the one hand, plus capital formation on the other. But while a commercial revolution facilitates industrialization, it is neither sufficient—as the case of Holland illustrates—nor necessary—as Germany proves.

Gerschenkron's theory of backwardness calls for the state to substitute in backward countries for the initiative that came in Britain from a widespread entrepreneurial class. Part of the task is to clear away barriers, as just indicated. Part of the effort of the state, however, had negative effects in the provision of patents and privileges that inhibited enterprise. Still, a number of positive steps were taken in general and industrial education, in stimulating technical advances, in guiding certain industries such as mining, and in the provision of capital, especially to ailing industry, via *Seehandlung,* a state corporation engaged in finance and trade, not unlike the British East India Company of the nineteenth century.

The educational drive took place at all levels: against illiteracy, to reform the gymnasium and to develop new universities, and to teach industrial skills. Like the French, the Germans responded to defeat with educational reform. After Jena the drive was so enormous that in 1819 Jacob stated that many students could not find situations which required their attainments.[23] Not only were new schools and universities built, but their principles changed. There was a decline in theology and a rise in science, and a connection established by Humboldt between research and teaching.[24] The role of mathematics was expanded. All this took place during a period when science and technology were excluded from the curriculum of Oxford and Cambridge and left to the Scottish universities, the dissenting academies, and as an avenue for social advancement of the marginal nonconformist members of the Lunar Society of Birmingham or the Philosophical and Literary Society of Manchester. The British traveler Banfield, in the Rhineland in 1848, observed that "education of people is a powerful influence on development of industry — and a most material and beneficial influence on the industrial occupations." He went further and made the "bold assertion" that the inhabitants of the Rhineland districts of Prussia, Nassau, Hesse-Darmstadt (with few exceptions), and Baden formed a mass of the best-educated inhabitants of Europe. There were 124 gymnasia in Prussia, 17 in the Rhenish Provinces alone. But the elementary schools were what the Prussians with most reason prided themselves on.[25]

The universities were created in Berlin, Breslau, Greifswald, Bonn, Halle, and Königsberg in Prussia, in competition with Göttingen, Tübingen, Heidelberg, and the like. Established in separate principalities, which had been reduced under Napoleonic occupation from three hundred to sixty-five or so, they provided competition and widespread initiative at the intellectual level.

One of the most famous institutions was the *Gewerbeinstitut* established by Beuth in Berlin, which trained artisans in 1820. It brought machinery from Britain, distributed subventions and prizes, and stimulated the growth of four shops. Borsig, the locomotive manufacturer of Berlin, along with Freund in steam engines, Egells in machinery, and Hollauer and Ehling in mechanical working, was a graduate of the Gewerbeinstitut. He dedicated his twenty-fourth locomotive to his old teacher, Beuth,[26] who had provided him with machinery on more than one occasion; perhaps helped to arrange a mortgage from Seehandlung to buy a factory; and submitted his forty-fourth locomotive to the 1844 Berlin Exhibition where it was a success.[27] All the technical schools, the 1871 *Jubelfest* of the *Gewerbeschule* noted, produced 3,500 technicians in fifty years, who "began in these years their superiority over the British."[28] Technical universities followed along after the Gewerbeinstitut. Hardach mentions that their establishment owed something to the spirit of competition among German states, as Karlsruhe in 1825 was followed by Darmstadt in 1826, Munich in 1827, Dresden in 1828, Stuttgart in 1829, and Hanover in 1831.[29]

Gewerbeförderung involved more than education. Bright young engineers were sent to England to study. As early as 1785 Bückling worked at Boulton and Watt "as a spy" to study the application of the steam engine to mines, and made a second trip in 1794 to bring back pieces of machinery and a British engineer. The latter, Richard, worked for thirty years in Silesian mining, making elevators and pumps.[30] Beuth himself made several trips to England, Belgium, and Holland, and his Gewerbeinstitut gave Egells 1,000 talers in 1817 to travel and work as a mechanic in England. When it proved difficult to find work, Egells asked for a greater subvention and received it, staying on for two years before starting his machine foundry in Berlin in 1821. Beuth bought a great deal of machinery in England, with capital provided by Seehandlung.

Industry, says Redlich,[31] needed spies to acquire machinery. Machine methods were secret at the company level, and prohibitions were imposed by Britain on the export of models, drawings, and machinery. "Even a man of the rank and ethical greatness of Baron vom Stein used dubious methods on his trips to England to acquire industrial knowledge."[32] But there was often little need to spy or to bribe local workers to obtain information. Fischer, the Swiss metallurgist mentioned earlier, had letters to Wedgwood, Lee, Faraday, Perkins, and the Woolich arsenal, and possessed an impressive personality and technical wisdom that his host often wished to obtain. He seems never to have had difficulty in learning about technical advances.[33]

Diffusion of technology took place largely via visits of German entrepreneurs and artisans to Britain, plus the short or long stays in Germany of British industrialists. Wilkinson, who had worked in Le Creusot in France in 1785, later came to Breslau to establish an iron foundry. From the Rhineland visits were paid to France, Belgium, and Holland as well as to Britain. In Baden there were visits back and forth to Switzerland and Alsace. In 1830 German chemists from Liebig to Kekulé went to Paris to study under Gay-Lussac, Frémy, and Berthollet "because they preferred the practical, laboratory-centered approach to the sterile idealism of the German universities at that time."[34] The situation later changed in both countries.

Not only in technical subjects, but also in banking, German young people went abroad to learn (or came from abroad to practice). Oppenheim was a French Jew, expelled from France at the time of the Restoration, brother-in-law of the French banker Fould, and closely connected with Isaac and Emile Pereire. He established an important private bank in Cologne. David Hansemann had lived abroad for seven years after 1810, traveling everywhere in Europe and bringing back ideas for insurance companies and chambers of commerce, as well as banking. Mevissen, Camphausen, and von der Heydt, the great names of mid-century German banking, lived and worked abroad for varying lengths of time — in France, Belgium, and England — and acquired both technique and ideas, in the case of Mevissen notions about limited liability and expansionist technocratic principles of the Saint Simoniens. There was a danger. The Junker Yorck said about Stein, "That man to our sorrow has been in Britain and brings thence his principles of government; but the institutions established in the course of centuries in Great Britain whose wealth rests on naval strength, commerce and factories, must be acclimated to our poor Prussian agriculture."[35]

In addition to these steps toward economic growth taken in response to Napoleon during the occupation and after the defeat, the German, or in some instances the Prussian, economy responded directly to Britain in several ways. The largest impact came in 1819 with the British Corn Laws' worsening of the terms of trade of Prussia, which normally sold sizable amounts of grain and wood to Britain. Hit by substantial harvests in 1822 and 1823, as well as by the Corn Laws, the price of grain fell continuously from 1817 to 1825 by more than two-thirds. The Junker farming aristocracy was in difficulty. Land prices fell, mortgages rose, and with them foreclosures. State banks entered to assist. Writing at the end of the century, Ucke compared the agriculture depression of the 1820s with that of the 1880s and claimed it was worse.[36] Recovery set in at the end of the 1820s. Many people in East and West Prussia thought the depression in agriculture was the result of natural phenomena, including the destruction of crops by hailstorms and animals, but others blamed the British.

The Zollverein is usually thought of as more a political than an economic step, with Prussia taking the lead to promote her political authority and accepting an unduly small share of the revenues from the common pool as the price of her leadership. Bowring in 1840 noted that in Germany the move was generally felt to have been a first step in the germanization of the people.[37] That the leader of an alliance bears a disproportionate share of the costs, or receives too small a share of the benefits, is a finding of modern political theory and the principle of the "free rider," which states that those states less directly concerned in an alliance are able to pay less, or get more, than their proportionate share.[38] More recently an economic-political reason has been found for Zollverein: the gains to the participating states from reducing the cost of managing their customs borders.[39]

Many but not all British, however, regarded Zollverein as an attack on the Corn Laws. Bowring states that the Zollverein was not "formed in hostility to the commercial interests of other states, it was not intended prematurely to create a manufacturing population in rivalry with or opposition to the manufacturing aptitudes of Great Britain," but he adds that if "in the natural progress of things, the tariffs of the Zollverein have become hostile to the importation of foreign, and especially of British, produce, it is because [of] *our* laws."[40] Other views have been noted: Evans—"The Zollverein is the product of our destructive policy"; Palmerston—"One of the motives of Prussia in Zollverein was to induce England to diminish the duties on wheat and timber"; Bowring—"We have made the Germans trade with each other because we would not buy from them."[41] But British commercial policy was not all malign. In 1824 Britain signed a treaty with Prussia that removed discrimination against her in shipping. By 1828 Huskisson was starting to dismantle the restrictions on the export of machinery, which were swept away in 1842 along with reductions of tariffs. In 1846, of course, the Corn Laws fell; and by the mid-fifties, Germany was supplying 25 percent of wheat imports to Britain compared to 18 percent from the United States.[42]

British policy was directed against the Zollverein. Hanover, which was allied to the British crown, refused to consent to any sacrifice to facilitate the expansion of German trade.[43] A tax league was formed in 1834 among Austria, Hanover, Brunswick, Oldenburg, and the Hansa cities to counter the fiscal benefits of the Zollverein. Brunswick withdrew in 1844 to join the Zollverein, and by 1851 Hanover itself yielded to Prussian political pressure and economic enticements. Hanover was slow also in acquiescing to designs for railroad connections across its territory and in lifting its tolls on the Elbe, whether encouraged or not in these views by Britain.

In addition to restricting Prussian and other German exports until the 1840s, Britain made life hard for nascent German industry through her own exports. There were accusations of dumping immediately after the Congress of Vienna, and again in the early 1840s. The Zollverein was widely regarded as a response to this dumping. In an industry such as linen, where the Silesian cottage industry was driven to despair by the machine-spun yarns of Leeds and Belfast, not to mention the competition of cheap cotton textiles, the response was adulteration on the one hand and starvation on the other.

Linen provides a telling contrast between British and German growth in the first quarter of the nineteenth century. Prussia imposed a tariff on textiles, clothing, hardware, sugar, and coffee in 1821, and the British retaliated by enacting a tariff on raw linen. This led to mechanization of the British industry, with the aid of the Girard (French) machines,[44] and little further need for cloth imports from Germany. Germany tried to respond to machine yarns by lowering price, underbidding, and using cotton in linen mixtures.

"Schmoller says with irony that 'the only technical progress they made was in disguising cotton so that hardly the most practiced eye could distinguish it from pure linen.' "[45] Linen declined from 23 percent by value of total German exports in 1828 to 11 percent in 1837, 9 percent in 1850, and 3 percent in 1864.[46]

There was continuous pressure for higher tariffs in the Zollverein, continuously resisted by Prussia. Changes in tariffs required a unanimous vote, and Prussia could apply a veto to any upward movement that threatened the export interests of the Junker decision makers. Palmerston had threatened retaliation against the Zollverein's formation in 1833.[47] Prussia was wary of substantial tariff increases on English iron, which appeared on the market in increasing quantities in the late 1830s and early 1840s, and on cotton yarn. But the Leipzig consul reported a new duty on iron to the Board of Trade in February 1837 and observed that the switch from imports of cloth to imports of yarn pointed to the ultimate exclusion of both.[48]

In some views, the Zollverein tariff increases of 1844 on iron and of 1846 on cotton yarns were significant policy actions designed to accelerate industrialization in what Crouzet, quoting Lévy-Leboyer, regards as the typical Continental as opposed to the British manner —upstream, rather than downstream—that is, industrialization that progressed from finished goods to components and inputs, rather than from iron to steel to machinery, or from yarn to cloth to clothing.[49] British manufacturers originally tried to prevent exports of yarn to inhibit weaving abroad, and for a long while managed to restrict exports of machinery. A strong case can be made that the repeal of the Corn Laws was "free-trade imperialism," to halt the move to industrialization on the Continent by enlarging the market for agricultural produce and primary materials.[50] But von Delbrück's account of the increases of 1844 and 1846 makes them appear as small concessions by Prussia to the other states, and almost accidental. In any event, Switzerland industrialized in the same directions as Germany without benefit of protection.

In addition to the connections through trade, the economic fortunes of Germany and Britain were tied through investment. Soon after the Napoleonic wars Prussia borrowed in London—in 1822 and 1832.[51] Between those dates a conversion loan was issued in London for Prussia by the Rothschilds. Thereafter for a time the flow of capital moved in the other direction, through amortization, and possibly through positive lending. Borchardt tends to doubt that Berlin exported capital on balance during the early 1840s,[52] and most sources agree that late in the decade there were capital imports in the form of subscription to railroad securities and investments in Rhenish mines, iron foundries, and nonferrous metalworks.

These connections were at best sporadic. Brockhage was surprised to find capital exports before 1850[53] and to determine that the Berlin capital market achieved importance at all. Frankfurt was the market par excellence for state loans, Hamburg for commercial lending, and Cologne for industrial loans. Political disintegration and the absence of a well-developed communication and transport network kept the capital market fragmented — a handicap to development theoretically analyzed in recent years by Shaw[54] and McKinnon[55] and already historically well understood by Borchardt[56] — and led to dealings with foreign sources of supply in both directions. The occasional purchase of foreign bonds seems to have been a result of lack of domestic investment opportunities, rather than a cause. The development of railroads after 1842 changed all this, along with the associated expansion of deposit banking after 1851.

The level of living in Germany to 1850 seems not to have risen perceptibly — though the data are even less reliable than those for the British standard-of-living controversy. Moreover, it is likely that total output per capita had not risen greatly, so that there were no substantial profits (for instance, from textiles, iron, agriculture, or commerce) available for capital formation, as there were in Britain. But the groundwork was being laid. The extension of the market took place in two ways — Zollverein on the one hand, and development of the railroad network on the other. These had trade-diversion as well as trade-creation effects, and the development of the railroads produced linkages to the iron and machinery industries. Even before the railroad, however, mechanization was under way, as Bowring observed:[57] "In some respects Germany may boast superiority to Great Britain in her means for manufactures. The arts of design and their application . . . are more successfully wrought and worked; chemical knowledge is farther advanced than with us. Steam-engines are found on all sides, and mechanical improvements have made rapid strides, and have served to open a wide field for the characteristic development of German intelligence; which, if not specially distinguished for invention and discovery, seems particularly fitted to laborious and thoughtful application, and for the unwearied pursuit of any object which strongly interests its attention." But new industries were embryonic, as evidenced by the foundation of Siemens and Halske, the union of a military engineer and an artisan, in 1847.

The disruptions caused by the transition from the traditional economy to the market, which Britain had undergone earlier with the Luddites, along with the unrest led by Cobbett, Peterloo, and later the Chartists, were disturbing Germany in the late forties. These upheavals resulted from the dissolution of the guild system, the beginnings of factory work, and the dismissal of casual labor from the countryside as agriculture reorganized—combined with the potato crop failure and high food prices. By 1850 social unrest had been dissipated, partly through substantial emigration; the bourgeoisie had made its peace with the Hohenzollerns; and rising national consciousness was producing a motive for industrialization.

Germany was resolved to industrialize, but in a different way than Britain. It was felt that British industrialization had been socially disastrous for unprotected groups like women and children working in mines and factories, and unesthetic insofar as it led to belching chimneys, grimy villages, and squalid jerry-built housing. The sentiment was rooted in the Junker agriculturalist's distaste for the city with its egotism and immoderate ambition, speculation, and greed.[58] Even liberal thought had misgivings about industrial society with its blemishes of poor housing, alcoholism, and prostitution.[59] Part of the view was based on visits to England, part on anti-British prejudice. But industrialization was on its way. The period from 1820 to 1848 has been described as an "undynamic time, almost untouched by the breath of the capitalist spirit."[60]

Economic rivalry touches the emotions. In the seventeenth century, Britain was notorious for her hatred of the Dutch, "the abominable rival,"[61] and from that century there remains in the English language a series of expressions that use the adjective "Dutch" in an uncomplimentary way.[62] Kehr claimed that every connection with England in the 1840s was hailed in Germany[63] but this seems exaggerated in the light of Engels' "Die Lage der arbeitenden Klasse in England," as Tilly points out.[64] Love and hate were doubtless both involved.[65] If Kehr was right for the 1840s, however, the sentiment favorable to England was not to last, any more than the economy was to remain undynamic.

Germany as Journeyman, 1850 to 1871

In his theory of backwardness, Gerschenkron states that the greater the backwardness, (*1*) the sharper the kink and the more sustained the subsequent spurt; (*2*) the greater the stress on producers' goods; (*3*) the greater the scale of industrial plant and enterprise; (*4*) the greater the pressure on consumption levels of the populace; (*5*) the less active agriculture as a market for industrial goods and as a source of increased productivity; and (*6*) the more active the role of banks and beyond that of the state.[66] This is a more developed, if terse, statement than his earlier formulations, which concentrated on banks and government; it still leaves no room for the development of commerce, which presumably assisted economic development in the British case, but led nowhere in the case of the Netherlands.[67] Nor do foreign entrepreneurs, technology, or capital have a place in it. Britain, the first country to experience the industrial revolution, is the benchmark. In order of backwardness in Gerschenkron's schema come France, Germany, Italy, and Russia. France relies more on banks than government, Russia at the other end of the spectrum more on government than banks. Germany and Italy lie between.

The role of government in Germany was largely confined in the first half of the nineteenth century to clearing away the heritage of traditional society and preparing the groundwork for advance through education, support of technological acquisitions, and some limited capital formation. For the most part, government advanced the economic interest of the Junker aristocracy and pursued national political ends. Despite the mining engineer service, the German government was far from the technocratic planning agency represented by the Corps des ponts et chaussées in France, or the Saint-Simonien tradition. In fact it opposed the extension of banks. Tilly's study of "Financial Institutions and Industrialization in the Rhineland" concludes that, contrary to Henderson (and Gerschenkron) on the state and industrialization, Prussia hindered the Rhineland, and it was "decentralized, profit-oriented, decision-making by bankers which had to overcome the opposition of the state to industry." He goes further and asserts that Gerschenkron's thesis cannot be supported, since the Bank of Darmstadt failed to develop Hesse, Baden, and Württemberg.[68]

It may be doubted that the bankers' decisions were in fact decentralized. Oppenheim, Hansemann, Mevissen, von der Heydt in Cologne; Bleichroeder, Mendelssohn in Berlin; Rothschild in Frankfurt were tied into one another's activities, as well as into industry. Mevissen was an officer or director of six banks, eight industrial corporations, and a railroad.[69] He admitted that the government wanted to develop industry, but to keep it in tutelage.[70] His intimate friend, Vierson, had eight directorships further.

Government, moreover, opposed the development of banking. The first breakthrough came when the Schaaffhausen'scher Bankverein began to fail and was allowed to reorganize as a joint-stock bank in 1848. This was the first, and Mevissen used the new form to explore new means of financing. Subsequent requests for permission to start further banks were turned down by the Prussian government in Berlin, although Blumberg asserts that 1848 moderated the Prussian government opposition to companies.[71] It was not until 1851, when Hansemann found a loophole in the law, that large banks could be organized along the lines of a *Kommanditgesellschaft,* with silent partners and transferable shares rather than stockholders. Five years later a series of such banks was formed, six in Prussia alone and others elsewhere in Germany. The episode is parallel to the conclusion by Thomas Joplin in 1833 that the law of 1826, prohibiting note-issue banks within 65 miles of London, could not be applied to joint-stock banks, which did not issue notes — a conclusion that broke through the restriction set up by the Bank of England. The movement took place twenty years later in Germany.

Mevissen and Oppenheim had intimate French associations and were early aware of the departure represented by the establishment of the Crédit mobilier in Paris in 1852. In 1853 they founded the Bank of Darmstadt, with some French, but mostly Cologne, money. Darmstadt was chosen because it lay outside Prussia, the government of which had rejected a request to establish the Bank of Berlin (and refused to allow the Schaaffhausen'scher Bankverein to transfer from Cologne to Berlin on the ground that anything not explicitly provided in the articles of incorporation was expressly forbidden).[72] In addition, Darmstadt was near Frankfurt, a financial center, which also refused permission to locate within its jurisdiction. The Darmstädter was intensely active, with agencies all over Germany and ultimately in Vienna and New York. At the end of 1856 Mevissen said that Germany, which had lagged a century behind

France and England, had now surpassed them, thanks to the Darm-städter.[73] The judgment was premature in timing and excessive in causation. Böhme quotes Engels that Germany was not yet up to the English standard in 1860, but altogether changed from the past[74] and expanding rapidly.

The emphasis on banks and government as a substitute for entre-preneurship in Germany is perhaps a little overdone. German entre-preneurs were different from the British in their political backward-ness. Kisch points out that the merchant-manufacturers of the Wupper Valley were devoid of political power.[75] It is claimed that the lack of power stems from the fact that they were scattered about in separate states.[76] Whatever the reason, whereas in Britain in 1865, 23 percent of the Members of Parliament were merchants and industrialists and 29.2 percent more were financial men, German entrepreneurs from all three sources in the Reichstag of 1871 amounted only to 8 percent of the total.[77] Merchants governed the Hansa cities such as Hamburg, but their grasp was limited. When the revolution of 1848 had run its course, the bourgeois classes, including the bankers to be sure, became frightened of the pro-letariat and let themselves be bluffed out of real political reform, both in the Frankfurt parliament and in separate constitutional crises, as in Hamburg. Regardless of their political weakness, how-ever, the merchant class did provide recruits for the ranks of in-dustrial entrepreneurship, especially in the Rhineland and West-phalia.

Krupp's ancestors were well-to-do merchants, as were those of the Haniel family in coal and ultimately iron. The textile industry on both banks of the Rhine was run by manufacturers who developed out of merchants. A few ironmasters came from the ranks of arti-sans, as did entrepreneurs in machinery. Chemists came from the drug business. All flourished more or less without government sup-port, although with the assistance of banks, except in the case of Krupp. (He went to the moneylenders in the early 1840s, but not to the banks.) Moreover, the government occasionally singled out a would-be businessman, as it did in the case of a director of a com-pany for the production of railway materials, who had taken part in the 1848 uprising. It threatened to withdraw the concession and the company collapsed. The year 1848 is said to have changed the atti-tude of the Prussian government to companies, on the ground that heavy industry was necessary in the interest of the state, and heavy industry required financing through limited liability.[78] In some views, the traditional antipathy of the landed aristocrats to industry was overcome only later, after the demonstration by Krupp in 1870 of his usefulness to German armed might.

Blumberg has provided the backgrounds of the professions of the 480 founders of 61 companies: 32 percent of them were merchants; 14 percent manufacturers, in which class I believe are included artisans who produce goods for the market by fairly primitive means; 12 percent state officials; 11 percent bankers; 7 percent large land-holders; and 1.3 percent military. The figures were rather consistent by industry and region, except that artisans were sharply underrepresented in mining in Silesia—5 percent against 15 percent nationally. The rest were scattered or unknown.[79] One may find the list of the backgrounds interesting for the small number of merchants as compared, for example, with Britain, or because merchants have such a prominent position after all that has been said about backwardness. The role of the state officials is remarkable since even under the backwardness thesis, the state assists in industrialization qua state and not through the formation of enterprises by state officials in an individual capacity.[80]

Wutzmer emphasizes the merchant origins of Prussian industrial entrepreneurship in the 1840s, although in many cases the merchant roots go farther back, as do significant instances of entrepreneurship. The case of Schmölder in Rheydt, who imported British yarn in the 1840s but started in 1846 with 113,000 talers in capital, a mill site, and a row of machines to undertake spinning,[81] is matched sixty years earlier by Brügelmann, "the prototype of a Schumpeterian entrepreneur," who in 1780 smuggled a spinning machine from Arkwright's factory to Elberfeld, built in 1783 a five-story water-powered spinning mill for 20,000 Rhein talers, and shortly set up weaving and dyeing facilities.[82] Import substitution, with or without smuggling, was a classic mode of development.

Moreover, after industrialization had gone a certain distance, innovation was possible. In the first half of the nineteenth century Britain took over inventions from the Continent, including the Girard machine for spinning flax, the Jacquard loom for fancy patterns in silk—both from France—and as early as 1810 the Friedrich König printing press from Germany.[83] By the late 1840s Germany was innovating in electrical equipment, as well as rapidly applying British inventions and innovations. In the second half of the century Solingen factories—the largest with eight hundred men—were pioneers in the process of forging cutlery by mechanical methods instead of by hand, a process that Sheffield was slow to adopt.[84] The turnabout may be compressed into a shorter period of time if one notes a Krupp's visit to Liverpool in 1839 to observe a rolling mill for copper plates, and the purchase in 1851 by Elkington of Birmingham of a Krupp machine for the mass production of spoons and forks.[85]

Import substitution occurred somewhat earlier in locomotives, with the assistance of the government that has already been described. Borsig's first locomotive was built in 1841. In that year there were only twenty locomotives in service in Germany, all foreign made. (An earlier 1840 locomotive, made by Poensgen at Aachen with the help of an English mechanic Dobbs, went out of service in 1841.) The major suppliers were Stephenson and Company of Newcastle, Robert Sharp of Manchester, and Norris of Philadelphia—a make preferred by the nascent Prussian railways. Borsig took a Norris model in 1841, perfected it, delivered it to the Berlin-Anhalt line in July of that year, and outperformed a British rival. In 1843, on the Berlin-Stettin line, another Borsig model beat an English make.[86] Borsig's forty-fourth locomotive, submitted to the Berlin Exhibition of 1844, won a prize on the basis of using less water than other machines, thus saving fuel, and costing less— 12,000 talers as against 12,900.

By 1846 there were more German than foreign machines on the German railroad lines. By the end of 1847 Borsig had delivered 187 locomotives to German lines, out of a total park of 332. In 1846 and 1847 alone, it furnished 128 out of 187 machines. The turning point in import substitution was 1847, with imports of 30 machines from abroad representing the maximum. From 1848 to 1854 Borsig produced 335 locomotives (instead of 187 as in the previous decade), other German firms 65, and all foreign firms together 37. No foreign locomotives at all were bought in 1854; in that year Borsig sold 6 machines to Poland and 4 to Denmark. Import substitution is complete when the industry moves to exporting.[87] Of the 1,036 locomotives produced from 1864 to 1869 by Borsig, one-quarter were exported, notably to Russia, Austria, and Scandinavia.[88]

The locomotive industry of Germany is interesting not only as a case study in import substitution, but also for the light it throws on the advantages of market disintegration. Borsig in Berlin was by all odds the dominant supplier in Germany, but tariffs, especially discrimination against Prussian suppliers by other political entities, provided sheltered markets in which local machinery manufacturers could get a start. Until 1867 Borsig had a virtual monopoly in Prussia, excluding the Rhineland. German companies outside Prussia delivered only 6 locomotives to Prussian railroads in 1861. On the other hand, 3 small railroad lines in the Rhineland had no Borsig locomotives and the Bergische-Märkische line only 4 of its park of 16. Outside of Prussia, however, there were machinery producers who went in for locomotive construction in Aachen (Regnier and Poncelet, plus Dobbs and Poensgen), Sterkade (Jacobi, Haniel, and Huyssen), Buckau (the Magdeburg-Hamburg steamship company), Munich (Maffei), Württemberg (Maschinenfabrik Esslingen), Kassel (Henschel), Hanover (Hanómag), and Stettin (Wöhlert, Schwarzkopf, Stettinger A.G.). Maffei of Munich was helped by being located in a large state that discriminated in its favor (as Prussia did for Borsig); Henschel and Maschinenfabrik Esslingen specialized in industrial locomotives for short hauls in plant yards and in powerful engines for mountain traction, including some innovative engines such as an Esslingen engine with six axles.

In other industries German producers successfully imitated and ultimately improved on English methods. The British introduced the first coke-oven in 1832. German foundries started to substitute coke for charcoal in about 1840 and achieved decisive success in 1852-1853.[89] Krupp's reputation in steel was based on perfecting French and English discoveries, especially the rapid development of Bessemer after 1856. The Thomas process developed in England in 1878 was avidly sought after by many manufacturers in France and Germany, though by none in Britain. The controversy among Burn, Hopkins and Burnham, Andrews and Brunner, Temin, McClosky, and others over whether it was economically feasible to cut back on acid Martin and expand basic openhearth in the Sheffield area is touched upon later. For myself, I am not intellectually satisfied by static models of profit maximization in a given state of the arts when the growth process is advanced by dynamic adaptation of new technology to given situations.

Imitation, followed by adaptation, followed by innovation are at their most conspicuous in the synthetic dye industry. Beer's account,[90] which is closely followed by such scholars of the chemical industry as Hohenberg and of technical change as Lilley, is well known and there is little need to reproduce it at length. Perkins made the initial breakthrough in aniline purple dye in 1856 at the Royal College of Chemistry in London. A student of Liebig named Hofmann, who had been brought to the Royal College in 1845 by the prince consort, went on in the search for other colors as Perkins withdrew from industrial research into pure academic work. Other discoveries took place in France and Britain, and these two countries were still on top in the Paris Exhibition of 1867. But France was falling rapidly behind: her bankers were unwilling to finance research, her patent laws were unfavorable, and, as Beer puts it, the French were poor at drudgery and preferred to search for ideas rather than processes. Perkins made a fortune and sold out at the age of thirty-five (he had been eighteen when he made his discovery) to devote his time to pure science. In 1865 Hoffmann went back to Germany to the University of Berlin to set up a methodical attack on synthetics. A new patent law sought by the industry helped in 1876. Universities and synthetic-dye companies teamed up, laboratories organized larger and larger battalions. Having started out in imitation, the German chemical industry remained to innovate.

The rise of German industrial output in the 1850s had significant impact on international movements of the factors of production that affected British-German relations. In the question of migration the British direct role was small, to be sure. There were three avenues for emigrants from Germany to the Western Hemisphere, via Hamburg and London or Liverpool, direct from Bremen, or overland to Cherbourg and thence by boat. The social turmoil of the 1840s — the dissolution of traditional agricultural ties, the collapse of the guild system, and the rise of the factory, all combined with the cholera of the 1840s and potato disease and poor crops — led to a swelling movement abroad. For the most part, the emigration was limited to artisans and peasants with some means to pay the passage. Whole villages would sell the forest to the nobles and head for America.[91] There is a tradition in the United States that this migration was in response to political oppression leading to and after the revolution of 1848, but this is overstated. The desire to escape military conscription was a contributory factor, and several hundred political refugees came to the United States after 1848. Largely, however, it was the agricultural depression in the years after 1845 that fed the emigration once it had started; what was remarkable was the manner in which it dried up under the blast of expansion. A standard question in migration analysis is whether the push was greater than the pull. German emigration reached 250,000 in the year 1854 after successive bad harvests from 1850 to 1853 and then dropped away to 100,000 in 1855 to 1857 with a good harvest and rapidly expanding industrial employment.[92] "The emigration from Germany was the most important single factor leading Germany to enter the North Atlantic trades" in competition with Britain.[93]

The indirect connection of this migration with England is that many of the emigrants went to dominions like Canada and Australia, or the former colony represented by the United States, and formed new, largely non-German loyalties. Britain's head start in world settlement of open spaces meant that there was no possibility of German migrants establishing Wakefield-like colonies or independent countries in which they exerted large influence to support the fatherland. When Germany acquired colonies later on, they were in native-populated and resource-poor areas in Africa, or islands in the Pacific, useful for coaling stations and a few colonial goods, but far from the dominions and the United States, which offered England large markets in peacetime and military support in war. Even after World War I, Hjalmar Schacht was continuously grumbling about Germany's lack of colonies. Germany is said to have overcome its inferiority complex with respect to French, Belgian, and especially British industry at the end of the 1850s and the beginning of the 1860s,[94] but there was always a sense of injustice that German emigrants were lost to the old country, whereas British emigrants located all over the world supported the homeland.

The other direct connection between Britain and Germany in factor movements concerned capital inflow. There is some debate about whether French, Belgian, and British capital exports to Germany were significant in the railroad investment boom of the 1840s, or only in the 1850s when investment shifted to coal, iron, and steel. Brockhage quotes contemporary observers on both sides of the question of whether foreign investors, especially British, bought German railroad paper.[95] One who believed it did not, Rother of Seehandlung, was possibly in a good position to judge. On the other hand, a modern study suggests that as much as 5 million talers (15 million marks) a year might have been investment in railroads; estimates total capital imports in the 1840s as 17 million talers; but asserts, against the weight of evidence, that capital imports stopped shortly after 1850.[96] The dominant current view is that capital imports were not important before 1850[97] and perhaps not important afterward either—contrary to what Haussherr, Jenks, Blumberg, Cameron, Legge, and Fischer (for Baden) say[98]—but were concentrated in mining. Benaerts gives the total mining to 1857 as 100 million marks (33 million talers),[99] presents extensive lists, and even sets out a *cri de coeur* from Gustav Mevissen published in the Köln-Neu-Essener Gewerbeverein Festschrift of 1852:

This field of action so productive, mining, a source scarcely explored in our national wealth, that our country, for lack of the spirit of enterprise has decided not to exploit, threatens more and more in these last few years to become the object of foreign speculation. It is a notorious fact that in the Rhineland for several years, many mining pits have been acquired for the account of French and English capitalists and are going to be exploited for their profit . . . The treasures which the soil of our country embraces thus serve to augment the capitalistic preponderance that foreigners already possess elsewhere and to nourish the foreign capitalist through the fruit of German labor. It would seem to be in the supreme interest of our economy to keep for it as much as possible not only of the remuneration, but also of the capital.[100]

This statement is contemporary with the 1970s in spirit, if not in rhetoric—translated from German to French and from French to English—in the spirit of *Überfremdung*. A book published in 1924 with Überfremdung in the title mentions that there were 49 companies in mining and ore production controlled from abroad, for a total of 140 million gold marks (26 Belgian, 13 English, 6 French, 4 Dutch), having begun in 1851 and with investments taking place mostly in the 1850s and 1860s.[101]

Of particular interest in this experience is the fact that by and large it unwound without the intervention of the government policy. This sounds surprising by today's analysis of the multinational corporation. Direct foreign investments have been compared first with trees, which are long-lived, and then with redwoods. Some early direct investments follow that pattern, but with a difference from today's multinational corporation. So great were difficulties of communication that the investor, with his money, settled down abroad and ultimately became a citizen. Thus Thomas Mulvaney, who raised capital in Dublin for investment in what were called the Hibernia and the Shamrock mines (founded in 1856-1857) and who pioneered in new techniques for bracing the mine shaft with iron instead of brick, became a resident of Westphalia. For the most part, however, the investments were simply bought out. Some of the railroad securities were acquired in nationalization measures. It may be that the industrial banks, like the Darmstädter, founded the year after Mevissen's complaint about the German lack of spirit of enterprise, made a special point of buying up foreign holdings — although there is no evidence, and French investments in Ruhr coal continued as late as 1908 with the purpose of securing coking coal for the de Wendel interests in Lorraine.[102] It would seem rather that as companies came up for sale they went to the highest bidders. In the 1850s these proved to be foreign investors in a number of cases; beginning in the 1860s,[103] the highest bidder was generally a German enterprise except in special cases such as the Phoenix, "one of those pompous Paris speculative enterprises,"[104] or the cases above in which de Wendel wanted to buy into the coke cartel and was probably forced to pay a high price.

Foreign capital thus apparently played only a modest role in German economic development, despite Cameron's claim,[105] and its role in coal and iron lasted only briefly in the 1850s and part of the 1860s.

The 1850s saw a further step in the direction of Anglo-German rivalry as the All-English City of Hamburg began to assert its independence from London, and British banking houses missed a chance to keep Hamburg in its sphere of influence. The Hamburg-American Packet Line AG (Hapag) was created in 1848, but shifted out of sail into steam in 1856. (The North German Lloyd Company of Bremen, which was more truly a transatlantic company, was founded in 1857.) Although London remained the world's leading port, Hamburg was on its way to becoming the most important port on the Continent and began to import raw sugar, coffee, and other tropical products directly, instead of over London.[106] Hamburg finance staked out a position of some importance in Scandinavia, which had been a British preserve, especially after the Crimean war[107] — an expansion that was, in 1857, destined to produce difficulty.

The panic of 1857 started with the collapse of a small bank in the U.S. Midwest, spread through the falling price of wheat to Liverpool, then London, to Scandinavia, where English credits were called, and then to Hamburg, which had extended large-scale credits to Sweden. As a number of large trading and banking houses stood on the verge of collapse, Hamburg emissaries sought loans from Rothschild, Baring, and Hambro in London, Fould in Paris, and also in Amsterdam, Copenhagen, Brussels, Berlin, Dresden, and Hanover.[108] Bank rates went to 10 percent, and ship captains hesitated to unload their wares because merchant houses might be unwilling to pay the freight.[109] The last two loan rejections had come from Fould in Paris ("Your dispatch is not sufficiently clear") and from the Hamburg ambassador at Berlin ("Bruck and the Emperor are not ambitious financially"), when the minister at Vienna cabled that the Austrians were providing a loan in the form of needed cash, in silver, which came to be called the Silver Train. It amounted to 12 million mark banco (plus another 4 million private credit to M. M. Warburg & Co., whose brother-in-law Schiff of the Austrian Credit-Anstalt had helped plead the case).[110] The episode was part of Hamburg's maturation. Böhme notes that the crisis kept coming back into the discussion of both Hamburgers and non-Hamburgers when discussing exchange, and even reading about it would make peoples' hair stand on end. Thereafter Hamburg merchants became more sophisticated and specialized more fully by banking, shipping, or trade.[111] It seems unlikely that Britain had a real opportunity to rediscount in the crisis for the Hamburg banks, at that rudimentary stage of the development of the international banking system. But international finance proved to be one more dimension in which German interests achieved comparatively early independence, if not rivalry.[112] Germany was again somewhat slowed down industrially by the financial crisis of May 1866, which started over the German-Austrian war and deepened after the outbreak of crisis in England when Overend, Gurney & Co. failed. Germany's recovery was speedy, and after the successful war against France its expansion was rapid.

It is of great interest that Prussia and Germany held to free trade ideals during all of the 1860s and in fact to 1875. The reasons were not analytical but ideological. The Junkers still clung to free-trade doctrines, and until Rudolph von Delbrück was dropped or voluntarily resigned as the president of the imperial chancellery in April 1876, these views dominated the civil service. Bismarck was interested in free trade less for its economic than for its diplomatic advantages. Low tariffs discomfited Austria with its exposed inefficient manufacturing, and prevented it from joining the Zollverein and rivaling Prussian leadership among the southern tier of German states.

With the conclusion of the Anglo-French Commercial Treaty of 1860, moreover, there was a competitive reason to join the movement to free trade, and this Prussia did in a trade agreement with France. A subsequent agreement with Russia carried an implied threat of favoring Russian over Austrian feed grains. In addition to the Stolper-Samuelson argument for free trade, which the Junkers subconsciously favored, there were the additional needs to keep up with Britain and to keep down Austria.

However, the Junker market in Britain was not to be sustained despite the repeal of the Corn Laws. Grain grew from 8 percent of German exports in 1828 to 11.5 percent in 1837 to 15.2 percent in 1850, while linen exports were falling, under the pressure of competition from Leeds, Belfast, and cotton textiles, from 23.4 to 11.1 to 8.9 percent.[113] But the gain did not last. It would be poetically just if the story told by Lambi that the Danish blockade of the Baltic and Hamburg during the war of 1864 over Schleswig and Holstein started the downfall.[114] The Junkers were for war and for grain exports. By choosing the former, they would have lost the latter (in this formulation). Bondi gives a figure for 1864 of grain as 7.3 percent of German exports, rising to 8.3 percent in 1869, which would support the view (his figures are given only for separate disjointed years). Despite Sering, on whom Lambi relies, there is little evidence for this contention. Knowledgeable historians are aware of a brief blockade of German exports by Denmark in the revolution of 1848, which had no lasting effects. It is likely that the loss of the British grain market by East Prussia was the result rather of American expansion, especially after the Civil War when the railroad was built west and veterans were given homesteads in the Northwest territories that now make up Minnesota and Nebraska. Whatever the reason, the German share of the British grain market compared to the American dropped precipitously after the end of the Civil War after peaking in 1861-1862:[115]

	German states	United States
1856 to 1860	25.9%	18.0%
1871 to 1875	8.2%	40.9%
1875	2.9%	60.2%

(From Lambi, *Free Trade and Protection,* pp. 10, 133.)

We may conclude by noting the economic implications of Prussia's three wars of the 1860s (if 1870 belongs to the 1860s), against Denmark, Austria, and France. Rostow makes a great deal of nationalism as a "most important and powerful motive force in the transition from traditional to modern societies,"[116] but he refers to "reactive nationalism — reacting against intrusion from more advanced nations" and, insofar as Germany is concerned, to the defeat at Jena in 1806. Again "it was German nationalism which stole the revolution of 1848 at Frankfurt and made the framework within which the German take-off occurred — the Junkers and men of the East, more than the men of trade and the liberals of the West."[117] To Harry Johnson, nationalism is a public good of collective consumption, rather than an investment that yields output in dedication to work and expansion.[118] In the German case, though it is difficult to make much of Rostow's statement that takeoff owed more to the Junkers than to the industrialists, it is fair to say that military success led to economic drive and expansion. The defeat of Austria in 1866 clinched the support of the southern tier. Victory over France stilled the last vestige of dissent of the "English" city, Hamburg, and made Prussian leadership in the newly founded Reich unanimous.

Germany as Master, 1873 to 1913

The smashing victory of Prussia over France in 1870 touched off a short-lived boom based on (*1*) unification of the German states under Prussian leadership; (*2*) receipt of a substantial sum in cash —

742 million marks of gold, silver, and French and German bank-notes—under the Franco-Prussian indemnity; (3) unification of German money with bimetallism giving way to the gold standard; but above all (4) a nationalist euphoria that produced a speculative rise in prices of commodities and securities. In the course of the transfer of the full indemnity of 5 billion marks, Germany accumulated 90 million in short-term claims on London. When the Jay Cooke failure in the United States led to a liquidity squeeze, the withdrawal of this amount precipitated the recession of 1873 and ushered in the Great Depression in England. After the collapse of stock markets, first in Vienna, then in Berlin and Frankfurt, the German economy was quiescent for a few years, accumulating strength for the expansion of the 1880s and 1890s. Britain, on the other hand, experienced a continuation of the investment boom of the early 1870s into and immediately past the middle of the decade. It then settled into depression in the 1880s. The contrast of German and British experience in the 1880s and 1890s produced the sense in both countries that Germany was catching up with and even over-taking Britain in economic expansion.

Even though it does not bear directly on our theme, it will be useful to observe the change in German tariff policy in 1879. This "fateful turning point,"[119] one of the most important in the history of modern Germany,"[120] was accomplished by the switch of the Junkers from alliance with the commercial interests of the northern cities to alliance with heavy industry. The ultimate cause was the loss of export markets for grain and the threat of imports. There is considerable discussion in the literature on whether the 1873 depression produced the change of attitude. Lambi says yes;[121] Barkin says no.[122] Gerschenkron notes that the depression increased the protectionism of industry,[123] but this was always high. Epstein perhaps has the point right: that the depression discredited laissez-faire and encouraged the organization of pressure groups, such as the Zentralverband deutscher Industrieller (1876). There was some good in the tariff; it prevented Germany from becoming a lopsided industrial country like England and required Bismarck in the political maneuvering to abandon his fight against the Catholics with whom he became allied.[124] Still, the shift consolidated all the anachronistic elements in the system at the top and buried the subservient interests that were hurt by the tariff under this feudal leadership. The peasant who benefited from cheap grain to feed his animals followed the leadership of the Junker who grew only grain. The small metal processors took their cue from the large vertically integrated processors who owned iron and made common cause with the iron interests.

The change took place with bewildering speed after 1877. Up to that time, Prussia and the Zollverein had been for low tariffs. The nationalist Friederich List was always opposed to tariffs on agriculture and, as an infant-industry protectionist, saw the ultimate end of protection in free trade. Tariffs had been raised on textiles and iron products in the 1840s, when Prussia yielded her principles and interests to accommodate the other members of the Zollverein. A later attempt to raise duties on manufactures in the 1850s obtained a grudging consent from Prussia to appease the southern tier. Britain started to intervene, but her ally Brunswick inside the Zollverein provided the necessary veto.[125] The single-veto system applicable to all members was abandoned in 1867 when the Zollverein was reorganized, but Prussia retained a presidential veto. Prussia was firmly wedded to liberal principles at the time, and the reduction of duties in connection with the trade agreement in France in 1862 was extended in the 1868 treaty with Austria, when duties were reduced on iron, cotton cloth, linen, chemicals, and wines.[126]

The boom of the early 1870s led to a movement to reduce still further the import duties on iron and to eliminate them altogether on iron manufactures (thus producing negative rates of protection for the latter). The iron producers were aided in resisting this pressure by the French system of "titres d'acquit à caution" for iron exported gross (while iron was imported on balance into France). This was regarded in Germany as an export subsidy. The device, later employed by the Germans in maintaining the export of grain when the country was on balance an importer, enabled exporters near the border in one part of the country to raise their price above the world level by selling certificates attesting to their exports to importers, who in turn used them to pay the duty. In this way exporters received and importers had to pay a price above the world market. As such it was a subsidy to export, but not one that lowered the price of an existing exporter.

The acquisition of Alsace-Lorraine in 1871 hurt the cotton interests of Saxony by bringing Mulhouse into the Zollverein. In iron ore it benefited the producers of iron and steel by providing them with a cheap source of iron—the French minette ores—and temporarily eliminating the supply of a commercial rival, until further exploration on the French side of the new border uncovered broad new fields. (While Germany was winning World War I, industrial war aims included acquisition of Briey-Longwy to add to the gains of 1871.)[127] At the peak of the boom the decision was taken to lower duties on iron—but later. Free-traders pressed for reduction, but with the passage of time the case for lowering tariffs weakened as the depression grew, and increasingly a positive case was expressed to raise the duties on iron. In 1876 Rudolph Delbrück, president of the imperialist chancellery under Bismarck, "resigned." As he was in good health and had no apparent reason, it seems evident that he was dismissed, rather than submitted his resignation voluntarily, because as a strong free-trader he inhibited the change of policy that was building in Bismarck's mind.

If the tariff did not have its origin largely in depression, it further had little to do with subsequent recovery. Overall it may be said to have slowed down expansion by tending to hold on the farm some of the thousands who were fleeing to the mines of the Ruhr and Silesia or the factories of Berlin. (Very quickly in the 1880s the problems of the Junkers were not solely those of falling prices and declining exports, on the side of demand, but also the supply of labor.) It also reduced real incomes and effective demands on workers and iron processors. The tariff may, however, have made some contribution to growth through higher profits for integrated iron and steel producers.

A more likely candidate for the role of contributor to growth is the German propensity to form cartels, concerns, and trusts. This tendency to amalgamate, to look after joint interests—in German, *Kartellfähigkeit*[128]—was an established German tradition. The Rheinisch Westfälische Kohlen Syndikat had a 33-paragraph agreement at the time of its formation in 1835. (A still older coal cartel, of course, was the famous Newcastle Vend of the seventeenth century in Britain.) The depression of 1873 led to rapid formation of cartels. Only 6 agreements have been traced to earlier than 1870, 14 to the period up to 1877. Thereafter many cartels were formed, 350 to the turn of the century, of which 275 survived,[129] and 1,500 to 1925.[130]

Of greater interest than the cartels is the push for vertical integration, a movement very different from what was happening in Britain. At a very early stage the steel industry of the Ruhr, supported by banks of the Ruhr, went backward into coal mining, later into the production of iron ore, then forward into machinery. Siemens and Halske bought a copper mine in 1864 and were encouraged by the prosperity of 1871 to move more widely into raw materials.[131] In the dyestuff industry one step on the way to the formation of the I. G. Farben trust occurred when three of the seven companies that ultimately participated got together to buy a coal mine.[132] Earlier the separate companies had branched into drug making, when they discovered that they had the raw materials and equipment to make active compounds, and into heavy chemicals to make themselves independent of other producers (and to save money).[133] In contrast with the British propensity to have separate stages of production separately owned, in Germany vertical integration was a common practice.

Moreover, the rise of large industrial organizations saw the elimination of the merchant. As Siemens in 1871 bought a shopful of equipment from the United States because of long delivery dates in Germany — five or six months — and set up an "American shop" with mass production methods, it began to change selling methods. Siemens decided to write to customers in advance of producing their "constructions," and to put pressure on them to order them as Siemens indicated, without alteration, to get them cheaply, well-made, and quickly.[134] This direct selling, in contrast to marketing through merchants, enabled the company to work out technical improvements acceptable to its customers, with an optimization that took into account both performance and cost, as contrasted with Britain where the merchant, standing between producer and customer, often impeded technical progress, telling the producer, "They don't want them like that," and the customer, "They don't make them like that."[135]

Until about 1885, according to Beer,[136] German dye companies marketed abroad through wholesalers whom, however, they permitted to carry the line of only one firm. From 1885 on, dyestuffs moved to direct selling, with firms wholesaling their own products, sending salesmen and consultants abroad to establish local sales corporations headed by Germans but otherwise employing local personnel.[137]

All this time the quality of German goods was improving. From slavish imitation and adulteration in the first half of the century, German industry was moving to autonomy—not always, as it happens, in a straight line. At the Great Exhibition of 1851, Britain led the world,[138] but Krupp exhibited a six-pounder cannon and a steel casting of 4,300 pounds.[139] In 1855 at the Paris Exhibition Krupp had a twelve-pound cannon, lighter than the French bronze and able to fire 3,000 rounds without buckling, and also a 10,000-pound steel casting.[140] Borsig won a prize for locomotives at Paris in 1855.[141]

The path of improvement was not always wide or steady. In Paris in 1865, German products were distinguished by being shoddy and cheap. The showing was regarded as a disaster for German exporters. In 1868 the Paris World Exhibition brought no significant success to the exporters of Barmen and Elberfeld,[142] although the inferiority against British goods observable in 1851 had been overcome.

The German exhibit at the Centennial Exhibition at Philadelphia was regarded as disastrously ineffective, with German goods cheap and poor except for Krupp artillery, which consisted of killing machines.[143] Even the chief German Commissioner to the Exhibition denounced his compatriots' showing.[144] Thereafter the performance changed rapidly. By the end of the century German products were scoring triumphs at Chicago in 1893, and at Paris in 1900 and 1901.[145]

Some shoddy goods were disguised as British, and from as early as the 1830s a number of British manufacturers were continuously engaged in litigation to protect trademarks. In the mid-1880s, complaints against foreign, and especially German, frauds against British trademarks blew into such a storm that the Merchandise Marks Act of 1887 was passed by Parliament, requiring imported goods to be marked to indicate their country of origin.[146] The law forbade misrepresentation and required that foreign goods marked with the name of an English dealer carry indication or place name of their foreign origin as well. The mark "Made in Germany," later the title of a book excoriating slipshod British commercial methods,[147] surprised the British by the ubiquity of goods available in Britain and in Europe, goods of rapidly rising quality. It quickly became apparent that the defensive measure had boomeranged and aided the offensive. Like Japanese goods in the twentieth century, which started out with a reputation for inferiority, and British woolens in the eighteenth century, German wares ultimately became known for their solid quality.

A similar defensive measure backfired somewhat later. In 1909, smarting under the import competition of German dyestuffs and chemicals, the British government enacted legislation requiring that patents be worked or licensed. This had the effect of encouraging foreign firms to establish subsidiaries in England and produce dyes on the basis of imported intermediate goods, rather than stimulating British production. Most of the British consumption of dyes continued to be imported — 80 percent — and a large part from domestic production was the output of foreign-owned firms.[148]

The last quarter of the century saw German goods squeeze British products out of a number of markets. Historians who denigrate the climacteric and the alleged failure of the Victorian entrepreneur tend to explain the relative decline in British exports to the Continent and to the United States in terms of the rise of protection. This explanation is not proof against the mass of evidence adduced by Hoffman of German gains at British expense, or faster than Britain, in a series of markets in Latin America and the Middle and Far East, outside of the colonies. Hoffman asserts that it is difficult to exaggerate the commercial preponderance of Britain in the 1880s and 1890s.[149] By 1900 pushy German exporters, giving undue lines of credit, selling in any quantity, and descending to the "petty ways and details of a shop,"[150] but also providing special rail and sea through-rates where these helped, were eating into British markets.

The difference in economic vitality is suggested by the difference in reaction to foreign tariffs: the British typically accepted exclusion from the foreign market as the Welsh tinmakers[151] and the Nottingham and Leicester hosiery trade[152] did after the United States McKinley tariff of 1890. The German reaction tended to be different and to consist in search for new goods that could, at given costs, surmount or circumvent the barrier. Baron von Richthofen told Sir Francis Lascelles in 1900 that he was not disturbed by a possible increase in Chinese tariffs, stating: "Germany has had considerable experience in dealing with countries which imposed a high tariff, such as the United States and the South American Republics," and found that "it was quite possible to carry on a large business in spite of such tariffs."[153]

This equanimity in the face of prospective tariff increases was

not maintained for long. In 1900 Canada adopted imperial preference, and Sir Joseph Chamberlain and a tariff reform movement
advocated imperial preference on a wider scale for the entire
empire. Germany took the occasion to denounce the 1865 trade
treaty with Britain on the ground that it provided England with
most-favored nation (MFN) treatment, not only for the mother
country but also for the dominions. Furthermore, Germany threatened to withdraw MFN treatment on her own from the United
Kingdom and other dominions than Canada, from whom she did
withdraw it. The German press followed the progress of the Trade
Reform debate in Britain with avid interest and the strong conviction that reform would lead to a decline of German prosperity.[154]
One of the reasons for the construction of the German navy was to
keep doors open, to maintain colonies, and to guard against an unfavorable trade conspiracy. (Germany had never fully recovered
from the exclusion of German ships from the Mediterranean in the
1830s, or the refusal of a British cruiser to come to the aid of a Prussian merchantman captured by pirates and held for ransom back in
1815.)[155] When he tried to negotiate the forestalling of the war in
1913 and 1914, Ballin laid down as one of the conditions of German
cooperation that Britain continue to adhere to free trade, "a commitment so valuable to German commerce."[156] Brentano, the free-
trader, put the issue sharply in political-economic terms: "What
good is a fleet to protect our goods when foreign countries can raise
tariffs against us," adding "and we can reduce our exports through
our own tariffs."[157]

A number of observers insist that the 1850s were the watershed of
German economic development and the period when Germany
made its major gains in closing the gap with the British economy.[158]
The period 1873 to 1896, moreover, is characterized as the Great
Depression, in Germany as well as in Britain, to judge from the
overall statistics. There is nonetheless good reason to maintain that
the later period was the one in which German economic growth,
and especially structural change, brought about a forward economic spurt that put Germany in a class with Britain as a major economic power, even if it did not bring the German economy entirely
abreast of the British.

To break down the period, there were three short depressions—
1873 to 1878, 1882 to 1886, and 1890 to 1894—and three recovery

periods — 1879 to 1882, 1886 to 1889, plus the period from 1894 to 1896. There were two especially good years, according to Spiethoff, 1889 and 1896, as contrasted with ten from 1849 to 1873.[159] Agriculture was depressed, but that no longer mattered in the overall economic position — though it was politically decisive. The movement off the farm became a flood. At the end of the 1870s Germany was still an agricultural country, with the majority living on the land. The proportion of the working force in agriculture, however, declined from 43.5 percent in 1882 to 36 percent in 1895. One and a half million emigrated, and vast numbers moved from agriculture in the east to mining in the west, a unique long-distance internal migration, as contrasted with short-range migration within Britain and France (except to Paris in the case of France).[160]

While the rate of growth was slower than in the earlier and subsequent periods, there were great additions to efficiency of plant and productivity of labor, creative innovations in business methods, and a wholesale adoption of improvements in technology and organization.[161] The number of artisans grew from 2.88 million to 2.93 million between 1882 and 1895, but middle-sized industry (from 5 to 50 workers) grew from 1.39 million to 2.45 million, and large industry (over 50) from 1.61 million to 3.04 million. Within the last group giant firms of more than 1,000 workers increased from 213,000 to 449,000. This was the period of growth of new industries in chemicals and electricity and the forward push of heavy industry that led Germany to match British output in iron and steel in the 1890s.

The upsurge in industry from 1894 to 1896 produced a halt in emigration, which echoed that of 1854 to 1855.[162] What is new and contrasts sharply with experience in Britain is the similar halt in foreign lending from Germany in the 1880s, at a time when British loans, especially to the Argentine, were flourishing.

The years 1871 to 1873 in Germany produced a boom in both domestic and foreign investment. The foreign-investment boom went in considerable degree to Russia. According to one estimate, in the mid-1880s Germany owned six-tenths of the sizable Russian debt of 6.25 billion rubles (about 3 billion marks). It is characteristic of neophyte foreign lenders (such as the United States in the 1930s) that foreign lending is positively correlated with the domestic cycle and not counterposed to it. These loans helped Germany find a prominent place in the Russian market for heavy goods—60 to 65 percent of imported pig iron, 50 percent of steel, 50 percent of instruments, and 70 percent of agricultural machinery. Beginning in 1886, however, German investment houses sold their Russian securities, or let them run off as the maturities of 1871-1873 were converted by a French loan of 1889. Berlin sold while Paris bought Russian securities,[163] which accounts for the curious phenomenon that French lending of billions of francs to Russia was accompanied by an export surplus only one-twelfth of that amount.[164] The halt of German lending to Russia had political overtones associated with the rise of Russian tariffs on pig iron in 1884-1885 and again in 1887, breaking out in general industrial protection and a tariff war in 1891 and 1893.[165] But Girault, the historian of French lending to Russia, is persuaded (no doubt rightly) that Berlin bankers would have been willing to refinance the Russian loans if the price had been right. Abundant French capital and the need for funds to finance German expansion cut off the flow of capital abroad, as the boom was to do to the emigration of workers in a few years. In Britain lending abroad continued to grow to a peak in 1913.

It is tempting to suggest that large-scale foreign lending—by the Dutch in the eighteenth century, the British at the end of the nineteenth, and the United States from 1958—is a symptom of industrial decline.

At about the middle of the 1890s the commercial and industrial rivalry of Germany with England broke out into more conscious political and military competition. On each side there was sharp awareness of the economic and military moves of the other. There is no need to detail the exact sequence of political steps leading to war, but it is of considerable interest to trace the relationship of various economic groups to the rising nationalism in Germany, and the German hatred of England, which rapidly replaced the earlier sense of inferiority.

Bankers, merchants, the Hansa cities, and the agrarians had little economic reason to oppose Britain. Independence was sought, but not mastery; Hamburg and Bremen had worked for direct commercial links with overseas areas and for independence in shipping to all parts of the world. The Deutsche Bank in 1872 was founded with the express purpose of freeing German trade from dependence on British banking. The same interests of banking, shipping, and

trade sought colonies, especially after 1885. And the agrarian interests were socially scornful of British bourgeois commercial and
industrial mentality, as well as distrustful of the processes of industrialization that led to grime, slums, a proletariat, and social unrest. In the initial stages these groups opposed building the fleet.
Hansa cities and bankers were friendly to Britain and believed that
their commercial success depended on British prosperity and commitment to free trade, and particularly on the avoidance of tariff
reform. Agrarians opposed the navy on two social grounds: because
the army was the senior and aristocratic service in Germany, and
because of the tension in the 1890s between the industrial and the
agrarian state. The Kanitz Bill called for raising grain prices to the
1850-1890 average and holding labor on the farm; the agrarians at
one stage argued, *kein Kanitz, keine Kähne*—no Kanitz motion, not
a single barge for the navy.[166]

A series of nationalist organizations was formed: the Kolonialver-
ein in 1887, the Alldeutsche Verband in 1891, and the Flottenverein
in 1898. Gradually they were taken over by the steel interests, and
gradually in turn they won the support of the merchant classes,
Hansa cities, bankers, and Junkers. Up to 1897 Hamburg opposed
naval construction, wondering what a navy would do against free-
trade England. By the fall of that year its opinion had swung
over.[167] The banker von der Heydt withdrew from the Alldeutsche
Verband shortly after its founding in 1891, because of its enmity to
England. Only 18 percent of the members of the organization were
entrepreneurs, and only one-quarter in all were businessmen. As the
decade wore on, however, the banking community began to ally itself with nationalism; the proprietor of the Bleichschröder Bank,
P. von Schwabach, although British consul general in Berlin, was a
member of both the Alldeutsche Verband and the Flottenverein.[168]
The Bankhaus Mendelssohn was closely allied with the Flottenverein. Kehr, who is a political polemicist, maintains that the banks
stopped opposing the fleet with the second naval building law of
1900.

Agrarian opposition to the fleet is said to have faded as a result of
the Boer War, in which the Germans as a whole sided strongly with
the Boers and against Britain. The modern analogue of the Boer
War in the United States was of course the long and unpopular conflict in Vietnam.

In due course commercial rivalry, colonies, shipping, financial competition with Britain in such regions as the Middle East, big steel, and naval building were all fused in a harmonious, highly nationalist relationship. In 1913, on the occasion of the twenty-fifth anniversary of Kaiser Wilhelm II's accession to the imperial throne, plans were made for the foundation of the Königliche Institut für Seeverkehr und Weltwirtschaft, located in Kiel, which was to be dedicated to the study of world trade. (These plans were finally realized in 1914, and in 1919 the buildings were bought from Krupp for a nominal sum.) There were merchants and bankers like Ballin and Warburg of Hamburg who did not share in the rapidly spreading hatred of England; they formed part of a rapidly dwindling minority.

Hardach ascribes the rise of anglophobia to the years 1850 to 1873.[169] In that period the warnings in Germany to avoid anglicization of the economy, which had been weak and isolated in the first half of the century, accumulated force. But the intensity of feeling grew sharply beginning in the 1880s and reached a peak at the end of the century, at a time when Britain in its turn felt threatened by German commercial rivalry. The *Agrarstaat* versus *Industriestaat* debate brought the English example to the fore. With their scornful contrast between *Händler und Helden* (tradesmen and heroes), the Junkers finally turned their detestation of the city and industry against the British as a means of preserving their position of leadership. Big steel prospered on this diet. "For conservatives, agrarians, bureaucrats and academics, their social inferiority to England, partly living, partly unconscious, was decisive in the rejection of England"[170]—with ultimately fateful consequences.

British Slowdown after 1875

There is no doubt that German economic growth after 1873 was fast, faster than that of Great Britain. The question that is unsettled is whether the British economy slowed down, suffered a "climacteric" —a maturing or aging process—and lost its capacity to adapt and to respond to economic signals. Answers to the question turn partly on methodology and separate the traditional economic historians from the "new," who use explicit economic models and econometric analysis.

It is perhaps foolhardy of one who is neither an econometrician nor a bona fide economic historian to enter the debate, a literary economist who is more historical economist than economic historian, interested in testing economic models against historical .fact more than using particular economic models to understand history. Nevertheless, it seems to me important to try to resolve the conflict. The traditional economic historians—with some distinguished exceptions—tend to believe that Britain slowed down after 1875 for reasons that Landes summarizes as social and institutional[171] and Habakkuk ascribes to the early start and the complexity of the industrial structure.[172] The new economic historians, on the other hand, tend to conclude from their models and regressions that the British economy, and especially British industry, did as well throughout the period as it was able, given the constraints of exogenous conditions, that it maximized profits—with limited exceptions—and that where it failed to adopt foreign innovations or domestic inventions, there were sound reasons of lack of profitability to explain it.

The methodological issue turns on whether one argues by example, as Saul and Richardson assert is true of traditional economic historians,[173] or whether the econometricians draw out of their models little more than the assumption they put in to begin with, as can perhaps be claimed. In a private letter McCloskey says that the use of evidence by traditional economic historians at a casual level is much below the standards to which their profession holds up the medieval historians, who of course have to rely on much less copious information. As a tu quoque reply, one can suggest that econometrics runs the risk of circular reasoning. It is perhaps a mistake to go outside the scope of Germany and Britain, but I have been struck by the triviality of Fogel's finding that railroads made little contribution to the economic growth of the United States after he assumed that both railroads and canals had constant-cost functions.[174] If two processes have constant costs over the whole range of possible outputs and are both in use at a given time, one (or the other) can be thrown away. In the case of many of the essays in the book edited by McCloskey,[175] and in his own study of British iron and steel,[176] if one assumes a competitive model in which technical change is exogenous it is quite easy to find in the usual case that companies were maximizing. The McCloskey demonstration in iron and steel goes further than this, to be sure, into comparative rates of labor productivity. But no consideration is given to the possible relevance of a model in which firms "satisficed" rather than maximized profits; or maximized a function that included among its arguments the desire for a quiet life; or maximized profits competitively in a model in which among the ways to maximize profits were to alter technology so as to reduce costs, economize on a scarce resource, make more effective use of an abundant resource, or reorder institutions (such as substituting direct selling for the merchant) in an effort to overcome barriers to still higher profits. As Pollard has said,[177] there are questions of dynamics. In a static model the problem is to maximize some function within given constraints. But dynamic models are available in which it is possible to break down such constraints. Bottlenecks can be limiting in a static model, or stimulating in a dynamic one.[178] Which is relevant in a given case is a question of judgment. The new economics seems usually to choose the static model.

Some years ago, John R. Meyer ascribed the slowdown of British growth to the falling off of export demand.[179] He constructed an input-output table for the British economy on the basis of the Census of Manufactures data for 1907 and suggested that if export demand had grown from 1875 to 1913 at the same rate as it had in the third quarter of the century, British growth would have been much higher. But an input-output table for a given year with its fixed coefficients is evidently an inappropriate tool to use over a forty-year period of changing technology, and the inference that demand must always come from the same place to sustain the same rate of growth is surely unacceptable. Britain in this period had too high a rate of growth of exports, rather than too low, since exports of standard goods to the countries of the empire enabled the economy to evade the exigencies of dynamic change, away from cotton textiles, iron and steel rails, galvanized iron sheets, and the like, to production for export or for the home market of the products of the new industries. It should be added that McCloskey is not attracted to the Meyer explanation based on demand.[180]

Whatever the shortcomings of the new economic history, what is required of more traditional methods, if they are not to be casual empiricism or anecdotal history—two highly pejorative characterizations? There is nothing wrong with the use of illustrative examples, provided that the generalizations they decorate or illuminate are soundly drawn from a representative sample of the universe under discussion, and that they properly illustrate the point. The use of an example presupposes that the scholar has first undertaken a study of the total body of material under discussion, or a carefully drawn and representative sample, and that the example is suggestive of a mean or model case, and not one or three standard deviations away—or a boundary case.

It is not necessary to recite the numbers that illustrate the faster growth of Germany than Britain during the forty years prior to 1914, nor to do more than recapitulate the useful discussion of Landes, already referred to, from which McCloskey and the new economic historians (plus a few more traditional economic historians such as Saul) are dissenting. If we take the statistics as read, the Landes argument consists in dismissing objective reasons for British backwardness—lack of resources, smaller population, high wages, and availability of capital, and stressing rather the disadvantages of the head start, with interrelatedness of technical capital increments; running down of entrepreneurial vigor after the founder's generation; scarcity of venture capital; and lack of technical education.[181] Saul regards the notion of technical decline between 1851 and 1867 as "entirely mistaken" and cites evidence of "brilliant newcomers," "pioneering first-generation firms," the rise of the bicycle industry to world dominance in ten years, and "strikingly good performance" in stationary engines.[182]

The provision of example and counterexample without description of the entire population from which the samples are drawn is a vapid procedure. For a Marshall of Leeds illustration, in which the second generation crippled the most efficient flax-spinning plant in the world in 1848 and the third generation brought it to bankruptcy in 1881,[183] one can counter with a Pilkington illustration where the new generation provided a vigorous sales effort, adopted Siemens gas-fired tank furnaces, and met foreign competition.[184] It is not enough to cite the failure of old companies—Hawks Crawshaw, Maudlays, Boulton & Watt, and Napier[185]—if new firms are rising to take their place. Nor is it appropriate for McCloskey to cite Lowthian Bell as an example of a trained scientist in the steel industry of Britain,[186] whereas Erickson indicates that he was the only one or at best one of two.[187] Or to claim with Temin that the steel industry failed to innovate or sustain technical progress because of lack of demand[188] without noting the failure of the tinplate industry to change its scale or technique over a hundred years despite an expansion of demand by one hundred fifty times between 1800 and 1891 — and of exports by four times between 1872 and 1891.[189]

The following succinct discussion will cover several dimensions of the problem: technical change, including invention, innovation, and imitation, and within the group the speed of solving technical problems, overcoming technical difficulties, or adopting a process that is dominant; the advantages and disadvantages of specialization, including the merchant system, the independent engineer, and their opposites — direct buying and selling and vertical integration — and related to both, the role of industrial standards; and lastly the Victorian entrepreneur and his education, including its technical content.

Technical Change

In the period from 1770 to at least 1851, technical change took place in Britain and imitation, with delay, took place on the Continent. A variety of cases has been cited earlier, including those in which inventions occurred in Europe, but the first useful applications were taken up in Britain: the König printing press, the Girard flax spinner, the Jacquard loom. In the period after 1875 the record is replete with the statement of new industries where innovations occurred in Europe or the United States, even when the invention was given birth in Britain; German imitation of British innovation was rapid, whereas British imitation of Germany was slow. It is only necessary to cite Bessemer, Gilchrist Thomas (and the French and German races to Britain to obtain the patents), mauve dyes, and the Parsons steam turbine on one side; and the diesel engine, Solvay process, hot blast coke ovens, Linotype, turret lathe, Owens Bottling machine, tabor molding machine, Northrop automatic loom, ring spindles, three-phase current, and reduction of aluminum on the other.

The classic case of course is the British delay in adopting the Gilchrist Thomas process and developing East Midland ores. McCloskey maintains that it was not profitable within the existing technology, the state of demand, and the location of the ores in relation to consuming centers.[190] The question arises, however, why it was necessary to wait from 1878 to 1915 until the Americans solved the technical problem — as far as the Northhamptonshire ores of Stewart and Lloyd at Corby were concerned.[191] A problem of coking fines at Frodingham did not find full solution for thirty years.[192] The experience of United Steel at Appleby-Frodingham in the 1920s and 1930s is not relevant to our subject, as McCloskey points out in relation to Clapham's strictures,[193] but it is of interest to note that the annual reports of United Steel point out that while Frodingham was fully employed and making substantial profits in each year from 1923 to 1928,[194] and again in the 1930s, expansion there was not undertaken until late in the 1930s.[195]

The record has further examples: the tunnel kiln developed for pottery in 1912, which took forty years to become general;[196] and the 100-inch twin grinders and continuous twin polisher at Pilkington's plate glass which took "the short time of seventeen years" to develop.[197] The defenders of United Steel speak of "necessary time lags" and claim that technical change takes time.[198] In the earlier stages of the industrial revolution, however, enormous changes were crowded into relatively few years — the cotton textiles in the 1760s, iron and steel in the 1850s, shipbuilding in the 1880s. By contrast the late nineteenth and early twentieth century performance of Britain seems deliberate.

As noted, there were successes: textile machinery, specialty steel, bicycles, machine tools for bicycles, paints, explosives, pharmaceuticals, soap, and the Parsons steam turbine (though it was ultimately surpassed by the Curtis, Rateau, and Zoelly turbines). In bicycles, moreover, there was speed. The new industry of Coventry and Birmingham rose to world dominance in ten years and responded positively to the financial setback of 1897.[199] This approaches the hub of the question. In a static model, depressions hurt; in a dynamic one, they evoke creative response from which come growth and profits. The contrast is between the Keynesian and the Schumpeterian models. In most industries, Britain followed the former.

A significant question is whether the British entrepreneur failed to understand the importance of research and development (R & D), as Richardson claims is true of the chemical industry and the British nation in general,[200] or was unsuccessful at it. Failure can be the consequence of general ineffectuality, or of one critical error at an important turning point. Richardson supports the view that R & D were held in low esteem in Britain by citing numbers of patents there and in Germany.[201] In other industries one can find statements of scorn for innovation in general,[202] and industries bemused with past successes that ignored new developments, as in steam, which inhibited interest in internal combustion, or groups of engineers who failed to be aroused by striking events: for example, the English electrical engineers' failure to respond to the long-distance demonstration of transmission of three-phase current.[203] But there are instances on the other side, where there was great interest but a wrong choice, notably heroic and successful efforts to improve the Leblanc soda process when it should have been abandoned; and example after example of attempts to adopt or adapt machinery, which failed for want of competence. An early example is the effort of James Marshall in the 1850s and 1860s to change from mechanical retting of flax for linen, and to make effective use of the Schlumberger combing machine. Efforts were extensive but unsuccessful and in the end, in 1874, the French equipment was discarded.[204] Byatt cites instances of companies that failed to overcome teething troubles in electric lighting and in electric supply, and abandoned the fields.[205] Experiments undertaken by the Brush company with the Swedish Ljundström machine proved to be "expensive."[206] It is difficult to devise an adequate classification scheme to enable one to weigh how much lack of Schumpeterian response at the end of the century was the result of disinterest, gross errors, or low levels of competence. Presumably all three obtained, as well as cases of effective entrepreneurial innovation.

There remains the competitive model in which research activity is not undertaken because it does not pay; it is more profitable to let others invent and innovate and to imitate slowly because the mean of the probability distribution of going down the wrong path is high. To the Chicago school, in which everyone is always maximizing profits, this explanation for limited invention, innovation, and slow imitation or solution of production problems is appealing. One particular form of the argument is that skilled labor was so cheap in Britain that it did not pay to innovate or imitate in labor-saving techniques.[207] But this argument can run either way, depending on whether one uses a static or a dynamic model. Cheap skilled labor will enable a country to build complex machinery in a static model, obviate the necessity for so doing in a dynamic one. In the same way that one can find economic historians saying that high wages are good[208] or bad[209] or for growth, high or low prices, more or less exports and imports, and the like can stimulate or retard depending upon the model chosen.

The new economics, moreover, might have been expected to take note of the finding that economic growth has a large residual component, whether investment in human capital, technical change, or learning by doing. At the very least, speed of imitation of innovations that can be recognized as likely to be successful has a payoff. The return to electricity may be less when there is a gas network for lighting; the Leblanc process should be abandoned when it is clear that the Solvay method dominates it, even though economies are being achieved in the former,[210] and solution of the problems of the East Midlands ores has a high payoff after the Thomas process shows the way. When the "residual" is so large a contribution to growth, the a priori view that technical change does not pay is difficult to accept.

Specialization and Standardization

Standardization achieves economies of scale in production. In contrast, thirty grades of low-grade poplins, when the ultimate user can distinguish at best three grades;[211] two hundred types of axle boxes and forty different handbrakes; fifty different systems of electrical supply, twenty-four voltages, and ten different frequencies; one hundred twenty-two channel and angle sections in steel when the Germans made thirty four;[212] "an almost unbelievable lack of standardization" on the part of British makers of plows;[213] and other examples all suggest difficulties in achieving scale economies. Specialization is limited by the size of the market, to be sure, but the question is not wholly out of the hands of the entrepreneur if he succeeds in achieving standardization of design. For this purpose he needs to have direct contact with the consumer. A filter in the form of a system of merchants or consulting engineers is likely to prevent technical change that settles on a standard design, which in turn optimizes economies of production and efficiency in use.

In a static model the merchant is efficient because he prevents the diseconomy of too large an administrative scale and permits specialization. The producer specializes in production; the merchant in selling. Each looks after his end of the process independently. Without technological change, the disintegration works — although Allen believes that in cotton, it works well in expansion but poorly when demand is declining.[214] When the time comes to contemplate change, however, the merchant acts as a filter between producer and consumer, preventing them from getting together to agree on how the product should be modified to enable it to be produced as cheaply as possible within the requirements of the consumer. The great specialization of Britain, which was a strength as new products became refined in such industries as cotton textiles, became a handicap when the problem was to streamline, simplify, and standardize. When companies rose to national size in the United States, they tended to give up dependence on wholesalers and jobbers and go in for direct selling.[215] At an early stage in American retailing, department stores stopped reliance on commission merchants and turned to direct buying, first through permanent agents, then by sending buyers to the producers even in Europe. The abandonment of the merchant by Siemens and the chemical companies in Germany in the 1880s has been mentioned.[216] Hohenberg's thesis is that the chemical industry could grow in size and profitability only by educating the consumer companies in the use of intermediate goods, and, for fertilizers, by educating the ultimate consumer.[217] In the third quarter of the twentieth century a distinction is made between hardware and software, the latter needed for the effective use of the former. In a merchant system software must be kept to a minimum because it requires direct selling by "commercial engineers."

It is not only the merchant who filters and screens effective communication between producer and user. The wrong type of engineer can equally impede standardization. Railroad lines with superintending engineers laid down specific standards for locomotives, based on professional judgments, which prevented British companies from producing stock models on a mass basis.[218] Consulting engineers hired by municipalities ordering electric lighting systems laid down rigid specifications with heavy penalty clauses, which inhibited fixing standards.[219] Saul generalizes this experience and notes that in northeastern England Charles Mertz both provided electrical supply and acted as the consulting engineer, without separation of function, with the result that electrification achieved its most notable progress in the area where he concentrated.[220] Vertical integration, which brought the merchant and the design function under the same roof with production, offered the opportunity for achieving standardization of design, or the provision of special modifications for special needs — which the British economy lacked. But only the opportunity. A laissez-faire system with many small companies, and no organization of the trade or dominant companies, lacks a mechanism for setting standards unless government is willing to undertake it. In Britain Parliament laid down the Standard Gauge Act in 1846, but failed to apply it to the Great Western Railroad. For the most part the public good of standards was provided in Germany and the United States by large companies. "The big firms rammed it through."[221] Contrast the British example with that of two large firms in Germany. Each British muncipality hired its own consulting engineer with his own idea and ordered a specially designed system. In Germany, Siemens responded rapidly in the 1890s to AEG's demonstration of the superiority of high-voltage, three-phase alternating current, and the two firms offered the public an identical standardized product.

One municipal engineer in Glasgow, John Young, pushed through the use of the overhead trolley at the end of the nineteenth century. Whereas in France, standardization in this field came from the outstanding producing company (Thomson-Huston), which operated some tramway lines but made its profits on equipment, the dynamism of Glasgow under the leadership of one individual seems to have enabled the street railway industry to avoid the proliferation of standards found in most other items of municipal equipment.[222]

The clash between the old economic history and the new is sharply revealed in steel and the role played by the merchant system. Old-fashioned economic history, which the new history dismisses summarily, ascribes a role in slowing down technological change and maintaining exports of standardized rails, galvanized sheets, and the like to the dominance of the industry by merchants, "gradually less suited" to the needs of the industry,[223] with no technical capacity, and responsible for a large part of domestic and home sales.[224] The industry was competitive, says McCloskey, and while steel users based their judgments of steel qualities not on chemical analysis but on experience and reputation, they were right in preferring first wrought to cast iron, then mild steel to hard steel, and then acid open-hearth to basic Bessemer. The fact that the admiralty fastened on the acid-basic difference rather than the open-hearth/Bessemer, and rejected basic open-hearth steel for ships until well into the First World War, is not explained. By implication there is no need for an institutional arrangement that links up producer and consumer without intermediaries. Technical information circulates perfectly when developed and made public, and price is all that is needed to direct choices. Contemporary observers who complain that producers and consumers are failing to take advantage of their opportunities, on the other hand, lack an appreciation of the effectiveness of competitive markets. It is not explained why these observers lack information, whereas consumers and producers have all they need.

The issue then is one of the existence or absence of market failure. The new economic historians believe markets work. Apart from a rare case like the Leblanc process, competition, adequacy of information, and rational behavior result in economic solutions. Externalities, like the dissemination of technical information through direct selling (software) and public goods like standards, are not needed; continuous profit maximization with adequate foresight is forthcoming under any and all circumstances. The alternative view for which a great deal of qualitative evidence exists, but which is difficult if not impossible to pose in quantitative form, is that at one level, everyone is maximizing subject to constraints; but at a less tautological and trivial level, periods of rapid technical change may lead to market failure through a lack of positive externalities and public goods, through institutions that inhibit profit maximization and, as the next section proposes to show, through actors who maximize objective functions other than profits.

The Victorian Entrepreneur

First, a small point. In a 1970 paper,[225] McCloskey uses macroeconomic statistics of productivity in Britain to suggest that Coppock was wrong in trying to correct the dating of the climacteric from the 1870s to the 1890s,[226] and that in fact it should be brought forward to the first decade of the twentieth century. It was not the Victorian entrepreneur who failed but the Edwardian. (Later it proved to be the case that no entrepreneur at all failed.) McCloskey's conclusion seems to rest on a failure to understand Coppock's argument, which turns on the choice of deflators for converting money to real income. McCloskey seems to believe that Coppock's criticism was based on the difference in weights of the price deflator between one based on national product and one based on value added. He suggests that these are the same, and of course this is correct. But Coppock's actual position rests on the difference, in an open economy with changing terms of trade, between income produced and income consumed. In the 1880s and 1890s income consumed was rising rapidly because of improvement in the terms of trade. Income produced, however, did less well. If instead of a deflator for national income, one for net national product were used, the climacteric is pushed back before the 1880s. The period from 1900 to 1913 is one of declining income despite improved output because of worsening terms of trade, and not one of newly arrived entrepreneurial failure.

Timing aside, there is the question of whether in three generations from clogs to clogs the British entrepreneur was spoiled by success and failed to develop from a brilliant amateur, who achieved the industrial revolution, into an accomplished professional technical manager, who kept it going.

The new economic historians have a powerful a priori argument on their side. It is insufficient to point out the decline of firms. It is possible for firms to decline, for family firms to fail, and for the sons of self-made men to go to Oxford and Cambridge and then into the professions or government rather than business, without economic decline or even a slowdown of growth, so long as those who leave industry are replaced by newcomers. It is not gross movements that count, but net; and not the quality of old owner-managers, but the average quality, including dynamism, of industrial managers as a whole. Everything said about the interest in the quiet life, trustee securities, three-day weekends in the country, and the like is of no importance if the *élan vital* of industry is maintained on balance by a flow of recruits.

There were newcomers. Saul points to them in textile machinery, high-speed engines, machine tools, bicycles, soap, alkalis, electrical companies.[227] And there were successes for old firms in hydraulic machinery and the like. But many firms in electrical products and chemicals were foreign, as were a number of critical technical people in various companies—in automobiles,[228] Short in Dick, Kerr and Co.,[229] and Levenstein and Dreyfus in dyestuffs.[230] It would appear that the number of domestic newcomers was not sufficient to fill the ranks left by those departing.

In *Economic Growth in France and Britain* I put together a table of nineteenth-century business dynasties drawn from *Fortunes Made in Business,* which showed that sons, grandsons, and great-grand-sons were drawn more and more out of business into Parliament and other forms of public life.[231] The list could have been made much longer for public life had I not wanted other indications of change of interest including education, religion, charitable works, and the like. It would be interesting to extend the list also to include the movement out of industry into the professions.

Habakkuk cites the case of William Morris, who started in the automobile business because his father could not afford to send him to the university to study medicine.[232] This is highly evocative of the last half of the eighteenth century, when entrepreneurs were re-cruited in large part from the ranks of Dissenters and Scots who were prevented from studying at Oxford and Cambridge, and thus from qualifying for the professions. A century later the barrier of religion in education and the professions had been broken down. Civil service, the law, medicine, and even engineering as an inde-pendent profession were recruiting many of the dynamic individuals who would have been available for the ranks of industry in the eigh-teenth century.

A recent paper by Thackray notes that science was studied by such persons as the members of the Philosophical and Literary So-ciety of Manchester in the eighteenth century, not for the purpose of solving industrial problems, as the conventional wisdom has it, but to achieve social advance.[233] Successful manufacturers would study spiders, and not for what they could learn about weaving from them. Thackray's thesis is that the provincial scientific societies— outside of the Royal Society in London—had the function of legiti-mizing marginal men. In this they were successful. The first genera-tion, which was self-educated and successful in business, turned to science in middle age, but to study such nonuseful subjects as (at that time) astronomy. The second generation in a modal family would be educated at Edinburgh and engage to some degree in business, but mostly study science. The third generation, however, converted to anglicanism, attended public school and Oxford or

Cambridge, engaged in political life, lived in the country, and stayed in society. This same third generation moved to put more science into Oxford and Cambridge, especially Cambridge, and to support Darwin, Huxley, and technical education—for others. There was great interest in scientific and technical education, but few engaged in practical applications.

Musgrave claims that science and technological education were not on the agenda of Victorian Britain.[234] The statement seems exaggerated if one contemplates the Select Committee on Scientific Instruction (1868), the Royal Commission on Scientific Instruction and the Advancement of Science (1870-1875), the reorganization of the Royal School of Mines (1882), the Royal Commission on Technical Instruction (1883), the Technical Instruction Act of 1889, its finance with whiskey money in 1891, and so on, including the expansion of examinations in mathematics, chemistry both practical and theoretical, and metallurgy, between 1875 and 1895. The question of technical and scientific instruction was not addressed in Britain in the eighteenth century, as in France, or in the first half of the nineteenth century, as in Germany; but as German competition rose, it was by no means overlooked. More apposite is Cotgrove's view that the social structure did not favor technical education of the elite for application in business.[235] There was widespread support for the idea of technical education, little opportunity to achieve social advance by means of it.

The contrast is with France, where established firms were identified with the Ecole polytechnique, with the Ecole centrale des arts et manufactures, and even certain banking families who went, generation after generation, to the Hautes Etudes commerciales. This is not to claim that French technical education was admirably suited for success in business: its Cartesian quality, emphasis on mathematics, and elitism produced a succession of brilliant and arrogant technocrats who did best in the army and public works and less well, unless they had apprenticed abroad, in the family firm. Nonetheless, the point of contrast is that scientific and technical education were approved *for* the elite in France, *by* the elite in Britain. If a son was intended for trade, he would not be sent to the public school or the university.[236] Leadership in industry was left to "players," while "gentlemen" went into public life, the civil service, the professions—medicine, law, ministry, the military services—or rusticated. This explains why in steel, an industry where most of the leading manufacturers were recruited from sons of businessmen and gentry, including professionals, the average age of these sons was rising rapidly between 1865 and 1895 — the mean from 38 to 46 and later to as high as 55, and the lower limit of the third quartile from 54 to 65.[237]

The brilliant newcomers in bicycles, from whose ranks came most of the less brilliant newcomers in automobiles (apart from William Morris), rose from the players as did Lever in soap. The gentlemen failed to furnish an adequate number of new recruits for industry, and in fact drew them off. The supply of replacements was insufficient. This is why, while it was possible for British industry as a whole to continue to grow while given firms were declining, and a number of large firms were emerging to industry dominance — Distillers Company, Imperial Tobacco, Courtaulds, J. P. Coats, Bryant and May, in addition to those already mentioned — on the whole, growth was unspectacular.

But it is time to return to the question of Germany. When did Germany overtake Britain? Certainly not until well after World War II. Rapid growth of the German economy as a whole, and leadership in new industries at the end of the nineteenth century were not sufficient to offset the long lag in efficiency in agriculture, textiles, shipping, banking, and foreign investments. In a world of S-curves, more rapid growth of one country than another does not inevitably mean overtaking via linear extrapolation, so that the slower growing country should resign like a chess master who loses a pawn against a peer. Much can supervene to delay an outcome that is in any case inevitable. The United States can perhaps take some comfort in this thought as it contemplates Japan. But not much.

Conclusion

8. The purpose of the six "short stories" tucked between the introduction and this final chapter has been to demonstrate that comparative history is a useful laboratory in which to test various economic models for generality. It is not, perhaps, history. Lawrence Stone has recently insisted that history "deals with a *particular* problem and a *particular* set of actors at a *particular* time in a *particular* place" (emphasis in original).[1] Social sciences, on the contrary, are interested in establishing uniformities and general laws of human interaction. Yet the historical method of searching for hypotheses to test, and testing hypotheses derived deductively, I claim, is a useful one. Historical economics rather than economic history (and presumably also historical sociology, historical demography, historical political science) constitutes a legitimate and fruitful approach to the study of man.

The passage of time, continued reading, conversation with experts, and further reflection have led me to modify in varying degrees some of the statements in the previously published essays here reproduced virtually without change. The oldest paper, on the responses to the price of wheat, raises questions today about timing. The conversion from wheat to dairy products, eggs, and bacon was probably underway in Denmark well before the decline in the price of wheat in the 1880s. The fall in price accelerated, rather than initiated, it.[2] Similarly, there is a question of whether the cumulative process of emigration from Italy, which picked up speed in 1881, was coterminous with the agricultural crisis that Luzzato asserts broke out only in 1885.[3] The point is debatable and doubtless deserves further investigation. Wheat and other agricultural prices had declined by 17 percent between 1878-1880 and 1881, and another 20 percent by 1885. The poor harvest of 1881 combined with the fall in price reduced total agricultural income from 6.2 billion lire in 1880 to 4.8 billion in 1881.[4] If one were to disaggregate between citrus and wine (which were relatively prosperous) on the one hand, and wheat on the other, one would probably find an even more catastrophic fall in the incomes and prospects of the peasants on the wheat-growing latifundia.

A purely antiquarian point perhaps has arisen in connection with the statement in Chapter 4 that New York's challenge to the dominance of London has been traced back to 1900. Historical gamesmanship has, in addition to the remark, "It was not like that in Breslau," the comment "Oh, no. That goes back at least another hundred years." In this case I find a challenge by New York to London's financial supremacy forty-three years earlier than 1900, in a *New York Herald* statement on "The Revulsion of 1857":

Each panic has resulted in making the city of New York the centre of finance and of trade for this continent. In 1837 it stood on a sort of struggling emulation with Philadelphia and Boston. The revulsion of that period decided its position and gave it an advance over them which it not only maintained, but has increased ever since. The rivalry between New York and other cities on this continent has ceased. The late struggle of 1857 was in great degree between New York and London, and has terminated to the advantage of the former city. And the time must not ere long arrive, when New York, and not London, will become the financial centre, not only of the New World, but also to a great extent, of the Old World.[5]

But this is mere chutzpah.

In the discussion of Canadian banking in the same chapter, the pace at which Toronto was winning out over Montreal was underestimated. There was a hint of the transfer of some activities of the Royal Bank of Canada and the Bank of Montreal. Today, three years later, the Royal Bank is still talking of moving the biggest part of three departments—investments, international money markets, and corporate marketing and development—that seem to be the same as those mentioned by Professor Ryba in May 1974 (see note 183 to Chapter 4). Despite the insistence of the Royal Bank that its actions had nothing to do with the victory at the polls of the separatist Parti québecois, the role of language may well have been under-rated.[6]

A more serious challenge, this time to the position set out in Chapter 5, comes from a new book by Fernand Braudel, who has insisted again on the critical role of generations and generations of capital accumulation among merchant families as a key factor in the industrialization of the Western World.[7] As of the date this is written, I have not been able to get hold of Braudel's book, and it would be foolish to anticipate its argument. Capital accumulation by merchants doubtless laid the basis for industrialization indirectly — through improving agriculture, contributing to infrastructure, developing banking — each in their turn important for industrialization. The contention of Chapter 5 is that the commercial revolution did not contribute to the industrial revolution *directly*.

Apart from emendations, modifications, extensions, and foot-notes, the chapters above seem to me to make some important sub-stantive points:

(*a*) It is virtually impossible to use economic models for predicting policy responses to major structural shifts in the world economy. Not only is general equilibrium in economics underdetermined; the nature of the reaction will depend in many cases on the political power of given sectors, regions, factors, classes, and the like, and their readiness to use it. Ideology and culture will play a role, often with delay — that is, cultural lag. Economic determinism is some-times supported, sometimes undermined. The positions in Chapters 2 and 3, moreover, differ rather fundamentally with those set forth in a new interpretation of the role of tariff policy in Europe in the nineteenth century.[8]

(*b*) Even where the reaction of a society to a given stimulus is wholly economic in character, the existence of a unique solution is doubtful because of the possibility of static and dynamic responses. In a static model, lower prices, reduced exports, increased imports, and hence lower tariffs at home on imports, higher tariffs abroad, home export taxes, and so on all depress income, employment, and economic activity generally. In a dynamic model, they may stimu-late. A static society folds under handicaps; a dynamic one over-comes at least some of them, if the challenge is not too great. The social scientist on the whole is not in a position to indicate when a static and when a dynamic response will be forthcoming, nor is the historian in such a position before the event.

(*c*) Viewed in historical perspective, the economic process appears to resemble the continuous repetition of production of new knowledge, its use in monopoly, erosion of the monopoly through diffusion of the knowledge, and often displacement of the activity. Some years ago in an essay on the history of transport in Europe, Girard suggested that each new means of transport was defeated by another new one because it charged monopoly rents and encouraged new entry. Thus turnpikes gave way to canals, canals to railroads, railroads to trucking.[9] It is not necessary to insist on excess monopoly rent. Monopolies erode unless based, as in finance, on economies of scale that are technologically impervious to change. As knowledge is diffused, old emporia, relays, and entrepôt centers lose their function. The old network fails to earn its keep and falls into disuse. Transport, trade, finance, and—though at a far slower pace—industrial technology, follow a process cycle not unlike Vernon's product cycle.

(*d*) With monopolies comes hierarchical organization. Trade and finance are dominated at any one time by one country, and within a country, by one city. In growth, countries move at different paces. Hierarchy is efficient. It may be necessary for stability, as I have tried to show elsewhere. It decays, then is replaced.

(*e*) It is hardly necessary to emphasize the need, in economic history, to reject monocausality or insistence on the primacy of natural resources, the money supply, the social role of the entrepreneur, technological change, the class struggle, or what you will. The studies above do not attack monocausality, but they offer it no support. Nor do they support overarching theories of stages of growth, or backwardness, or, except incidentally in Chapter 6, the institutional approach to economic history.

The conclusion I draw from the foregoing is that economics at its present stage of development is much better at partial-equilibrium problems of the "if this, then that" type, than at general-equilibrium issues of causation.[10] More and more, I am reminded of Keynes' advice to economists to seek to resemble dentists. In large part, Keynes had in mind that a dentist is highly professional, with sophisticated techniques useful for only a part of the problem of health, and not on the whole ambitious to unravel the secrets of the human mind and body. I would add to this that dentists today have drawers full of different tools that they use in different ways for different types of problems too painful to contemplate. In earlier times the barber-dentist, if that is what he was, knew only how to extract. He had one model, and one tool. Today, to be sure, there are specialists who work consistently at one or another problem rather than the general practice of dentisty. Few of them, I would hope, think of their specialty as having general explanatory value in the history of medicine, or even of dentistry.

General practitioners of economic history, moreover, are not free to choose their tools at random, or because they happen to feel like working with a certain one today, regardless of the problem. Stone has a great deal of sound advice to offer historians, telling them not to be overawed by methodological sophistication in the social sciences, and to use common sense to compensate for technical ignorance; it is perhaps excessive to recommend that the historian "pick and choose what suits him best" from the social sciences and "select what seems to him to be most immediately illuminating and helpful" without requiring him to justify the model chosen.[11] Why a static model now, a dynamic model then? What makes him think that economic outcomes are socially determined here, and social outcomes economically determined there? To pick and choose particular models for particular problems without justification is implicit theorizing, against which my generation was cautioned by Wesley C. Mitchell fifty years ago.

History, I assert, is an excellent laboratory in which economists can test their models and learn what those models explain and what their limitations are. I would want the history to be comparative, since the object is to improve economic understanding in general, not that of a particular past. The economies studied must not be vastly dissimilar, since that broadens the field too widely to encompass all knowledge and prevents useful thought experiments on how small differences in social, cultural, and political conditions affect economic outcomes.

It is in the nature of man to evangelize, to urge others to behave as he does, and I am no exception. It is my considered opinion, as well as my passionate conviction, that economics needs history — perhaps even more than history needs economics.

Notes

Bibliography

Index

Notes

1. Comparative Economic History

1. See Fogel, *Railroads and American Economic Growth.*
2. Hufbauer, *Overseas Investment.*
3. Gerschenkron, *Economic Backwardness;* North and Thomas, *Rise of the Western World;* Rostow, *Stages of Economic Growth;* Schumpeter, *Business Cycles.*
4. Reynolds, *Three Worlds of Economics.*
5. Gerschenkron, *Continuity in History,* p. 121.
6. *The Economic Development of France and Germany, 1815-1914.*
7. "Croissances comparées."
8. Kindleberger, *Economic Growth in France and Britain.*
9. Mokyr, "Industrial Revolution in the Low Countries."
10. Boserup, *Conditions of Agricultural Growth;* Dovring, *Land and Labor in Europe;* Moore, *Demography of Eastern Europe;* Slicher van Bath, *Agrarian History of Western Europe.*
11. Cameron, *Banking and Development* and *Banking and Industrialization;* Goldsmith, *Financial Structure and Development.*
12. Anderson and Bowman, "Education in Development"; Musgrave, *Technical Change and Education.*
13. Aitken, *State and Economic Growth.*
14. Burn, *Economic History of Steelmaking;* Hohenberg, *Chemicals in Western Europe;* Kisch, "Textiles in Silesia."
15. Hobsbawm, *Labouring Men;* Kerr and Siegel, "Propensity to Strike"; Lorwin, "Labor Organizations in Belgium and France"; Rimlinger, "Strike Propensity of Coal Miners"; Tilly et al., *Rebellious Century.*
16. Böhme, *Frankfurt und Hamburg;* Van Houtte, "Belgium and the Netherlands."
17. Landes, "Technological Change and Development"; Musson, *Science, Technology and Growth.*
18. Girard, "Transport."
19. Chenery, "Patterns of Growth"; Denison, *Why Growth Rates Differ;*

Hoffmann, *Growth of Economies;* Kuznets, *Modern Economic Growth* and *Growth of Nations;* Maddison, *Growth in the West;* Woytinsky and Woytinsky, *World Commerce and Government* and *World Population and Production.*

20. Cameron, *Banking and Development* and *Banking and Industrialization.*

21. Redlich, "Comparative Historiography."

22. Bouvier, *Krach de l'Union générale;* Bonelli, *Crisi del 1907.*

23. Gourevitch, "Trade and Coalitions."

24. Lund, "Land Clearance in 18th Century." Professor Bonelli of the University of Torino has a book on land clearance in the nineteenth century in Marche, Italy, but I lack the reference.

25. North and Thomas, *Rise of the Western World.*

26. Gerschenkron, *Economic Backwardness* and "Typology of Industrial Development."

27. Bendix, *State and Society;* Crozier, *Bureaucratic Phenomenon;* Weber, *Theory of Social Organization.*

28. Rosenberg, *Bureaucracy, Aristocracy and Autocracy.*

29. Istituto per la Scienza, *Burocrazia in Italia.*

30. Abramovitz and Eliasberg, *Public Employment in Britain.*

31. Robson, *Civil Service in Britain and France.*

32. See note 11 above.

33. See note 22 above.

34. Tortella, "Banking in Spain."

35. Romeo, *Risorgimento and capitalismo.*

36. Halbwachs, *Les Traces de voies à Paris.*

37. Tilly, *Financial Institutions in the Rhineland,* p. 55.

38. Checkland, *The Gladstones.*

39. Fischer, *Der Staat und Industrialisierung,* pp. 208 ff.

40. Crouzet, *Capital Formation.*

41. Pouthas, *La Population française.*

42. Ariès, *Populations françaises;* Haines, *Economic-Demographic Interrelation;* Kollmann, "Population of Barmen."

43. "Technical Education and the French Entrepreneur."

44. Artz, *Technical Education in France;* Ben-David, *Fundamental Research* and *Scientists' Role;* Cotgrove, *Technical Education and Social Change;* Parker, "French and German Ore Mining"; Redlich, "Academic Education for Business" and "Business Leadership"; Ringer, *German Mandarins;* Wilkinson, *Governing Elites.*

45. Kindleberger, "Technical Education," p. 23.

46. Kisch, "Textile Industries in Silesia."

47. Hufbauer, *Synthetic Materials;* Stobaugh, "Product Life Cycle"; Tilton, *International Diffusion of Technology;* Vernon, "Product Cycle."

48. Hoffmann, *Growth of Economies.*

49. Braun, *Sozialer Wandel in einem Industriegebiet.*

50. Halbwachs, *Les Traces de voies à Paris.*

51. Redford, *Labour Migration in England.*

52. Bull, *Sozialgeschichte der norwegische Demokratie.*

53. Brepohl, *Der Aufbau des Ruhrvolkes;* Köllmann, "Population of Barmen."

54. "Monetary Integration."

55. *Two Postwar Recoveries.*

56. "Western Europe and Great Britain."

57. "Industrialization."

2. Group Behavior and International Trade

1. *From Economic Theory to Policy,* passim.

2. *The Great Transformation,* passim.

3. Especially helpful have been Duncan Ballantine, John Blum, K. W. Deutsch, A. Gerschenkron, Bert F. Hoselitz, G. K. Krulee, E. E. Morison, W. W. Rostow, and J. E. Sawyer.

4. See Nourse, *American Agriculture,* appendix A. An earlier and entirely orthodox account is furnished by Veblen in "Price of Wheat since 1867."

5. See Ensor, *England, 1870-1914,* p. 116; and Ernle, *English Farming,* pp. 379-381.

6. See Jensen, *Danish Agriculture,* pp. 192 ff., esp. p. 212.

7. Ibid., statistical appendix. For a series of interesting contemporary European views see the Report of the U.S. Commissioner of Agriculture (1883), pp. 326-351 (quoted by Nourse, *American Agriculture,* pp. 271 ff.).

8. Slight differences in range and timing existed in separate markets because of differing transfer costs and the accessibility of different sources of supply. In Sweden, for example, which is not covered here, the comparable decline was from $1.34 per bushel in 1881 to $0.78 in 1887. See table II of the appendix to the useful "Decline and Recovery of Wheat Prices" (Food Research Institute, p. 347), which gives annual figures for a large number of countries.

9. Lewis and Maude, *English Middle Classes,* p. 171.

10. See Ensor, *England, 1870-1914,* p. 117.

11. This statement should perhaps be qualified by reference to the fair-trade agitation of the 1880s and the rise of protectionist sentiment in the 1890s under Joseph Chamberlain. Both these movements, however, were industrial in origin and sought to enlist rural support as an afterthought.

Some weight should perhaps also be given to the roles of bad weather and pestilence, which delayed recognition of the importance of overseas competition. It is not certain that the reaction would have been equally passive had the country as a whole clearly understood the deep-seated nature of agriculture's troubles.

12. See Gerschenkron, *Bread and Democracy,* p. 45.

13. Ibid., pp. 26-29 and 57-58.

14. Golob, *The Méline Tariff,* pp. 81-82. I rely heavily on Golob's treatment.

15. International Institute of Agriculture, *World Trade,* pp. 794-798.

16. Hourwich, *Immigration and Labor,* p. 201, notes for a somewhat later period that more than 70 percent of Italian immigrants to the United States came

from agricultural regions. Gross emigration rates differ from net, it may be observed, by rather sizable amounts because of the practice of transatlantic migration on a seasonal basis for harvesting, particularly to Argentina, by so-called *golondrinos* ("swallows").

17. For lack of readily available secondary material I have not investigated the course of events in Austria-Hungary, Sweden, Spain, and Portugal—which took action against new wheat imports—or in the Netherlands, Belgium, or Switzerland—which did not. A cursory examination of the tariff schedules (see Food Research Institute, "Decline and Recovery of Wheat Prices, table 7, p. 350) and of annual figures for gross emigration overseas (*Annuaire statistique de France,* 1914-15, pt. 3, p. 164) suggests that Austria-Hungary and Sweden were equally tardy in protecting agriculture and equally affected by emigration. Gerschenkron (*Bread and Democracy,* pp. 40-41) gives an interpretation of the Swiss experience.

18. See Jensen, *Danish Agriculture,* p. 133.

19. A more complete statement might attach importance to types of soil.

20. Jensen, *Danish Agriculture,* p. 101: "After the defeat in the war of 1864, the work which was already begun was taken up by able and enthusiastic men." See also Westergaard, *Economic Developments,* p. 13: "For the economic life of Denmark [the War of 1864] was of still greater importance in that it gave industry a strong impetus for attacking and solving the many problems which pressed upon it within the country's narrowed boundaries."

21. For an account of forerunners see Faber, *Co-operation in Danish Agriculture,* pp. 25-30.

22. See Golob, *The Méline Tariff,* pp. 145 ff.

23. I have discussed elsewhere the antithesis between the views of Keynes, who asserted that the world is ruled by little else than the theories of economists and political philosophers, and those of Arnold, who classes the economist with the lawyer and the scholar as performing a purely ceremonial role (see Arnold, *Folklore of Capitalism,* esp. chap. 4; and Keynes, *General Theory of Employment,* p. 383).

24. See his *Economic Adaptation to a Changing World Market.*

25. Ensor, *England, 1870-1914,* p. 117. It may be observed that some protection was afforded to British cattle interests by the sanitary regulations, passed in the 1890s, that forbade the import of live animals from the Continent and overseas. The principal competition for home-grown meat, even at this time, however, was in meat imported from the Southern Hemisphere, a trade that developed with the innovation of refrigerated ships in the 1880s. Beef grazing, however, is far less labor intensive than dairying and would have been, from the point of view of employment, a much less satisfactory adaptation.

26. In *Les Deux Europes.*

27. Delaisi, *Les Deux Europes,* p. 207. These sources are called "new," in contrast with Germany, Ireland, and Britain, in Jerome, *Migration and Business Cycles.* It may be noted that emigration from Ireland fluctuated parallel to that of Europe *A,* even though it lies in Europe *B* in Delaisi's scheme.

28. Golob, *The Méline Tariff,* p. 8.

29. Roepke (*Social Crisis of Our Times*) finds the clue to the development of

agriculture in the various countries of Europe in the existence or absence of a sturdy peasant body. Its absence accounts for the injury to British agriculture; its presence for the Danish success (pp. 245-246). The peasantry of Italy and "southeast Europe lacked soundness" (p. 204). Wheat protection favors large estates and is detrimental to peasant agriculture (p. 247). But this analysis fails to cover the French case, where peasants gained from protection; and Roepke himself fatally damages the consistency of his position in the statement, "Admittedly, agriculture is that part of the national economic system to which the principles of a free market economy could only be applied with broad reservations" (p. 205).

30. This statement is perhaps unfair to Talcott Parsons and Robert K. Merton and their structural-functional approach to sociology, with which I am inadequately acquainted. For an attempt to apply this to the French economy see Sawyer, "Strains in Modern France."

31. Delaisi, *Les Deux Europes,* pp. 46-47.

32. See, for example, Machlup, "Three Concepts of Balance of Payments," p. 59n.

33. An individual in the society, of course, will belong to a variety of subgroups based on his occupation, class, religion, avocations, age, sex, race, and so on.

34. *From Economic Theory to Policy,* p. 109.

35. This characterization is objected to as unfair to the Junkers, who—whatever their disagreeable attributes—were men of responsibility who energetically farmed their own land in the face of natural difficulties rather than live off the unearned increment in absentia. Yet they were backward in the sense that they clung to traditional crops farmed with traditional techniques. Perhaps a more appropriate adjective is "static."

36. Bateson, "Morale and National Character."

37. See, for example, Lewis and Maude, *English Middle Classes,* passim.

38. See Benedict, *Patterns of Culture;* Kardiner, *Psychological Frontiers of Society;* Kluckhohn, *Mirror for Man.* Given the emphasis on anthropological data, primary attention has been devoted to the personality types of culture rather than subcultures, and Kardiner, for example, regards Western man as a homogeneous type. This notion is in process of correction at the hands of Bateson, Gorer, Meade, and others.

39. See Innis, *Political Science in the Modern State,* p. 87.

40. A number of writers have referred to the alleged inability of the British farmer to cooperate because of his individualism. See, for instance, Russell, who states in his foreword to Faber's *Co-operation in Danish Agriculture,* pp. vii-viii: "The British method, in short, proved less capable of adaptation to new and adverse conditions than the Danish. Critics may argue . . . that the British farmer is so confirmed an individualist and so imbued with the idea of running his own farm in his own way that he cannot co-operate with his neighbor. It may or may not be so." See also Haggard, *Rural Denmark,* p. 273: "The Danes look upon their land as a principal means of livelihood . . . —in short, as a business proposition in which the Nation is most vitally concerned. In the main, although we [British] may not acknowledge it, we look upon our land, or much of it, as a pleasure proposition in

which the individual only is concerned." Haggard also cites (pp. 192-193) the sad case of a Norfolk honorable secretary of a rat and sparrow club who was unable to enlist any cooperation from potential benefactees.

41. See note 11 above.

42. Landes, "French Entrepreneurship."

43. *From Economic Theory to Policy,* pp. 123 and 222-223. Another case is probably that of the American Medical Association, which is unified in opposing expenditures on health by governmental bodies, which would increase the incomes of the vast majority of its members.

44. Faber, *Co-operation in Danish Agriculture,* pp. 31-32.

45. See Benedict, *Patterns of Culture,* pp. 53-56, and chap. 4 for a discussion of the Spenglerian contrast between Apollonian and Faustian cultures and the description of a self-balancing society. Bateson has described another such primitive society in *Naven.* Oppenheimer mentions other instances of the prevalence of small and medium-sized landholdings in Utah, Iowa, and New Zealand in "The Tendency of Development," in Calverton, *Making of Society,* pp. 40-42. Cf. Haggard's literary description of the Danes as "tolerant-minded" (*Rural Denmark,* p. 212).

46. See Faber, *Co-operation in Danish Agriculture,* p. 7.

47. Haggard, *Rural Denmark,* p. 190.

3. The Rise of Free Trade in Western Europe, 1820 to 1875

1. See Pincus, "A Positive Theory of Tariff Formation." For the theory of collective goods see Breton, *Economic Theory of Representative Democracy;* Olson, *Logic of Collective Action;* and, introducing leadership, Froelich et al., *Political Leadership and Collective Action.* Froelich and his colleagues view leaders as political entrepreneurs, interested in maximizing their "surplus" or profit in providing collective goods against taxes, extortions, donations, or purchases.

2. Cited by Gerschenkron, *Bread and Democracy,* p. 65.

3. Helleiner, *Free Trade and Frustration,* p. 63.

4. Johnson, "Economic Theory of Protectionism," p. 118.

5. Stuart, *Free Trade in Tuscany,* p. 24.

6. Fischer, *Der Staat und Industrialisierung.*

7. Bulferetti and Costanti, *Industria e Commercio in Liguria,* pp. 495-501.

8. Wright, *Free Trade and Protection,* pp. 58-59.

9. Ibid., p. 112.

10. Ibid., p. 139.

11. Ibid., p. 113.

12. Porter, *Progress of the Nation,* chap. 16.

13. Bläsing, *Das goldene Delta,* p. 85.

14. MacGregor, *Germany under Frederick William IV,* p. 246.

15. Bulferetti and Costanti, *Industria e Commercio in Liguria,* chap. 2.

16. Bowring, "Prussian Commercial Union," p. 38.

17. Wright, *Free Trade and Protection,* p. 124.

18. Böhme, *Frankfurt und Hamburg,* chap. 1.
19. Checkland, *The Gladstones,* pp. 139, 333.
20. Crouzet, "Western Europe and Great Britain," p. 120.
21. Bläsing, *Das goldene Delta,* p. 83.
22. Heaton, *Economic History of Europe,* p. 398-399.
23. Semmel, *Rise of Free Trade Imperialism,* pp. 181 ff.
24. Brebner, "Laissez-Faire and State Intervention," pp. 254-256.
25. Huskisson, *Speeches,* p. 328.
26. Ibid., pp. 503-505.
27. Labracherie, *Michel Chevalier,* p. 131.
28. Whyte, *Early Life and Letters of Cavour,* p. 131.
29. Select Committee on Export of Tools and Machinery, "Report," p. 12.
30. Wright, *Free Trade and Protection,* p. 130.
31. Select Committee on Exportation of Machinery, "First Report," p. 44.
32. Babbage, *The Economy of Machinery,* p. 363.
33. Polanyi, *The Great Transformation,* p. 136.
34. Select Committee on Exportation of Machinery, "Second Report," p. xx.
35. Ibid., p. xiv.
36. Babbage, *The Economy of Machinery,* p. 364.
37. Musson, "The 'Manchester School,' " p. 49.
38. Chambers, *Workshop of the World,* chap. 1.
39. "The Imperialism of Free Trade."
40. Polanyi, *The Great Transformation,* pp. 133-137.
41. Moore, "Corn Laws and High Farming."
42. Polanyi, *The Great Transformation,* pp. 152-153.
43. *Speeches on Questions of Public Policy,* pp. 4, 18.
44. Ibid., p. 57.
45. The Corn Laws "inflict the greatest amount of evil on the manufacturing and commercial community" (ibid., p. 57). "Silversmiths and jewellers get orders not from the Duke of Buckingham but from Manchester, from Glasgow or Liverpool or some other emporium of manufactures" (ibid., p. 90).
46. Ibid., p. 106.
47. Chambers, *Workshop of the World,* p. 71.
48. *Speeches,* p. 70.
49. Ibid., p. 100.
50. Ibid., p. 103.
51. *High Farming,* p. 374.
52. Moore, "Corn Laws and High Farming."
53. Bowring, "Prussian Commercial Union," p. 55.
54. Brown, *Board of Trade,* pp. 135, 171 ff.
55. Testimony of Thomas Ashton, in Select Committee on Exportation of Machinery, "First Report," par. 235.
56. MacGregor, *Germany under Frederick William IV,* p. 68.
57. Bowring, "Prussian Commercial Union," p. 287.
58. Select Committee on Import Duties, "Minutes of Evidence," p. 59, par. 782.
59. Semmel, *Rise of Free Trade Imperialism,* p. 149.

60. Platt, *Finance, Trade and Politics*, p. 87.

61. Clapham, "Last Years of the Navigation Acts," p. 161.

62. Woodham-Smith, *The Great Hunger*.

63. Cited by Semmel, *Rise of Free Trade Imperialism*, p. 207.

64. List, cited by Fielden, "Rise and Fall of Free Trade," p. 85.

65. Ibid., p. 78.

66. Gouraud, *La Politique commerciale de la France*, p. 198.

67. Ibid., p. 208.

68. Amé, *Les Tarifs de douanes*, vol. 1, pp. 170-174.

69. Lévy-Leboyer, *Histoire économique et sociale*, p. 96.

70. Augé-Laribé, *La Politique agricole*, p. 66.

71. *Histoire économique et sociale*, p. 92.

72. Lutfalla, "Aux origines du libéralisme économique," pp. 500, 515, 517.

73. Lévy-Leboyer, *Histoire économique et sociale*, p. 95.

74. Chevalier, *Cours d'économie politique*, p. 538.

75. Labracherie, *Michel Chevalier*, pp. 130-31.

76. Pollard and Holmes, *Documents of European Economic History*, vol 1, pp. 384-386.

77. Chevalier, *Cours d'économie politique*, p. 521.

78. Illasu, "The Cobden-Chevalier Commercial Treaty," p. 80.

79. Rist, "Une Expérience française," p. 937.

80. Dunham, *Anglo-French Treaty of Commerce*, p. 179.

81. Rosenberg, *Die Weltwirtschaftskrise*, pp. 24-26.

82. Most lists of treaties are given separately by country. For an overview, see Pollard, *European Economic Integration*, p. 117. The impact of repeal of the timber duties and the Navigation Acts in stimulating export-led growth in Scandinavia is treated by Norman, "Trade Liberalization and Industrial Growth." The stimulus to shipping in Norway and to timber exports in Sweden led via linkages to industrialization, which the free-trade imperialists were seeking to avoid.

83. Dunham, *Anglo-French Treaty of Commerce*, p. 333.

84. Consumers of imported materials and machinery are not included here. But Lhomme's view was that the state adopted free trade because it loved the *grande bourgeoisie* and knew its interests better than the members did; that the *grande bourgeoisie* recognized this fact and agreed with the tariff reductions except for a few intransigent protectionists like Pouyer-Quartier. See Lhomme, *La Grande Bourgeoisie au pouvoir*, p. 179. It is, however, impossible for me to accept this rationalization.

85. Huskisson, *Speeches*, p. 131; Pollard, *European Economic Integration*, p. 112.

86. Jacob, *Agriculture, Manufactures, Statistics and Society*, pp. 201-202.

87. Fischer, *Der Staat und Industrialisierung*, pp. 128, 134.

88. Pollard and Holmes, *Documents of Economic History*, vol. 1, p. 374.

89. MacGregor, *Germany under Frederick William IV*, p. 6.

90. Olson and Zeckhauser, "An Economic Theory of Alliances." For a view emphasizing the revenue aspects of the Zollverein, especially savings in the costs of collection and the reduction in smuggling, see Dumke, "Political Economy of Eco-

nomic Integration." Revenues available from the Zollverein permitted the petty princes to maintain their rule without democratic concessions to bourgeois interests.

91. Pollard, *European Economic Integration,* p. 112.
92. Von Delbrück, *Lebenserinnerungen,* vol. 1, pp. 142-144.
93. Fischer, *Der Staat und Industrialisierung,* p. 136.
94. Dawson, *Protection in Germany,* p. 20.
95. Brown, *Board of Trade,* p. 113.
96. Bowring, "Prussian Commercial Union," p. 287.
97. Von Delbrück, *Lebenserinnerungen,* vol. 1, p. 147.
98. Rosenberg, *Die Weltwirtschaftskrise,* p. 207.
99. Henderson, *Britain and Industrial Europe,* p. 171.
100. Von Delbrück, *Lebenserinnerungen,* vol. 1, pp. 162-164.
101. Ibid., p. 200.
102. Dawson, *Protection in Germany,* p. 21.
103. Lambi, *Free Trade and Protection,* p. 5.
104. Zorn, "Wirtschafts- und socialgeschichtliche Zusammenhänge," p. 296.
105. Barkin, *Controversy over German Industrialization,* p. 33.
106. Ibid.
107. *Free Trade and Protection,* pp. 83, 113.
108. Rosenberg, *Die Weltwirtschaftskrise,* p. 195.
109. Lambi, *Free Trade and Protection,* p. 57.
110. Ibid., p. 191.
111. Williams, *British Commercial Policy,* p. 199.
112. Thiedig, *Englands Übergang zum Freihandel,* pp. 31-32.
113. Greenfield, *Economics and Liberalism,* p. 113.
114. Clough, *Economic History of Modern Italy,* p. 27.
115. Whyte, *Political Life and Letters of Cavour,* p. 73.
116. Thayer, *Life and Times of Cavour,* p. 133.
117. Pedone, "La Politica del commercio-estere," in Fua, *Le Sviluppo Economico in Italia,* vol. 2, p. 242.
118. Castronovo, *Economia e societa in Piemonte,* p. 16.
119. Mori, quoted by Luzzato, *L'Economia italiana,* vol. 1, p. 28n.
120. Prodi, "Il Protezionismo," pp. 1-10.
121. *Economic History of Modern Italy,* p. 114.
122. Sachs, *L'Italie,* p. 748.
123. Norsa and Pozzo, *Imposte e tasse in Piemonte,* pp. 16, 17.
124. Parravicini, *Archivo economico,* p. 326.
125. Luzzato, *L'Economia italiana,* p. 28.
126. Coppa, "The Italian Tariff."

4. The Formation of Financial Centers

1. Kerr, "Geography of Finance" and "Metropolitan Dominance in Canada."

2. Labasse, *Les Capitaux et la région.*

3. Pred, *Spatial Dynamics.*

4. Goldstein and Moses, "A Survey of Urban Economics."

5. Vernon, *Metropolis, 1985.*

6. Goldsmith, *Financial Structure and Development;* McKinnon, *Money and Capital;* Sametz, *Financial Development;* Shaw, *Financial Deepening.*

7. *Money and Capital.*

8. *Financial Deepening.*

9. An up-to-date report on the subject is Interbank Research Organisation, *The Future of London.* There are, moreover, indications that the U.S. government is interested in contemplating the steps that would be required to restore the supremacy of New York as the leading world financial center.

10. Fanno, *La Banche e il mercato monetario.*

11. Powell, *Evolution of the Money Market.*

12. Gras, *Introduction of Economic History,* chaps. 5 and 6.

13. Goldsmith, *Financial Structure and Development.*

14. Gerschenkron, "Economic Backwardness" (1952); Hoselitz, "Entrepreneurship and Capital Formation."

15. Gerschenkron, *Economic Backwardness* (1962).

16. Cameron, *France and the Economic Development of Europe; Banking in the Early Stages of Industrialization; Banking and Economic Development.*

17. Cameron, *Banking and Economic Development,* p. 8.

18. Fohlen, "France, 1700-1914," vol. 4, p. 37.

19. Goldsmith, *Financial Structure and Development,* p. 400.

20. Shaw, *Financial Deepening,* p. 10.

21. McKinnon, *Money and Capital.*

22. Shaw, *Financial Deepening.*

23. Powell, *Evolution of the Money Market,* p. 274.

24. Taylor, *Gilletts, Bankers at Banbury,* p. 229.

25. I cannot refrain from pointing out that these economies tend to be lost in the international system when there are fluctuating exchange rates, no international money, and a disintegrated international capital market.

26. Pressnell, *Country Banking,* p. 49.

27. Duncan et al., *Metropolis and Region,* p. 39.

28. Henning, "Standorte und Spezialisierung."

29. Goldstein and Moses, "A Survey of Urban Economics," p. 485, n. 40.

30. Madden and Nadler, *International Money Markets,* p. 110.

31. Gras, *Introduction to Economic History.*

32. Duncan et al., *Metropolis and Region,* p. 84.

33. McKenzie, *The Metropolitan Community,* 1933, p. 62.

34. Duncan et al., *Metropolis and Region,* p. 117.

35. Vernon, *Metropolis, 1985,* pp. 70, 73.

36. Ibid., p. 80.

37. Robbins and Terleckyj, *Money Metropolis,* p. 38.

38. Kindleberger, "European Integration," pp. 191-192.

39. Robbins and Terleckyj, *Money Metropolis,* chap. 6.

40. Bisschop, *Rise of the London Money Market,* pp. 150, 163.

41. Wechsberg, *The Merchant Bankers,* p. 102.

42. Leighton-Boyce, *Smiths, the Bankers,* p. 20.

43. Bisschop, *Rise of the London Money Market,* p. 156.

44. Anderson, "The Attorney and the Early Capital Market," p. 251.

45. Bagehot, *Lombard Street,* p. 138.

46. Ibid., p. 140.

47. Ibid., p. 6.

48. Sayers, *Lloyds Banks,* p. 35. The general manager from 1871 to 1902, Howard Lloyd, went to London from Birmingham once a week after 1884; his successor made it his business to concentrate the head office in London (ibid., p. 50). From 1899 the board met alternately in Birmingham and London, and by 1910 met only in London (ibid., p. 272).

49. Ibid., p. 237.

50. Ibid., p. 269.

51. Ibid., pp. 165, 270. References to the ability and willingness of depositors to move funds between the provinces and London are found elsewhere in Sayers' account of Lloyds for Birmingham (ibid., p. 110), and Leighton-Boyce's account of Nottingham (*Smiths, the Bankers,* p. 36).

52. Crick and Wadsworth, *Joint-Stock Banking,* p. 311.

53. Ibid., pp. 312, 316.

54. Ibid., pp. 329, 342.

55. Ibid., p. 345.

56. Ibid., p. 188.

57. Gregory, *Westminster Bank,* p. 184.

58. Powell, *Evolution of the Money Market,* p. 286.

59. Withers, *National Provincial Bank,* pp. 61, 62.

60. Taylor, *Gilletts, Bankers at Banbury,* p. 229.

61. Matthews and Tuke, *History of Barclay's Bank,* pp. 1-9.

62. Sayers, *Lloyds Bank,* p. 50.

63. Leighton-Boyce, *Smiths, the Bankers,* p. 279.

64. Hidy, *George Peabody,* p. 84.

65. Sayers, *Lloyds Bank,* p. 261.

66. Ibid., p. 263.

67. Ibid., pp. 79-80.

68. Chandler, *Four Centuries of Banking,* vol. 1, pp. 420 ff.

69. Leighton-Boyce, *Smiths, the Bankers,* p. 279; Sayers, *Lloyds Bank,* pp. 58, 232.

70. Bisschop, *Rise of the London Money Market,* p. 217.

71. Powell, *Evolution of the Money Market,* pp. 370, 372.

72. Lévy-Leboyer, *Les Banques européennes,* pp. 436-437.

73. Bigo, *Les Banques françaises,* p. 21.

74. Gille, *La Banque en France,* pp. 57, 77.

75. Bigo, *Les Banques françaises,* p. 101.

76. Gille, *La Banque en France,* pp. 1-101.

77. Ibid., p. 24.

78. Lévy-Leboyer, *Les Banques européennes*, p. 429.

79. Gille, *La Banque en France*, pp. 67-68.

80. Thuillier, "Pour une histoire bancaire régionale," p. 512.

81. Bouvier, *Le Crédit lyonnais*.

82. Labasse, *Les Capitaux et la région*.

83. Gille, *La Banque en France*, p. 36.

84. Brocard, "Les Marchés financiers du province," p. 106.

85. Madden and Nadler, *International Money Markets*, p. 327.

86. *Crédit du nord centenaire*.

87. Buffet, *Du régionalisme au nationalisme financier*; Charpenay, *Les Banques régionalistes*.

88. Dauphin-Meunier, *La Banque de France*, pp. 165-166.

89. Fanno, *Le Banche e il mercato monetario*, p. 74.

90. Labasse, *Les Capitaux et la région*, p. 446.

91. Ibid., pp. 493, 500.

92. Helfferich, *Georg von Siemens*, p. 30.

93. Riesser, *The Great German Banks*, p. 509.

94. Tilly, *Financial Institutions*, p. 115.

95. Cameron, "Founding the Bank of Darmstadt"; Riesser, *The Great German Banks*, pp. 56-57.

96. Benaerts, *Les Origines de la grande industrie allemande*, p. 275.

97. Compare the British episode of 1833 (described earlier in this chapter) when joint-stock banks were created in England within 65 miles of London, over the objection of the Bank of England, through the discovery of a loophole in the 1826 law.

98. Tilly, *Financial Institutions*, p. 115.

99. Ibid., p. 118.

100. Böhme, *Deutschlands Weg zur Grossmacht*, p. 219; *Frankfurt und Hamburg*, pp. 151-153. For a discussion of the Frankfurt money and capital market more generally, see Heyn, "Private Banking and Industrialization."

101. Tilly, *Financial Institutions*, p. 138.

102. Quoted by Blumberg, "Die Finanzierung der Neugründungen," p. 172.

103. Ibid., pp. 199-200.

104. Landes, "The Bleichröder Bank," p. 206.

105. Böhme, *Frankfurt und Hamburg*, p. 254.

106. Ibid., pp. 266-270; Rosenberg, *Die Weltwirtschaftskrise*, pp. 128 ff.

107. Böhme, *Deutschlands Weg zur Grossmacht*, p. 219; *Frankfurt und Hamburg*, p. 236.

108. Helfferich, *Georg von Siemens*, p. 27.

109. Brockhage, *Zur Entwicklung des preussischdeutschen Kapitalexports*, p. 56.

110. Ibid., pp. 208-209.

111. Helfferich, *Georg von Siemens*, pp. 31, 38, 41.

112. Ibid., p. 34.

113. Wiskemann, *Hamburg und die Welthandelspolitik*, p. 206.

114. Helfferich, *Georg von Siemens*, p. 43.

115. Ibid., p. 58.

116. Ibid., p. 111.

117. Whale, *Joint-Stock Banking in Germany,* pp. 27-28.

118. *Hundert Jahre im Dienst der Deutschen Wirtschaft.*

119. Ibid., p. 42.

120. Ibid., p. 48.

121. Riesser, *The Great German Banks,* p. 654.

122. In 1900, for example, the Midlands Bank, finding itself with few branches south of a London-Bath line, created a network in the area (Crick and Wadsworth, *Joint-Stock Banking,* p. 341).

123. Brockhage, *Zur Entwicklung des preussischdeutschen Kapitalexports.*

124. Wiskemann, *Hamburg und die Welthandelspolitik,* p. 237.

125. Ibid., p. 238.

126. Baar, "Probleme der industriellen Revolution," p. 531.

127. Böhme, *Deutschlands Weg zur Grossmacht,* p. 333; Borchardt, "Industrial Revolution in Germany," p. 152.

128. Duncan et al., *Metropolis and Region,* p. 81.

129. Deutsche Bank, letter of Jan. 25, 1973; Seidenzahl, *100 Jahre Deutsche Bank,* pp. 375 ff.; Wechsberg, *The Merchant Bankers,* pp. 260 ff.

130. Myers, *New York Money Market,* p. 6.

131. Luzzatto, *Storia economica,* p. 160.

132. Romani, *Italia nel secolo XIX,* p. 591.

133. Greenfield, *Economics and Liberalism,* p. 142.

134. Luzzatto, *L'economia italiana,* pp. 63 ff.

135. Gerschenkron, *Continuity in History,* p. 88.

136. Cameron, *Banking and Economic Development,* p. 18.

137. Cohen, "Financing Industrialization."

138. Cohen, in Cameron, *Banking and Economic Development,* p. 60.

139. Clough, *Economic History of Modern Italy,* p. 125.

140. Luzzatto, *L'economia italiana,* p. 105.

141. Clough, *Economic History of Modern Italy,* p. 12.

142. Luzzatto, *L'economia italiana,* pp. 211-212.

143. Smith, *Italy,* p. 163.

144. Pareto, *Le Marché financier italien* 1894, p. 59.

145. Luzzatto, *L'economia italiana,* p. 266.

146. Ibid., p. 250. An earlier failure of the Banca di Milano was the result of the failure in 1882 of the Union génerále of Paris, which had created it.

147. Fanno, *Le Banche e il mercato monetario,* p. 92n.

148. Luzzatto, *Storia economica,* p. 465.

149. Bonelli, *La Crisi del 1907,* pp. 29-37.

150. There is irony in the fact that the Banca di Torino (the Società delle Ferrovie de Gottardo) helped finance the Gotthard route (Castronovo, *Economia e societa in Piemonte,* p. 116).

151. Ibid., pp. 200 ff., 215 ff., 243.

152. Schwarzenbach, "The Swiss Money Market," pp. 482-483.

153. Ibid., p. 497.

154. Ibid., p. 519.

155. Iklé, *Switzerland,* p. 10.

156. Lévy-Leboyer, *Les Banques européennes,* pp. 425, 431.

157. Ibid., p. 432n.

158. Iklé, *Switzerland,* p. 14.

159. Gille, *La Banque en France,* p. 88.

160. *Union Bank of Switzerland,* p. 55.

161. Iklé, *Switzerland,* p. 18.

162. *Union Bank of Switzerland,* pp. 38-39.

163. Iklé, *Switzerland,* p. 15.

164. *Union Bank of Switzerland,* p. 74.

165. Ibid., pp. 86-88, 132.

166. Schwarzenbach, "The Swiss Money Market," pp. 484-486.

167. Jöhr, *Die schweizerischen Notenbanken,* p. 457.

168. Neufeld, *Financial System of Canada,* p. 39.

169. Bank of Montreal, *Centenary,* p. 14.

170. Neufeld, *Financial System of Canada,* p. 123.

171. Ross, *Canadian Bank of Commerce,* vol. 1, p. 22.

172. *Royal Bank of Canada,* p. 17.

173. It is significant that in the same year, poised on the brink of decline, Halifax established the first clearinghouse in Canada; this example was quickly followed by Montreal (1889), Toronto and Hamilton (1891), and Winnipeg (Jamieson, *Chartered Banking in Canada,* p. 25).

174. Ibid., pp. 17-24.

175. *Bank of Nova Scotia,* pp. 81, 83.

176. Neufeld, *Financial System of Canada,* pp. 488-489.

177. Ibid., p. 573.

178. Botha, "Canadian Money Market," pp. 138, 143.

179. *Report,* pp. 294-315.

180. For size in selected years from 1870 to 1970, see Neufeld, *Financial System of Canada,* table 4.6, p. 98.

181. Royal Commission on Banking and Finance, *Report,* p. 343.

182. *Rise of Toronto,* p. 211.

183. As this study was being prepared for publication, Dr. Irving Silver of the Canadian Ministry of State for Urban Affairs kindly called my attention to an article that appeared in the *Montreal Gazette* on May 28, 1974. It reported that a study by Professor Andre Ryba of the University of Montreal established that stock-market, money-market, bond-market, and banking activities are all gradually shifting to Toronto. In particular, both the Royal Bank of Canada and the Bank of Montreal have shifted their "vital money market 'trading desks' to Toronto."

184. Gras, *Introduction to Economic History.*

185. Masters, *Rise of Toronto.*

186. Glazebrook, *Story of Toronto,* pp. 193-194.

187. Masters, *Rise of Toronto,* p. 59.

188. Ibid., p. 97.

189. Ray, "Regional Aspects of Foreign Ownership," pp. 40, 41.

190. Royal Commission on Banking and Finance, *Report,* pp. 322-323.

191. Kerr, "Metropolitan Dominance in Canada," p. 538.

192. Ibid., p. 545.

193. Note that in Australia there are two main money markets—an old one, Melbourne, and a new one, Sydney, with "Sydney tending to become the more important of the two, partly because the Head Office of the Reserve Bank is there" (Wilson, "Australian Money Market," p. 49). This case is worth comparing with that of Canada and may help determine the role in the slow rise of Toronto played by the cultural differences between French Montreal and British Toronto.

194. Masters, *Rise of Toronto,* p. 212.

195. Botha, "Canadian Money Market," pp. 138-143; Eaton and Bond, "Canada's Newest Money Market," p. 15.

196. Royal Commission on Banking and Finance, *Report,* p. 344.

197. *Royal Bank of Canada,* p. 17.

198. Albion, *Rise of New York Port.*

199. Gras, *Introduction to Economic History.*

200. Myers, *New York Money Market.*

201. Robbins and Terleckyj, *Money Metropolis.*

202. Albion, *Rise of New York Port,* pp. 1-93.

203. Ibid., pp. 378-381.

204. Kouwenhoven, *Partners in Banking,* pp. 20-31.

205. Hidy, "George Peabody," pp. 15, 95, 136, 237.

206. Albion, *Rise of New York Port,* pp. 238-242.

207. Myers, *New York Money Market,* chap. 6.

208. Ibid., chap. 11.

209. Ibid., p. 240.

210. Gras, *Introduction to Economic History,* p. 266.

211. Ibid.

212. Lösch, *Economics of Location,* pp. 461 ff; Riefler, *Money Rates and Money Markets* pp. 65, 72.

213. Riefler, *Money Rates and Money Markets,* p. 74.

214. Robbins and Terleckyj, *Money Metropolis,* p. 85.

215. Brown, *A Hundred Years of Merchant Banking.*

216. Redlich, *American Banking, Men and Ideas,* pt. 2, p. 60.

217. *In Memoriam, Jesse Seligmann,* p. 115.

218. Hopkinson, *Drexel & Co.*

219. Brockhage, *Zur Entwicklung des preussischdeutschen Kapitalexports,* pp. 34-35.

220. Ibid., p. 54.

221. Leighton-Boyce, *Smiths, the Bankers,* pp. 10, 61, 205.

222. Rosenberg, *Die Weltwirtschaftskrise,* p. 38.

223. Crick and Wadsworth, *Joint-Stock Banking,* p. 307.

224. Cameron, *France and the Economic Development of Europe.*

225. Bagehot, *Lombard Street,* p. 16.

226. Newbold, "Beginnings of World Crisis," p. 438.

227. Jeffrys, "Business Organisation in Great Britain," pp. 62, 121.

228. Kindleberger, *Economic Growth in France and Britain,* pp. 61-64.

229. Cecil, *Albert Ballin.*

230. Wiskemann, *Hamburg und die Welthandelspolitik,* p. 273.

231. Abrahams, "Foreign Expansion of American Finance," p. 10.

232. *Foreign Expansion of American Banks,* p. iii.

233. Abrahams, "Foreign Expansion of American Finance," p. 53.

234. Kindleberger, *The World in Depression.*

235. U.S. Department of State, *Foreign Relations,* vol. 3, pp. 269, 272.

236. *Development of a European Capital Market.*

237. "Report to the Council and the Commission on the Realization by Stages of Economic and Monetary Union."

238. De Mattia, *L'unificazione monetaria italiana;* Luzzatto, *L'economia italiana,* pp. 60 ff.

239. Interbank Research Organization, *The Future of London,* pp. 1-8.

240. Robbins and Terleckyj, *Money Metropolis,* p. 35.

241. Ibid.

242. Robinson, *Money and Capital Markets,* pp. 19, 202.

243. Yassukovich, "International Capital Market"; see also Low, "Improving the Secondary Market"; Lutz, "Problems of the Secondary Market."

244. Low, "Improving the Secondary Market," pp. 1157-1158.

245. McRae, "Barclay's Euro-clearing System."

246. Low, "Euroclear Opens Up," p. 31.

247. Kohn, "Eurobonds," p. 70.

248. Ibid., p. 68.

249. Duncan et al., *Metropolis and Region.*

250. "U.S. Manufacturing Subsidiaries in Canada."

251. "In all, some 450 international companies have their main European offices in Brussels, a total rivalled only by Paris" (International Research Organisation, *The Future of London,* pp. 22). And following them, two American banks — the Chase Manhattan and the Security Pacific — have located their European headquarters in Brussels rather than London.

5. Commercial Expansion and the Industrial Revolution

1. I have been aided in writing this paper by comments and suggestions from Rondo Cameron, François Crouzet, Robert Forster, Donald N. McCloskey, Franklin F. Mendels, Joel Mokyr, and R. G. Wilson. They are, however, absolved of all responsibility for errors of fact or judgment.

2. Minchinton, *Growth of English Overseas Trade,* p. 51.

3. Bairoch, "Commerce international," p. 544; Deane, *First Industrial Revolution,* p. 68.

4. Gras, *Business and Capitalism,* passim.

5. Smith, *Wealth of Nations,* pp. 113-114.

6. Ibid., p. 112.

7. Marshall, *Industry and Trade,* p. 33.

8. Wright, *Free Trade and Protection*, pp. 1-6.

9. Haley, *Dutch in the Seventeenth Century*, p. 19.

10. Barbour, "Dutch and English Merchant Shipping," pp. 119-124.

11. Ibid., p. 132.

12. Scoville, *Persecution of Huguenots*, pp. 341-347.

13. Wilson, *Dutch Republic*, chap. 5.

14. Smith, *Wealth of Nations*, p. 354.

15. Wright, *Free Trade and Protection*, p. 59.

16. Boxer, "Dutch Economic Decline," pp. 245, 259.

17. Cipolla, *Economic Decline of Empires*, pp. 8-9.

18. Mokyr, *Industrial Growth* and "Industrial Revolution." See also Smith, *Wealth of Nations*, pp. 826-827, 837.

19. Mokyr, "Industrial Revolution," chap. 6; Wright, *Free Trade and Protection*, passim.

20. Habakkuk, *American and British Technology*, passim; Crouzet, "Croissances comparées," p. 288.

21. Gee, *Trade and Navigation of Great Britain*, p. 128, quoted by Smith in *Wealth of Nations*, p. 96.

22. Hoskins, *Industry, Trade and People in Exeter*, pp. 69-74; Wilson, *Anglo-Dutch Commerce*, p. 39.

23. Wilson, *Anglo-Dutch Commerce*, pp. 55-56.

24. Crouzet, "Economie et société," p. 256.

25. Wright, *Free Trade and Protection*, p. 171.

26. Wilson, *Anglo-Dutch Commerce*, p. 187.

27. Olivieri, "An Urban Case History," pp. 454-456.

28. Smith, *Wealth of Nations*, p. 395.

29. Ibid., pp. 421-422.

30. Ibid., p. 403.

31. Haley, *Dutch in the Seventeenth Century*, p. 49; Wilson, *Dutch Republic*, p. 35; for a contrary view see Geyl, *Netherlands in the Seventeenth Century*, p. 164.

32. *Anglo-Dutch Commerce*, p. 188.

33. McNeill, *Venice*.

34. Williams, *Ancien Régime in Europe*, p. 484.

35. Wilson, *England's Apprenticeship*, p. 40.

36. Mantoux, *Industrial Revolution*, p. 92.

37. Wilson, *Dutch Republic*, p. 31.

38. Barbour, "Dutch and English Merchant Shipping," p. 114.

39. Williams, *Ancien Régime in Europe*, p. 484.

40. Davis, "English Foreign Trade, 1660-1700," p. 94.

41. Ibid., p. 95.

42. Price, *France and the Chesapeake*, vol. 1, p. 590.

43. Pares, *A West-India Fortune*.

44. Checkland, *The Gladstones*.

45. Pares, *A West-India Fortune*, p. 141.

46. Ibid., p. 331.

47. Ibid., p. 319.
48. Checkland, *The Gladstones,* p. 176.
49. Ibid., pp. 182-123.
50. Ibid., p. 198.
51. Minchinton, *Growth of English Overseas Trade,* p. 43.
52. Minchinton, *Trade of Bristol,* p. xv.
53. Minchinton, *Growth of English Overseas Trade,* p. 44.
54. Campbell, "Economic History of Scotland," pp. 17-19.
55. Devine, "Glasgow Colonial Merchants," passim.
56. Minchinton, *Growth of English Overseas Trade,* p. 47.
57. Crouzet, *Capital Formation,* passim.
58. Westerfield, *Middlemen in English Business,* pp. 413, 417, 419.
59. Court, *Rise of the Midland Industries,* chap. 9.
60. Wilson, "Denisons and Milneses," p. 147.
61. Wilson, *Gentlemen Merchants,* p. 82.
62. Prest, *Industrial Revolution in Coventry,* p. 49.
63. Wadsworth and Mann, *Cotton Trade and Lancashire,* p. 237.
64. Edwards, *Growth of British Cotton Trade,* pp. 107, 151, 171, 176.
65. Ibid., p. 181.
66. Wilson, "Entrepreneur in the Industrial Revolution," p. 180.
67. Allen, *British Industries,* p. 260.
68. Robson, *Cotton Industry in Britain,* pp. 92-95.
69. Mantoux, *Industrial Revolution,* p. 65.
70. Hoskins, *Industry, Trade and People in Exeter,* chaps. 2, 3.
71. Wilson, "Entrepreneur in the Industrial Revolution," p. 177.
72. Hoskins, *Industry, Trade and People in Exeter,* p. 53.
73. Heaton, *Yorkshire Woollen and Worsted Industries,* p. xix.
74. Gras, *Business and Capitalism,* p. 178.
75. Heaton, *Yorkshire Woollen and Worsted Industries,* p. xx.
76. Wilson, *Gentlemen Merchants,* p. 60.
77. Wilson, "Denisons and Milneses," p. 151.
78. Wilson, *Gentlemen Merchants,* pp. 6-7.
79. Ibid., pp. 56, 75.
80. Ibid., p. 57.
81. "English Foreign Trade, 1700-1774," p. 106.
82. Court, *Rise of the Midland Industries,* pp. 199-206.
83. John, *Industrial Development of South Wales,* chaps. 2, 6.
84. Hughes, *North Country Life,* vol. 1, pp. 7, 51, 58, 59, 69.
85. *Hull in the Eighteenth Century,* p. 101.
86. Fitton and Wadsworth, *The Strutts and the Arkwrights,* pp. 63-64.
87. Wadsworth and Mann, *Cotton Trade and Lancashire,* p. 239.
88. *Fortunes Made in Business.*
89. Fox Bourne, *English Merchants,* p. 189.
90. "Commerce international," passim.
91. Meyer, *L'Armement nantais,* pp. 66, 252.
92. Dornic, *L'Industrie textile dans Le Maine,* p. 103.

93. "Economie et société," p. 210.

94. Ibid., p. 275.

95. "Croissances comparées" p. 265.

96. Meyer, *L'Armement nantais,* pp. 164, 225.

97. Quoted ibid., p. 207.

98. Crouzet, "Economie et société," pp. 213-214; Poussou, "Structures demographiques," p. 345.

99. Carrière, *Négociants marseillais,* p. 280.

100. Scoville, *Persecution of Huguenots,* chap. 2.

101. Meyer, *L'Armement nantais,* p. 173.

102. Dermigny, *Cargaisons indiennes,* vol. 1, p. 209.

103. Carrière, *Négociants marseillais,* pp. 930 ff.

104. Carrière, *Négociants marseillais,* p. 279; Cavignac, *Jean Pellet,* p. 30.

105. Carrière, *Négociants marseillais,* p. 274.

106. Mathorez, *Les Etrangers en France,* chap. 2, sec. 1.

107. Cavignac, *Jean Pellet,* p. 30; Thésée, *Négociants bordelais,* p. 10.

108. Poussou, "Structures demographiques," pp. 349-350.

109. Léon, *Marchands et speculateurs dauphinois,* p. 87.

110. Dermigny, *Cargaisons indiennes,* passim.

111. Dornic, *L'Industrie textile dans Le Maine,* p. 171.

112. Daumard, *Les Bourgeois de Paris,* p. 368.

113. Price, *France and the Chesapeake,* vol. 1, p. 368.

114. Dardel, *Commerce, industrie et navigation,* p. 119.

115. Ladurie, *Les Paysans de Languedoc,* pp. 123-126.

116. Goubert, *Familles marchands sous l'Ancien Régime,* pp. 29, 71, 103.

117. Bergeron, "Paris dans l'organisation des échanges intérieurs," p. 19.

118. Ibid.

119. Garden, "Le Commerce lyonnais," p. 20.

120. Ibid., p. 24.

121. Dornic, *L'Industrie textile dans Le Maine,* pp. 45, 59.

122. Ibid., p. 53.

123. Ibid., pp. 1, 43, 100, 105.

124. Ibid., p. 109.

125. Cavignac, *Jean Pellet,* p. 132.

126. Ibid.

127. Borchardt, "Industrial Revolution in Germany," pp. 89-90, 145-146; Kocka, "Expansion, Integration, Diversifikation," p. 9.

128. Jacob, *Agriculture, Manufactures, Statistics and Society,* pp. 94, 116, 225.

129. Schremmer, *Die Wirtschaft Bayerns,* p. 594.

130. Fischer, *Der Staat und Industrialisierung,* p. 79.

131. Rauers, *Bremer Handelsgeschichte,* pp. 13-15.

132. Eckardt, *Lebenserinnungen,* vol. 1, p. 200.

133. Schramm, "Hamburg und die Adelsfrage," p. 82.

134. Böhme, *Frankfurt und Hamburg,* passim.

135. Kisch, "From Monopoly to Laissez-Faire," pp. 347, 363, 383, 387.

136. Kisch, "Textile Industries in Silesia," p. 543.

137. Ibid., p. 552.

138. Blumberg, "Geschichte der deutschen Leinenindustrie," p. 99.

139. Zunkel, *Der rheinische-westfälische Unternehmer*, chap. 11.

140. Ibid., p. 25.

141. Adelmann, "Structural Change," p. 86.

142. Wutzmer, "Die Herkunft der industrielle Bourgeoisie Preussens," pp. 148-150.

143. Zunkel, *Der rheinische-westfälische Unternehmer*, p. 26.

144. Aycoberry, "Probleme der Sozialschichtung in Köln," p. 518.

145. Braun, *Sozialer Wandel in einem Industriegebiet*, p. 78.

146. Ibid., pp. 263-264.

147. Kehr, *Der Primat der Innenpolitik*, p. 153.

148. Zunkel, *Der rheinische-westfälische Unternehmer*, p. 13.

149. Ucke, *Die Agrarkrise in Preussen*, pp. 8, 11.

150. Kisch, "Textile Industries in Silesia," p. 552.

151. Abel, *Geschichte der deutschen Landwirtschaft*, p. 304.

152. Bramsted, *Aristocracy and the Middle-Classes in Germany*, p. 54.

153. Hardach, "German Economic Historiography," pp. 67 ff.

154. Jankowski, "Law, Economic Policy and Private Enterprise," pp. 718 ff.

155. Hatzfeld, "Kaufmannische Probleme," p. 204.

156. Kocka, *Unternehmungsverwaltung und Angestelltenschaft*, p. 126.

157. Ibid., p. 165.

158. Beer, *Emergence of the German Dye Industry*, p. 95.

159. Hohenburg, *Chemicals in Western Europe*, pp. 127 ff.

160. Benaerts, *Les Origines de la grande industrie allemande*, pp. 121-122.

161. Quoted in ibid., p. 123.

162. Aycoberry, "Probleme der Sozialschichtung in Köln," p. 515.

163. Borchardt, "Zur Frage des Kapitalmangels," passim.

164. Westerfield, *Middlemen in English Business*, p. 412.

165. Daumard, *Les Bourgeois de Paris*, p. 8.

6. European Port Cities

1. This chapter was originally presented as the Marc Bloch lecture at the International Center for European Studies at the University of Quebec at Montreal, on April 14, 1976. Its revised form benefited from the comments and suggestions of Jake Knoppers, Josef Konvitz, and Arthur Schweitzer.

2. *Economy and Society*, vol. 3, p. 1289.

3. *The Mediterranean*, vol. 1, p. 38, n. 60.

4. *Travels through Germany*, pp. 314-315.

5. *La Révolution industrielle*, chap. 1.

6. Young, *Travels in France*, p. 55.

7. Braudel, *The Mediterranean*, vol. 1, p. 39.

8. Bull, *Sozialgeschichte der norwegische Demokratie*, pp. 22-23.

9. Kellenbenz, forward to Beutin, p. xxiii. Even in the twentieth century, this coast still has tidal waves, most recently in 1963, and it was heavily threatened again in January 1976. Cf. "North Sea Coast Super-Floods Cause Anxiety," from the *Munich Mercury,* January 23, 1976, summarized in the *German Tribune,* February 8, 1976, p. 9.

10. Glick, *Irrigation in Medieval Valencia,* pp. 1-12.

11. Clifford, *Draining of the Fens,* pp. 1-5.

12. Ibid., p. 40. Mr. Knoppers informs me that in Dutch Friesland, the king had to impose a solution because various landowners would not contribute their share of the cost of draining — in fact, actually resisted it — and this led to disputes between abutters and king about who owned the land. This may be relevant to the historical record of the royal house preventing strength among the nobles in Denmark, as discussed in Chapter 2.

13. Drake, *Population in Norway,* pp. 82-84.

14. Braudel, *The Mediterranean,* vol. 1, p. 68.

15. Weber, *Economy and Society,* vol. 3, pp. 1323, 1326.

16. Fox, *History in Geographic Perspective,* passim. Adam Smith makes much the same distinction.

17. Ibid., p. 47.

18. Weber, *Economy and Society,* vol. 3, p. 1215.

19. Vernon, *Metropolis, 1985.*

20. Price, "Economic Function of American Ports," p. 139.

21. Cecil, *Albert Ballin,* p. 9.

22. Price, "Economic Function of American Ports," pp. 138-172.

23. Van Houtte, "Belgium and the Netherlands," p. 107; Wiskemann, *Hamburg und die Welthandelspolitik,* p. 259.

24. For Bremen and Hamburg see Engelsing, "Technik in der deutschen Seeschiffahrt," p. 500. The Nantes-Bordeaux comparison is implicit in Crouzet, "Economie et société," and Meyer, *L'Armement nantais.*

25. The inclusion of Marseille in this list seems misleading unless the twentieth century is meant. See Braudel, *The Mediterranean,* vol. 1, p. 220.

26. Ibid., p. 108.

27. McNeill, *Venice,* pp. 56, 76, 132.

28. Ibid., p. 22.

29. Rapp, "Unmaking of Mediterranean Trade Hegemony."

30. Luzzatto, *Storia economica,* p. 166. But see Pullen, "Crisis in the Venetian Economy," who objects to the view that the Venetians misinvested their capital in mainland properties and villas and insists that they invested in Spain through the Genoese, speculated on the money markets of Europe, and served as a clearing house for bills of exchange.

31. Braudel, *The Mediterranean,* vol. 1, p. 389.

32. *Storia economica,* p. 151.

33. Bulferetti and Costanti, *Industria e commercio in Liguria,* p. 122.

34. Braudel, *The Mediterranean,* vol. 1, pp. 342-344.

35. Bulferetti and Costanti, *Industria e commercio in Liguria,* pp. 223-227.

36. Smith, *Italy*, pp. 35-37.

37. Roberts, "Lombardy," p. 65.

38. McNeill, *Venice*, p. 227.

39. Even in banking the Genoese ultimately lost their perspective. Cavour notes that the Genoese bankers thought that Turin would never become a banking center. See Romani, *Storia economica d'Italia*, p. 591.

40. See Barbour, "Dutch and English Merchant Shipping."

41. See page 143 above.

42. Carter, *Getting, Spending and Investing*, pp. 40-41. On p. 122 she suggests that the movement from Amsterdam occurred at the end of the eighteenth century.

43. Buist, *Hope & Co.*, p. 18. A further discussion of the aristocratization of the Dutch oligarchs is given in Swart, "Holland's Bourgeoisie," p. 46.

44. See Krantz and Hohenberg, *Failed Transitions*, pp. 62, 65.

45. Van Houtte, "Belgium and the Netherlands," pp. 102-103.

46. *Economy and Society*, vol. 2, p. 479.

47. Price, "Economic Function of American Ports," p. 149.

48. Schramm, "Hamburg und die Adelsfrage," p. 89. Eckardt wrote in 1910 that a few daughters of the highest society who married Prussian officers were regarded as curiosities. See *Lebenserinnerungen*, vol. 1, p. 200. These references were kindly furnished me by Edouard Rosenbaum.

49. Eckardt, *Lebenserinnerungen*, vol. 1, p. 205.

50. Böhme, *Frankfurt und Hamburg*.

51. Ibid., p. 200.

52. Ibid., pp. 39, 67.

53. Young, *Travels in France*, p. 56.

54. Ibid., p. 96.

55. Cavignac, *Jean Pellet*, p. 304.

56. Young, *Travels in France*, p. 83.

57. Moore, *Social Origins of Dictatorship and Democracy*, p. 64.

58. Meyer, *L'Armement nantais*, p. 64.

59. Moore, *Social Origins of Dictatorship and Democracy*, pp. 47-49.

60. Smith, *Wealth of Nations*, p. 384.

61. Ibid., p. 319.

62. See Forster, review of Carrière, p. 164.

63. Benaerts, "Les Hommes," p. 231.

64. Poussou, "Structures demographiques et sociales," p. 357. Note that of the five family groups ennobled in Nantes in the first half of the eighteenth century and the nine in the second half, a number were foreign—generally Irish, and hence Catholic, with some English (presumably also Catholic) refugees. See Meyer, *L'Armement nantais*, p. 91.

65. Cavignac, *Jean Pellet*, p. 325.

66. Forster, review of Carrière, p. 164.

67. Konvitz, "Grandeur in French City Planning." This essay is part of a larger work on "Port City Planning in Early Modern Europe" that Professor Konvitz is engaged in.

7. Germany's Overtaking of England, 1806 to 1914

1. This chapter is based on four lectures given in Professor S. B. Saul's seminar in economic history at the University of Edinburgh in January 1974. The superficial excuse for choosing the topic is set out in the first paragraph. The underlying reason is that in 1971 I read German economic history for four months at the Institut für Weltwirtschaft at the University of Kiel, and the seminar afforded an opportunity to organize that material.

2. Crouzet, "Western Europe and Great Britain," pp. 98 ff.

3. Rostow, *Stages of Economic Growth;* Hardach, "German Economic Historiography," pp. 60-61, 66-70.

4. *Economic Aspects of Sovereignty.*

5. Kocka, *Unternehmungsverwaltung und Angestelltenschaft,* vol. 2, p. 79.

6. Redlich, "Frühindustrielle Unternehmer," p. 408. (Translations of all quotations in this chapter taken from non-English sources are my own.)

7. For the contemporaneous view of another German-Swiss engineer, J. G. Bodmer, who visited Birmingham in 1816-1817 and found some unevenness in British development, with much handwork of a primitive kind side by side with much more elaborate technical process, see Court, *Rise of the Midland Industries.*

8. Crouzet, "Croissances comparées," pp. 139, 147, 150.

9. *The German People,* pp. 50-52.

10. Ritter, *Die Rolle des Staates,* p. 34.

11. *Les Origines de la grande industrie allemande,* p. 119.

12. Ibid., p. 369.

13. Adelmann, "Structural Change," p. 88.

14. Abel, *Geschichte der deutschen Landwirtschaft,* pp. 258 ff.

15. The absence of commerce is stressed by William Jacob, a visitor to Germany in 1819. Of Münster, he says "little commerce" (*Agriculture, Manufactures, Statistics and Society,* p. 94); further, "Commerce, of Hanover inconsiderable despite connection to Bremen" (p. 116); "Berlin is not a commercial city, there is no great enterprise, and no great efforts diverted to make it become one" (p. 204); "A body of merchants and manufacturers, who by their capital give employment to numerous workmen, and who like country gentlemen are too rich to be dependent on the smiles or frowns of the court, is not to be found in Prussia" (p. 225).

16. *Der Staat und Industrialisierung,* p. 49.

17. Ibid., p. 90.

18. Benaerts, *Les Origines de la grande industrie allemande,* p. 57.

19. Riesser, *The Great German Banks,* p. 39.

20. Böhme, *Frankfurt und Hamburg,* p. 172; Banfield, *Industry of the Rhine,* ser. 2, p. 196; Bowring, "Prussian Commercial Union," p. 38.

21. Henderson, *Britain and Industrial Europe,* p. 92.

22. Von Bodelschwingh, *Leben des Ober-Präsidenten Vincke,* p. 96.

23. *Agriculture, Manufactures, Statistics and Society,* p. 231.

24. Ritter, *Die Rolle des Staates,* p. 25.

25. Banfield, *Industry of the Rhine,* ser. 2, pp. 222, 224.

26. Ritter, *Die Rolle des Staates,* p. 25.

27. Benaerts, *Borsig et les locomotives en Allemagne,* p. 51.

28. Ritter, *Die Rolle des Staates,* p. 25.

29. "German Economic Historiography," p. 77.

30. Benaerts, *Les Origines de la grande industrie allemande,* p. 344.

31. "Frühindustrielle Unternehmer," p. 342.

32. Ibid.

33. Ibid., p. 368.

34. Hohenberg, *Chemicals in Western Europe,* p. 68.

35. Benaerts, *Les Origines de la grande industrie allemande,* p. 337.

36. *Die Agrarkrise in Preussen,* p. 32.

37. "Prussian Commercial Union," p. 7.

38. Froelich et al., *Political Leadership and Collective Action;* Olson and Zeckhauser, "An Economic Theory of Alliance," pp. 266 ff.

39. Dumke, "Political Economy of Economic Integration."

40. "Prussian Commercial Union," p. 2.

41. Benaerts, *Les Origines de la grande industrie allemande,* p. 74.

42. Lambi, *Free Trade and Protection,* p. 20.

43. Benaerts, *Les Origines de la grande industrie allemande,* p. 66.

44. Williams, *British Commercial Policy,* p. 200.

45. Blumberg, "Geschichte der deutschen Leinenindustrie," p. 99.

46. Bondi, *Deutschlands Aussenhandel,* p. 146.

47. Ibid., p. 44.

48. Brown, *Board of Trade,* p. 113.

49. Crouzet, "Western Europe and Great Britain," pp. 121-122.

50. Semmel, *Rise of Free Trade Imperialism.*

51. Brockhage, *Zur Entwicklung des preussischdeutschen Kapitalexports,* pt. 1, pp. 106, 117, 128.

52. "Zur Frage des Kapitalmangels," p. 412.

53. *Zur Entwicklung des preussischdeutschen Kapitalexports,* pt. 1, p. 52.

54. *Financial Deepening.*

55. *Money and Capital.*

56. "Zur Frage des Kapitalmangels."

57. "Prussian Commercial Union," p. 38.

58. Barkin, *Controversy over German Industrialization,* pp. 150 ff.

59. Ibid., p. 132.

60. Hardach, "German Economic Historiography," p. 51.

61. Wilson, *Anglo-Dutch Commerce,* p. 29.

62. For instance, a "Dutch uncle" is not an uncle, but a harsh and overbearing elder; a "Dutch treat" is not a treat, but an event in which the guest pays his own way; "Dutch courage" is alcohol; "Dutch arithmetic" results in a total larger than the constituent entries; a "Dutch wife" is a pillow; a "Dutch concert" is cacophony; a "Dutch nightingale" is a frog; and so on. Even the opprobrious term "boor" in English is the neutral word in Dutch for a farmer.

63. "Imperialismus und deutscher Schlachtflottenbau," p. 295.

64. Tilly, "Los von England," p. 182.

65. Hardach, "Anglomanie und Anglophobie," pp. 153 ff.

66. Gerschenkron, "Typology of Industrial Development," pp. 499 ff.

67. Rostow, "Beginnings of Modern Growth," p. 573, n. 45.

68. Tilly, *Financial Institutions*, p. 138.

69. Blumberg, "Die Finanzierung der Neugründungen," p. 199.

70. Benaerts, *Les Origines de la grande industrie allemande*, p. 256.

71. "Die Finanzierung der Neugründungen," p. 174.

72. Riesser, *The Great German Banks*, p. 509.

73. Benaerts, *Les Origines de la grande industrie allemande*, p. 277.

74. Böhme, *Prolegomena*, p. 54.

75. "From Monopoly to Laissez-Faire," p. 390.

76. Zunkel, *Der rheinische-westfälische Unternehmer*, p. 252.

77. Ibid., p. 189.

78. Blumberg, "Die Finanzierung der Neugründungen," p. 174.

79. Ibid., p. 196.

80. Details for a few companies (Blumberg, "Die Finanzierung der Neugründungen," pp. 201 ff; Zunkel, *Der rheinische-westfälische Unternehmer*, p. 52) suggest that differences existed between manufacturing and mining, and between the Rhineland and Silesia, with mining and Silesia having the greater numbers of government officials among the original shareholders.

81. Wutzmur, "Die Herkunft der industrielle Bourgeoisie Preussens," p. 148.

82. Kisch, "From Monopoly to Laissez-Faire," pp. 400 ff.

83. Henderson, *Britain and Industrial Europe*, p. 161. On the question of British invention and innovation in the first half of the nineteenth century, consider the statement by Porter, *Progress of the Nation*, p. 262: "Some part of our cotton-spinning is of foreign invention; but the state of mechanical arts not being sufficiently advanced for that purpose in their own countries, the inventors have been obliged to resort to English workshops for the means of perfecting their conceptions."

84. Clapham, *Economic Development of France and Germany*, p. 288.

85. Henderson, *Britain and Industrial Europe*, p. 161.

86. Benaerts, *Borsig et les locomotives en allemagne*, pp. 48-51.

87. Ibid., pp. 51 ff.

88. Ibid., p. 40.

89. Benaerts, *Les Origines de la grande industrie allemande*, p. 358.

90. *Emergence of the German Dye Industry*.

91. Walker, *Germany and the Emigration*, p. 77.

92. Wiskemann, *Hamburg und die Welthandelspolitik*, p. 186.

93. Sturmey, *British Shipping and World Competition*, p. 17.

94. Aycoberry, "Probleme der Sozialschichtung in Köln," p. 513.

95. *Zur Entwicklung des preussischdeutschen Kapitalexports*, pt. 1, pp. 220 ff.

96. Von Borries, *Deutschlands Aussenhandel*, pp. 238 ff.

97. Semmel, *Rise of Free Trade Imperialism*; p. 412.

98. Ibid.

99. *Les Origines de la grande industrie allemande*, p. 353.

100. Ibid.

101. Legge, *Kapital- und Verwaltungsüberfremdung*, p. 45.

102. Sédillot, *La Maison de Wendel*, p. 250.

103. Benaerts, *Les Origines de la grande industrie allemande*, p. 355; but see Legge, *Kapital- und Verwaltungsüberfremdung*, p. 46, who dates the return flow as 1875.

104. Cameron, *France and the Economic Development of Europe*, p. 395.

105. Ibid., p. 403.

106. Wiskemann, *Hamburg und die Welthandelspolitik*, p. 189.

107. Rosenberg, *Die Weltwirtschaftskrise*, p. 128.

108. Böhme, *Frankfurt und Hamburg*, p. 235.

109. Ibid., pp. 266 ff.

110. Rosenbaum, "M. M. Warburg & Co.," p. 126.

111. Böhme, *Frankfurt und Hamburg*, pp. 272-273.

112. A previous example of import substitution can be seen in the period 1830 to 1850, as Rhineland banks began at an early stage to compete with Dutch banks for the finance of Rhenish linen and cotton exports and by 1850 had replaced them (Adelmann, "Structural Change," p. 89).

113. Bondi, *Deutschlands Aussenhandel*, p. 146.

114. Lambi, *Free Trade and Protection*, p. 19.

115. Zorn, "Wirtschafts- und sozialgeschichtliche Zusammenhänge," p. 259.

116. *Stages of Economic Growth*, p. 26.

117. Ibid., p. 27.

118. "Efficiency and Welfare Implications," pp. 49-50.

119. Epstein, "Socio-economic History," p. 111.

120. Lambi, *Free Trade and Protection*, p. 340.

121. Ibid., p. 73.

122. *Controversy over German Industrialization*, p. 33.

123. *Bread and Democracy*, p. 42.

124. Epstein, "Socio-economic History," p. 111.

125. Williams, *British Commercial Policy*, p. 200.

126. Barkin, *Controversy over German Industrialization*, p. 33.

127. Cecil, *Albert Ballin*, p. 264.

128. Levy, *Industrial Germany*, p. 7.

129. Clapham, *Economic Development of France and Germany*, p. 311.

130. Levy, *Industrial Germany*, p. 15.

131. Kocka, *Unternehmungsverwaltung und Angestelltenschaft*, p. 125.

132. Beer, *German Dye Industry*, p. 130.

133. Ibid., p. 99.

134. Kocka, *Unternehmungsverwaltung und Angestelltenschaft*, p. 128.

135. Kindleberger, *Economic Growth in France and Britain*, p. 148.

136. *German Dye Industry*, p. 95.

137. Ibid., p. 96.

138. J. C. Fischer, the Swiss-German metallurgist who visited England frequently between 1794 and 1851, when he was 78 regarded the 1851 exhibition as the peak of materialist development and felt obliged to say, "That's enough, let us

quiet down so that we can once again hear the human spirit" (Redlich, "Frühindustrielle Unternehmer," p. 407).

139. Batty, *The House of Krupp*, p. 61.

140. Ibid., pp. 62 ff.

141. Benaerts, *Borsig et les locomotives en allemagne*, p. 22.

142. Köllmann, *Sozialgeschichte der Stadt Barmen*, pp. 44-45.

143. Beer, *German Dye Industry*, p. 110.

144. Hoffman, *Great Britain and German Trade Rivalry*, p. 77.

145. Beer, *German Dye Industry*, p. 110; Hoffman, *Great Britain and German Trade Rivalry*, p. 119.

146. Hoffman, *Great Britain and German Trade Rivalry*, pp. 45 ff.

147. By E. E. Williams.

148. Beer, *German Dye Industry*, p. 47.

149. Hoffman, *Great Britain and German Trade Rivalry*, p. 168.

150. Ibid., p. 177.

151. Minchinton, *British Tinplate Industry*, pp. 63-71.

152. Saul, *Studies in British Overseas Trade*, pp. 160-161.

153. Hoffman, *Great Britain and German Trade Rivalry*, p. 185.

154. Ibid., p. 285.

155. Bondi, *Deutschlands Aussenhandel*, vol. 5, p. 53.

156. Cecil, *Albert Ballin*, p. 171.

157. Kehr, "Imperialismus und deutscher Schlachtflottenbau."

158. Benaerts, *Les Origines de la grande industrie allemandle*, p. 626.

159. Rosenberg, *Grosse Depression*, vol. 2, p. 55.

160. Böhme, *Prolegomena*, p. 85.

161. Rosenberg, "Political and Social Consequences of the Great Depression," p. 59.

162. Inoki, "Aspects of German Peasant Emigration," p. 214.

163. Girault, *Empruntes russes*, pp. 139 ff.

164. White, *French International Accounts*.

165. Barkin, *Contoversy over German Industrialization*, p. 75.

166. Kehr, *Der Primat der Innenpolitik*, p. 135.

167. Ibid., pp. 133-134.

168. Zorn, "Wirtschaft und Politik," p. 353.

169. "German Economic Historiography."

170. Fogel, *Railroads and American Economic Growth*.

171. In McCloskey, *Essays on a Mature Economy*.

172. McCloskey, *Economic Maturity and Entrepreneurial Decline*.

173. In McCloskey, *Essays on a Mature Economy*, p. 106.

174. Fogel, *Railroads and American Economic Growth*.

175. *Essays on a Mature Economy*.

176. *Economic Maturity and Entrepreneurial Decline*.

177. McCloskey, *Essays on a Mature Economy*, p. 106.

178. Kindleberger, *Economic Growth in France and Britain*, p. 325.

179. "An Input-Output Approach," pp. 12-15.

180. McCloskey, "Did Victorian Britain Fail?", pp. 446 ff.

181. Saul, "Engineering Industry," p. 191.

182. Ibid., pp. 192, 206, 215, 216.

183. Rimmer, *Marshall of Leeds.*

184. Barker, "Glass Industry," p. 318.

185. Saul, "Engineering Industry," pp. 187, 233.

186. *Economic Maturity and Entrepreneurial Decline,* p. 56, note.

187. *British Industrialists,* pp. 35, 59.

188. "Relative Decline of the British Steel Industry," pp. 140 ff.

189. Minchinton, *British Tinplate Industry,* pp. 24, 29.

190. *Essays on a Mature Economy.*

191. Burn, *Economic History of Steelmaking,* p. 169, note.

192. Andrews and Brunner, *Capital Development in Steel,* p. 135.

193. "Did Victorian Britain Fail?", p. 447.

194. Andrews and Brunner, *Capital Development in Steel,* pp. 125-130.

195. Ibid., pp. 204-207.

196. Carter and Williams, *Industry and Technical Progress,* p. 206.

197. Cook, *Effects of Mergers,* p. 305.

198. Andrews and Brunner, *Capital Development in Steel,* p. 96.

199. Saul, "Engineering Industry," p. 215. The bicycle industry rose in Coventry on the ruins of the ribbon trade, which had been overwhelmed by French competition consequent to the Anglo-French Commercial Treaty of 1860. It took advantage of cheap labor from the prostrate textile industry and skilled labor previously engaged in watch- and clockmaking. See Prest, *Industrial Revolution in Coventry,* p. 4.

200. Richardson, "Chemicals," p. 302.

201. Ibid.

202. Burn, *Economic History of Steelmaking,* p. 296; Minchinton, *British Tinplate Industry,* p. 195.

203. Byatt, "Electrical Products," p. 252.

204. Rimmer, *Marshall of Leeds,* pp. 265, 267.

205. "Electrical Products," pp. 245, 249.

206. Saul, "Engineering Industry," p. 207.

207. Harley, "Skilled Labour," pp. 391 ff.

208. Crouzet, "Croissances comparées," pp. 139. ff.

209. Mokyr, "Industrial Revolution," pp. 365 ff.

210. The drawn-out replacement of the Leblanc by the Solvay process in the production of caustic, bleach, and soda ash is one of the few examples of nonprofit-maximizing behavior found by the new economic historians. See Lindert and Trace, "Yardsticks for Victorian Entrepreneurs," pp. 239 ff. A post-World War I example has been presented by Henning and Trace, "Britain and the Motorship," pp. 353 ff. They conclude that it would have been profitable for British shipowners like Danish to shift to motorships, but the decision and actions to change were taken much more slowly.

211. Robson, *Cotton Industry in Britain,* pp. 92-95.

212. Landes, "Technological Change," p. 495.

213. Saul, "Engineering Industry," p. 212.

214. *British Industries and Their Organization,* pp. 229, 238. This author believes that Lancashire was slow in adopting mechanical improvements—ring spindles, automatic looms, and high-speed winding (p. 247)—but a later economic historian argues that the failure of the industry in the interwar period cannot be blamed on technological backwardness or entrepreneurial ineptitude (Sandberg, *Lancashire in Decline*).

215. Chandler, *Strategy and Structure.*

216. The absence of a highly developed commercial network of merchants outside the Rhineland and the Hanseatic cities may have been a benefit for Germany in an age of technological complexity, since it required emerging firms to perform the merchanting functions (assembling inputs and marketing outputs) largely by themselves. This accounts for the larger average size of German, compared with British, firms.

217. *Chemicals in Western Europe.*

218. Saul, "Engineering Industry," p. 202.

219. Byatt, "Electrical Products," pp. 269, 272.

220. Byatt, "Electrical Products," p. 272; Saul, "Engineering Industry," p. 231 ff.

221. Burn, *Economic History of Steelmaking,* p. 199.

222. See McKay, *Tramways and Trolleys,* pp. 181-184.

223. Burnham and Hoskins, *Iron and Steel in Britain,* p. 80.

224. Ibid., pp. 210-211.

225. "Did Victorian Britain Fail?"

226. Coppock, "Climacteric of the 1890's," pp. 1 ff.

227. "Engineering Industry," pp. 192, 200, 206, 213. See also Byatt, "Electrical Products," pp. 244 ff.

228. Saul, "Engineering Industry," p. 226.

229. Byatt, "Electrical Products," p. 255.

230. Richardson, "Chemicals," p. 287.

231. *Economic Growth in France and Britain,* pp. 128 ff.

232. Habakkuk, *American and British Technology,* p. 191.

233. Thackray, "Natural Knowledge in Cultural Context," pp. 672 ff.

234. *Technical Change and Education,* p. 120.

235. *Technical Education and Social Change.*

236. Coleman, "Gentlemen and Players," pp. 105-107.

237. Erickson, *British Industrialists,* pp. 12, 73.

8. Conclusion

1. "History and the Social Sciences," p. 28.

2. Conversation with Professor Pedersen at the Sixth International Congress of Economic History, Copenhagen, August 1974.

3. *L'Economia italiana,* p. 219.

4. Romeo, *Risorgimento and capitalismo,* pp. 167-169.

5. Evans, *History of the Commercial Crisis,* pp. 113-114.

6. "Quebec's New Government."

7. *Afterthoughts on Material Life.*

8. See Bairoch, *Commerce exterieur et développement économique.* While Bairoch recognizes that the response of an economy to external stimuli is conditioned by its structure, he concludes rather too facilely that a leading developed country benefits from free trade, a lagging country from tariffs.

9. See Girard, "Transport."

10. For a discussion of causality in economic history that takes swipes at mathematical model building and at counterfactual speculation, see McClelland, *Causal Explanation.*

11. Stone, "History and the Social Sciences," p. 19.

Bibliography

Abel, Wilhelm. *Geschichte der deutsche Landwirtschaft vom frühen Mittelalter bis zum 19. Jahrhundert*. Deutsche Agrargeschichte 2. Stuttgart, 1962.

Abrahams, Paul P. "The Foreign Expansion of American Finance and Its Relation to the Foreign Economic Polities of the United States, 1907-1921." Ph.D. Dissertation, University of Wisconsin, 1967. Published in New York: Arno, 1974.

Abramovitz, Moses, and V. F. Eliasberg. *The Growth of Public Employment in Great Britain*. Princeton, N.J.: Princeton University Press, 1957.

Adelmann, Gerhard. "Structural Change in the Rhenish Linen and Cotton Trades at the Outset of Industrialization." In F. Crouzet, W. H. Chaloner, and F. Stern, eds., *Essays in European Economic History, 1789-1914*, pp. 82-97. New York: St. Martin's, 1970.

Aitken, Hugh G. J., ed. *The State and Economic Growth*. New York: Social Science Research Council, 1959.

Albion, Robert Greenhalgh. *The Rise of New York Port (1815-1860)*. New York: Schribner, 1939.

Allen, G. C. *British Industries and Their Organization*. 2nd ed. London: Longmans, Green, 1939.

Amé, Léon. *Etudes sur les tarifs de douanes et sur les traités de commerce*. Vols. 1 and 2. Paris: Imprimerie nationale, 1876.

Anderson, B. L. "The Attorney and the Early Capital Market in Lancashire." In François Crouzet, ed., *Capital Formation in the Industrial Revolution*. London: Methuen, 1972.

Anderson, C. A., and Mary J. Bowman. "Concerning the Role of Education in Development." In *Research Needs for Development Assistance Programs*, August 1961. Reprinted in C. Geertz, ed., *Old Societies and New States*. New York: Free Press of Glencoe, 1963.

Andrews, P. W. S., and Brunner, Elizabeth. *Capital Development in Steel: A Study of the United Steel Companies, Ltd*. Oxford: Basil Blackwell, 1952.

Ariès, Philippe. *Histoire des populations françaises et leurs attitudes devant la vie depuis le XVIIIe siècle*. Paris: Self, 1948.

Arnold, Thurman W. *The Folklore of Capitalism*. New Haven, Conn.: Yale University Press, 1937.

Artz, Frederick B. *The Development of Technical Education in France, 1500-*

1850. Cambridge, Mass., and London: MIT Press and Society for the History of Technology, 1966.

Augé-Laribé, Michel. *La Politique agricole de la France de 1880 à 1940*. Paris: Presses universitaires de France, 1950.

Aycoberry, Pierre. "Probleme der Sozialschichtung in Köln im Zeitalter der Früh-industrialisierung." In W. Fischer, ed., *Wirtschafts- und sozialgeschichtliche Probleme der frühen Industrialisierung*, pp. 512-528. Berlin: Colloquium Verlag, 1968.

Baar, Lothar. "Probleme der industriellen Revolution in grosstädtischen Indus-triezentren: das berliner Beispiel." In W. Fischer, ed., *Wirtschafts- und sozial-geschichtliche Probleme der frühen Industrialisierung*, pp. 529-542. Berlin: Colloquium Verlag, 1968.

Babbage, Charles. *The Economy of Machinery and Manufactures*. 4th ed., London: Charles Knight, 1835.

Bagehot, Walter. *Lombard Street: A Description of the Money Market*. New York: Scribner, Armstrong, 1873. Reprinted Homewood, Ill.: Irwin, 1966.

Bairoch, Paul. *Commerce exterieur et développement économique de l'Europe au XIXe siècle*. Paris: Mouton et Cie, et Ecoles des hautes études en sciences sociales, 1976.

———— "Commerce international et genèse de la revolution industrielle anglaise." *Annales, économies, sociétés, civilisations* 28 (1973): 541-571.

Banfield, Thomas C. *Industry of the Rhine*. Ser. 1, *Agriculture*, 1846; ser. 2, *Manufactures*, 1848. New York: Augustus Kelley, 1969.

Bank of Montreal. *The Centenary of the Bank of Montreal, 1817-1917*. Montreal: privately printed, 1917.

Bank of Nova Scotia, 1832-1932. Toronto: privately printed, 1932.

Barbour, Violet. "Dutch and English Merchant Shipping in the Seventeenth Century." *Economic History Review* 2 (1930). Reprinted in Warren C. Scoville and J. Clayburn La Force, eds., *The Economic Development of Western Europe*, vol. 2, pp. 108-137. Lexington, Mass.: Heath, 1970.

Barker, T. C. "The Glass Industry." In D. H. Aldcroft, ed., *The Development of British Industry and Foreign Competition, 1875-1914*, pp. 307-325. London: Allen & Unwin, 1968.

Barkin, Kenneth D. *The Controversy over German Industrialization, 1890-1902*. Chicago: University of Chicago Press, 1970.

Bateson, Gregory. "Morale and National Character." In G. Watson, ed., *Civilian Morale*, pp. 71-81. Cambridge: Cambridge University Press, 1942.

———— *Naven*. Cambridge: Cambridge University Press, 1936.

Batty, Peter. *The House of Krupp*. London: Secker and Warburg, 1967.

Beer, John Joseph. *The Emergence of the German Dye Industry*. Urbana: University of Illinois Press, 1959.

Benaerts, Pierre. *Borsig et les débuts de la fabrication des locomotives en Alle-magne*. Paris: Editions F. H. Turot, 1933.

———— *Les Origines de la grande industrie allemande*. Paris: Editions F. H. Turot, 1933.

Ben-David, Joseph. *Fundamental Research and the Universities: Some Comments on International Differences*. Paris: Organization for Economic Cooperation and Development, 1968.

———— *The Scientists' Role in Society: A Comparative Study*. Englewood Cliffs, N.J.: Prentice-Hall, 1971.

Bendix, Reinhold, ed. *State and Society: A Reader in Comparative Politics*. Boston: Little, Brown, 1968.

Benedict, Ruth. *Patterns of Culture*. Cambridge, Mass.: Houghton Mifflin, 1934.

Bergeron, Louis. "Paris dans l'organisation des échanges interieurs à la fin du XVIIIe siècle." Paper presented to the Colloque national de l'association française des historiens économistes at Paris, Oct. 6, 1973, entitled *Aires et structures du commerce français au XVIIIe siècle*.

Bigo, Robert, *Les Banques françaises au cours du XIXe siècle*. Paris: Sirey, 1947.

Bisschop, W. R. *The Rise of the London Money Market, 1640-1826*. London: Frank Cass, 1968 (first Dutch edition, 1896; first English translation, 1910).

Bläsing, Joachim F. E. *Das golden Delta und sein eisernes Hinterland, 1815-1841, von niederländisch-preussischen zu deutschniederländischen Wirtschaftsbeziehungen*. Leiden: H. E. Stenfert Kreese, 1973.

Blumberg, Horst. "Die Finanzierung der Neugründungen und Erweiterungen von Industriebetrieben in Form der Aktiengesellschaften während der fünfziger Jahrhunderts in Deutschland, am Beispiel der preussischen Verhältnisse erläutert." In Hans Mottek, ed., *Studien zur Geschichte der industriellen Revolution in Deutschland*, pp. 165-208. Berlin: Akademie Verlag, 1960.

———— "Ein Beitrag zur Geschichte der deutschen Leinenindustrie von 1834 bis 1870." In Hans Mottek, ed., *Studien zur Geschichte der industriellen Revolution in Deutschland*, pp. 65-143. Berlin: Akademie Verlag, 1960.

Bodelschwingh, E. von. *Leben des Ober-Präsidenten Vincke, nach seiner Tagebüchern bearbeitet*, vol. 1. Berlin: Georg Reimer, 1853.

Böhme, Helmut. *Deutschlands Weg zur Grossmacht, Studien zum Verhältnis von Wirtschaft und Staat wahrend der Reichsgründerzeit, 1848-1881*. Cologne: Kiepenheuer and Witsch, 1966.

———— *Frankfurt und Hamburg, des deutsches Reiches Silber- und Goldloch und die allerenglischste Stadt des Kontinents*. Frankfurt: Europaïsche Verlagsanstalt, 1968.

———— *Prolegomena zu einer Sozial- und Wirtschaftsgeschichte Deutschlands, in 19. und 20. Jahrhundert*. Frankfurt: Suhrkamp Verlag, 1968.

Bondi, Gerhard. *Deutschlands Aussenhandel, 1815-1870*. Berlin: Akademie Verlag, 1958.

Bonelli, Franco. *La Crisi del 1907: una tappa dello sviluppo industriale in Italia*. Turin: Fondazione Luigi Einaudi, 1971.

Borchardt, Knut. "The Industrial Revolution in Germany, 1700-1914." In C. M. Cipolla, ed., *The Fontana Economic History of Europe*, vol. 4, pp. 76-160. N.p.: Collins/Fontana Books (1972).

———— "Zur Frage des Kapitalmangels in der ersten Halfte des 19. Jahrhunderts in Deutschland." In *Jahrbücher für Nationalökonomie und Statistik* 173 (1961): 401-421.

Borries, Bodo von. *Deutschlands Aussenhandel, 1836 bis 1856*. Stuttgart: Gustav

Fischer Verlag, 1970.

Boserup, Esther. *The Conditions of Agricultural Growth: The Economics of Agricultural Change under Population Pressure.* Chicago: Aldine, 1966.

Botha, D. J. J. "The Canadian Money Market, I: Institutional Developments." *South African Journal of Economics* 40 (1972): 119-143.

Bouvier, Jean. *Le Crédit lyonnais de 1863 à 1882, les années de formation d'une banque de depôts.* Vols. 1 and 2. Paris: SEVPEN, 1961.

——— *Le Krach de l'Union générale, 1878-1885.* Paris: Presses universitaires de France, 1960.

Bowring, John. "Report on the Prussian Commercial Union, 1840." In *British Parliamentary Papers*, vol. 21, 1840.

Boxer, C. R. "The Dutch Economic Decline." In M. Cipolla, ed., *The Economic Decline of Empires*, pp. 235-263. London: Methuen, 1970.

Bramsted, Ernest K. *Aristocracy and the Middle-Classes in Germany: Social Types in German Literature, 1830-1900.* Rev. ed. Chicago: University of Chicago Press, 1964.

Braudel, Fernand. *Afterthoughts on Material Life and Capitalism.* Baltimore, Md.: Johns Hopkins University Press, 1977.

——— *The Mediterranean and the Mediterranean World in the Age of Philip II.* Vols. 1 and 2. New York: Harper & Row, 1972.

Braun, Rudolf. *Sozialer und kultureller Wandel in einem ländlichen Industriegebiet im 19. und 20. Jahrhundert.* Erlenbach-Zurich: Eugen Rentch Verlag, 1965.

Brebner, J. Bartlett. "Laissez-Faire and State Intervention in Nineteenth-Century Britain." In E. M. Carus-Wilson, ed. *Essays in Economic History,* vol. 3, pp. 252-262. London: Edward Arnold, 1962.

Brepohl, Wilhelm. *Der Aufbau des Ruhrvolkes im Zuge der Ost-West-Wanderung, Beiträge zur deutschen Sozialgeschichte des 19. und 20. Jahrhunderts.* Recklinghausen: Verlag Bitter, 1948.

Breton, Albert. *The Economic Theory of Representative Democracy.* Chicago: Aldine, 1974.

Brocard, Lucien. "Les Marchés financiers du province." In A. Aupetit et al., *Les Grands Marchés financiers*, pp. 105-152. Paris: Alcan, 1912.

Brockhage, Bernhard. *Zur Entwicklung des preussischdeutschen Kapitalexports.* Leipzig: Duncker u. Humblot, 1910.

Brown, John Crosby. *A Hundred Years of Merchant Banking: A History of Brown Brothers & Co.* New York: privately printed, 1909.

Brown, Lucy. *The Board of Trade and the Free-Trade Movement, 1830-1842.* Oxford: Clarendon Press, 1958.

Buffet, Jean. *Du régionalisme au nationalisme financier.* Paris: Berger-Levrault, 1917.

Buist, Marten G. *At Spes Non Fracta, Hope & Co., 1700-1815, Merchant Bankers and Diplomats at Work.* The Hague: Martinus Nijhoff, 1974.

Bulferetti, Luigi, and Claudio Costanti. *Industria e commercio in Liguria nell'età del Risorgimento (1700-1861).* Milan: Banca Commerciale Italiana, 1966.

Bull, Edvard. *Sozialgeschichte der norwegische Demokratie.* Stuttgart: Ernst Klett Verlag, 1969.

Burn, Duncan L. *Economic History of Steelmaking, 1867-1939*. Cambridge: Cambridge University Press, 1940.

Burnham, T. H., and G. O. Hoskins. *Iron and Steel in Britain, 1870-1930*. London: Allen & Unwin, 1943.

Byatt, I. C. R. "Electrical Products." In D. H. Aldcroft, ed., *The Development of British Industry and Foreign Competition, 1875-1914*, pp. 238-273. London: Allen & Unwin, 1968.

Caird, Sir James. *High Farming . . . The Best Substitute for Protection*. Pamphlet, 1848. Cited in Lord Ernle, *English Farming Past and Present*. 4th ed., p. 374. London: Longmans, Green, 1937.

Cameron, Rondo E. "Founding the Bank of Darmstadt." *Explorations in Entrepreneurial History* 13 (1956): 113-130.

—— *France and the Economic Development of Europe*. Princeton, N.J.: Princeton University Press, 1961.

—— "L'Exportation des capitaux francais, 1850-1880," *Revue d'histoire économique et sociale* 33 (1955): 346-353.

—— with the collaboration of Olga Crisp, Hugh T. Patrick, and Richard Tilly. *Banking in the Early Stages of Industrialization: A Comparative Study*. New York: Oxford University Press, 1967.

——, ed. *Banking and Economic Development: Some Lessons of History*. New York: Oxford University Press, 1972.

Campbell, R. H. "An Economic History of Scotland in the Eighteenth Century." *Scottish Journal of Political Economy* 11 (1964): 17-24.

Carrière, Charles. *Négociants marseillais au XVIIIe siècle: contribution à l'étude des économies maritimes*. Marseille: Institut historique de Provence, 1973.

Carter, Alice Clare. *Getting, Spending and Investing in Early Modern Times: Essays on Dutch, English and Huguenot History*. Assen, the Netherlands: Von Gorcum, 1975.

Carter, C. F., and B. R. Williams. *Industry and Technical Progress: Factors Governing the Speed of Application of Science*. London: Oxford University Press, 1957.

Castronovo, Valerie. *Economia e societa in Piemonte dell'unita al 1914*. Milan: Banca Commerciale Italiana, 1969.

Cavignac, Jean. *Jean Pellet, commerçant de gros, 1694-1772, contribution à l'étude du négoce du XVIIIe siècle*. Paris: SEVPEN, 1967.

Cecil, Lamar. *Albert Ballin, Business and Politics in Imperial Germany*. Princeton, N.J.: Princeton University Press, 1967.

Chambers, J. D. *The Workshop of the World, British Economic History, 1820-1880*. 2nd ed. London: Oxford University Press, 1968.

Chandler, Alfred D. *Strategy and Structure: Chapters in the History of Industrial Enterprise*. Cambridge, Mass.: Harvard University Press, 1962.

Chandler, George. *Four Centuries of Banking (Martin's Bank)*. London: Batsford, vol. 1, 1964; vol. 2, 1968.

Charpenay, Georges. *Les Banques régionalistes*. Paris: Nouvelle Revue critique, 1939.

Checkland, S. G. *The Gladstones: A Family Biography, 1764-1851*. Cambridge: Cambridge University Press, 1971.

Chenery, Hollis. "Patterns of Industrial Growth." *American Economic Review* 50 (1960): 624-654.

Chevalier, Michel. *Cours d'économie politique, fait au Collège de France.* Vols. 1-3. 2nd ed. N.p.: 1855.

Cippola, C. M., ed. *The Economic Decline of Empires*, pp. 1-15. London: Methuen, 1970.

Clapham, J. H. *The Economic Development of France and Germany, 1815-1914.* 4th ed. Cambridge: Cambridge University Press, 1953.

————— "The Last Years of the Navigation Acts." In E. M. Carus-Wilson, ed., *Essays in Economic History*, vol. 3, pp. 144-178. London: Edward Arnold, 1962.

Clifford, Henry C. *The Draining of the Fens.* 2nd ed. Cambridge: Cambridge University Press, 1956.

Clough, Shepherd B. *The Economic History of Modern Italy.* New York: Columbia University Press, 1964.

Cobden, Richard. *Speeches on Questions of Public Policy.* Vol. 1. John Bright and James E. Thorold Rogers, eds. London: Macmillan, 1870.

Cohen, Jon S. "Financing Industrialization in Italy, 1894-1914: The Partial Transformation of the Late Comer." *Journal of Economic History* 27 (1967): 363-382.

Coleman, D. C. "Gentlemen and Players." *Economic History Review* 26 (1973): 92-116.

Cook, P. Lesley. *Effects of Mergers: Six Studies with the Collaboration of Ruth Cohen.* London: Allen & Unwin, 1958.

Coppa, Frank J. "The Italian Tariff and the Conflict between Agriculture and Industry: The Commercial Policy of Liberal Italy, 1860-1922," *Journal of Economic History* 30 (1970): 742-769.

Coppock, D. J. "The Climacteric of the 1890s: A Critical Note." *Manchester School* 24 (1956): 1-31.

Cotgrove, Stephen E. *Technical Education and Social Change.* London: Allen & Unwin, 1958.

Court, W. H. B. *The Rise of the Midland Industries, 1600-1838.* London: Oxford University Press, 1938.

Crédit du nord centenaire. Lille: privately printed, 1948.

Crick, W. F., and J. E. Wadsworth. *A Hundred Years of Joint-Stock Banking (Midlands Bank).* London: Hodder & Stoughton, 1936.

Crouzet, François, "Croissances comparées de l'Angleterre et de la France au XVIIIe siècle: essai d'analyse comparée de deux croissances économiques." Reproduced in edited form in R. M. Hartwell, ed., *The Causes of the Industrial Revolution in England,* pp. 139-174. London: Methuen, 1967.

————— "Economie et société (1715-1789)." In François-George Pariset, ed., *Bordeaux au XVIIIe siècle,* vol. 6. Bordeaux: Féderation historique de Sud-Ouest. 1968.

————— "Western Europe and Great Britain: 'Catching Up' in the First Half of the Nineteenth Century." In A. J. Youngson, ed., *Economic Development in the*

Long Run, pp. 98-125. London: Allen & Unwin, 1972.

————, ed. *Capital Formation in the Industrial Revolution.* London: Methuen, 1972.

Crozier, Michel. *The Bureaucratic Phenomenon.* Chicago: University of Chicago Press, 1964.

Dardel, Pierre. *Commerce, industrie et navigation à Rouen et au Havre au XVIIIᵉ siècle. Rivalité croissante entre ces deux ports.* Rouen: Société libre d'émulation de la Seine-Maritime, 1966.

Daumard, Adeline. *Les Bourgeois de Paris au XIXᵉ siècle.* Paris: Flammarion, 1970.

Dauphin-Meunier, A. *La Banque de France.* Paris: Gallimard, 1936.

Davis, Ralph. "English Foreign Trade, 1660-1700." *Economic History Review,* ser. 2, 6 (1954). Reprinted in W. E. Minchinton, ed., *The Growth of English Overseas Trade in the 17th and 18th Centuries,* pp. 78-98. London: Methuen, 1969.

———— "English Foreign Trade, 1700-1774," *Economic History Review,* ser. 2, 15 (1962). Reprinted in W. W. Minchinton, ed., *The Growth of English Overseas Trade in the 17th and 18th Centuries,* pp. 99-120. London: Methuen, 1969.

Dawson, William H. *Protection in Germany: A History of German Fiscal Policy during the Nineteenth Century.* London: P. S. King and Son, 1904.

Deane, Phyllis. *The First Industrial Revolution.* Cambridge: Cambridge University Press, 1965.

Delaisi, F. *Les deux Europes.* Paris: Payot, 1929.

Delbrück, Rudolph von. *Lebenserinnerungen.* Vols. 1 and 2. Leipzig: Duncker u. Humblot, 1905.

Denison, Edward, assisted by Jean-Pierre Poullier. *Why Growth Rates Differ: Experience in Nine Western Countries.* Washington, D.C.: Brookings Institution, 1967.

Dermigny, Louis. *Cargaisons indiennes, Solier et Cie, 1781-1793.* Vols. 1 and 2. Paris: SEVPEN, 1960.

Devine, T. M. "Glasgow Colonial Merchants and Land, 1770-1815." In J. T. Ward and R. G. Wilson, eds., *Land and Industry: The Landed Estate and the Industrial Revolution,* pp. 205-265. New York: Barnes & Noble, 1971.

Dornic, François. *L'Industrie textile dans Le Maine et ses débouches internationaux (1650-1815).* Le Mans: Editions Pierre-Belon, 1955.

Dovring, Folke. *Land and Labor in Europe, 1900-1950: A Comparative Study of Recent Agrarian History.* 3rd ed. The Hague: Martinius Nijhoff, 1964.

Drake, Michael. *Population and Society in Norway, 1735-1865.* Cambridge: Cambridge University Press, 1969.

Dumke, Rolf H. "The Political Economy of Economic Integration: The Case of the Zollverein of 1834." Queen's University *Discussion Paper* no. 153, presented to the Canadian Economics Association June 5, 1974.

Duncan, O. D., et al. *Metropolis and Region.* Baltimore, Md.: Johns Hopkins University Press, 1960.

Dunham, Arthur L. *The Anglo-French Treaty of Commerce of 1860 and the Progress of the Industrial Revolution in France.* Ann Arbor: University of Michigan Press, 1930.

Eaton, G. Howard, and David E. Bond. "Canada's Newest Money Market—Vancouver." *Canadian Banker* 77 (1970): 14-15.

Eckardt, Julius V. *Lebenserinnerungen.* Vols. 1 and 2. Leipzig: Verlag S. Hirzel, 1910.

Edwards, Michael M. *The Growth of the British Cotton Trade, 1780-1815.* Manchester: Manchester University Press, 1967.

Engelsing, Rolf. "Technik, Unternehmensorganization and Kapitalinvestition in der deutschen Seeschiffahrt des 19. Jahrhundert." In W. Fischer, ed., *Wirtschafts- und sozialgeschichtliche Probleme der frühen Industrialisierung.* Berlin: Colloquium Verlag, 1958.

Ensor, R. C. K. *England, 1870-1914.* Oxford: Oxford University Press, 1936.

Epstein, Klaus. "The Socio-economic History of the Second German Empire." *Review of Politics* 29 (1967): 100-112.

Erickson, Charlotte. *British Industrialists: Steel and Hosiery, 1850-1950.* Cambridge: Cambridge University Press, 1959.

Ernle, Lord. *English Farming, Past and Present.* 5th ed. New York: Longmans, Green, 1936.

Evans, D. Morier. *The History of the Commercial Crisis, 1857-1858 and the Stock Exchange Panic of 1859.* London: Groombridge & Sons, 1859. Reprinted Augustus M. Kelley, 1969.

Faber, Harald. *Co-operation in Danish Agriculture.* 2nd ed. London: Longmans, Green, 1931.

Fanno, Marco. *Le Banche e il mercato monetario.* Rome: Athenaem, 1913.

Fielden, Kenneth. "The Rise and Fall of Free Trade." In C. J. Bartlett, ed., *Britain Pre-eminent: Studies in British World Influence in the Nineteenth Century,* pp. 76-100. London: Macmillan, 1969.

Fischer, Wolfram. *Der Staat und die Anfänge der Industrialisierung in Baden, 1800-1850.* Berlin: Duncker u. Humblot, 1962.

Fitton, R. S., and A. P. Wadsworth. *The Strutts and the Arkwrights, 1758-1830: A Study of the Early Factory System.* Manchester: Manchester University Press, 1958.

Fogel, Robert W. *Railroads and American Economic Growth: Essays in Econometric History.* Baltimore, Md.: Johns Hopkins University Press, 1964.

Fohlen, Claude. "France, 1700-1914." In C. M. Cipolla, ed., *The Fontana Economic History of Europe,* vol. 4, pp. 7-75. N.p.: Collins/Fontana Books, 1972(?).

Food Research Institute. "Decline and Recovery of Wheat Prices in the Nineties." *Wheat Studies* 10 (1934).

Forster, Robert. Review of Charles Carrière, *Négociants marseillais au XVIIIe siècle. Journal of Modern History* 47 (1975):162-165.

Fortunes Made in Business. Vols. 1-3. London: n.p., 1883.

Fox, Edward Whiting. *History in Geographic Perspective: The Other France.* New York: Norton, 1971.

Fox Bourne, H. R. *English Merchants: Memories in Illustration of the Progress of British Commerce*. London: Richard Bentley, 1866.

Froelich, N., J. A. Oppenheimer, and O. R. Young. *Political Leadership and Collective Action*. Princeton, N.J.: Princeton University Press, 1971.

Gallagher, John, and Ronald Robinson. "The Imperialism of Free Trade." *Economic History Review*, ser. 2. 6 (1953): 1-15.

Garden, Maurice. "Le Commerce lyonnais au XVIIIe siècle." Paper presented to the Colloque national de l'association française des historiens économistes at Paris, Oct. 6, 1973, entitled *Aires et structures du commerce français au XVIIIe siècle*.

Gee, Joshua. *Trade and Navigation of Great Britain Considered*. London: S. Buckley, 1729.

Gerschenkron, Alexander. *Bread and Democracy in Germany*. Berkeley: University of California Press, 1943.

——— "Comments." In Universities—National Bureau of Economic Research, *Capital Formation and Economic Growth*, pp. 373-378. Princeton, N.J.: Princeton University Press, 1955.

——— *Continuity in History and Other Essays*. Cambridge, Mass.: Harvard University Press, Belknap Press, 1968.

——— "Economic Backwardness in Historical Perspective." In B. F. Hoselitz, ed., *The Progress of Underdeveloped Areas*. Chicago: University of Chicago Press, 1952.

——— *Economic Backwardness in Historical Perspective: A Book of Essays*. Cambridge, Mass.: Harvard University Press, Belknap Press, 1962.

——— "Typology of Industrial Development as a Tool of Analysis." In *Second International Conference on Economic History*, pp. 487-505. Paris/The Hague: Mouton, 1965.

Geyl, Pieter. *The Netherlands in the Seventeenth Century*. Pt. 1, *1609-1648*. New York: Barnes & Noble, 1961.

Gille, Bertrand. *La Banque en France au XIXe siècle: recherches historiques*. Geneva: Librairie Droz, 1970.

Girard, L. "Transport." In *The Cambridge Economic History of Europe*. Vol. 6, pp. 212-273. Cambridge: Cambridge University Press, 1965.

Girault, René. *Empruntes russes et investissements français en Russie, 1887-1914*. Paris: A. Colin, 1973.

Glazebrook, G. P. deT. *The Story of Toronto*. Toronto: University of Toronto Press, 1971.

Glick, Thomas F. *Irrigation and Society in Medieval Valencia*. Cambridge, Mass.: Harvard University Press, Belknap Press, 1970.

Goldsmith, Raymond. *Financial Structure and Development*. New Haven, Conn: Yale University Press, 1969.

Goldstein, Gerald S., and Leon N. Moses. "A Survey of Urban Economics." *Journal of Economic Literature* 11 (1973):471-515.

Golob, E. O. *The Méline Tariff: French Agriculture and Nationalist Economic Policy*. New York: Columbia University Press, 1944.

Goubert, Pierre. *Familles marchands sous l'Ancien Régime: les Danse et les Motte de Beauvais.* Paris: SEVPEN, 1959.

Gouraud, Charles. *Histoire de la politique commerciale de la France et son influ-ence sur le progrès de la richesse publique depuis les moyen ages jusqu'à nos jours.* Vols. 1 and 2. Paris: August Durand, 1854.

Gourevitch, Peter Alexis. "International Trade, Domestic Coalitions, and Liberty: Comparative Responses to the Great Depression of 1873-1896." *Journal of Interdisciplinary History,* forthcoming.

Gras, N. S. B. *An Introduction to Economic History.* New York: Harper, 1922.

———— *Business and Capitalism: An Introduction to Business History.* New York: Crofts, 1939.

Greenfield, Kent Roberts. *Economics and Liberalism in the Risorgimento: A Study of Nationalism in Lombardy, 1814-1848.* Rev. ed. Baltimore, Md.: Johns Hopkins University Press, 1965.

Gregory, T. E. *The Westminister Bank through a Century.* Vols. 1 and 2. London: Westminister Bank, 1936.

Habakkuk, H. J. *American and British Technology in the Nineteenth Century.* Cambridge: Cambridge University Press, 1962.

———— and P. Deane. "The 'Take-off' in Britain." In W. W. Rostow, ed., *The Economics of Take-off into Sustained Growth,* pp. 63-82. London: Macmil-lan, 1963.

Haggard, H. Rider. *Rural Denmark and Its Lessons.* London: Longmans, Green, 1911.

Haines, Michael R. "Economic-Demographic Interrelation in Agricultural Regions: A Case Study of Prussian Upper Silesia, 1840-1914." Ph.D. dissertation, Uni-versity of Pennsylvania, 1971.

Halbwachs, Maurice. *La Population et les traces de voies à Paris depuis une siècle.* Paris: Presses universitaires de France, 1928.

Haley, K. H. D. *The Dutch in the Seventeenth Century.* London: Thames and Hudson, 1972.

Hamada, Koichi. "On the Political Economy of Monetary Integration: A Public Economics Approach." In R. Z. Aliber, ed., *The Political Economy of Mone-tary Reform.* London: Macmillan, 1977.

Hardach, K. W. "Anglomanie und Anglophobie während der industriellen Revo-lution in Deutschland." *Schmollers Jahrbuch* 91 (1971):153-181.

———— "Some Remarks on German Economic Historiography and Its Understand-ing of the Industrial Revolution in Germany." *Journal of European Economic History* 1 (1972):37-99.

Harley, C. K. "Skilled Labor and the Choice of Techniques in Edwardian Indus-try." *Explorations in Economic History,* ser. 2, 2(1973/74):391-414.

Hatzfeld, Lutz. "Kaufmannische Probleme der Rohrenfabrik Poensgen & Schoel-ler, 1844-1850." In Karl Erich Born, ed., *Moderne deutsche Wirtschaft-geschichte,* pp. 203-213. Cologne-Berlin: Kiepenheuer und Witsch, 1966.

Hawtrey, R. G. *Economic Aspects of Sovereignty.* 2nd ed. London: Longmans, Green, 1952.

Heaton, Herbert. *Economic History of Europe.* New York: Harper, 1936.

———— *The Yorkshire Woollen and Worsted Industries.* 2nd ed. Oxford: Claren-don Press, 1965.

Helfferich, Karl, *Georg von Siemens, Ein Lebensbild aus Deutschlands grosser Zeit.* Revised and abridged edition of the 1921-1923 work in 3 vols. Krefeld: Richard Serpe, 1956.

Helleiner, Karl F. *Free Trade and Frustration: Anglo-Austrian Negotiations, 1860-70.* Toronto: University of Toronto Press, 1973.

Henderson, W. O. *Britain and Industrial Europe, 1750-1870: Studies in British Influence on the Industrial Revolution in Western Europe.* Liverpool: University Press, 1954.

Henning, Friedrich-Wilhelm. "Standorte und Spezialisierung des Handels und des Transportwesens in der Mark Brandenburg um 1800." *Scripta Mercaturae* (1/1971):1-44.

Henning, Graydon R., and Keith Trace. "Britain and the Motorship: A Case of the Delayed Adoption of New Technology." *Journal of Economic History* 35 (1975):353-385.

Heyn, Udo E. "Private Banking and Industrialization, The Case of Frankfurt am Main, 1825-1875." Ph.D. dissertation, University of Wisconsin, 1969.

Hidy, Muriel E. "George Peabody, Merchant and Financier, 1829-1854." Ph.D dissertation, Radcliffe College, 1939. Published New York: Arno, 1974.

Hobsbawm, Eric J. *Labouring Men: Studies in the History of Labour.* London: Weidenfeld, 1964.

Hoffman, Ross J. S. *Great Britain and the German Trade Rivalry, 1875-1914.* Philadelphia: University of Pennsylvania Press, 1933.

Hoffmann, Walther G. *The Growth of Industrial Economies.* Translated from the 1931 original. Manchester: Manchester University Press, 1958.

Hohenberg, Paul M. *Chemicals in Western Europe, 1850-1914: An Economic Study of Technical Change.* Chicago: Rand McNally, 1967.

Hopkinson, Edward, Jr. *Drexel & Co. over a Century of History.* New York: Newcomen Society of North America, 1952.

Hoselitz, Bert F. "Entrepreneurship and Capital Formation in France and Britain since 1700." In *Capital Formation and Economic Growth.* Princeton, N.J.: Princeton University Press for the National Bureau of Economic Research, 1956.

Hoskins, W. G. *Industry, Trade and People in Exeter, 1688-1800, with Special Reference to the Serge Industry.* Manchester: Manchester University Press, 1935.

Hourwich, I. A. *Immigration and Labor.* New York: Huebsch, 1922.

Hufbauer, Gary C. *Synthetic Materials and the Theory of International Trade.* Cambridge, Mass.: Harvard University Press, 1966.

—— and F. M. Adler, *Overseas Manufacturing Investment and the Balance of Payments.* Washington, D.C.: U.S. Treasury Department, 1968.

Hughes, Edward. *North Country Life in the Eighteenth Century.* London: Oxford University Press, vol. 1, 1952; vol. 2, 1965.

Hundert Jahre im Dienst der deutschen Wirtschaft: ein Rückblick zur Erinnerung an die Gründung der mitteldeutschen Creditbank. Frankfurt-am-Main: privately printed, 1956.

Huskisson, William. *The Speeches of the Right Honorable William Huskisson.* London: John Murray, 1832.

Iklé, Max. *Switzerland: An International Banking and Finance Center.* Strouds-
berg, Penn.: Dowden, Hutchinson & Ross, 1972.
Illasu, A. A. "The Cobden-Chevalier Commercial Treaty of 1860." *Historical Jour-
nal* 14 (1971):67-98.
In Memoriam, Jesse Seligmann. New York: privately printed, 1894.
Innis, Harold A. *Political Science in the Modern State.* Toronto: University of To-
ronto Press, 1946.
Inoki, Takenori. "Aspects of German Peasant Migration to the United States,
1815-1914: A Re-examination of Some Behavioral Hypotheses in Migration
Theory." Ph.D. dissertation, Massachusetts Institute of Technology, 1973.
Interbank Research Organisation. *The Future of London as an International Fi-
nancial Centre.* London: Her Majesty's Stationery Office, 1973.
International Institute of Agriculture. *World Trade in Agricultural Products.*
Rome: IIA, 1940.
Istituto per la Scienza del'Amministrazione Pubblica, Dipartimento di Sociologia.
La burocrazia centrale in Italia, analisi sociologica. Milan: Editore Guiffre,
1965.
Jackson, Gordon. *Hull in the Eighteenth Century: A Study in Economic and Social
History.* London: Oxford University Press for the University of Hull, 1972.
Jacob, William. *A View of the Agriculture, Manufactures, Statistics and Society
in the State of Germany and Parts of Holland and France, taken during a
journey through those countries in 1819.* London: John Murray, 1820.
Jamieson, A. B. *Chartered Banking in Canada.* Toronto: Ryerson, 1953.
Jankowski, Manfred D. "Law, Economic Policy and Private Entreprise: The Case
of the Early Ruhr Mining Region, 1766-1865." *Journal of European Economic
History,* ser. 2, 3 (1973):688-727.
Jeffrys, J. B. "Trends in Business Organization in Great Britain since 1856, with
special reference to the financial structure of the companies, the mechanism
of investment, and the relations between the shareholder and the company."
Doctoral thesis, London School of Economics, 1938.
Jensen, Einar. *Danish Agriculture: Its Economic Development.* Copenhagen:
Munksgaard, 1937.
Jerome, H. *Migration and Business Cycles.* New York: National Bureau of Eco-
nomic Research, 1926.
John, A. H. *The Industrial Development of South Wales, 1750-1850, An Essay.*
Cardiff: University of Wales Press, 1950.
Johnson, Harry G. "An Economic Theory of Protectionism, Tariff Bargaining and
the Formation of Customs Unions." *Journal of Political Economy* 73 (1965):
256-283. Reprinted in P. Robson, ed., *International Economic Integration,*
pp. 99-142. Harmondswoth: Penguin, 1972.
——— "The Efficiency and Welfare Implications of the International Corporation." In C. P. Kindleberger, ed., *The International Corporation.* Cambridge, Mass.: MIT Press, 1970.
Jöhr, Adolf. *Die schwiezerischen Notenbanken, 1826-1913.* Zurich: Orell Füssli,
1915.
Kardiner, A. *The Psychological Frontiers of Society.* New York: Columbia University Press, 1943.

Kehr, Eckhart. *Der Primat der Innenpolitik, gesammelte Aufsätze zur preussisch-deutschen Sozialgeschichte im 19. und 20. Jahrhundert.* H. U. Wehler, ed. Berlin: Walter de Gruyter, 1965.

———— "Imperialismus und deutscher Schlachtflottenbau." Excerpts from *Schlachtflottenbau und Parteipolitik, Berlin, 1930,* in H. U. Wehler, ed., *Imperialismus,* pp. 289-308. Cologne and Berlin: Kiepenhener u. Witsch, 1970.

Kellenbenz, Hermann. Foreword to Ludwig Beutin, *Gesammelte Schriften zur Wirtschafts- und Sozialgeschichte.* Cologne: Böhlau Verlag, 1963.

Kerr, Clark, and Abraham Siegel. "The Interindustry Propensity to Strike: An International Comparison." In A. Kornhauser, R. Dubin, and A. M. Ross, eds., *Industrial Conflict.* New York: McGraw-Hill, 1954.

Kerr, Donald P. "Metropolitan Dominance in Canada." In John Warkentin, ed., *A Geographical Interpretation of Canada,* pp. 531-555. Toronto: Methuen, 1967.

———— "Some Aspects of the Geography of Finance in Canada." *Canadian Geographer* 9 (1965):175-192. Also in Robert M. Irving, ed., *Readings in Canadian Geography.* Toronto: Holt, Rinehart & Winston, 1965.

Keynes, John Maynard. *The General Theory of Employment, Interest and Money.* New York: Harcourt, Brace, 1936.

Kindleberger, Charles P. *Economic Growth in France and Britain, 1851-1950.* Cambridge, Mass.: Harvard University Press, 1964.

———— "European Integration and the Development of a Single Financial Center for Long-Term Capital." *Weltwirtschaftliches Archiv* 90 (1963):189-210.

———— "Technical Education and the French Entrepreneur." In Edward C. Carter II, Robert Forster, and Joseph N. Moody, eds., *Enterprise and Entrepreneurs in Nineteenth and Twentieth-Century France,* pp. 3-39. Baltimore, Md.: Johns Hopkins University Press, 1976.

———— *The World in Depression, 1929-1939.* Berkeley: University of California Press, 1973.

Kisch, Herbert. "From Monopoly to Laissez-Faire: The Early Growth of the Wupper Valley Textile Trades." *Journal of European Economic History* (Fall 1972):298-407.

———— "The Textile Industries in Silesia and the Rhineland: A Comparative Study of Industrialization." *Journal of Economic History* 19 (1959):541-564.

Kluckhohn, Clyde. *Mirror for Man.* New York: Whittlesey House, 1949.

Kocka, Jürgen. "Expansion, Integration, Diversifikation: Wachstumstrategien industrieller Grossunternehmen in Deutschland vor 1914." Comment on Theme 2 of the Sixth International Congress on Economic History, Copenhagen, 1974.

———— *Unternehmungsverwaltung und Angestelltenschaft am Beispiel Siemens, 1847-1914: zum Verhältnis von Kapitalismus und Bürokratie in der deutschen Industrialisierung.* Stuttgart: Ernst Klett Verlag, 1969.

Kohn, Eric D. "Eurobonds—What Sort of Market?" *Euromoney* 3 (1971):68-70.

Köllmann, Wolfgang. *Sozialgeschichte der Stadt Barmen im 19. Jahrhundert.* Tübingen: J. C. B. Mohr (Paul Siebeck), 1960.

———— "The Population of Barmen before and during the Period of Industrialization." In D. Glass and D. E. C. Eversley, eds., *Population in History: Essays in Historical Demography*, pp. 588-607. London: Edward Arnold, 1964.

Konvitz, Josef, "Grandeur in French City Planning under Louis XIV: Rochefort and Marseille." *Journal of Urban History* 2 (1975):3-42.

Kouwenhoven, John A. *Partners in Banking: An Historical Portrait of a Great Private Bank, Brown Brothers, Harriman & Company, 1818-1968.* New York: Doubleday, 1968.

Krantz, Frederick, and Paul M. Hohenberg, eds. *Failed Transitions to Modern Industrial Society: Renaissance Italy and Seventeenth Century Holland.* Montreal: Interuniversity Centre for European Studies, 1975.

Kuznets, Simon S. *Economic Growth of Nations: Total Output and Production Structure.* Cambridge, Mass.: Harvard University Press, 1971.

——— *Modern Economic Growth: Rate, Structure and Spread.* New Haven, Conn.: Yale University Press, 1966.

Labasse, Jean. *Les Capitaux et la région, étude géographique: essai sur le commerce et la circulation des capitaux dans la région lyonnaise.* Paris: Colin, 1955.

Labracherie, Pierre. *Michel Chevalier et ses idées économiques.* Paris: Picart, 1929.

Ladurie, Emmanuel LeRoy. *Les Paysans de Languedoc.* Paris: SEVPEN, 1966.

Lambi, Ivo Nikolai. *Free Trade and Protection in Germany, 1868-1879.* Wiesbaden: Franz Steiner Verlag, 1963.

Landes, David S. "French Entrepreneurship and Industrial Growth in the Nineteenth Century." *Journal of Economic History* 9 (1949):45-61.

——— "Technological Change and the Development of Western Europe, 1750-1914." In *The Cambridge Economic History of Europe, VI, The Industrial Revolution and After: Incomes, Population and Technological Change,* vol. 1, pp. 274-601. Cambridge: Cambridge University Press, 1965.

——— "The Bleichröder Bank: An Interim Report." In *Yearbook V* publication of the Leo Baeck Institute, pp. 201-220. London: East and West Library, 1960.

Legge, Joseph. *Kapital- und Verwaltungsüberfremdung bei der Industrie und den Verkehrsanstalten Deutschlands von 1800 bis 1923/24.* Halberstadt: Meyer, 1924.

Leighton-Boyce, J. A. S. L. *Smiths, the Bankers, 1658-1958.* London: National Provincial Bank, 1958.

Léon, Pierre. *Marchands et spéculateurs dauphinois dans le monde antillais du XVIIIe siècle, les Dolle et les Raby.* Paris: Belles Lettres, 1963.

Levi, Leone. *The History of British Commerce.* 2nd ed. London: Murray, 1880.

Levy, Hermann. *Industrial Germany: A Study of Its Monopoly Organizations and Their Control by the State.* Cambridge: Cambridge University Press, 1935. Reprinted 1966.

Lévy-Leboyer, Maurice. *Histoire économique et sociale de la France depuis 1848.* Paris: Les Cours de droit, Institut d'études politiques, 1951-52.

——— *Les Banques européennes et l'industrialisation internationale dans la première moitié du XIXe siècle.* Paris: Presses universitaires de France, 1964.

Lewis, Roy, and Angus Maude. *The English Middle Classes*. London: Phoenix House, 1949.

Lhomme, J. *La Grande Bourgeoisie au pouvoir, 1830-1880*. Paris: Presses universitaires de France, 1960.

Lindert, Peter H., and Peter Trace. "Yardsticks for Victorian Entrepreneurs." In D. N. McCloskey, ed., *Essays in a Mature Economy: Britain after 1840*. Princeton, N.J.: Princeton University Press, 1971.

Lorwin, Val. R. "Labor Organizations and Politics in Belgium and France." In E. M. Kassalow, ed., *National Labor Movements in the Postwar World*, pp. 142-168. Evanston, Ill.: Northwestern University Press, 1963.

———— "Working Class Politics and Economic Development in Western Europe." *American Historical Review* 63 (1958):338-351.

Lösch, August. *The Economics of Location*. New Haven, Conn.: Yale University Press, 1954.

Low, William F. "Euroclear Opens Up." *Euromoney* 4 (1972):31, 33.

———— "Improving the Secondary Market." *The Banker* (1972):1157-1159.

Lowie, Robert H. *The German People, A Social Portrait of 1914*. New York: Rinehart, 1946.

Lund, N. Windfield. "Land Clearance and New Settlements on the Waste Lands of Europe in the 18th Century." Paper presented at an informal meeting, organized by Professor Lund, at the Sixth International Congress on Economic History, Copenhagen, August 1974.

Lutfalla, Michel. "Aux origines de la libéralisme économique de la France." *Revue d'histoire économique et sociale* 50 (1972):494-517.

Lutz, Alfred. "Problems of the Secondary Market—Has it Really come of Age?" *Euromoney* 5 (1973):19, 21.

Luzzatto, Gino. *L'Economia italiana dal 1861 al 1914,* vol. 1 (1861-1894). Milan: Banca Commerciale Italiana, 1963.

———— *Storia economica dell'età moderna e contemporanea*. Vol. 2. Padua: CEDAN, 1960.

McClelland, Peter D. *Causal Explanation of Model Buildings in Economics, and the New Economic History*. Ithaca, N.Y.: Cornell University Press, 1975.

McCloskey, Donald N. "Did Victorian Britain Fail?" *Economic History Review* 23 (1970):446-459.

———— *Economic Maturity and Entrepreneurial Decline: British Iron and Steel, 1870-1913*. Cambridge, Mass.: Harvard University Press, 1973.

————, ed. *Essays on a Mature Economy: Britain after 1840*. Princeton, N.J.: Princeton University Press, 1971.

MacGregor, John. *Germany, Her Resources, Government, Union of Customs and Power under Frederick William IV*. London: Whittaker, 1848.

Machlup, Fritz. "Three Concepts of Balance of Payments and the So-Called Dollar Shortage." *Economic Journal* 60 (1950):46-68.

McKay, John P. *Tramways and Trolleys: The Rise of Urban Mass Transport in Europe*. Princeton, N.J.: Princeton University Press, 1976.

McKenzie, R. D. *The Metropolitan Community*. New York: McGraw-Hill, 1933.

McKinnon, Ronald I. *Money and Capital in Economic Development*. Washington,

D.C.: Brookings Institution, 1973.

McNeill, William H. *Venice: The Hinge of Europe, 1081-1797.* Chicago: University of Chicago Press, 1974.

McRae, Hamish. "Barclay's Euro-clearing System-Mark II" *Euromoney* 4 (1972):33.

Madden, John T., and Marcus Nadler. *The International Money Markets.* New York: Prentice-Hall, 1935.

Maddison, Angus. *Economic Growth in the West: Comparative Experience in Europe and North America.* New York: Twentieth Century Fund, 1964.

Mantoux, Paul. *The Industrial Revolution in the Eighteenth Century: An Outline of the Beginnings of the Modern Factory System in Britain.* Rev. ed. New York: Harper & Row Torchbooks, 1961.

Marshall, Alfred. *Industry and Trade: A Study of Industrial Technique and Business Organization, and of Their Influence on the Conditions of Various Classes and Nations.* London: Macmillan, 1920.

Marshall, Joseph. *Travels through Germany, Russia and Poland in the Years 1769 and 1770.* From the original. London: J. Almon, 1772. Reprinted New York: Arno, 1971.

Masters, D. C. *The Rise of Toronto, 1850-1890.* Toronto: University of Toronto Press, 1947.

Mathias, Peter. *The First Industrial Nation: An Economic History of Britain, 1700-1914.* London: Methuen, 1969.

Mathorez, J. *Les Etrangers en France sous l'Ancien Régime, histoire de la population française.* Vol. 1. Paris: Edouard Chapinon, 1919.

Matthews, P. W., and Anthony W. Tuke. *History of Barclay's Bank, Ltd.* London: Blades and Blades, 1926.

Mendershausen, Horst. *Two Postwar Recoveries of the German Economy.* Amsterdam: North-Holland, 1955.

Meyer, Jean. *L'Armement nantais dans la deuxième moitié du XVIIIe siècle.* Paris: SEVPEN, 1969.

Meyer, John R. "An Input-Output Approach to Evaluating the Influence of Exports on British Industrial Production in the Late 19th Century." *Explorations in Entrepreneurial History* 8 (1955):12-34.

Minchinton, W. E. *The British Tinplate Industry: A History.* Oxford: Clarendon Press, 1957.

———— "The Merchants in England in the Eighteenth Century." *Explorations in Entrepreneurial History* 10 (1957):62-71. Reprinted in Hugh G. J. Aitken, ed., *Explorations in Enterprise,* pp. 278-295. Cambridge, Mass.: Harvard University Press, 1965.

————, ed. *The Growth of English Overseas Trade in the 17th and 18th Centuries.* London: Methuen, 1969.

————, ed. *The Trade of Bristol in the 18th Century.* Vol. 20. Bristol: Record Society's Publication, 1957.

Mokyr, Joel. *Industrial Growth and Stagnation in the Low Countries, 1800-1850.* New Haven, Conn.: Yale University Press, 1977.

———— "The Industrial Revolution in the Low Countries in the First Half of the Nineteenth Century: A Comparative Case Study." *Journal of Economic History* 34 (1974):365-391.

Moore, Barrington, Jr. *Social Origins of Dictatorship and Democracy.* Boston: Beacon Press, 1966.

Moore, D. C. "The Corn Laws and High Farming." *Economic History Review* ser. 2, 18 (1965):544-561.

Moore, W. E. *Economic Demography of Eastern and Southeastern Europe.* New York: Columbia University Press, 1945.

Musgrave, P. W. *Technical Change, the Labour Force and Education: A Study of the British and German Iron and Steel Industries, 1860-1964.* Oxford: Pergamon Press, 1967.

Musson, A. E. "The 'Manchester School' and Exportation of Machinery." *Business History* 14 (1972):17-50.

————, ed. *Science, Technology and Economic Growth in the Eighteenth Century.* London: Methuen, 1972.

Myers, Margaret G. *The New York Money Market.* Vol. 1. New York: Columbia University Press, 1931. Reprinted 1971.

Neufeld, E. P. *The Financial System of Canada, Its Growth and Development.* New York: St. Martin's 1972.

Newbold, J. T. W. "The Beginnings of the World Crisis, 1873-1896." *Economic History* 2 (1932):425-441.

Norman, Victor D. "Trade Liberalization and Industrial Growth: The Impact of British Trade Liberalization in the 1840s on Industrialization in the Scandinavian Countries." Unpublished. Cambridge, Mass.: Massachusetts Institute of Technology, December 1970.

Norsa, Paolo, and Pozzo, Mario. *Imposte e tasse in Piemonte durante il periodo cavouriano.* Turin: Museo nazionale del Risorgimento, 1961.

North, Douglass C., and Robert Paul Thomas. *The Rise of the Western World: A New Economic History.* Cambridge: Cambridge University Press, 1973.

Nourse, E. G. *American Agriculture and the European Market.* New York: McGraw-Hill, 1924.

Olivieri, Angelo. "An Urban Case History: Bordeaux." *Journal of European Economic History* 2 (1973):447-456.

Olson, Mancur, Jr. *The Logic of Collective Action: Public Goods and the Theory of Groups.* Rev. ed. Cambridge, Mass.: Harvard University Press, 1971.

———— and Richard Zeckhauser. "An Economic Theory of Alliances." *Review of Economics and Statistics* 48 (1966):266-279.

Oppenheimer, Franz. "The Tendency of the Development of the States." In V. F. Calverton, *The Making of Society.* New York: Random House, 1937.

Pares, Richard. *A West-India Fortune.* London: Longmans, Green, 1950. Reprinted New York: Archon Books, 1968.

Pareto, Vilfredo. *Le Marché financier italien, 1891-1899.* Annual articles. Reprinted Geneva: Droz, 1965.

Parker, William N. "National States and National Development: French and German Ore Mining in the Late Nineteenth Century." In H. G. J. Aitken, ed., *The State and Economic Growth,* pp. 201-212. New York: Social Science Research Council, 1959.

Parravicini, Giannino. *Archivo economico dell'unificazione italiana.* Turin: ILTE, 1958.

Pedone, Antonio. "La Political del commercio-estere." In Giorgio Fua, ed., *Le sviluppo economico in Italia.* Vol. 2. Milan: France Angelli, 1969.

Phelps, Clyde William. *The Foreign Expansion of American Banks: American Branch Banking Abroad.* New York: Ronald, 1927.

Pincus, Jonathan J. "A Positive Theory of Tariff Formation Applied to Nineteenth Century United States." Ph.D. dissertation, Stanford University, 1972. New York: Columbia University Press, forthcoming.

Platt, D. C. M. *Finance, Trade and Politics in British Foreign Policy, 1815-1914.* Oxford: Clarendon Press, 1968.

Polanyi, Karl. *The Great Transformation.* New York: Farrar & Rinehart, 1944.

Pollard, Sidney. *European Economic Integration, 1815-1870.* New York: Harcourt Brace Jovanovich, 1974.

———— "Industrialization and the European Economy." *Economic History Review* 26 (1973):636-648.

———— and C. Holmes. *Documents of European Economic History.* Vol. 1. New York: St. Martin's, 1968.

Porter, G. R., *The Progress of the Nation.* New ed. London: John Murray, 1847.

Poussou, J. P. "Structures demographiques et sociales." In François-George Pariset, ed., *Bordeaux au XVIIIe siècle,* chap. 5. Bordeaux: Fédération historique de Sud-Ouest, 1968.

Pouthas, Charles. *La Population française pendant la première moitié du XIXe siècle.* Paris: Presses universitaires de France, 1956.

Powell, Ellis T. *The Evolution of the Money Market (1384-1915): An Historical and Analytical Study of the Rise and Development of Finance as a Central, Coordinated Force.* London: Financial News, 1915. Reprinted New York: Augustus Kelley, 1966.

Pred, Allan R. *The Spatial Dynamics of U.S. Urban-Industrial Growth, 1900-1914: Interpretive and Theoretical Essays.* Cambridge, Mass.: MIT Press, 1966.

Pressnell, L. S. *Country Banking in the Industrial Revolution.* Oxford: Clarendon Press, 1957.

Prest, John. *The Industrial Revolution in Coventry.* London: Oxford University Press, 1960.

Price, Jacob M. "Economic Function and the Growth of American Port Towns in the Eighteenth Century." *Perspectives in American History* 8 (1974):123-186.

———— *France and the Chesapeake: A History of the French Monopoly and of Its Relationship to the British and American Tobacco Traders.* 2 vols. Ann Arbor: University of Michigan Press, 1973.

Prodi, Romano. "Il Protezionismo nella politica e nell'industria italiana dall'unificazione al 1886." *Nuova Rivista Storica* 1-2 (1966):1-74.

Pullen, Brian. "Crisis and Change in the Venetian Economy in the 16th and 17th Centuries." In B. Pullen, ed., *Crisis and Change in the Venetian Economy.* London: Methuen, 1968.

"Quebec's New Government, Plagued by Language Policy Problem, Is Trying to Find the Right Words, *New York Times,* February 18, 1977, p. A9.

Rapp, Richard T. "The Unmaking of Mediterranean Trade Hegemony: International Trade Rivalry and the Commercial Revolution." *Journal of Economic History* 35 (1975):499-525.

Rappard, William E. *La Révolution industrielle et les origines de la protection légale du travail en Suisse.* Bern: Stämfli, 1914.

Rauers, Friederich. *Bremer Handelsgeschichte im 19. Jahrhundert.* Bremen: Franz Leuwer, 1913.

Ray, D. Michael. "Regional Aspects of Foreign Ownership of Manufacturing in Canada." Waterloo, Canada: unpublished paper prepared for the Task Force on the Structure of Canadian Industry (Watkins Committee), 1967.

——— "The Location of United States Manufacturing Subsidiaries in Canada." *Economic Geography* 47 (1971):389-400.

Redford, Arthur. *Labour Migration in England, 1800-1850.* Manchester: Manchester University Press, 1926.

Redlich, Fritz. "Academic Education for Business: Its Development and the Contribution of Ignaz Jastrow (1856-1937)." *Business History Review* 31 (1961):35-91. Reprinted in F. Redlich, *Steeped in Two Cultures,* pp. 199-257. New York: Harper Torchbooks, 1971.

——— "Business Leadership: Diverse Origins and Variant Forms." *Economic Development and Cultural Change* 6 (1958):177-190. Reprinted in F. Redlich, *Steeped in Two Cultures,* pp. 88-111. New York: Harper Torchbooks, 1971.

——— "Frühindustrielle Unternehmer und ihre Probleme in Lichte ihrer Selbtszeugnisse." In W. Fischer, ed., *Wirtschafts- und sozialgeschichtliche Probleme der frühen Industrialisierung,* pp. 339-413. Berlin: Colloquium Verlag, 1968.

——— *The Molding of American Banking, Men and Ideas.* Pts. 1 and 2. New York: Hafner, 1951.

——— "Toward Comparative Historiography: Background and Problems." *Kyklos* 11 (3, 1958):362-389. Reprinted in F. Redlich, *Steeped in Two Cultures,* pp. 312-338. New York: Harper Torchbooks, 1971.

Reynolds, Lloyd G. *The Three Worlds of Economics.* New Haven, Conn.: Yale University Press, 1971.

Richardson, H. W. "Chemicals." In D. H. Aldcroft, ed., *The Development of British Industry and Foreign Competition, 1875-1914,* pp. 274-306. London: Allen & Unwin, 1968.

Riefler, Winfield W. *Money Rates and Money Markets in the United States.* New York: Harper, 1930.

Riesser, Jacob. *The Great German Banks and Their Concentration, in Connection with the Economic Development of Germany.* Translation of German 3rd ed., completely revised and enlarged. Washington, D.C.: U.S. Government Printing Office (National Monetary Commission), 1911.

Rimlinger, Gaston V. "The International Differences in the Strike Propensity of Coal Miners: Experience in Four Countries." *Industrial and Labor Relations Review* 12 (1959):389-405.

Rimmer, W. G. *Marshall of Leeds, Flaxspinners, 1788-1886.* Cambridge: Cambridge University Press, 1960.

Ringer, Fritz K. *The Decline of the German Mandarins: The German Academic Community, 1890-1913.* Cambridge, Mass.: Harvard University Press, 1969.

Rist, Marcel. "Une Expérience française de libération des échanges au dix-neuvième siècle: le traité de 1860." *Revue d'économie politique* 66 (1956):908-961.

Ritter, Ulrich Peter. *Die Rolle des Staates in der Industrialisierung.* Berlin: Duncker u. Humblot, 1961.

Robbins, Sidney M., and Nestor E. Terleckyj. *Money Metropolis: A Location Study of the Financial Activities in the New York Region.* Cambridge, Mass.: Harvard University Press, 1960.

Roberts, J. M. "Lombardy." In A. Goodwin, ed., *The European Nobility in the Eighteenth Century.* London: Adam and Charles Black, 1953.

Robinson, Roland I. *Money and Capital Markets.* New York: McGraw-Hill, 1964.

Robson, R. *The Cotton Industry in Britain.* London: Macmillan, 1957.

Robson, William A. *The Civil Service in Britain and France.* London: Hogarth, 1956.

Roepke, Wilhelm. *The Social Crisis of Our Times.* Chicago: University of Chicago Press, 1950.

Romani, Mario. *Storia economica d'Italia nel secolo XIX, 1815-1914.* Vol. 1. Milano: Dott. A. Giuffre Editora, 1968.

Romeo, Rosario. *Risorgimento and captialismo.* Bari: Editori Laterza, 1959.

Rosenbaum, Eduard. "M. M. Warburg & Co., Merchant Bankers of Hamburg: A Survey of the First 140 Years, 1798 to 1938." Reprinted from Leon Baeck Institute of Jews from Germany, *Yearbook VII.* London: 1962.

Rosenberg, Hans, *Bureaucracy, Aristocracy and Autocracy, 1650-1815.* Cambridge, Mass.: Harvard University Press, 1958.

―――― *Die Weltwirtschaftskrise von 1857-1859.* Stuttgart-Berlin: Verlag von W. Kohlhammer, 1934.

―――― *Grosse Depression und Bismarckzeit, Wirtschaftsablauf, Gesellschaft und Politik in Mitteleuropa.* Berlin: de Gruyter, 1967.

―――― "Political and Social Consequences of the Great Depression of 1873-1896 in Central Europe," *Economic History Review* 13 (1943):58-73.

Ross, Victor A. *A History of the Canadian Bank of Commerce.* Toronto: Oxford University Press, vol. 1, 1920; vol. 2, 1922.

Rostow, Walt W. "The Beginnings of Modern Growth in Europe: An Essay in Synthesis." *Journal of Economic History* 33 (1973):547-580.

―――― *The Stages of Economic Growth.* Cambridge: Cambridge University Press, 1960.

Royal Bank of Canada, Fiftieth Anniversary, 1869-1919. Montreal: privately printed, 1920.

Royal Commission on Banking and Finance. *Report* (Porter Report). Ottawa: Queen's Printer, 1964.

Russell, E. J. Foreword to Harald Faber, *Co-operation in Danish Agriculture.* 2nd ed. London: Longmans, Green, 1931.

Sachs, Isidore. *L'Italie, ses finances et son développement économique depuis l'unification du royaume, 1859-1884, d'après des documents officiels.* Paris: Librairie Guillaumin, 1885.

Sametz, Arnold W., ed. *Financial Development and Economic Growth.* New York: New York University Press, 1972.

Sandberg, Lars G. *Lancashire in Decline; a Study in Entrepreneurship, Technology and International Trade.* Columbus: Ohio State University Press, 1973.

Saul, S. B. *Studies in British Overseas Trade, 1870-1914.* Liverpool: Liverpool University Press, 1960.

——— "The Engineering Industry." "In Derek H. Aldcroft, ed., *The Development of British Industry, 1875-1914,* pp. 186-277. London: Allen & Unwin, 1968.

Sawyer, John E. "Strains in the Social Structure of Modern France." In E. M. Earle, ed., *Modern France.* Princeton, N.J.: Princeton University Press, 1951.

Sayers, R. S. *Lloyds Bank in the History of English Banking.* Oxford: Clarendon, 1957.

Schramm, Percy Ernest. "Hamburg und die Adelsfrage (bis 1806)." *Zeitschrift des Vereins für hamburgische Geschichte* 55 (1969):81-93.

Schremmer, Eckart. *Die Wirtschaft Bayerns vom hohen Mittelalter bis zum Beginn der Industrialisierung: Bergbau, Gewerbe, Handel.* Munich: C. H. Beck, 1970.

Schumpeter, Joseph A. *Business Cycles: A Theoretical, Historical and Statistical Analysis of the Capitalist Process.* Vols. 1 and 2. New York: McGraw-Hill, 1939.

Schwarzenbach, Ernst. "The Swiss Money Market." In J. T. Madden and M. Nadler, eds., *The International Money Markets,* pp. 481-523. New York: Prentice-Hall, 1935.

Scoville, Warren C. *The Persecution of Huguenots and French Economic Development, 1680-1720.* Los Angeles: University of California Press, 1960.

Sédillot, René. *La Maison de Wendel de mille sept cents quatre à nos jours.* Paris: privately printed, 1958.

[Segré Report.] *The Development of a European Capital Market.* Brussels: European Economic Community, 1967.

Seidenzahl, Fritz. *100 Jahre Deutsche Bank, 1870-1970.* Frankfurt am Main: Deutsche Bank, 1970.

Select Committee Appointed to Inquire into the Operation of the Existing Laws Affecting the Exportation of Machinery. "First Report," with Minutes of Evidence and Appendix, 1 April 1841, *Parliamentary Papers,* 1841, vol. 7; "Second Report," 11 June 1841, ibid.

Select Committee on Import Duties. "Minutes of Evidence," 15 July 1840, *Parliamentary Papers, Reports of Committees,* 1840, vol. 5.

Select Committee on the Laws Relating to the Export of Tools and Machinery. "Report," 30 June 1825, *Parliamentary Papers, Reports of Committees,* 1825, vol. 5.

Semmel, Bernard. *The Rise of the Free Trade Imperialism: Classical Political Economy, the Empire of Free Trade, and Imperialism, 1750-1850.* Cambridge: Cambridge University Press, 1970.

Shaw, Edward S. *Financial Deepening in Economic Development.* New York: Oxford University Press, 1973.

Slicher van Bath, B. H. *The Agrarian History of Western Europe, 500-1850.* London: Edward Arnold, 1963.

Smith, Adam. *An Inquiry into the Nature and Causes of the Wealth of Nations*

[1776]. Cannan ed. New York: Modern Library, 1937.

Smith, Denis Mack. *Italy: A Modern History.* Ann Arbor: University of Michigan Press, 1959.

Stobaugh, Robert B., Jr. "The Product Life Cycle, U.S. Exports and International Investment." Ph.D. dissertation, Harvard Graduate School of Business Administration, 1968.

Stone, Lawrence. "History and the Social Sciences in the Twentieth Century." In C. F. Delzell, *The Future of History,* pp. 3-42. Nashville, Tenn.: Vanderbilt University Press, 1977.

Stuart, James Montgomery. *The History of Free Trade in Tuscany, with Remarks on Its Progress in the Rest of Italy.* London: Cassell, Potter & Galpin, 1876.

Sturmey, S. G. *British Shipping and World Competition.* London: Athlone Press, 1962.

Swart, K. W. "Holland's Bourgeoisie and the Retarded Industrialization of the Netherlands." In Frederick Krantz and Paul M. Hohenberg, eds., *Failed Transitions to Modern Industrial Society: Renaissance Italy and Seventeenth Century Holland.* Montreal: Interuniversity Centre for European Studies, 1975.

Taylor, Audrey M. *Gilletts, Bankers at Banbury and Oxford: A Study in Local Economic History.* Oxford: Clarendon, 1964.

Temin, Peter. "The Relative Decline of the British Steel Industry, 1880-1913." In Henry Rosovsky, ed., *Industrialization in Two Systems: Essays in Honor of Alexander Gerschenkron.* New York: Wiley, 1966.

Thackray, A. "Natural Knowledge in Cultural Context, The Manchester Model." *American Historical Review* 79 (1974):671-684.

Thayer, William Roscoe. *The Life and Times of Cavour.* Boston: Houghton Mifflin, 1921.

Thésée, Françoise. *Négociants bordelais et colons de Saint-Domique, liaisons d'habitations, la Maison Henry Romberg, Bapst et Cie.* Paris: Société française de histoire d'outre-mer, 1972.

Thiedig, Werner. *Englands Übergang zum Freihandel und die deutsche Handelspolitik, 1840-1856.* 40-page summary of thesis. Giessen: n. p., 1927.

Thuillier, Guy. "Pour une histoire bancaire régionale: Nivernais de 1800 à 1880." *Annales, économies, sociétés, civilisations* 10 (1955):494-512.

Tilly, Charles, Louise Tilly, and Richard Tilly. *The Rebellious Century, 1830-1930.* Cambridge, Mass.: Harvard University Press, 1975.

Tilly, Richard H. *Financial Institutions and Industrialization in the Rhineland, 1815-1870.* Madison: University of Wisconsin Press, 1966.

———— "Los von England: Probleme des Nationalismus in der deutschen Wirtschaftsgeschichte." *Zeitschrift für die gesamte Staatswissenschaft* 124 (1968): 179-196.

Tilton, John E. *International Diffusion of Technology: The Case of Semi-Conductors.* Washington, D.C.: Brookings Institution, 1971.

Tortella, Gabriel. "Banking and Industry in Spain, 1829-74." *Journal of Economic History* 29 (1969):163-166.

Ucke, Arnold. *Die Agrarkrise in Preussen während zwanziger Jahre dieses Jahrhundert.* Halle: Maz Niemeyer, 1888.

Union Bank of Switzerland, 1862, 1912, 1962. Zurich: privately printed, 1962.

Van Houtte, Jan A. "Economic Development of Belgium and the Netherlands from the Beginning of the Modern Era." *Journal of European Economic History* 1 (1927):100-120.

Veblen, Thorstein B. "The Price of Wheat since 1867." *Journal of Political Economy* 1 (1890):70-103.

Vernon, Raymond. "International Investment and International Trade in the Product Cycle." *Quarterly Journal of Economics* 80 (1966):190-207.

——— *Metropolis, 1985.* Cambridge, Mass.: Harvard University Press, 1960.

Wadsworth, Alfred P., and Julia deL. Mann. *The Cotton Trade and Industrial Lancashire, 1600-1780.* Manchester: Manchester University Press, 1931.

Walker, E. Ronald. *From Economic Theory to Policy.* Chicago: University of Chicago Press, 1943.

Walker, Mack. *Germany and the Emigration, 1816-1885.* Cambridge, Mass.: Harvard University Press, 1964.

Weber Max. *Economy and Society: An Outline of Interpretative Sociology.* Vols. 1-3. Guenther Roth and Claus Wittlich, eds. New York: Bedminister Press, 1968.

——— *The Theory of Social and Economic Organization.* Introduction by T. Parsons, ed. New York: Oxford University Press, 1947.

Wechsberg, Joseph. *The Merchant Bankers.* Boston: Little, Brown, 1966.

[Werner Report.] "Report to the Council and the Commission on the Realization by Stages of Economic and Monetary Union." European Communities *Bulletin*, suppl. 11, 1970.

Westerfield, Ray B. *Middlemen in English Business, Particularly between 1660 and 1760.* New Haven, Conn.: Yale University Press, 1915.

Westergaard, Harald. *Economic Developments in Denmark.* London: Oxford University Press, 1922.

Whale, F. Barrett. *Joint-Stock Banking in Germany: A Study in the German Credit Banks before and after the War.* London: Cass, 1930. Reprinted New York: Augustus Kelley, 1968.

White, Harry D. *The French International Accounts, 1880-1913.* Cambridge, Mass.: Harvard University Press, 1933.

Whyte, A. J. *Early Life and Letters of Cavour, 1810-1848.* London: Oxford University Press, 1925.

——— *The Political Life and Letters of Cavour, 1848-1861.* London: Oxford University Press, 1930.

Wilkinson, Rupert, ed. *Governing Elites: Studies in Training and Selection.* New York: Oxford University Press, 1969.

Williams, E. E. *Made in Germany.* 2nd ed. London: Heinemann, 1896.

Williams, E. N. *The Ancien Régime in Europe: Government and Society in the Major States, 1648-1879.* New York: Harper & Row, 1970.

Williams, John H. "The Theory of International Trade Reconsidered." *Economic Journal* 39 (1929):195-209.

Williams, Judith Blow. *British Commercial Policy and Trade Expansion, 1750-1850.* London: Oxford University Press, 1973.

Wilson, Charles. *Anglo-Dutch Commerce and Finance in the Eighteenth Century.*

Cambridge: Cambridge University Press, 1941.

────── *England's Apprenticeship 1663-1763*. New York: St. Martin's, 1965.

────── *The Dutch Republic and the Civilisation of the Seventeenth Century*. London: Weidenfeld and Nicholson, 1968.

────── "The Entrepreneur in the Industrial Revolution in Britain." *Explorations in Entrepreneurial History* 7 (1955):229-245. Reprinted with omissions in Barry E. Supple, ed., *The Experience of Economic Growth: Case Studies in Economic History*, pp. 171-188. New York: Random House, 1963.

Wilson, J. S. G. "The Australian Money Market." *Banca Nazionale del Lavoro Quarterly Review* 104 (1973):46-59.

Wilson, R. G. *Gentlemen Merchants: The Merchant Community of Leeds, 1700-1830*. Manchester: Manchester University Press, 1971.

────── "The Denisons and Milneses: Eighteenth Century Merchant Landowners." In J. T. Ward and R. G. Wilson, eds., *Land and Industry: The Landed Estate and the Industrial Revolution*, pp. 145-172. New York: Barnes & Noble, 1971.

Wiskemann, Erwin. *Hamburg und die Welthandelspolitik von den Anfängen bis zur Gegenwart*. Hamburg: Friederischsen, de Gruytar, 1929.

Withers, Hartley. *National Provincial Bank, 1833-1933*. London: privately printed, 1933.

Woodham-Smith, Cecil. *The Great Hunger: Ireland, 1845-1849*. New York: Harper and Row, 1962.

Woytinsky, W. S., and E. S. Woytinsky. *World Commerce and Governments*. New York: Twentieth Century Fund, 1955.

────── *World Population and Production*. New York: Twentieth Century Fund, 1953.

Wright, Carl Major. *Economic Adaptation to a Changing World Market*. Copenhagen: Munksgaard, 1939.

Wright, Gordon. "The Origins of Napoleon's III's Free Trade." *Economic History Review* 9 (1938-39):64-67.

Wright, H. R. C. *Free Trade and Protection in the Netherlands, 1816-39: A Study of the First Benelux*. Cambridge: Cambridge University Press, 1955.

Wutzmer, Heinz. "Die Herkunft der industrielle Bourgeoisie Preussens in den vierziger Jahren des 19. Jahrhunderts." In Hans Mottek, ed., *Studien zur Geschichte der industriellen Revolution in Deutschland*, pp. 145-163. Berlin: Akademie-Verlag, 1960.

Yassukovich, Stanislas M. "The Development of an International Capital Market." *Euromoney* 2 (1971):16, 18-20.

Young, Arthur. *Travels in France during the Years 1787, 1788 and 1789 (1790)*, Garden City, N.Y.: Doubleday Anchor Books, 1969.

Zorn, Wolfgang. "Wirtschaft und Politik in deutschen Imperialismus." In W. Abel, K. Borchardt, H. Kellenbenz, and W. Zorn, eds., *Wirtschaft, Geschichte und Wirtschaftsgeschichte*, pp. 340-354. Stuttgart: Gustav Fischer Verlag, 1955.

────── "Wirtschafts- und sozialgeschichtliche Zusammenhänge der deutschen Reichsgrundüngszeit (1850-1879)." In Helmut Böhme, Hg., *Probleme der*

Reichsgrundüngszeit, 1848-1879, pp. 296-309. Cologne-Berlin: Kiepenheuer & Witsch, 1968.

Zunkel, Friederich. *Der rheinische-westfälische Unternehmer, 1834-1879, ein Beitrag zur Geschichte des deutsche Bürgertums im 19. Jahrhundert.* Cologne and Opladen: Westdeutscher Verlag, 1962.

Index

y